Praise for Ian Mackersey

'A splendid addition to the literature'

Stand To! on *No Empty Chairs*

'I find it impossible to over-praise a book which reads like a superior detective story while bringing a totally new depth of understanding to this extraordinary woman'

Daily Mail on *Jean Batton: The Garbo of the Skies*

'This harrowing and detailed history, written by a former pilot, looks at the terrible toll that the war took on these young men'

Catholic Herald on *No Empty Chairs*

'An interesting overview . . . I enjoyed this well-written and researched book'

Cross and Cockade International on *No Empty Chairs*

'A brilliant amalgam of high adventure and psychological probing'

Independent on Sunday on
Smithy: The Life of Sir Charles Kingsford Smith

'Vivid detail . . . has a very human feel, in that it does not simply look at the combat or the planes, but at the people who flew them . . . moving'

Warfare Magazine on *No Empty Chairs*

'A wonderful human story, set in the most romantic era of invention the world has ever known'

Ian Mackersey is a writer and documentary filmmaker. He began his career as a writer for *The Dominion* and later the *New Zealand Herald*, and lived in Britain and Zambia before returning to New Zealand. His biographies of the tragic life of the beautiful pioneer aviator Jean Batten, the 'Garbo of the Skies', of 'Smithy' the great Australian ocean pilot Charles Kingsford Smith, and the Wright Brothers, the geniuses who, invented the powered flying machine, were widely acclaimed.

By Ian Mackersey

No Empty Chairs

Crusader Fox King

Rescue Below Zero

Pacific Ordeal
(With Captain Kenneth Ainslie)

Into the Silk

Long Night's Journey

Tom Rolt and the Cressy Years

Jean Batton: The Garbo of the Skies

Smithy: The Life of Sir Charles Kingsford Smith

The Wright Brothers

NO EMPTY CHAIRS

The Short and Heroic Lives
of the Young Aviators Who Fought
and Died in the First World War

IAN MACKERSEY

PHOENIX

AN PHOENIX PAPERBACK

First published in Great Britain in 2012
by Weidenfeld & Nicolson
This paperback edition published in 2013
by Phoenix
an imprint of The Orion Publishing Group Ltd,
Orion House, 5 Upper St Martin's Lane,
London WC2H 9EA

An Hachette UK company

3 5 7 9 10 8 6 4

Copyright © Ian Mackersey 2012

A CIP catalogue record for this book
is available from the British Library.

ISBN 978–0–7538–2813–7

Contents

List of Illustrations

Duncan Grinnell-Milne (*with thanks to Alex Revell*)
Arthur Gould Lee (*with thanks to Alex Revell*)
Bernard W Keymer (*with thanks to Edward Keymer*)
Billy Bishop (*Canadian War Museum, Ottawa, Canada*)
Gotha aeroplanes (*Imperial War Museum*)
Elliot Springs (*National Museum of the US Air Force*)
Captain Roy Brown (*with thanks to Norman Franks*)
Dr William H. Rivers (*The Royal Society*)
Allied aircraft in flames (*with thanks to Terry Treadwell*)
Incinerated crew (*Mary Evans Picture Library*)
Mick Mannock (*with thanks to Alex Revell*)
Ira Jones and King George V (*RAF Museum*)
85 Squadron and their mascots (*Imperial War Museum*)
Aerial combat (*Mary Evans Picture Library*)
Everard Calthrop (*with thanks to Jonathan Rooper*)
Tower Bridge parachute demonstration (*with thanks to Flightglobal*)
Handley Page V/1500 bomber (*Corbis*)

Prologue

A moment came when even the most supremely self-confident aces began to wonder when their turn would come. You sat down to dinner faced by the empty chairs of men you had laughed and joked with at lunch. They were gone. The next day new men would laugh and joke from those chairs. Some might be lucky and stick it for a bit, some chairs would be empty very soon. And so it would go on. And always, miraculously, you were still there. Until tomorrow.

Thus Cecil Lewis, in his classic 1936 memoir of service as a fighter pilot on the Western Front,[1] described the slender thread on which life in the Royal Flying Corps hung. Lewis was one of the few lucky ones. He came through with his body and mind intact. After shooting down eight enemy aircraft he was spared by a posting back to England. Most of his colleagues had already been killed – or soon would be.

In the spring of 1917, when the world's first air war was raging in the skies above the great land battles on the Western Front, the British squadrons were losing 200 pilots a month. Life expectancy for a young flying officer, freshly arrived in France with just a handful of flying hours, was eleven days. Some squadrons suffered such huge losses all the faces had changed in the space of a couple of months. One squadron's entire aircrew was obliterated in thirty days.

The aeroplanes they took to war, barely a dozen years after the flying machine had been invented, were rudimentary open-cockpit biplanes. Aerial combat techniques didn't exist. The weapon with which their crew were expected to shoot down the equally frail German planes was a single machine gun bolted to the wood-and-fabric wing. Unlike the warfare raging in the Flanders mud below, where enormous armies anonymously slaughtered one another in holocausts of high-explosive shells, poison gas and machine-gun fire, the air battles overhead were intensely personal affairs. Deadly old-fashioned duels in which two pilots, their goggled faces often staring at each other, engaged in desperate contests of wit and skill to shoot the other down. The victim, if he didn't end it all with his revolver or by jumping out, would fry to death in a flaming, parachuteless cockpit.

In the squadron messes the empty chairs were filled by an unceasing flow of eager volunteers. Foot soldiers escaping from the killing fields of the trenches for a seemingly more comfortable mode of warfare. And, inspired by the exploits of a small elite of pilot heroes, a stream of public schoolboys, often falsifying their ages, rushing from the sixth form to fight for King and country. Cecil Lewis was barely seventeen when he signed up.

The Flying Corps may have provided a more civilised existence on the Western Front. Airmen would sleep in beds between clean sheets, would be waited upon by servants, sit down to four-course dinners with fine wines and flowers on the table. But for most it proved a much shorter life than the awful one they had left amid the terror, mud and sickening sights of the front line. Nor did it offer the hoped-for escape from the psychological traumas of war. Several times a day the pilots and observers were ordered into the air to attack fellow human beings with whom they had no quarrel – encounters from which, almost daily, some would not return. Few of these aerial warriors on either side remained unaffected by the fear and stress. However boldly, with bravado and enormous quantities of alcohol, they concealed their dread from their colleagues few, despite their skill and tally of victories, were not eventually emotionally damaged.

In the near-century that has passed since the First World War, books and movies about the air battles that raged over northern France have portrayed the grim and tragic reality of much of it as romantically heroic adventure. The truth was that it was a nerve-shattering, highly dangerous and utterly terrifying experience. The physical and mental strain of flying open-cockpit aircraft into combat over the Western Front was as painfully punishing as any other in the history of warfare.

Before he got his life-saving posting back to England, Cecil Lewis was sent home on sick leave. His vision had been damaged by open-cockpit flying. When, with a newly awarded Military Cross, he returned a fortnight later to his squadron in France he was shocked to discover how many of his colleagues had gone. Walking into the mess he found only four pilots there. 'Where were the others? Where's Rudd?' he asked.

'Killed. Archie [anti-aircraft shellfire]. This morning. Machine took fire. Couldn't recover the bodies.'

The boy who spoke was only eighteen. A good pilot. Brave. Rudd had been his room mate. God, how quiet the mess was!

'And Hoppy?'

'Wounded: gone home.'

'And Pip and Kidd?' I was almost frightened to ask.

'Done in last night. Direct hit. One of our own shells. Battery rang up to apologise. New pilots coming, By the way congrats on your Military Cross.'

Echoes. Congratulations. Five ghosts in the room. Five friends. Congrats!

'Thanks, I said.'[2]

Two weeks later Lewis's eye trouble returned. He went to see the squadron medical officer, who suspected he was suffering from much more than a vision problem. This time he was sent back to England for good.

I climbed into the train at Amiens with a wonderful feeling of relief. While I had been on the job, screwed up to the pitch of nervous control it demanded, all had been well. In fact, the only effect of a long spell at the front seemed to be to make me more reckless and contemptuous of the danger. But now that tension had been relaxed, I realised how shaky and good-for-nothing I was. Eight months overseas, four months of the Somme battle, three hundred and fifty hours in the air, and still alive! Pilots in 1916 were lasting on an average for three weeks. Today it seems incredible that I came through; but at that time I did not calculate the odds. I had an absolute and unshakable belief in my invulnerability.[3]

Few Flying Corps pilots placed their experiences on public record as intimately as Cecil Lewis did. Instead, in what for most were to be the final weeks of their lives, they shared their existence on the front line by unburdening their private thoughts and fears in letters to parents, wives, girlfriends, brothers and sisters. The sheer quantity of letters that poured out of the Western Front in WWI reflected the importance for all of contact with home. In 1916 alone an incredible 5 million letters were dispatched every week from France and Belgium by the British Expeditionary Force.

Some of these letters from the Great War's aviators make truly heart-rending reading. There are vivid descriptions of the fear and excitement of aerial combat, of the close companionship of friends, of the agony of watching them die. The trauma of war induced a constant need to communicate intensely private feelings probably, for many, rarely hitherto expressed. They talk of loneliness and the yearning to see again loved ones and the green and pleasant land of England. Not only did war seem to quicken affection for families and friends, it was also a powerful aphrodisiac, generating wonderful love letters. Girlfriends back home became fiancées and wives within weeks.

The correspondence in both directions reflected the heroic attitudes to war, less familiar today, of an era in which every class of British society believed implicitly in the nobility of the great and glorious cause; of acceptance of a duty, if necessary, to die for one's country. The almost universal vocabulary displayed the ideals of patriotism, stiff-upper-lip courage and an absolute belief that, despite the staggering toll of death and mutilation, the fate of the combatants lay in the hands of a higher power. God figures prominently in many letters. To question the need for the wholesale slaughter of millions was to suggest shameful pacifism. Yet the longer the seemingly pointless war went on, so more and more airmen began openly to question its purpose.

Knowing that every letter could be their last, many Flying Corps men wrote home every day – sometimes two or three times. The quality of some of the writing is astonishing. For these were letters written before the age of the fax, e-mail, staccato texting and social website chatting – an age when people communicated in proper letters, pages long, gently delivered by post.

Thousands of such dispatches were handed after the war by aviators' families into the safekeeping of museums and libraries around the world. Many, in folders, neatly bound with faded pink tape, have lain in boxes unread for more than nine decades. The story told by these letters, and by published and unpublished memoirs, is of an air war far removed from some of the glamorous depictions of it. Not only do they chillingly describe the sheer sustained terror of aerial combat and the punishing stress but, often in almost unbearable terms, they articulate the terrible grief at the loss of a much-loved son endured by some devastated family somewhere almost daily.

Unlike the land battles, the command and direction of the parallel air war had no precedent. When the Flying Corps and its separate sister naval air service had been created in 1912 the powered aeroplane had only been around, and in a still exceedingly rudimentary form, for nine years. Yet the British Army, which ran the military air service for most of the war, could have had flying machines much sooner. Back in 1905, offered the most significant war weapon invented since the discovery of gunpowder, it had, however, decided not to pursue negotiations with the Wright brothers. And even when public alarm at the threat to Britain of German airship bombers forced it at last to acquire aeroplanes, it did so with extraordinary reluctance.

Faced with attack from deadly new airborne weapons the British Army had, only just in time, created the brave little flying force whose pilot and observer heroes were to become a new military breed as their country's first aerial warriors. Their personal chronicles of the new means of war into which they were pitched in 1914 have left us with an intensely human record of a savage, now long-forgotten conflict fought for the first time in the sky.

Author's note

The 1914–18 air war was conducted on many fronts. On various scales, between a range of warring nations, it was fought mainly in north-western Europe, in Italy, the Balkans, Russia, the Middle East. This book is concerned principally with the men and operations of the British Royal Flying Corps and their German Air Service enemies with whom they clashed on the Western Front in France.

It is not a military history of the world's first air war nor of the RFC and its sister Royal Naval Air Service. For those in search of definitive records of the air campaigns and battles they both fought, of the deeds of the hundreds of pilots whose tallies of victories made them aces, of the records of individual squadrons, their bases and the aircraft they flew, there are extensive official histories and huge numbers of books within the aviation literature of the First World War devoted in great detail to seemingly every conceivable aspect of the war in the air.

Although many of their great-grandfathers may have fought in it, astonishing as it may seem, my research for *No Empty Chairs* very soon discovered the existence today of a generation in which relatively few had ever heard of the terrible Great War, let alone of its major parallel air war.

Ian Mackersey
August 2013

Chapter 1

The Reluctant Inventors

In October 1904 the British Army sent a senior officer to America to meet the two young bicyclemakers who had astounded the world ten months earlier with the first successful flight of a powered flying machine. The army was seriously interested in its military potential. Their emissary, Lieutenant-Colonel John Capper, a veteran of the Boer War with little understanding of the complexities of flight, worked at Farnborough in Hampshire for a small War Office research and development establishment called the Balloon Factory. Its function was to help the army develop the use of 'aerial vehicles'.

The current vehicles were an assortment of huge, man-lifting enemy observation kites, gliders, dirigible airships and balloons. In Dayton, Ohio, Capper was hospitably received by the Wright brothers, Wilbur and Orville. They talked to him openly about their aeroplane, the *Flyer*, proudly explaining how it worked. They showed him photos of it in flight. But they refused to demonstrate it, or even let him set eyes on the machine which, out of near-paranoid fear that someone would pirate its sacred design, they had locked up in a windowless shed at their airfield nearby. The nearest Capper got to the world's first aeroplane was to be shown its engine, which happened to be under repair in the brothers' bicycle shop. He wasn't even allowed to have copies of the tantalising pictures of the revolutionary device captured in flight. All he was able to achieve was to request that Britain be given an option to buy when they'd further developed their aeroplane.

Back in London the colonel, determined that the British Army should be the first to use this radical new means of reconnaissance, wrote a persuasive report for his War Office masters. The Wrights, he said, had produced a machine of very great military importance. They had created what could become 'accessories of warfare, scouting machines which will go at a great pace and be independent of ground obstacles, whilst offering from their elevated position unrivalled opportunities of ascertaining what is occurring in the heart of an enemy's country'.[1]

When, a few months later, the Wrights had further improved their aeroplane they felt obliged to offer it first to their own country. To their surprise and disappointment the US War Department wasn't interested. So they formally approached Colonel Capper. Capper enthusiastically passed their letter upwards to War Office headquarters where it arrived on the desk of the director of fortifications and works – who immediately shunted it sideways to a scientifically minded body called the Royal Engineer Committee. Concerned with the technical evaluation of new military devices, the committee was sufficiently interested to ask the British military attaché in Washington to go to Dayton and arrange some flight trials. But when the attaché got there, he was astounded to be told by its inventors that they would fly it for him only if they received an advance contract if it met the British military reconnaissance specifications. The Wrights trusted no one. Refusing to countenance a blind contract, the British Army gave up on the *Flyer* in exasperation.

However, the War Office was coming under growing pressure to equip itself for aerial warfare. The island nation, protected by the battleships of the Royal Navy and unconquered for over 800 years, was suddenly facing the unthinkable: the possibility of attack and invasion from the air. By 1908 the way in which this might come was being alarmingly presented to the public. A sensational science-fiction book, *The War in the Air*, by the influential author H.G. Wells, serialised in the popular *Pall Mall Magazine*, depicted with stark realism the world's first major air war. Its outcome was the destruction of all human civilisation. Aerial bombing forces, 'dripping death', systematically razed the planet's great cities. Giant German airships and big aeroplane bombers laid waste to Britain. Devoured episode by episode as eagerly as people today view their TV serials, the story had a tremendous impact on its readers. And in Edwardian England their nervousness was further fuelled by a relentless campaign launched by the great newspaper baron Lord Northcliffe. Through his influential *Daily Mail* and *The Times* he began to urge the country to wake up to the imminent risk it faced of invasion: 'COMMAND OF THE AIR – GERMANY AS THE AERIAL POWER – TEUTONIC VISION – A LANDING OF 350,000 MEN.'[2] The *Mail*'s Berlin correspondent reported that Germany could transport this great army in just half an hour during the night from Calais to Dover in 'motor airships' and aeroplanes. When such concerns were echoed in the House of Commons the Liberal prime minister, Herbert Asquith, was forced to act. He created a high-level committee to investigate whether the British military should invest in airships or aeroplanes. A powerful group, the Imperial Defence

Committee bristled with major political figures and top military brass. The war minister and two future prime ministers, Lloyd George and Winston Churchill, sat on it, along with the chiefs of the army and the navy.

The most extraordinary feature of this august body's historic hearings, which began in late 1908, was the way they were immediately dominated by one forceful figure: the head of the British Army, General Sir William Nicholson, chief of the general staff. He saw no role for the flying machine in his army. 'Aviation is a useless and expensive fad advocated by a few individuals whose ideas are unworthy of attention,' he once famously declared. An undistinguished soldier with untypically little active field service for his great rank, Nicholson was an aggressively quarrelsome and pedantic character known unaffectionately as 'Old Nick'. He monopolised the committee's proceedings with absurd arguments, tolerating no opposition to his rigidly fixed opinions on the techniques of warfare and vehemently opposing the introduction of any form of aerial vehicle, be it airships, kites, observation balloons or aeroplanes. He wanted none of them anywhere near his army.

Aeroplanes, Nicholson insisted, would be useless for reconnaissance of enemy positions and troop movements. He doubted that pilots would be able to breathe at cruising level and was convinced that no observer in an aeroplane 'travelling at 30 miles an hour could possibly see what an enemy was doing. He knew this from travelling at 30 miles an hour in his motor car.'[3] No one on the committee felt able to remind him that even in a train moving at 60 miles an hour, while telegraph poles whizzed by, cows in the nearby fields were plainly visible. Nicholson maintained that battle reconnaissance could only be satisfactorily carried out in the way he knew best: by men on horses, despite the serious concerns among his cavalry colleagues that the noise of aeroplanes would alarm the horses and make them difficult to handle.

Nicholson often crossed swords with the head of the navy, the first sea lord, Admiral Sir John Fisher. The admiral urgently wanted both airships and aeroplanes to operate as scouts for the fleet and as bombers to attack enemy warships, submarines, minefields and dockyards. Nicholson prevailed. The committee concluded in its report to Prime Minister Asquith that while more experimental work deserved to be done on airships, the aeroplane had yet to prove itself as a military vehicle. It recommended that all aeroplane development at the Balloon Factory cease forthwith.

But the aeroplane was now a fact of life. In Britain primitive sporting machines of all shapes and sizes had begun to emerge from the sheds of private experimenters to lurch into the air on flights of varying success. The first, undertaken in October 1908 on Farnborough Common in Hampshire by an American cowboy, Samuel Cody, in an aeroplane built of bamboo, fabric and piano wire, remained in the air for 27 seconds. It made him a national hero. Inventors with soon-to-be-famous names like A.V. Roe, the Short brothers, Handley-Page and Geoffrey de Havilland were all busy building aeroplanes. In October 1909 the War Office caved in. Its minister, Richard Haldane, now convinced that aircraft had a vital military application, reversed the Imperial Defence Committee's decision. He gave the Balloon Factory a new lease of life. It was dramatically expanded into a military aircraft production plant which quickly recruited on to its design teams some of the country's brightest burgeoning planemakers.

Britain was now lagging a long way behind in the international race to perfect the flying machine. Across the Channel French inventors were already making 40-minute journeys and Wilbur Wright (the brothers having at last decided to exhibit their aeronautical genius to the world) was soon in France, astonishing people with public flights of nearly two and a half hours. If proof were still needed that Britain had lost its invulnerability to invasion, the Frenchman Louis Blériot provided it when, in July 1909, he became the first aviator to fly the Channel, arriving in Dover from Calais in 37 minutes. Blériot's achievement was a sobering demonstration of the superiority of the French aircraft industry. It was producing planes with technical sophistication that would soon overtake the remarkable but difficult to fly Wright *Flyer*. Unlike its British counterparts, the French Army had been quick to use civilian flying schools to train pilots for a military air corps. The Aéronautique Militaire became the world's first air force in October 1910.

It wasn't until April 1911 that the British Army was forced at last to recognise the need for the distrusted aeroplane as its reconnaissance eyes in battle. Cautiously the War Office decided on a token gesture: it formed a small air battalion. An insignificant little unit of the Royal Engineers, commanded by a major, it began with just fourteen officers and 150 other ranks. It comprised two companies, each headed by a junior officer, one equipped with soon-to-be-abandoned army airships, the other, based at Larkhill on Salisbury Plain, with a handful of very rudimentary aeroplanes, most of them acquired from the French. The four British-made planes, looking distinctly like their 'Box Kite' name, had been built in a Bristol tramworks, unabashed copies of a French Henri Farman biplane.

Heightening the appearance of the battalion's birth at the dawn of aviation there was even a Wright brothers biplane, little changed from the one that had made the historic first flight in 1903, and a French monoplane virtually identical to that in which Blériot had flown the Channel two years earlier.

Miserably funded, the Air Battalion was not even given money to train its first pilots. Recruited from the army, they were required to learn to fly privately at their own expense at civilian flying schools. The £75 cost was refunded only if they qualified. The unexacting flight test for their Royal Aero Club certificate, known as the 'ticket', was easily passed. Observed by two instructors on the ground, a pilot was merely required to make two brief flights, each completing five figure-of-eight patterns above the aerodrome. They then had to land within 50 metres of a specified point, take off again and repeat the landing in a glide descent without the engine. Few pupils were ever failed.

The navy studiously remained at arm's length from the Air Battalion. It believed that flying soldiers couldn't possibly understand the unique requirements of maritime aviation. The admirals went their own way, commissioning their own airships, creating a naval flying school at Eastchurch on the Isle of Sheppey and experimenting with float planes that could go to sea aboard warships. They didn't want any of the products of the army's Farnborough factory, preferring to deal with the private manufacturers whose industry was growing by the month.

Meanwhile, at Larkhill, the diminutive nucleus of a British air force, the Air Battalion's No. 2 Company, commanded by an artillery captain, was beginning to create a tiny cadre of military aviators. Avoiding bad weather, through which they couldn't safely fly, their underpowered motorised kites cruised uncertainly about southern England at 40 miles an hour – so slow that in a strong headwind they were sometimes stationary in the air or even blown backwards. Strangely to modern eyes, the Box Kite's elevator was stuck out in front on the end of slender outriggers. In the absence of any sort of fuselage, the pilot sat precariously in the open, perched on the bottom wing immediately in front of the pusher engine.

During flying training the pupil sat behind his instructor, reaching his arms around him to grasp the control stick. When it was considered safe for him to go solo, forbidden to attempt any risky turning manoeuvres, he took off, climbed to around 50 feet and immediately landed straight ahead. In turbulence the aeroplane was so difficult to handle pilots risked being thrown out of their seats. They had no altimeters and no proper navigation training. In the absence of aeronautical maps, on cross-country flights some carried Bradshaw railway guides to check their position from station name boards.

The hope was that the machines of this unwelcomed appendage of the army would prove on military exercises their observation superiority over the cavalry. The yawning generational gulf between the exponents of aerial observation platforms and the cavalry is wonderfully symbolised in photographs of a military review that captured one of the planes cruising past a general and his staff officers, all sitting with elegantly plumed hats astride their magnificent horses. The cavalry officers are gazing up in disbelief at the phenomenon of a Maurice Farman Shorthorn – a contraption of wood and canvas held together by wire, mounted on bicycle wheels – lumbering by low in the air over the parade ground and looking for all the world like a mechanical stick insect.

At first these early aircraft had difficulty even making it to the location of the manoeuvres. In August 1911 five machines set out from Larkhill to fly the 100 miles to a big military exercise near Cambridge. Only two pilots arrived – and it took them two days. The unit's collection of barely a dozen elementary flying machines was a feeble manifestation of British air power. Senior officers sent by the War Office that summer to observe French Army exercises were staggered by the scale of the air support they saw demonstrated. The Aéronautique Militaire was equipped with more than 200 aeroplanes. They were successfully controlling artillery fire and photographing rival forces' positions. In Germany the army had already acquired the Zeppelin bomber airships against which the puny Larkhill aeroplane unit was powerless.

The anti-aviation zealots in the War Office were now forced to reconsider. The need for air supremacy in the looming war had become so undeniable that, under pressure from the prime minister and Cabinet, the army and the navy were made to form a unified air force. The result was the birth on 13 May 1912 of the Royal Flying Corps. The new corps was formed with separate army and naval wings plus a central flying school – to be based on Upavon Downs in Wiltshire – to train pilots for both. Its creators' bold vision was a new British air force. It was an ideal not to be realised for six years.

From the outset the Admiralty distanced itself from the army's 'military wing'. It continued to boycott the Farnborough Royal Aircraft Factory and sent only a few of its officers for pilot training at the new joint flying school. Instead it went on buying its own aeroplanes and training its own pilots at Eastchurch. Despite the efforts of a high-powered air committee set up to preside over them both, contact and co-ordination between the two wings remained uncomfortably minimal. Nor was the navy happy with its less than grand title as a mere wing. It soon had it changed to the Royal Naval Air Service, allowing the military wing to become the Royal Flying Corps. The first thing the latter did was to upgrade its motley collection of antiques, most of which still had no apparent fuselage, their cockpits being connected to the tail assembly by a slender skeleton of uncovered booms.

Desperate for more advanced machines, the War Office held trials on Salisbury Plain. After demonstrations of an assorted collection from both French and English private inventors a British two-seater biplane was chosen. With its engine at the front and its fabric-covered fuselage it was the first of the evolving vehicles to look anything like a modern aeroplane. Labelled the BE2, it was the creation of a talented young designer, Geoffrey de Havilland, whose company would go on to produce the Tiger Moth, the Second World War Mosquito and the world's first jet airliner, the Comet. De Havilland's wife used to stitch the fabric seams of his early inventions on her sewing machine. The War Office ordered a small batch of these basic but sturdy aeroplanes to become the workhorse of the Flying Corps, whose aerial vehicles were soon at last to prove their worth to the cynical generals. At the annual military war games held in East Anglia in September 1912 the opposing armies were, for the first time, supplied with a small clutch of aircraft to help observe each other's positions, a role the cavalry had for centuries traditionally performed – and would still determinedly do so at these exercises.

The biggest event in the peacetime British military calendar, the manoeuvres were attended by the war minister, accompanied by a sprinkling of foreign generals. King George V was there on horseback, observing the great four-day-long mock battle between the Red Army, commanded by Lieutenant-General Sir Douglas Haig, and the Blue forces, led by General Sir James Grierson. Hot favourites were Haig's Reds, whose crack cavalry division was expected to quickly locate and overrun Grierson's troops. It was thanks to the aeroplane that things did not go according to plan.

One of the Blue Army's spotter planes located a large force of Haig's unwisely unconcealed troops. From the air they were seen streaming down a road like a column of ants, their weapons and equipment glittering in the sun. The pilot and his observer, having no radio, sped triumphantly back to Grierson's headquarters to report their find. General Grierson was puzzled. He'd just sent his cavalry off in a completely different direction and there was no way of immediately changing their course. However, the aircraft's observer, Major Hugh Trenchard, offered a suggestion: that they fly the revised orders out to the cavalry. This had never been done before, but Grierson was persuaded.

His staff bustled round him. Orders were written and handed to Trenchard for personal delivery to Briggs, the cavalry commander; and five minutes later the aircraft was aloft again.

They eventually sighted horse-drawn transport and the flashing points of cavalry lances by the hedges of the Newmarket road. Heads turned up in curiosity, hands waved in greeting as the Farman circled above. Trenchard's eyes raked the area for a glimpse of braid and red tabs: 'How vulnerable they are,' he said to his pilot Longmore. 'And how far off course!'

The roof had been suddenly removed from the mock battlefield. No commander, Trenchard knew, could ever again depend entirely on luck or strength or skill; a regiment of the cavalry was no substitute for a single reconnaissance aircraft.

Longmore banked steeply and landed in a meadow. Trenchard handed the sealed message to General Briggs who acted on it at once. Afterwards it was admitted officially that the manoeuvres had been largely influenced by the 'intervention of aircraft' which secured the initiative for Grierson.[4]

The aeronautically aware general had also taken steps to conceal his soldiers from the Red Army's planes. 'I told them,' he said, 'to look as like toadstools as they could.'

This one small event, which today reads like an aerial adventure from *Biggles*, is credited by aviation historians as the moment the aeroplane transformed for ever the science of war. And not just for the military observation revolution it represented. It presaged, too, the violence of aerial combat, as General Grierson foresaw: 'So long as hostile aircraft are hovering over one's troops all movements are liable to be seen and reported, and therefore the first step in war will be to get rid of the hostile aircraft. He who does this first, or who keeps the last aeroplane afloat, will win.'[5] All too soon his prophesy was to be tested.

In August 1914 war, on a scale of destruction and suffering never before seen in human history, exploded across Europe. By midnight on 4 August five nations were in armed conflict: Austria–Hungary against Serbia;

Germany against France, Britain and Russia; Russia against German... Austria–Hungary. It was assumed on all sides that hostilities at this... could not be very long sustained by any of the participants: 'Every army believed that it could crush its opponents within a few months. German troops were as confident that they would soon be marching in triumph along the Champs-Elysées in Paris as French troops were that they would parade along the Unter den Linden in Berlin.'[6] The wide belief among the warring nations was that it would all be over by Christmas. In fact the fighting on all these and many other fronts within and beyond Europe, which eventually saw more than 60 million men mobilised, would go on for four years and three months. The conflagration would involve much of the world. It would see fighting in Africa and the Pacific. It would draw in Turkey, Italy, Bulgaria, Romania, Japan and ultimately the United States. It would bring naval battles on the world's oceans and destruction raining down on soldiers and civilians from the air. It would decimate a generation of young men.

In London Britain's declaration of war against Germany brought crowds on to the streets. Along the Mall and outside Buckingham Palace they enthusiastically sang 'God Save the King'. A few days earlier George V, who was a cousin of the German Emperor, Kaiser Wilhelm II, and of the Russian Tsar, Nicholas II, had vainly attempted to avert the war, sending a telegram to Nicholas saying it must all be a terrible mis-understanding between nations. 'I am most anxious not to miss any possibility of avoiding the terrible calamity which at present threatens the whole world,' he wrote.[7] But the march of events had never been within the control of the monarchs.

Throughout Britain thousands of young men, hearts swelling with pride and excitement at the prospect of a wonderful adventure in the cause of freedom and defence of their country, flocked to join up. Few had the least idea that within weeks passion and glory would be replaced by terror and death. None in this fervour of patriotism envisaged the toll of the human sacrifice the war would exact. The horrifying scale of the casualties about to be created by the first use of modern weaponry would leave over 15 million soldiers and civilians dead across Europe and more than 20 million people physically wounded and mentally damaged.

On that August day, as millions of soldiers were marching to war across Europe from Russia to the Channel coast, the German forces, their cavalry lances tipped with fluttering pennants, swept into neutral Belgium – and into battle with the French and British armies. With the small British

Expeditionary Force, rushed to France to support the French and hugely outnumbered by Germany's enormous advancing armies, went a tiny Royal Flying Corps contingent. The first great air war was about to begin.

Chapter 2
The Aeroplane Goes to War

The first contingent of the British Expeditionary Force (BEF), protected by nineteen battleships, had crossed the Channel in darkness on 12 August. The following day the first aeroplane of the army's minuscule air wing flew to France to join them. A fleet of wooden London buses with solid tyres and open-top decks had helped transport the troops up to the front. The whole operation was conducted with such secrecy the German high command wasn't even aware of their arrival to bolster the French armies until ten days later, when one of its forward units near the Belgian city of Mons was surprised to meet a squadron of the 4th Dragoon Guards. A British corporal fired on the German soldiers and his commanding officer, it is recorded, 'drew his sword and charged'.[1] The skirmish on 23 August was the beginning of the violence of the Battle of Mons, the first major clash of arms of the war by the British on the Western Front.

It erupted so unexpectedly for the inhabitants of the villages in the midst of it that people setting off for church that day in their Sunday best were caught in the crossfire and fled. Women still carrying their feathered hats joined the floods of terrified uprooted humanity wheeling prams, wheelbarrows and carts that clogged the roads ahead of the advancing German divisions. Reprisals in response to Belgian resistance snipers had been harsh: entire villages were burned to the ground, women raped and thousands of innocent hostages summarily shot. Armed with enormous siege artillery, the shells of the invaders' heavy mobile howitzers, called 'Big Berthas', crashed through the steel and concrete of the country's defence forts, smashing the garrisons into surrender. Although the battle lasted only a day the BEF suffered heavy casualties. Sixteen hundred of its men were killed or wounded, triggering the first of the sad telegrams to families back in England. Nobody dreamed that this was just the beginning of what would become a horrifying 3 million British and Empire casualties.

The sheer size of the forces that clashed in titanic battles on the Western Front in August 1914 is, nearly a century later, almost impossible to conceive. Between them Germany and France had mobilised a staggering 4 million men. In France and Belgium a million and three-quarter-strong German invasion force faced French armies totalling 2 million. The German strategy, created by a Prussian warlord, the former chief of the Imperial German staff, Field Marshal Count von Schlieffen, was enshrined in a famous document still studied and argued over by military historians. The plan, which foresaw simultaneous wars with France and Russia, was devised to avoid conflict on two fronts and deliver German victories on both. The bulk of the huge German army would first be concentrated in the west for the swift defeat of France before switching its mammoth forces in great convoys of trains to the eastern front to deal with the Russians. Things didn't work out so neatly, however.

According to the Schlieffen plan the main German force sent into Belgium was intended to drive rapidly down into north-western France, bypass Paris to the west and south before swinging east to execute a massive encirclement of the French Army, whose annihilation and surrender was confidently expected within six weeks. For France it was the second time in many people's memory of German armies in their threatening spiked helmets rolling towards Paris. In 1870 the capital had found itself under siege, facing mass starvation, in the Franco–Prussian war in which two French provinces, Alsace and Lorraine, had been lost to Germany. But in 1914, the Germans hadn't found it so easy. The Schlieffen plan had not reckoned on the ferocity of Belgian resistance, the unexpected speed of Russian mobilisation or British entry into the war at all.

Compared with the military juggernauts of the German and French armies the British Expeditionary land forces of barely 36,000 men that arrived in southern Belgium seemed pathetically few. Their battle-hardened regular professionals were not enough to help the much larger French forces stem the thrust of the German divisions. Both Allied armies were forced into steady retreat back into France, destroying railways and river bridges behind them.

The long withdrawal, 150 miles through the Pas de Calais, in the last week of August 1914 left the Allies teetering on the edge of calamity. Not only did it begin to look as if the war would indeed be over by Christmas, but that it would end with German victory and the BEF driven out of France. The battles and the exhausting marches without enough food and sleep in intense summer heat took a heavy toll of the Anglo–French forces. Their lines of retreat became littered with human graves and dead and dying horses. The French casualties were enormous – one general had to be talked out of committing suicide – and French troops running away were fired upon by their officers. The first British soldier of the war to be court-martialled for desertion was also shot.

Those calamitous weeks in the hot summer of 1914 saw the beginning of the world's first air war and the blooding of the Royal Flying Corps. Just getting to France was a hazardous business for the inadequately trained pilots of the four squadrons dispatched there in their unreliable machines. No. 3 Squadron, setting out at dawn on 13 August to fly to Dover from its aerodrome at Netheravon in Wiltshire, lost one of its aircraft on take-off. The pilot of the overloaded Blériot, Lieutenant Robert Skene, and his mechanic Keith Barlow were both killed. The crash was witnessed by another mechanic, James McCudden, then a humble figure in the Flying Corps hierarchy whose later exploits were to make him a household name. McCudden had swung the propeller of the ill-fated aeroplane.

They left the ground and I noticed the machine flying very tail low until it was lost to view behind our shed at about 80 feet. We then heard the engine stop and, following that, the awful crash which, once heard, is never forgotten. I ran for half a mile and found the machine in a small copse of firs, so I got over the fence and pulled the wreckage away from the occupants, and found them both dead ... I shall never forget that morning at about half past six, kneeling by poor Keith Barlow and looking at the rising sun and then again at poor Barlow who had no superficial injury and was killed purely by concussion, and wondering if war was going to be like this always.[2]

The pilots and mechanics who flew their assortment of BE2s, Farmans and Blériots over the Channel, nervously listening to every beat of their unreliable engines, were issued with inflated inner tubes for the crossing. Against all the odds they made it without mishap over the sea, but no sooner had No. 4 Squadron's flight leader, Captain Cogan, gained the French coast with his formation than his engine cut out. Spotting what looked like a suitable field he began to glide down, waving to the other pilots to fly on without him. But his vigorous hand signals were mis-understood and the whole flight followed him. Unfortunately the field proved to be newly ploughed and several of the machines were too damaged to get off again.

The four squadrons were surprised by the warmth of the French welcome. As the ground staff travelled inland from Boulogne in the

odd collection of hastily acquired motor vehicles they'd brought from
England – one was a large red van, its side still bearing the prominent
label 'H.P. Sauce' – they were everywhere heaped with bottles of wine
and cheered with shouts of 'Vive l'Angleterre!'. 'Whenever we stopped,
as we often did,' wrote Air Mechanic McCudden, 'we were piled up
with fruit and flowers and kissed by pretty French girls.' The pilots and
observers, expecting to be roughing it in France, hadn't bothered to pack
pyjamas. When, to their surprise, they found that they had been booked
into comfortable hotels in Amiens they had to make such a large bulk
purchase of nightwear they were said to have emptied the shops.

The other ranks of the Flying Corps were not equally pampered.
McCudden described a typical night for him. 'I decided to sleep under a
wing of my machine as I wanted to be close to it and not to leave it open
to any prowling spy to tamper with it ... About midnight a terrific
thunderstorm arrived and it rained in sheets for hours. However
I managed to get the machine's cockpit covered over and to keep fairly
dry.'[3]

By the middle of August Britain's infant flying corps had got all its
aeroplanes, intact or in wrecked pieces, to Amiens, where the RFC's field
commander, Brigadier-General Sir David Henderson, had established his
headquarters. Henderson was a long-serving army intelligence officer
who had been wounded and decorated in the Boer War. An authority on
the art of reconnaissance, he was a soldier passionately convinced that
aircraft were now an essential tool of reconnoitring. Henderson was
attracted to the potential of military aviation. In his fiftieth year he had
privately qualified as a pilot at a civilian flying school and been appointed
the first director-general of military aeronautics at the War Office. Here,
surrounded by generals rooted in the methods of nineteenth-century
warfare, he had found himself daily fighting for the Flying Corps in an
atmosphere where the role of the aeroplane was scarcely understood.
But in France, flung into a hot war, the flying machine, despite its still
primitive level of evolution, had begun to justify Henderson's faith.

The squadrons had arrived in time to support the British divisions in
the ferocious fighting in southern Belgium and the sad retreat back into
France. From landing grounds at the French town of Mauberge close to
the Belgian border they had for the first time faced a real enemy.

The German high command had also been contemptuous of the flying
machine, but had eventually attached bomber airships and reconnaissance
aeroplanes to all its individual armies. These aircraft were no more
advanced than those of the RFC and the French. Around half were

curious-looking machines called *Tauben* – Pigeons – strange-looking bird-shaped monoplanes with swept-back wings and fan-spread tails. They banked by twisting their wingtips, carried no armament and their top speed was barely 60 miles an hour. Nonetheless, in the war's first days, one had managed to create some brief consternation in Paris by dropping a small clutch of harmless little bombs and propaganda leaflets on the city. The German airships had proved only slightly more potent. One sprinkled a few bombs on the Belgian city of Antwerp then cruised down the Channel coast making ineffectual attacks on Zeebrugge, Dunkirk and Calais.

The British aircraft had no weapons to destroy the airships. They began instead to experiment with crude methods of harassing the German troops as they poured into northern France. They tried tossing hand grenades on to the marching enemy columns, but it usually did little more than stampede the horses. One enterprising pilot made some simple petrol bombs which he flung down on to a German lorry, causing it to veer into a ditch and catch fire. Even more desperate were small steel darts called flechettes, mediaeval needle-pointed, pencil-sized missiles with tail vanes that were packed into canisters under the fuselage. Released by a trigger in the cockpit, they were showered down on concentrations of enemy troops. In theory a flechette could penetrate a man's skull through his metal helmet. In practice they rarely hit anybody.

The aircraft were at greater risk than their targets. They were fired upon not only by German artillery and infantry rifles but by the retreating British and French battalions as well. Anything in the air in the early days of the war was immediately shot at by either side. To try to stop the friendly fire the RFC began painting Union Jacks on the undersides of their wings. Rifle fire was the most lethal. It brought the Flying Corps' first war fatalities when a pilot and his observer were hit and crashed. Earlier the same day another aircraft had returned to Mauberge with a wounded observer. Sergeant-Major David Jillings, shot through the leg by ground fire, acquired immortality as the RFC's first battle casualty.

Anti-aircraft fire posed less of a threat. It was so inaccurate the pilots had little difficulty avoiding the lethal black puffs viciously exploding shrapnel around them as the German gunners struggled to find their distance and height. The evasive technique to defeat the gunners' attempts to place them in the fatal middle of bracketing shots was simply to weave and make quick changes in flight level. The 1914 aircrew reacted to this shellfire with amusement and one pilot gave it a nickname that was to pass into aviation history. Lieutenant 'Biffy' Borton, 'a dapper,

monocled pilot with a reputation for being something of a dare-devil',
was said to have been so pleased at the ease with which he dodged the
fire of a four-gun unit that he began to sing to his observer an infamous
bawdy song popularised by the London music hall comedian George
Robey: 'Archibald, certainly not!' Within weeks anti-aircraft fire had
become known throughout the Royal Flying Corps as 'Archie', a name
that survived until the end of the war, though few pilots ever knew its
origin.*

The reconnaissance aircraft did not remain unarmed for very long.
Soon both sides' aeroplanes were meeting in the air. At first these encounters were friendly. Pilots would smile and wave at fellow aviators in a
spirit of camaraderie. But these gentlemanly gestures were soon replaced
by the need to prevent one another's spying activities. Pilots and their
observers began to carry revolvers, rifles and shotguns. Some flew with
hand grenades in the hope they could drop them on enemy aircraft from
above. One Flying Corps pilot is said to have attached a cable to a grenade
in the futile hope of dangling it into German propellers. The first, mostly
inconsequential, air-to-air duels were fought with hand-held rifles and
pistols. When his ammunition ran out one pilot decided to prolong the
fight with his Very pistol. He began firing the burning coloured signal
flares at his opponent, who promptly responded in kind. Circling each
other, they continued this ludicrous duel for several minutes, until both
airmen began laughing and broke off the engagement.

Most encounters, however, became lethal. Lieutenant Cuthbert Rabagliati, a bright and sharp-tongued No. 5 Squadron observer fondly known
as 'Ragbags 2', described how he succeeded in shooting down a German
aircraft with his army-issue Lee-Enfield:

> I was using a .303 service rifle and the German was using a Mauser
> pistol with a shoulder stock. We manoeuvred ourselves one against
> the other ... We couldn't shoot through the propeller in front so
> we had to shoot sideways ... None of us knew anything about how
> to lay off [aim ahead of the target aircraft]. It was purely a hit and

---

*One of the the verses ran: *A lady named Miss Hewitt got on friendly terms with me/She fell
in love with me at once and then fell in the sea!/My wife came on the scene as I threw coat and vest
aside/As other garments I slipped off to save the girl, she cried/'Archibald certainly not!/Desist at
once disrobing on the spot!/You may show your pluck and save Miss Hewitt/But if you've got to
strip to do it/Archibald – certainly not.'*
Anti-aircraft fire was also known as 'ack-ack' from the WWI phonetic alphabet. In
WWII it was generally called 'flak', from the German word *Flakfeuer*.

miss effort. We fired a great many rounds – I fired over a hundred – and then suddenly to my joy I saw the German pilot fall forward on his joystick and the machine tipped up and went down ... We were of course completely thrilled. We'd had our duel and we'd won. We watched him going down. We circled round and he finally crashed.[5]

During the German armies' unstoppable push into northern France the British pilots and their observers were plotting their hour-by-hour progress with an accuracy unprecedented in the history of military reconnaissance. Yet the commanding army generals remained stubbornly reluctant to accept the bird's-eye reports that could determine the fate of the retreating Allied armies. The gung-ho observer, Lieutenant Rabagliati, and his pilot returned to Mauberge excited by the discovery of a startling change in the direction of the German advance. They were immediately packed into a car and taken by their squadron commander straight to the BEF's commander-in-chief, Field Marshal Sir John French, headquartered in a nearby château. On arrival the pair were ushered into a room where Rabagliati found himself in the august presence of

a lot of elderly gentlemen covered in gold lace. The Field Marshal was in conference with his senior generals. Somebody announced us and he said, 'Well here's a boy from the Flying Corps, come here and sit down!' I was put to sit next to him, then he said, 'Now where have you been? Have you been flying? What have you been doing?' He called up to some man, 'Come here and just look at this!' I showed him a map all marked out. He said, 'Have you been over that area?' and I said, 'Yes, sir!' I explained what I had seen and they were enormously interested. They then began reading the figures [of German troop numbers] that I had estimated – whereupon I felt that their interest faded. They looked at each other and shrugged their shoulders.

The British commanding generals didn't believe him. They had more confidence in the conflicting reports of their cavalry patrols. Rabagliati was bewildered when French, who had distinguished himself as a cavalry commander in the Boer War, said, 'This is very interesting what you've got, but you know *our* information – which of course is correct – proves that I don't think you could have seen as much as you think! Well, of course I quite understand that you may imagine that you have, but it's not the case.'[6]

The retreat went on for fourteen days through late August 1914. It moved across northern France so quickly the squadrons had difficulty keeping up, forced to relocate almost daily from one makeshift landing ground to another. Pilots returning from reconnaissance would arrive overhead at the base from which they'd left to discover no trace of it. In their absence the cluster of portable canvas hangars, vehicles, tents and aeroplanes had vanished, transported south to another temporary base often hastily laid out, with just a landing direction T in a field of sugar beet or cabbages. Pilots got lost trying to find their squadrons. Their machines ploughed into crops and capsized on landing and were often damaged. Some, failing to find the new base, force-landed, destroyed their aeroplanes and completed their journey on foot.

The weather wreaked more havoc than the enemy on the wood and fabric of the fragile aeroplanes. Picketed out in the open, the flimsy Blériots were easily blown over and smashed by storms. After one such disaster, in which four machines were written off, the ground staff, recalled Air Mechanic Cecil King, 'were hauled before the Commander who said, "You men must guard these aircraft with your lives. Without them the Army is blind. We are the eyes of the Army. If it's between you and the aircraft, the aircraft comes first."'[7]

By early September the German divisions had marched to within thirty miles of Paris. There was panic in the city. On main boulevards trees were felled and trenches and barricades hurriedly built. The government, fearing the capital was about to be overrun, departed for Bordeaux. More than a million Parisians followed. The British commander, Field Marshal Sir John French, watched one of his 14,000-strong divisions reduced within days to a mere 8,000 men. Lord Kitchener, the British war minister, had to rush to France to dissuade him from taking his battered troops, who were falling asleep on the retreat march, out of the line to rest. The field marshal was persuaded to keep his exhausted army in action, but French, considered lacking in adequate 'offensive spirit', would later be replaced by a more aggressive general.

The Germans didn't make it to Paris. In a once-tranquil valley of champagne vineyards and leafy, wine-growing villages immediately to the east of the city their advance ran out of steam. The Allies, helped by thousands of French reinforcements delivered by a motorcade of Parisian taxis to the front line, finally held the invaders a few miles south of the river Marne. Within days the valley was the scene of another of the First World War's great battles.

The First Battle of the Marne, which lasted for less than a week in early September 1914, was one of the most decisive encounters of WWI. Books are still being written about it nearly a century later. The last great fluid battle for several years brought a desperately needed strategic victory for the Anglo–French Allies and saved France from catastrophic defeat. 'A confused, swaying struggle across open fields, over rivers, up and down wooded slopes, through old-fashioned, pretty villages',[8] it saw the German armies driven back north for more than sixty miles. Their commanders viewed the outcome as so strategically critical that the Kaiser himself was brought to the front to observe the fate of his now struggling military might.

The enormous number of troops involved at the Marne battle is utterly mind-boggling today. The Germans had a million and a quarter men. They faced a million French and 125,000 British soldiers. More than 500,000 casualties were suffered by the three armies in just a few weeks in August and early September. The Germans were forced to retreat back into southern Belgium where, in October, at the quiet Flemish market town of Ypres, in ferocious hand-to-hand fighting through thickets of barbed wire amid hails of machine-gun fire and storms of shrapnel, the war on the Western Front ground to a halt. Both sides, exhausted and deadlocked, dug themselves into facing trenches hastily scrabbled in the rain-sodden soil. These became part of the trench system that would sprawl across the map of western Europe, stretching in a 450-mile continuous line from the North Sea to Switzerland. This ugly, zig-zagging scar, stripped of every vestige of vegetation, remained essentially unchanged for four more terrible years. The stalemate spelled the end of the grand Schlieffen plan. The chief of the German general staff, Field Marshal Count von Moltke, suffered a nervous collapse. A few days before he was replaced he wrote an anguished letter to his wife, reflecting on the blood that had been spilled. 'Terror often overcomes me when I think of this, and the feeling I have is I must answer for this horror.'[9]

The trail of destruction that had so nearly seen Germany's armies reach the French Channel coast had been followed precariously from the air from Belgium through northern France and back again into Belgium. The handful of young British pilots and observers who had, against all the scepticism of the army commanders, continued to supply them with reconnaissance reports, finally convinced the cavalry-obsessed generals of the Flying Corps' worth. A mission flown on the eve of the Battle of the Marne did so particularly convincingly.

The British Army was still in retreat to the south-east of Paris. It had lost sight of the pursuing German General von Kluck's forces. The BEF's commander, Sir John French, impatient to know where the enemy was, had turned to the RFC for help. Among the aircraft sent out to look was a BE2a flown by Captain Philip Joubert de la Ferté and his observer. In the gathering dusk they found what they were looking for:

> thousands of twinkling bivouac fires. They both realised that the main German advance had swung toward the east and not toward the British forces in the south. They flew eastward while Allen marked off the fires on his map. Then, around a series of ponds, they saw horses being watered. The more they searched the ground the more horses they saw. Flying low over the area they saw them at every pond and stream and horse lines around every farmhouse. This was certainly von Kluck's cavalry. That night the accuracy of the RFC was not doubted. French made his plans to fall on the back of von Kluck's army.[10]

Beyond all doubt the Flying Corps had proved itself at last. Sir John French went to the length of commending his tiny flying force in a dispatch to War Minister Kitchener in London.

> I wish particularly to bring to your Lordship's notice the admirable work done by the Royal Flying Corps under Sir David Henderson. Their skill, energy and perseverance have been beyond all praise. They have furnished me with complete and accurate information which has been of incalculable value in the conduct of operations. Fired at by friend and foe, not hesitating to work in every kind of weather, they have remained undaunted throughout. Further, by actually fighting in the air they have succeeded in destroying five of the enemy's machines.[11]

It was remarkable that this small embryonic air force, struggling with crude, underpowered flying machines and making up the techniques of observation and air combat as it went along, had achieved what it had. By the end of the First Battle of Ypres there was not much of it left. Of the sixty-three aeroplanes brought to France, more than forty had been destroyed. By October 1914 it possessed just ten serviceable machines.

As the winter of 1914 brought its icy grip to the Western Front there was a pause in significant hostilities as both sides dug deeper into the frozen earth of the devastated war zone. Soldiers consolidated hundreds of miles of trench networks. Millions of men on opposite sides now faced each other, sometimes just a few yards apart, in this ungodly world, 'where nothing moved in the daytime, night was filled with feverish activity, and the sounds of war were never stilled'.[12] Trench warfare, with all its horrors, had begun.

Behind the lines the military air squadrons were at last able to establish more permanent bases from which, for the next three years, they would continue the war in the air. The value of aerial reconnaissance was now such that the commanding generals on both sides were forced to factor it into their day-to-day conduct of battle. They wanted not just more of this all-seeing intelligence service, but were asking urgently for air direction of their artillery fire as well.

Within less than four months the RFC, the unwanted child of the British Army, had become one of its most precious assets.

Chapter 3
Enter 'Boom'

Forced to expand, the Flying Corps suddenly needed many new and better aeroplanes. It needed aircraft fitted with machine guns, and wireless to communicate observations more swiftly to ground. It needed vastly more ground maintenance staff, pilots and observers. The acting head of the Directorate of Aeronautics, Major Sefton Brancker, ordered to prepare urgent plans for a dramatic increase in squadrons and pilot training schools, calculated that at least fifty squadrons were now required. He doubted this figure would be approved. He was astonished, therefore, when, on submitting his proposal to War Minister Lord Kitchener, the Field Marshal wrote on the memo: 'Double this. K.' The funds that the War Office had once so reluctantly spared for its aeronautical battalion were suddenly available, it seemed, in almost unlimited quantity.

But where were the personnel and the aeroplanes to man a hundred squadrons to come from? The government's own Royal Aircraft Factory at Farnborough couldn't help. It was principally an aeronautical research and design facility with limited capacity for aircraft construction. All this had to change.

Hugh Trenchard, the observer who had found the 'enemy' cavalry for General Grierson during the 1912 manoeuvres, now a lieutenant-colonel in command of what remained of the Flying Corps home establishment, tackled part of the expansion with gusto. He set up flying training schools all over the country. To deal with an acute instructor shortage he simply bought up the famous Brooklands aerodrome in Surrey, complete with its hangars, aeroplanes, equipment, flying schools, trained civilian pilots – and, as part of the package, a neighbouring pub, which included several casks of beer. At the same time the War Office embarked on a belated, enormous programme of aircraft construction, standardising initially on the sedate BE2 and ordering hundreds of these machines from private contractors and its own small factory. However, the British Army now paid a high price for its tardiness in recognising the revolutionary role of the military aeroplane. The country's neglected cottage aircraft manufacturing industry could not develop the know-how and capacity needed immediately and it never caught up during the four years of the war. The British air services continued to depend on French aeroplanes and engines to go on flying and fighting.

Trenchard none the less was not deterred from launching an aggressive recruiting drive for hundreds of mechanics. The simultaneous call for pilots and observers brought an immediate response from the trenches. Infantry, artillery and cavalry officers disenchanted, and in many cases psychologically traumatised, by the harrowing experiences of trench warfare seized the chance to escape the continuous shellfire, bitter weather and rat-infested conditions. The desire to seek a less unpleasant way of serving their country was very great indeed. However, not all of the recruits from the infantry were seeking a better life. Some were sent to the Flying Corps as a punishment. Lieutenant Alan Bell-Irving, serving with the Gordon Highlanders, was spotted by a visiting general one day standing in the trench wearing only his shirt and boots. He had taken off his kilt to burn the lice off it. Ordered to report to his company commander, he was told, 'You're not one of us.' He was instructed to apply immediately for transfer to the RFC, a destination viewed by his fellow officers as 'the suicide club'.

One of the voluntary applicants for transfer was an outspoken and opinionated young Royal Horse Artillery subaltern freshly down from Oxford, Sholto Douglas. Desperate to escape a major personality clash with his CO, Douglas was delighted to find that 'unexpected relief was at hand in the shape of an order that appeared one day inviting gunner subalterns to volunteer for duty as observers with the Royal Flying Corps'. He had watched their aeroplanes with envy as they flew out over the lines. 'It all seemed to me very exciting.' Running shells up to the line and watching his horses dying from exposure had proved too much. 'What with the tyranny of my Commanding Officer and the mud and the misery of the animals ... the life of a gunner subaltern was becoming a pretty depressing business.' His CO only too gladly approved his application for transfer. 'I doubt,' wrote Douglas, 'if any was ever approved quicker than that one.'[1]

On Boxing Day 1914, three days after his twenty-first birthday, 2nd Lieutenant Douglas left the trenches for the last time to report for duty with No. 2 Squadron, operating from a field several miles away. The deal was that he would be attached to the RFC for three weeks 'to see if I liked it and if they liked me'.

I mounted my treasured charger Tommy and, in company with my groom, rode across the flat, highly cultivated country which surrounds the River Lys and reported for duty at the airfield at Merville . . . I sent my groom back with Tommy to my old unit, and that was the last I was ever to see of either of them. The only adverse criticism that I received from anybody on the step I had taken came from my mother. In a letter she wrote: 'You must be mad.'

The first thing that struck Douglas on joining his Flying Corps squadron that leaden December day was the lack of formality.

After the rigid discipline that I had known in the Royal Horse Artillery the free and easy way in which things were done in the RFC was very much to my liking. Although most of the pilots were regular army officers . . . they were all men of a different breed from what I had become accustomed to since joining the artillery. I was now in the company of individualists, some of whom, I was soon to find, could even be regarded as at least eccentrics – if not downright crazy.

It was this informality that particularly amazed most of the officers newly arrived from the trenches. Almost every pilot in the Flying Corps seemed to have a nickname: 'Moley' Molesworth, 'Fluffy' Gibbons, 'Scruffy' Longton, 'Beery' Bowman, 'Spider' Atkinson. An especially reserved and shy pilot who spoke little was called 'Noisy' Lewis. A man who looked vaguely like the Kaiser was 'Wilhelm'. One Australian, owing to his suntanned complexion, was famously known as 'Nigger' Horn, a sobriquet that would be regarded as wholly unacceptable today. A South African, George Lloyd, found himself answering to 'Zulu'. And an unfortunate pilot who suffered from chronic haemorrhoids was universally addressed as 'Piles', an unkind label he bore in surprisingly good spirit.

Group pictures show pilots and observers with their assortment of pet dogs, goats and pigs, casually dressed in a confusing variety of uniforms, some wearing those of the army regiments from which they'd come, some in cavalry breeches and knee-high boots, others in shorts with long stockings or puttees wound up to their knees. Beside their aeroplanes they are in long leather flying coats with scarves and thigh-high sheepskin-lined 'fug' boots. Their tunics, often worn over their pyjamas, were frequently decorated with the stains of the castor oil that blew on to them from their rotary engines. They all look much older than their early twenties, are usually pictured holding cigarettes or pipes and the ubiquitous military moustaches make many of them almost indistinguishable from one another. New pilots were often intrigued by the superstitious rituals they found. One airman insisted on always turning round three times before climbing into the cockpit. Another never flew without a potato and a reel of cotton in his pocket.

'It was a wonderful life,' said William Fry (who came from the infantry to join No. 12 Squadron). 'We weren't bothered with parades nor with rules about uniform, nor were we expected to look after the welfare of the men in the flight – they could look after themselves better than we could. We were burdened with no responsibilities whatsoever. No senior officers in the mess were bent on keeping junior officers in their place. Those of us who had come from the regiments could hardly believe our luck.'[2]

For Sholto Douglas who, twenty-five years later in the Second World War, would become commander-in-chief of RAF Fighter Command, life was certainly more civilised than the awful one he'd just left. No. 2 Squadron, on the move almost daily since arriving in France, had at last come to roost on the outskirts of the village of Merville in a flat landscape scattered with the pyramid heaps of coal-waste dumps. The aerodrome was a large grass field near several small canvas hangars. The squadron headquarters was in a nearby farmhouse, the officers' mess and billets in the village. Douglas found the informality among his new colleagues also extended to his role as an observer. There appeared to be no definition of the job at all or, indeed, any formal training. It was often done haphazardly by another pilot or by one of the maintenance NCOs.

Douglas was told he would be flying on a contact patrol – spotting for the artillery, helping the gunners to direct their shells accurately on to their targets. There was as yet no air-to-ground wireless that worked well enough to do this. The sets existed but they were so heavy that to fly with them meant displacing the observer and overloading the pilot with work. Instead the observers had simply been firing off Very flares, using a code in which different sequences of red and green colours told the gunners whether to adjust their fire to the left, right, forward or back. The imprecision of this system was gradually being replaced with more accurate guidance transmitted by Aldis lamps flicking out the dots and dashes of Morse code. Douglas had to learn the code fast. He was still struggling to master it when the squadron commander told him at dinner one evening he'd be doing it for real in the morning in one of the squadron's two-seater BE2a machines that were beginning to succeed its antique Maurice Farmans.

It was actually the first time I had ever flown in an aeroplane and I had practically no idea at all where we were from the time we took off to the time we landed. Not being able to recognise the features on the ground – I had never even seen what the ground looked like from the air before – meant that as far as my contribution to the reconnaissance was concerned I was worthless. By the time we landed I felt that I'd made a complete hash of things.

His pilot came to his rescue, filling in the reconnaissance report and 'saved me from complete disgrace'.[3]

Douglas soon got the hang of it, teaching himself to map-read and getting used to flying patrols under heavy anti-aircraft fire. From the wireless and satellite world of twenty-first-century communication some of the methods of passing simple messages seem bizarre. 'The pilot sat in the back and the observer in front. We would fly over the batteries at a height of between three and four thousand feet. Calling them up by signalling with the lamp, which was always a struggle for the observer because he had to manipulate a cumbersome contraption in the full blast from the propeller ... we would continue signalling to them the results from the shells they would fling over, with any corrections that were needed.' The corrections couldn't have been more rudimentary: 'Over', 'Short', 'Left', 'Right'. The battery would correct and fire again. The procedure often produced a direct hit, signalled down with a triumphant 'OK'.

The adjustments were made with the help of maps on which the terrain was marked up in grid squares, each with an identifying letter and number. Alternatively, to indicate direction, the time-honoured clock reference system might be used: 12 o'clock was due north and the distance to the target – often an enemy artillery battery – was quoted from the codes of concentric radial circles drawn at fifty-yard intervals on the air and ground maps. Gun batteries without their own lamps would acknowledge receipt of the aircraft's messages using a system of white cloth panels laid out on the ground upon which code letters were ponderously arranged. Some of the panels had been developed into venetian blinds that opened white and closed black, enabling Morse messages of dots and dashes to be sent from the ground back to the aircraft.

But often as not the observer had to resort to simply dropping written target information in a message bag. And over the shrieking bedlam of the British trenches the aircraft would sometimes use battery-powered klaxon horns of high decibels to screech out their dots and dashes to the gunners below. Communication between the gun batteries and the trenches was equally primitive. As field telephone lines were frequently the first casualties of enemy shellfire, messages were routinely carried by runners or carrier pigeons.

The shells being fired in their direction were a very real danger to the reconnaissance machines. The pilots and their observers could often hear them, alarmingly close, rumbling invisibly past on their deadly journeys. The aircraft would actually be flying in a quite narrow tunnel created by the flight paths of both the British and enemy guns. It was a perilous place in which to fly and from time to time aeroplanes were hit. All in all, it was an unhealthy occupation.

Photographic reconnaissance with glass-plate cameras was just beginning to replace the sketches observers scribbled on maps and notebooks on their knees. The pictures they brought back revealed priceless details of the enemy's front-line dispositions – information that cavalry probes could never have obtained behind the impregnable German lines. Subtle day-by-day changes in enemy activity could be spotted on succeeding days' pictures. Tiny adjustments to the trench patterns might indicate the position of a new machine-gun post. Fresh digging exposed new trenches. The wheel marks of limbers recently hauled up to the line betrayed altered gun positions. New spreads of barbed wire were quickly noted. And miles behind the lines the cameras captured giveaway images of assembled soldiers and the troop trains bringing them up to the front.

The photos were assembled into mosaic maps by a photographic unit and rushed to the headquarters of the Flying Corps wing to which No. 2 Squadron, and its sister, No. 3, belonged. Sholto Douglas was surprised to find that his photos were in a quality competition with those of a 3 Squadron observer, Lieutenant Darley. The wing's newly appointed commander, Lieutenant-Colonel Trenchard, recently transferred to France from the RFC's Farnborough headquarters, was taking a sharp interest in the fruits of his squadrons' reconnaissance missions. Visiting No. 2 Squadron, Douglas wrote: 'He would pull out of his pocket a bunch of Darley's photographs which he would show me with encomiums, apparently believing that he was inciting me to better efforts. But, as Darley and I had discovered in talking with each other, that Trenchard used to do the same thing the other way round on his visits to No. 3 Squadron, showing Darley my best efforts, we soon agreed that the old boy was wasting his time.'[4]

The 'old boy', however, was a force to be reckoned with. Their wing commander, Hugh Trenchard, known to all as 'Boom' for his exceptionally sonorous voice, was on his way to becoming what he still remains: the most legendary figure in the history of the British military air services. Yet this unremarkable, far from naturally gifted man seemed the most unlikely candidate for the greatness he would achieve. A gruff, congenitally inarticulate and at times fearsome martinet who never learned to spell or write with any fluency, he had come to flying late in a far from spectacular military career in which his duties had been mixed with much polo and hunting.

The son of a bankrupt Somerset solicitor, Trenchard had struggled academically to get a military commission. He found exams almost impossible to pass. Rejected by both Dartmouth Royal Naval College and the Woolwich Royal Military Academy, he just managed at the third attempt to scrape a pass in the much less demanding test for militia candidates. Eventually commissioned into the Royal Scots Fusiliers, he had served in India and in the Boer War in South Africa where, severely wounded in the lungs and spine, he had been invalided back to England. Later he had been a cavalry officer fighting tribesmen in Nigeria, earning a DSO and a reputation 'as a man of formidable personality who never hesitated to criticise all and sundry in the bluntest terms'.[5]

In 1912, now a major, he had become a rather lonely and discontented figure, approaching forty, unmarried and too unclubbable and poor for much higher rank. He was urged by a friend who had joined the just formed Royal Flying Corps to learn to fly and become a military pilot. Trenchard was a big and rather clumsy pupil. He invested £75 in lessons at a Brooklands flying school, where he got his Royal Aero Club pilot's ticket after just 64 minutes in the air. With this minimal qualification he was accepted by the Central Flying School. Here, having proved an indifferent pilot and a positively dangerous instructor, he had been appointed the school's adjutant. Although he was never to become either an experienced or a competent pilot Trenchard, whose logbook in the RAF Museum at Hendon shows his total flying hours as only 91, had demonstrated his worth in another significant way: he quickly learned to recognise and promote the enormous military potential of the aeroplane. From here on it would be not as a pilot but as a commander with a passionate belief in the future of air power that his career would blossom.

In his latest role as a wing commander in the Flying Corps' front line in France Trenchard had acquired among his flying crews a reputation as a stern disciplinarian as well as for his sharp tongue. One of his pilots, an outstanding example of the individualism Sholto Douglas had noticed on his first day at Merville, was an old Harrovian, Lieutenant John Moore-

Brabazon. Unlike his pilot colleagues Moore-Brabazon was a true pioneer of aviation. He had learned to fly in France in 1908, had become friendly with the Wright brothers and had become the first person to qualify as a pilot in Britain, being awarded Royal Aero Club certificate No. 1. At Merville he had been put in charge of the wing's photographic section. On his very first day he had fallen foul of his wing commander:

It happened at lunch in the crowded mess when someone asked the time and someone else, consulting his watch, said it was ten past one. Moore-Brabazon, a man of many talents who regulated his own watch by the time signal from the Eiffel Tower, broke in at once: 'Oh, no,' he contradicted. 'It's just one o'clock. You must be fast here.'

Conscious that the penetrating eye of Trenchard was on him, he explained defensively why he could not be wrong. Then he lapsed into nerve-stricken silence.

'You're Moore-Brabazon, aren't you?' said Trenchard, still staring fixedly at him.

'I am, sir.'

'And you only got here today?'

'I did, sir.'

'Well, remember this, Moore-Brabazon. The correct time here is what I make it.'[6]

'We were all a little bit scared of him because he was very severe and his manner was quite frightening,' recalled Air Mechanic Cecil King in an interview around sixty years later.

I was often picked to be his orderly – he used to call you to him and tell you what you had to do: 'Now you'll follow twenty paces behind me wherever I go. If I go in a doorway and I want you to come, I'll beckon you. If not wait at the doorway until I come out. If I call you, you'll come at the double to receive your orders.' That was carried out strictly and he never said anything that was unnecessary. If he growled, 'Orderly!' you jumped to attention, flew up and stood stiffly to hear what he had to say. Then you went off at the double to obey.[7]

But this was just the public face of the complex Trenchard. Few ever knew that his testiness was often triggered by agonising bouts of migraine that had plagued him ever since he was wounded in South Africa. His flying officers at Merville came to learn that beneath the gruff and menacing exterior lay an inquiring and flexible mind. He wanted results and badgered people for suggestions, haunting the hangars at all hours questioning squadron and flight commanders, pilots and observers, picking their brains. He was determined to demonstrate the indispensability of his reconnaissance planes to his army commander, General Sir Douglas Haig. The original British Expeditionary Force had been split into two armies with Haig now commander-in-chief of the First Army, to which Trenchard's wing was attached. The newly enlightened Haig had long since ceased to rely on men on horses to spy out the enemy. A wholly converted believer in the power of aerial reconnaissance, he had acquired such faith in it that he'd decided to delay the launch of ground offensives to await suitable weather for his artillery fire to be directed at the German line at Neuve Chapelle, south-west of Lille.

Haig regarded the air support for this operation, the first British offensive of the war, as so important he brought Trenchard into his Merville headquarters. He told the wing commander: 'If you can't fly because of the weather, I shall probably put off the attack.'[8] At midnight on the eve of the scheduled battle on 8 March 1915 the general sent for him. The cloud base was low and it was raining. This historic meeting, possibly the first in which supporting air power was so fundamentally woven into the core of an attack plan, was conducted in classic secrecy.

> The general was already waiting, wearing a great-coat over pyjamas, when Trenchard arrived. Bareheaded and with coat collar turned up, Haig strolled with-him across the wet village square, past the sentries, over the canal bridge and back, discussing the one imponderable factor which could not be controlled. He had been pinning his hope on finer weather, he said. He doubted whether the RFC would be able to direct the fire of the artillery and follow the progress of the infantry in poor visibility. 'I want one of your pilots to go up early in the morning. If his report is favourable, the fight will be on.'[9]

The brief 6am flight reported persisting low cloud but adequate visibility beneath it. Haig ordered the assault to go ahead. The bombardment was to begin at 7.30, the infantry to attack at 8.05am. The initial advance went off like clockwork, followed from the air by Trenchard's aircraft flickering their dots and dashes to the artillery. But the German line held. The attack failed with the appalling loss of around 13,000 men. The British gained one wrecked village. Their gunners largely ignored the target information fed to them from the air and paid the high price of the loss of six aeroplanes. When Haig learned that his artillery commanders had ignored the target information he summoned them to his headquarters. Reprimanding them for their 'early Victorian' ideas he is recorded as ordering them all to use the air service 'or go'.

The dramatic expansion of the Flying Corps to a hundred squadrons authorised by Lord Kitchener's bold gesture was painfully slow to happen. By the end of March 1915 there were still only 112 aircraft in France equipping a pitiful seven hard-pressed squadrons. But slowly this brave little force began to extend its role and firepower. As the frequency of air combat increased rifles and revolvers were replaced at last by machine guns. And though they could inflict only insignificant damage, small bombs were being dropped on tactical targets behind the enemy lines. It was one such raid that brought the RFC's first Victoria Cross.

Chapter 4
Brave Lives Given for Others

The pilot whose bravery and sacrifice earned him Britain's highest gallantry award was 2nd Lieutenant William Rhodes-Moorhouse. A twenty-seven-year-old old Harrovian and Cambridge man of considerable inherited wealth, he had learned to fly before the war, had his own aeroplane and had made headlines by flying his bride across the Channel on their honeymoon.

On 26 April 1915, in an attempt to disrupt the flow of German troops to the front at the Ypres Salient (a notorious blood-stained chunk of Allied-gained land projecting into German-held territory), he and three other 2 Squadron pilots were ordered to bomb the German-controlled railway yards at Courtrai, thirty-five miles away in southern Belgium. Each of the four BE2 aircraft was loaded with a single 100lb (45kg) bomb and were, to the great disappointment of Sholto Douglas, unable to carry an observer. Douglas fulfilled that role for Rhodes-Moorhouse. 'I begged him to take me with him and we had quite an argument about it,' he wrote. 'But he firmly refused on the grounds that he simply would not be able to manage with my extra weight on board.'[1]

The night before he left, Rhodes-Moorhouse, convinced he was embarking on a suicidal mission, sat down and wrote a farewell letter to his family. The offensive spirit that had now become a military imperative on the Western Front drove the flying squadrons and was instilled into the pilots. It demanded, brutally, that the impossibility of a task was insufficient reason for not attempting it.

Rhodes-Moorhouse was the only one of the four pilots to reach the Courtrai target. The railway station was fearsomely defended and when he made his bombing run at the dangerously low height of barely 300 feet his aeroplane was hosed with rifle fire from the ground and, most withering of all, from a machine gun in the belfry of a nearby church. Although mortally wounded he held his course and dropped his bomb on the station, now flying so low that some of its fragments, as he had feared, exploded upwards on to his aircraft. Grievously wounded, his stomach and thigh ripped open and one hand torn by a bullet, he set course back to Merville.

His thirty-minute return flight back across the lines at low level was an epic of heroism. With blood flooding into the cockpit from his torn open stomach and gaping thigh wound he managed, despite the shock, pain and nausea, to stay on course and make a perfect landing at Merville. The mechanics who lifted him out of the cockpit found so much blood they thought at first his leg had been severed. Rhodes-Moorhouse, still conscious, refused medical attention until he had delivered his report of the attack. Carried to the squadron office he dictated it there from his stretcher in the hearing of Trenchard himself before being taken to the casualty clearing station. The doctor saw at once that the wounds were beyond surgical repair and called for the padre, who gave him holy communion. Rhodes-Moorhouse is reputed to have said to him, 'If I must die, give me a drink.' He survived the night but died next afternoon. His flight commander, Captain Maurice Blake, sat beside him through his final hours during which Rhodes-Moorhouse held a photograph of his young son. He said to Blake: 'It's strange dying, Blake old boy – unlike anything one has ever done before, like one's first solo.'[2]

On Trenchard's recommendation Rhodes-Moorhouse was awarded a posthumous VC. Sholto Douglas, who had helped lift his dying pilot from the cockpit, was shaken by the evidence of his narrow escape. Nearly a hundred bullet holes were counted in the aircraft. Douglas noticed that at least half a dozen had hit the observer's seat. 'It was quite obvious,' he wrote, 'that I would not have survived if I had been with him.'

Rhodes-Moorhouse left behind an extraordinarily touching farewell letter to his one-year-old son, William, to be read to him when he was older.

My dear Sonny,

This is the first and last letter I shall ever write to you. You are now just over a year old and the dearest happy little chap I have ever seen and thank God you don't realise the awful war that is going on now. Years hence you will be shown this letter and your Dad's photograph by your dear Mother who has always been the sweetest and dearest wife a man could possibly have. Your dear mother and I have never had a quarrel or a misunderstanding of any sort ever, and it is for you to fill up the gap by exerting all your energies to be a great comfort to her who has been so sweet to your Dad and yourself.

Tomorrow I am going out at a very early hour, long, long before you will be out of bed, on an expedition which, if this letter reaches home, I shall be dead. If things are as they are at present you will be fairly well off. It has always been my desire and wish that my son be an engineer ... But, my dear boy, it is for each of us to make his own way in this world and far be it for me to say now 'be an engineer' ... If you want any advice on <u>any</u> subject, don't forget any subject, <u>always</u> ask your dear mother ... Parnham [the family estate in Dorset] I hope will be yours in time to come. Always keep up your position as a land-owner and a gentleman and make your friends at school and the Varsity friends, true friends (not hangers on) ... not for what they can get but friends because they like you as a good fellow ... I am looking at your sweet little face now and God bless you my dear boy.

> Goodbye, Sonny,
> Your loving father,
> Will Rhodes-Moorhouse[3]

In a postscript to his wife, Linda, Rhodes-Moorhouse wrote: 'Goodbye darling. God bless you always. I am off on a trip from which I don't expect to return but which I hope will shorten the war a bit. I shall probably be blown up by my own bomb, or if not, killed by rifle fire. Well God bless you my darling. I have no regrets. We have never had a quarrel and dear old Sonny will help to fill the gap. Goodbye my Darling pet, God keep you always dear, From Will.*

While Rhodes-Moorhouse had been so valiantly sacrificing his life in that futile act of gallantry to disrupt German troop trains moving through Courtrai to the front line at Ypres, the rail junction had already seen the passage to the front of a sinister new war weapon: thousands of big cylinders of chlorine gas. They had been manhandled into the trenches

---

*Rhodes-Moorhouse was sometimes described as a New Zealander of native Maori ancestry. This was only partly true. His parents were New Zealanders and his mother was part Maori, but he was born in London and although he made a short visit to New Zealand in 1907 he never lived there. Rhodes-Moorhouse's son William was also to die for his country. He went to Eton, became an Olympic skier, and in the Second World War joined the RAF. A pilot with No. 601 Squadron, he served in France, flying from Merville, the base where his father had died twenty-five years earlier. He was killed when his Hurricane was shot down over Tunbridge Wells in the Battle of Britain in September 1940. At the family estate in Dorset his ashes were buried beside his father.

on 22 April, their valves opened and the deadly yellow-green vapour released on the prevailing wind towards the Allied lines. Hundreds of French soldiers, blinded and with their lungs destroyed, died within ten minutes. In another gas attack two days later many Canadians also died, despite being ordered to urinate into cloths and use these to cover their faces (the chemicals present in urine were thought to help neutralise the chlorine). The sight of the death cloud creeping across the bare, devastated earth of no-man's-land was observed with awe and disgust from the air by Flying Corps pilots. 'I saw a long creeping wraith of yellow mist,' wrote Cecil Lewis as he watched a later retaliatory Allied gas attack on the German lines.

> I stared for a moment before I realised: Gas! Then instinctively, although I was a mile above the earth, I pulled back the stick to climb higher, away from the horror.
>
> In the light westerly wind it slid slowly down the German trenches, creeping panther-like over the scarred earth, curling down into dugouts, coiling and uncoiling at the wind's whim. Men were dying there, under me, from a whiff of it: not dying quickly, nor even maimed or shattered, but dying whole, retching and vomiting blood and guts; and those who lived would be wrecks with seared, poisoned lungs, rotten for life.[4]

Despite their wrecked nerves, one of the remarkable features of the young army officers arriving in the Flying Corps from the squalor and terror of the trenches was the way they continued to demonstrate in the air the qualities that had already earned them medals for outstanding gallantry on the ground. Captain Aidan Liddell, the much-loved son of an immensely wealthy Durham coal mine-owner, had come to the war from a world of Edwardian luxury. His family home, abounding in chandeliers and hunting trophies, was a fourteen-bedroomed Hampshire mansion which, surrounded by tennis and croquet courts, stood among trout lakes in over 800 acres of parkland near Basingstoke. The devoutly Catholic Liddells employed thirty-five servants, including a coachman, butler, liveried footmen and a housekeeper called Beckley, whose first task of the day was 'to iron the master's daily paper'. Aidan had gone to Stonyhurst College for a classical education from the Jesuits and on to Balliol College, Oxford, where most of his contemporaries were equally rich and privileged. He had been enormously popular at Oxford but some unspecified chronic ailment prevented him from shining academically and he avoided all team sports. Graduating with only third-class honours in zoology, he had returned home in 1912 to assume the role of Sherfield Manor's young squire whose days, it seems, were occupied with hunting, fishing and billiards.

As war approached Aidan Liddell had decided to amuse himself by learning to fly. He got his pilot's ticket at the Vickers flying school at Brooklands and then, surprisingly perhaps, joined the army. He took a commission in the Argyll and Sutherland Highlanders. With this celebrated Scottish regiment, his rosary tucked into his sporran, he had gone to fight in France in August 1914. As a machine-gun subaltern he had been awarded a Military Cross early in 1915 for his bravery in holding the line, continuing to fire his guns while hundreds around him were being mown down by fusillades of shrapnel and his gun team was reduced to just three men. 'My dear old Flum,' he had written to an old Stonyhurst friend, 'You don't know how boring and nerve-racking this trench business is . . . this is a dreadful war, and now they've started using grenades and bombs with great frequency it's a little worse than before. Some of the lines of trenches are only 25 yards apart and are full of water and mud . . . I'm sure none of the 10,000,000 or so combatants would mind if peace was declared tomorrow.'[5]

From a trench flooded by a burst river stopbank, in places up to their necks, Aidan wrote to his mother:

All the ground is full of dead bodies and when the wall of a dugout falls in there is generally a body exposed. One man wanted to cut some ends of roots that were sticking out of his dugout wall, and discovered they were a corpse's fingers![6]

In his next letter he reported:

It's impossible to get along the trench without going over one's knees in several places . . . I haven't had dry feet, or even boots without water slushing in them for a week, and our dugout leaks terribly in spite of waterproof sheets hung on the ceiling, which have to be emptied every three hours or so. So with wet straw to sleep on, and soaked blankets to cover one, and perpetual wet feet one would rather be elsewhere than soldiering . . .[7]

Liddell's leave back in England in the middle of January 1915 was an ungenerous single week. Strangely, he spent nearly half of those freezing midwinter days subjecting himself to more wet and cold, choosing to go salmon fishing on an uncle's estate in Cumberland.

Back on the Western Front the accumulated toll of physical hardship and of five months in continuous action at last caught up with him. He collapsed, so ill he was shipped back to England. The army medical officer who examined him diagnosed the convenient catch-all 'influenza'. A medical board, adding rheumatism 'from standing in a wet trench', declared him temporarily unfit for service and sent him on extended leave. None of these doctors had considered that the most acute of their patient's conditions was the psychological injury that had stretched his nervous system beyond endurance; that he was, in truth, simply emotionally burned out. The most significant element of his illness – traumatic stress, or shellshock, already affecting hundreds of thousands of battle-shattered men on both sides on the Western Front – was then scarcely understood.

When he was finally declared fit to resume active service Liddell decided to switch to what seemed the more comfortable life of the Royal Flying Corps. With his pilot's ticket, his upper-class background and his Military Cross he was immediately accepted. In July 1915 he was back in France, with RFC wings, posted as a captain to No. 7 Squadron based at St Omer. This was a reconnaissance squadron equipped with one of the Flying Corps' less nimble aircraft, the RE5, a clumsy two-seat tractor biplane, memorably said by one of its pilots to have 'resembled a blowzy old woman that floundered about the sky in a safe if unattractive manner'.[8]

Liddell was now far removed from the misery of the trenches. The squadron's mess was in a local estaminet, where the pilots enjoyed plentiful hot water, leisurely breakfasts with the previous day's London newspapers and tennis, which they played with Madame's attractive young daughters. But Liddell quickly found himself on operations, reconnoitring enemy activity deep inside the lines in occupied Belgium. Within a few days of his arrival he and his observer flew a long mission to Bruges on which they were attacked by an enemy aircraft. Their machine gun, fired backwards from the front cockpit to avoid the propeller, jammed and they could retaliate only ineffectively with a rifle and automatic pistol. They arrived back at St Omer with a bullet-damaged aircraft, lucky to have survived.

Three days later, on 31 July, Liddell was sent again to Bruges. His observer on this flight, Lieutenant Roland Peck, added to his Lewis machine gun a loaded .303 rifle. Approaching Bruges at 5,000 feet they were again attacked. They didn't see the German two-seater that twice struck from above. Its gunner poured machine-gun fire on to the RE5, severing the throttle-control line, smashing the wheel of the control column, shooting away an aileron and part of the rudder and tearing open Liddell's right thigh.

Liddell blacked out and lost control of the aircraft. It flipped on to its back, nearly tipping out Peck, who had unstrapped himself to stand up to fire his Lewis gun. They dived for 3,000 feet before Liddell regained consciousness and somehow managed to get the machine back into level flight, now barely 2,000 feet above the ground. With the controls damaged the only way he could keep it there was by wrestling the smashed wheel with one hand and juggling the rudder bar with his good left foot.

They were half an hour from St Omer. Liddell's thigh wound, exposed to the mangled bone, was pouring blood and they were over enemy territory. He seriously doubted he could remain conscious long enough to get them home. As an immediate landing to seek medical help would have meant imprisonment for the rest of the war, Liddell decided to press on. He scribbled a note to Peck saying that he intended to head for the Channel coast beach west of Nieuport in unoccupied Belgium. Peck replied that there was a closer alternative: a Belgian Flying Corps base at La Panne near Furnes.

Somehow Liddell got them safely down at La Panne. The aircraft was immediately surrounded by people anxious to rush him to hospital but he refused to go, demanding that a doctor be brought to supervise his removal from the cockpit to prevent further damage to his leg. In the meantime he is said to have fashioned a splint and applied a tourniquet while berating a Belgian officer for the failure of the airfield's landing direction marker to be pointing into wind. During the half-hour that they waited for the medical officer a photographer took some remarkable pictures. These dramatic images, splashed a few days later across the front page of the *Daily Mirror*, show Liddell being lifted from the cockpit and lying on the ground on a stretcher. He is smoking a cigarette, smiling and waving.

Liddell's feat made him an instant local hero. The French president, Monsieur Poincaré, came to see him in hospital. So did several Belgian and British generals. The commandant of the La Panne base wrote to Liddell's squadron commander, Major Hoare: 'Thanks to his coolness and conspicuous energy he has saved his aeroplane, his companion and himself from the hands of the enemy, having had the incredible strength of will necessary to make a faultless landing on our camp. He has thus given us all a magnificent example of endurance which deserves to be rewarded.'[9]

Major Hoare wrote to Liddell:

Dear Liddell,

Just a line to say how damned sorry I am that you've been so badly winged. I'm afraid you will have a bad time, but you will have this much to buck you up, that you have done one of the finest feats that has been done in the Corps since the beginning of the war. How you managed to get back God only knows, but it was a magnificent effort and the General is giving a detailed report on it today to [Field Marshal] French ... You have set a standard of pluck and determination which may be equalled, but certainly will not be surpassed during this war ...

Yours

C. Hoare[10]

The Belgian surgeons struggled to save Liddell's leg, removing four inches of bone. But in the absence of yet-to-be-discovered antibiotics gangrene set in. His leg had to be amputated. As he came round from the anaesthetic he was told he had been awarded the Victoria Cross.

The amputation failed to arrest the spread of infection. When his temperature soared and he developed shivering fits the doctors, fearing they couldn't save him, summoned his mother. Emily Liddell rushed to Belgium, where she sat at Aidan's bedside for a week. On 31 August 1915, after receiving extreme unction from a Catholic priest, he told Emily it was getting dark. 'Mummy, I want to go home,' he said.

'You are going home, sonny,' she replied.

Squeezing her hand in acknowledgement, Aidan died.[11]

In addition to the usual official telegrams of regret from the King and Queen and the war minister, the Liddell family was overwhelmed by more than a thousand letters of condolence. They are filled with admiration and patriotism. 'From the smallest drummer boy to the Colonel, this battalion asks only to be given the chance to avenge Aidan's death,' wrote his Argyll and Sutherland Highlanders former commander, Major Maxwell Rouse.[12] 'His splendid sacrifice – for that's what it was – was finer far than the world will ever guess ... we all feel as if the light had gone out – the light of our battalion.' From Oxford a former Balliol tutor wrote: 'There is something so extraordinarily complete about his death. First, a magnificent expression of the power of action that was in him, then a month of suffering ... to bring out the other side of a complete man. Suffering ... which does so much to make a man fit for heaven! How proud you must be of him.'[13]

A parchment scroll arrived from Buckingham Palace. It was a circular sent in hundreds of thousands to the next-of-kin of war dead. 'I join with my grateful people,' George V declared, 'in sending you this memorial of a brave life given for others in the Great War.'

Chapter 5
The Fokker Scourge

By the spring of 1915 the war was going badly for the British. After Turkey attacked Russia in the Caucasus the Allies had tried to bombard Constantinople with a naval assault through the narrow Dardanelles Strait linking the Mediterranean with the Black Sea. The operation was undertaken at Russia's request in the hope that it would divert the Turks away from the Caucasus. The combined British and French naval mission failed. It was left to British, Australian and New Zealand soldiers now to land at Gallipoli to try to take the Turkish capital by land. This attempt, too, ended in disaster. The British and Empire troops suffered dreadful losses. And the familiar columns of the casualty lists were joined by further grim tallies of dead and wounded from a separate appalling battle failure on the Western Front.

Here the BEF was running out of shells and the shrapnel-firing field artillery guns urgently needed replacing with much heavier, more destructive howitzers able to blast open the barbed-wire entanglements with high-explosive shells. But before the heavier-calibre guns could arrive from the overwhelmed British armaments factories the BEF found itself, in September 1915, forced back into action and more bloodshed.

To draw German forces away from the hard-pressed Russian armies on the Eastern Front the British and French launched major attacks in France. The French delivered theirs in Artois and also in Champagne north-east of Paris; the BEF struck near the mining town of Loos. The British began hostilities with chlorine gas – their first use of the hideous weapon. Tragically, the wind blew it back on to one of the battalions releasing it. In the middle of the choking clouds a Scottish piper marched back and forth playing 'Scotland the Brave'. Desperately needed British reserve troops failed to arrive in time. For the BEF and the French the Battle of Loos achieved nothing but death and dismembered bodies. In a ferocious counter-attack German machine guns made casualties of nearly 200,000 men. By the time the assault was called off the British had lost 50,000 soldiers, the French a horrifying 145,000. In all something like 400,000 more young Allied and German men had been killed or wounded.

As the casualty lists yet again sprawled shockingly across columns of the English newspapers they triggered widespread anger and government unease at the military leadership of the war. Already under a cloud for his perceived lack of aggression in the retreat from Mons, the BEF's commander, Sir John French, was replaced at the end of the year by General Haig.

During the Battle of Loos the Flying Corps and the French Air Service had worked together to bomb the moving trains bringing German troops to the front. But with their pathetically small bombs and the difficulty of aiming against moving targets the raids had done little to stem the flow of enemy reinforcements. The RFC's role remained essentially artillery ranging and photo reconnaissance for the army. But by the end of the Battle of Loos these operations were suddenly threatened by a new peril in the sky: German fighter aircraft that could fire their machine guns straight ahead through their spinning propellers.

The machine was the single-winged Eindecker, built by a little-known Dutchman, Anthony Fokker, whose company was later to make some of the world's most widely used airliners. Although said to have been personally lacking in great technical design skills, Fokker possessed a special ability to attract and inspire teams of brilliant technicians to his company. Before the war he had offered his services to the British War Office but the generals had expressed no interest. Finding more encouragement in Germany he had moved there and, at the age of twenty-two, set up a factory near Berlin. When war came he found himself deluged with military orders for his aeroplanes from the German Army Air Service. One of these orders, in April 1915, came with a very specific requirement.

Fokker was presented with a captured French Air Service aeroplane whose wooden propeller, to prevent it being chopped off by bullets, had been fitted with steel deflector plates that allowed its machine gun to fire directly through it, enabling the pilot to shoot in more accurate and deadly fashion in the direction of flight. The plane had been unofficially customised by its French pilot, Roland Garros, who had been taken prisoner. Garros had been surprised to discover that only a small proportion of machine-gun rounds failed to pass through the momentary gaps created as the blades spun round. With his plates fitted, the bullets that did strike the propeller simply bounced off in arcs that, happily, missed the cockpit. Despite the alarming vibration whenever a bullet hit the plates, Garros, with this crude device, had begun to shoot down a string of German machines. But his missions had come to an early end when engine failure had forced him to land in enemy territory – and make a gift of his invention to the Germans.

When Fokker, asked to copy the system, had examined the French aeroplane he decided that this was an inefficient arrangement. He and his team knew of something much better. Before the war, a Swiss engineer, Franz Schneider, working for a German aircraft manufacturer, the LVG company, had designed and patented, but never built, a mechanical device that cleverly synchronised propeller and machine gun. It relied on the fact that while one of the two propeller blades passed the gun's trajectory at something like 1,200 times a minute, the gun would fire only about 500 to 600 times.* To ensure the bullets went only through the gaps – 'like kicking a football through the sails of a windmill' – a mechanical interrupter physically stopped the gun for a split second each time a blade was directly in front of the muzzle.

Seizing on the Schneider system Fokker produced his own version of it, installing the synchronised gun on one of his own single-seater monoplanes. In his autobiography he claimed to have personally designed the interrupter gear, creating it from scratch. But was he really the inventor? Franz Schneider certainly didn't think so. He sued Fokker for infringement of his 1913 patent.†

Unconcerned by Schneider's demands for damages, Fokker had proudly taken his device for approval to the Imperial German Air Service. The inspecting officers greeted it with scepticism. Although he demonstrated that it would fire streams of bullets faultlessly through the

---

*At this firing rate the 500-bullet belt of Fokker's Eindecker machine gun gave its pilot barely a minute's worth of shooting. As a comparison the Browning gun of the WWII Battle of Britain Spitfire had a fire rate of around 1,100 rounds per minute. But the 350 bullets it carried in each of its eight wing-mounted guns gave it a mere 17 or so seconds of fire.

†Fokker sought refuge in a law that he believed gave him immunity from such claims where the product was manufactured for military purposes. But the court ruled that the German Army had merely ordered an aeroplane that could fire through its propeller; that the means by which it did so was Fokker's responsibility, as was any patent liability involved. Fokker was ordered to pay damages but legal wrangling in the German courts went on for the next eighteen years and there is no record that Schneider was ever paid anything. Meanwhile, in 1919, Fokker, in a masterly plot, bribing scores of German and Dutch police, frontier and railway officials, had taken advantage of the collapse of the German administration to smuggle his factory back to his native Holland. Chartering six trains each hauling sixty wagons he had with incredible audacity, by disguising the freight, shipped 200 aeroplanes and 400 engines across the border to launch a civil aviation business that was to become one of the world's biggest.

whirling propeller, they demanded proof that it would work in combat. 'The suggestion was made that I, a foreigner and a civilian, go to the front, find a French or British flyer, and demonstrate by actually bringing down an enemy plane that my gun was practical.'[1]

Despite his protests Fokker was driven to the Western Front, to the headquarters of General von Heeringen. The general arranged for the unhappy Dutchman to be dressed in German air corps uniform and issued with a false ID card for a real sortie over the front line. For several days he flew up and down the lines searching for a test victim in vain. It was not until his fifth mission that, at 6,000 feet near Douai, he spotted a French Farman two-seater on a reconnaissance. 'It was my opportunity to show what the gun would do, and I dived rapidly towards it,' Fokker said. 'Even though they had seen me, they would have had no reason to fear bullets through my propeller. While approaching I thought of what a deadly stream of lead I could send into the plane. It would be just like shooting a sitting rabbit, because the pilot couldn't shoot back through his pusher propeller at me.'

It didn't happen. At the last moment, on the point of firing, Fokker decided he couldn't go through with it. 'I had no personal animosity towards the French. Suddenly I decided the whole job could go to hell. It was too much like "cold meat" to suit me. I had no stomach for the whole business, nor any wish to kill Frenchmen for Germans. Let them do their own killing!'

Fokker landed at the German airfield at Douai and confessed to the base commander his moral dilemma. He suggested a German pilot take the killer aeroplane hunting instead. The man assigned to the task was Lieutenant Oswald Boelcke, one of his squadron's most experienced pilots, whose two Iron Crosses testified to his success as a two-seater reconnaissance pilot. Fokker talked him through the firing system and Boelcke, never having shot down an aeroplane, set off keen to put it to work. In the summer of 1915, with the air war in its early stages, still relatively few aeroplanes were operating above the battlefields, and Boelcke didn't immediately score any victories. It was not until later in the summer, and into the spring of 1916, that he and a fellow pilot, Max Immelmann, began at last to shoot down British and French pilots, doing so in such numbers and with such impunity that the Allied air commands became seriously alarmed by the scale of their losses.

The Eindecker was not a particularly wonderful flying machine. Its single wing curiously braced by a stubby mast adorned with what looked like the spokes of an umbrella, it had a somewhat fragile appearance.

It was initially under-powered and banked inefficiently by warping its wingtips. But its forward-firing guns were destined to more than compensate for these disadvantages. At a stroke this mediocre aeroplane with its lethal armament handed air superiority decisively to the German squadrons. They dominated the skies over the Western Front, denying British and French reconnaissance aircraft the airspace they needed to take their vital photographs behind the lines. To prevent the secret mechanism falling into Allied hands the German pilots were ordered not to cross into enemy territory.

Their widely publicised successes within Germany made national heroes of Boelcke and Immelmann, who began to compete to top each other's tally of kills. They stalked the prey they nicknamed 'cold meat' with the patience and precision of pigeon-hunting falcons. 'I let him fly on eastward for a while,' reported Immelmann to his mother, describing an attack on a British reconnaissance two-seater near Arras:

> Then I took up the pursuit, hiding behind his tail all the time. I followed him for about a quarter of an hour in this fashion. My fingers were itching to shoot, but I controlled myself and withheld my fire until I was within 60 metres of him. I could plainly see the observer in the front seat peering out downward. Knack-knack-knack ... went my gun. Fifty rounds, and then a long flame shot out of his engine. Another fifty rounds at the pilot. Now his fate was sealed. He went down in long spirals to land. The pilot had a bullet in the right upper arm. I also shot his right thumb away ... The observer was unwounded. His machine gun was in perfect working order, but he had not fired a single shot – so complete was the surprise I sprung on him.[2]

Immelmann knew these details of the damage his gun had inflicted because he had landed close to the British pilot's aeroplane and gone to his aid. The German introduced himself and instructed some cavalrymen to arrange for a car to drive the captured crew to hospital. Later he flew over the lines to drop a note at a British aerodrome advising that the pilot and his observer had survived and were being well treated in captivity.

The Flying Corps and the French Air Service were virtually impotent to respond to the depredations of the Fokker. The slow, gentle, unmanoeuvrable British workhorses, the BE2 reconnaissance biplanes, were never designed to fight for their lives: they were simply picked off at random by the Eindeckers which, through the latter half of 1915, Anthony Fokker continued to make more and more dangerous with increasingly powerful engines and the addition of a second forward-firing gun. By the end of the year the Eindecker had become, temporarily at least, the most formidable fighting machine in the world. It took the British and French more than six months to acquire their own synchronously equipped fighters.

Meanwhile the BE2 victims struggled to survive. The reconnaissance machines had now been fitted with Lewis machine guns operated by the observer/gunner in the front cockpit. They also had lighter-weight wireless sets with which the observers, reeling out a long copper-wire aerial, tapped out Morse code ranging instructions to the artillery batteries, now supported by Flying Corps wireless operators attached to them. When the Fokkers tried to terminate the ranging process the British observers found themselves in a one-sided battle. Not only could their guns not fire forward, the directions in which they could do so were heavily restricted by the mass of surrounding struts and bracing wires holding the aircraft together. To deal with this there was a clumsy and awkward option: the gun could be detached from its mounting socket and moved to one of three other brackets to get the best line of fire in a dogfight.

The RFC's commanders appeared helpless in their search for the gun-firing solution. Instead of channelling resources urgently into the creation of their own interrupter gear the military aeronautics department simply ducked the issue, rushing instead to acquire an array of pusher-driven aeroplanes for the sole reason that they didn't need to fire forwards through propellers. One of them was the BE9. Its unofficial name, 'the Pulpit', wrote a cynical young Flying Corps pilot, 2nd Lieutenant Duncan Grinnell-Milne, was all too obvious.

> A little three-ply box projected from the front of the machine. The wretched man in this box had indeed an unrestricted forward view, but just behind his head revolved the four deadly blades of the propeller. There was no communication possible between front and back seat; if anything happened, if the pilot were wounded, or even if nothing more serious occurred than a bad landing in which the machine tipped over on its nose, the man in the box could but say his prayers: he would inevitably be crushed by the engine behind him. One of these machines was attached to the squadron in which I served; but by the merciful dispensation of Providence it never succeeded in defeating an enemy craft.[3]

As its reconnaissance aeroplanes were being steadily shot out of the sky that summer of 1915 the Royal Flying Corps was making some major command changes. Sir David Henderson, now a major-general, was brought back to London to become overall commander-in-chief of the corps at the War Office and Lieutenant-Colonel Trenchard, promoted to brigadier-general and acquiring his predecessor's personal horse, George, took command of the RFC's operations in France.

To some of his fellow officers the extraordinarily incoherent Trenchard was a surprising appointment. 'His mind always worked quicker than his tongue; he was almost physically incapable of expressing his thoughts on paper – his handwriting had to be seen to be believed – his dictating was a nightmare to his stenographers, and his instructions were often a cause of puzzlement (and sometimes amusement) to his staff officers. His closest friends (or worst enemies) could hardly accuse him of being an intellectual type of officer.'[4] But Trenchard, who, it was said, probably never read the codified principles of war defined in military manuals, possessed one important quality that was to sustain him in high command: his unerring instinct to concentrate the force of air power where it contributed most to the success of the land armies who would win or lose the war.

With no machines capable of tackling the Fokkers and morale sagging among the pilots watching their numbers decline by the day, Trenchard's inheritance was bleak. As there was no way the air corps could discontinue its reconnaissance and gun-spotting for the ever-expanding artillery bat-teries, he decided to call for a major change in operational tactics 'until,' he said, 'the RFC are in possession of a machine as good as the German Fokker'. He ordered that all reconnaissance aircraft were henceforth to be escorted by at least three other machines. They were all to be flown in close formation and the reconnaissance abandoned if even one of the aircraft for any reason couldn't stay with the group. As the army demanded longer and longer missions to report on troop train activity further and further behind the lines, the risks to the survival of the observation planes increased so dramatically that the size of the escort force sometimes grew to ludicrous proportions. For one of these missions, deep into Belgium, such was the fear of Fokker attack that, although the operation was eventually cancelled, no less than twelve escorting aeroplanes were assigned to the task.[5]

The escort edict drastically cut the number of daily operations the squadrons could fly. In the winter of 1915 the Flying Corps in France was not only bereft of forward-firing aeroplanes to hold its own in the air, it didn't have enough machines of any description, nor enough pilots to fly them. When the French Air Service offered a batch of Morane biplanes there weren't any pilots to go to Paris to collect them. The flow of newly trained aircrew from England was barely keeping up with the Fokker casualties. And there weren't enough competent instructors to teach the pilot recruits to fly properly. Some were arriving in France with so little experience they were a menace to their squadrons, wrecking their machines even before they'd crossed the lines. 'A reserve pilot has just smashed his fourth machine, so I'm sending him back for further training,' the exasperated Trenchard complained to Henderson.[6]

In Britain the newspapers called the rising toll of victims the 'Fokker Scourge', describing Flying Corps pilots as 'Fokker fodder'. In the House of Commons the crisis was seized upon by a colourful eccentric, Noel Pemberton-Billing. This commanding, flamboyant figure, once described as a 'cantankerous patriot', who styled himself 'the First Air Member', began a crusade in which he persistently questioned the capability of the RFC's leadership. He criticised the way it was managing and losing the air war and its failure to produce adequate aeroplanes with enough properly trained pilots. Headlines followed his allegation that RFC pilots in France were daily, through the blundering incompetence of their leaders, being 'rather murdered than killed'. Pemberton-Billing spoke with the authority he had acquired as the owner of a pre-war aircraft construction company which he had run before becoming a squadron commander in the Royal Naval Air Service and, later, an MP.*

The Flying Corps commander-in-chief took the complaints personally. Sir David Henderson, who had sat in the Commons listening to Pemberton-Billing's murder accusations, promptly offered his resignation. He demanded that the under-secretary for war hold a public inquiry to give the aviation generals the opportunity to defend themselves. His resignation was refused, but the government agreed to the inquiry. Among scores of allegations it was charged with investigating was the highly sensitive claim that the RFC's field commander, General Trenchard 'had no sufficient training in flying'. A judge, Sir Clement Bailhache, was appointed to run the inquiry which would go on for months. Nor was this the only committee to have been let loose to pronounce upon the ills besetting the Flying Corps. Another was already at work looking into the management and role of the monopoly the government had created with its Farnborough factory. This group was headed by a

---

*Pemberton-Billing sold his company (Pemberton-Billing Ltd) in 1916 to his factory manager, who renamed it Supermarine Aviation Works. The company became famous for its high-speed seaplanes and the immortal Spitfire.

baronet, Sir Richard Burbidge, better known as the managing director of Harrods than for his knowledge of aviation.

The crisis of confidence in the military air service did little for the morale of the front-line aircrew or the anxieties of their families. It also put additional pressure on the commanders, whose careers were rooted in ground warfare for which the upstart flying machine was still struggling to prove itself.

Among the impediments to the rapid equipment of the Flying Corps with machines to tackle the Fokkers was the competition it continued to face for such aeroplanes from the Royal Naval Air Service. Unhampered by the bottleneck of the army's Farnborough aeroplane factory, the navy's admirals simply went on buying the best available directly from independent manufacturers. But the manufacturers, all of them small firms, a lot of them car-makers used to turning out mere handfuls of planes for the recreational market and powering them with French engines, couldn't keep up with the war's demands. The two air arms were having to turn to the French for both aeroplanes and the engines the British were only just beginning to learn how to build. The worry and pressure of it all began to affect General Henderson's health. 'The doctor has got at me,' he confided to Trenchard, 'and says I must go away for a fortnight. You need not tell anybody this . . . the rest is only a precautionary measure . . . I hope we shall soon have plenty of machines for you, but the lack of a big engine is turning my hair grey.'[7]

The machines didn't materialise. Aeroplanes and pilots were being destroyed faster than either could be replaced. Back on duty early in 1916, Henderson was forced to resume his flow of disappointing news to Trenchard. 'We cannot send out the squadrons promised this month and at the same time keep you up to strength in pilots,' he wrote in March. 'I am sorry for this but the combination of bad weather and casualties has brought us down for the moment to bedrock in pilots.'[8]

Trenchard replied: 'I am, as you say, frightfully worried over the loss of pilots out here. You can imagine it is not quite an easy game at present . . .' In desperation he suggested to Henderson they borrow some aircraft and pilots from the Royal Naval Air Service. 'What do the Navy want with all these machines and pilots sitting about all over the world doing nothing, when we are overworking everybody . . . It is really, and I am not panicking, very serious.' When Henderson approached his opposite number, the director of air services at the Admiralty, he helpfully offered fifteen pilots. But the naval aviators themselves were far from happy about the proposal. 'This morning,' Henderson had to write to

Trenchard, 'Admiral Vaughan-Lee told me that the pilots who had been
warned for this duty were unwilling to fly our aeroplanes, as they considered them unsuitable for flying in the presence of the enemy.' In the
end three navy pilots agreed to the attachment, but only on condition they
took their own French-built Nieuport machines. 'Three beastly Nieuports
with their attendants are going to you at once,' Henderson informed
Trenchard. 'Gawd help you.'[9] 'It will be a great nuisance,' responded
Trenchard. 'But as you ask it I will do it . . . I sometimes think it would be
better if Pemberton-Billing was put in command out here.'

The already overstretched Henderson was also burdened with the
chore of collecting evidence for the looming inquiry into his alleged
incompetence. He needed his field commander to help explain to the
committee why the army's demands for intelligence forced him to go on
sending his pilots into doomed combat. But the painfully inarticulate
Trenchard shrank from the task. He agreed to send operational statistics,
but was unwilling 'to give written information for the sake of political
agitators to pull to pieces unless I am ordered to do so'.[10]

Trenchard had difficulty understanding why the flow of aircraft he so
badly needed couldn't be speeded up simply by hassling the struggling
suppliers. He began to direct his frustrations to one of Henderson's
lieutenants, the director of air organisation, William Sefton Brancker,
now a brigadier-general. In Brancker he found a sympathetic ear and a
kindred aeronautically inclined spirit. The brigadier-general had moved
from the army to the air corps bringing with him a reputation as a rather
unconventional officer of unusual vision and shrewd common sense who
regularly shocked his superiors with buccaneering methods that cut
through War Office red tape and got things done. A short, stylish, monocled man of enormous charm, exuding endless positivity, Brancker had
become a legend in the Flying Corps, both for his engaging personality
and for his renowned lack of skill as a pilot. But Brancker was no more
successful than Henderson in providing aircraft that didn't exist in the
numbers Trenchard demanded. The letters that passed between them
through the RFC's dark days of 1916 developed into a private correspondence that ran in parallel to their more stiffly formal official letters.
Increasingly they had to do with individual pilots in Trenchard's squadrons, sometimes seeking a favour: 'Dear Brancker, I am sending home
young Captain Bolton in my regiment to learn to fly. I would be very
much obliged if you would keep an eye on the boy. He used to hunt with
me and we were great guns. But he should be kept hard at work as he is
a young gentleman, blessed with a certain amount of money.'[11]

But more frequently Trenchard was writing about pilots who were cracking under the strain of daily aerial combat. Lieutenant Strugnall was one who was approaching his limits. 'He is one of the best pilots I have got out here and can fly anything. He is not "tired", but he has been out here a long time and I think he had better go home as I do not want to run the risk of breaking him up.'[12]

Lieutenant Allen was already beyond the boundaries of his endurance. He 'had his observer killed in the air on the 31st May and suffered very badly from nerves afterwards. They tried to make him pull himself together but he was no good, and whenever he went out to work he returned without doing any work. He stated to his squadron commander that he did not want to fly any more. As fighting in the air is a normal thing he would be of no use to the Flying Corps.'[13]

Had Lieutenant Allen been ordered to carry on flying he would inevitably have joined the mounting statistics of pilots and observers killed or wounded over the Western Front. People at home no longer needed Pemberton-Billing to draw their attention to the shocking figures: the casualty lists told their own story almost daily in the British newspapers. Yet amazingly, the stream of young applicants bursting to serve with the Flying Corps continued unabated.

Chapter 6
Public Schoolboys Wanted

The biggest pool of Flying Corps recruits were eager English public schoolboys. Undeterred by the sensational coverage of the Fokker carnage, many were cutting short their education and falsifying their ages to join up before the war ended and denied them their romantic adventure. The ethos of the RFC was firmly public-school. Its squadrons, at least initially, were elite establishments in which grammar-school, lower-middle and, most emphatically, working-class applicants found scant welcome.

But though the public-school products were viewed by the officer-class hierarchy at the War Office almost automatically as the right material to serve their country in the air as commissioned pilots, they didn't always find it easy to get in to the Flying Corps. There were, as yet, no recruiting offices for pilots and observers and the selection process was unusually informal and haphazard. It helped to have privately acquired the Royal Aero Club's flying ticket; indeed, this was a virtual guarantee of entry. Those without the ticket would seek letters of introduction from distinguished military relatives, if they were lucky enough to have them – the higher the rank the better. Better still if, as ex-Boer War colleagues, they were on close terms with the commander-in-chief himself.

'Dear Ajax,' wrote a Colonel Cavendish from London's Hanover Square. 'Do you remember at Cape Town in 1883 Ryk Myburgh who was in the Colonial Office there? He is now Resident Magistrate at Bulawayo and his 2nd boy is here now wanting to get into the Flying Corps. He is a very nice boy, age 19, and if you could help him to it I think he might be useful. The boy's name is John A Myburgh . . . doubtless a word from you would grease the wheels.'[1] It did. 'Dear Shaver,' General Henderson wrote back, 'I saw this boy and I said he was to be taken if medically fit. He was a good stamp of lad.'[2]

Of course not everyone was blessed with an influential friend or relative. For those who were not, the only option was to go in person to the War Office in its huge baroque stone building in Whitehall to plead for acceptance. In this bewildering and intimidating warren of a thousand rooms, two and a half miles of corridors swarming with red-tabbed staff officers and blue-clad messengers, the applicants would be directed to Room 613A. Here would sit one of several captains of impeccable breeding who vetted applicants for the Directorate of Military Aeronautics. One of the best known was Lord Hugh Cecil.

Later Baron Quickwood, Cecil was the son of the Marquess of Salisbury, three times British prime minister. Educated at Eton and Oxford, he had become the member of Parliament for Oxford University, acquiring a reputation in the Commons for the power of his classical oratory, delivered in a high-pitched voice. One of his closest friends was Winston Churchill, at whose wedding he had been best man. In 1915, at the ripe age of forty-six, he had joined the Royal Flying Corps. Although he had trained as a pilot and earned his military wings, his performance in the cockpit was said to have been so ham-fisted he was not considered competent to be let loose in a squadron; instead he was found the safer selection job in the War Office. Identifying candidates for their suitability as war pilots was a role for which, beyond establishing the quality of their pedigree, he had little aptitude, either. Cecil Lewis recalled his own memorable interview with Lord Cecil – 'bald and mild, with good hands and a most charming manner'.

'So you were at Oundle?'
  'Yes, sir.'
  'Under the great Sanderson?'
  'Er – yes, sir.' (Old Beans the great Sanderson! Well I'm blowed!)
  'Were you in the Sixth?'
  'Yes, sir – Upper Sixth. Er – a year under the average, sir.'
  'I see. How old are you?'
  'Almost eighteen, sir.' (Liar! You were seventeen last month.)
  'Play any games?'
  'Yes, sir. I got my school colours at fives, and I captained the House on the river. I should have got my house colours for rugger this year if I'd stayed; but—'
  'Fives you say? You should have a good eye then.'
  'Yes, I suppose so, sir.'
  'You're very tall.'
  'Six foot three, sir.' [He was actually six foot four.]
  'I don't think you could get into a machine.'
  'Why, sir?' (Oh Lord! He's going to turn me down. He *mustn't* turn me down.)

'Well, they're not built for young giants like you, you know.'

'Couldn't I try, sir?'

A slow smile, a pause, then: 'Yes, I suppose so. I'll write a note to the O.C. at Hounslow.'

'Oh, thank you so much, sir. I'm awfully keen, sir.'

He wrote rapidly. 'Here, take this with you and show it to the O.C. Hounslow.'[3]

A few weeks later Lewis was starting his pilot training.

The difference the right connections could make is demonstrated by the contrasting experiences of Arthur Harris. Back in England in 1915 from the German South-west Africa campaign in which he'd served as a boy bugler with a Rhodesian regiment, he had gone to the War Office in London to try and join the RFC. 'I was interviewed,' he said, 'by a rather supercilious young man. When I said I would like to fly he said, "Well, so would 6,000 other people! Would you like to be 6,001 on the waiting list?" So I retired rather disgruntled.' When Harris told his father what had happened, he said, 'Well, why didn't you go and see your uncle Charlie?'

Harris had never heard of his uncle Charlie, but was grateful for a letter of introduction from him arranged by his father. He went back to the War Office with it. 'When I handed the note to the same supercilious young fellow he said, "Oh, please sit down a minute, sir!" Which was rather a change from his reception the day before. He came back about ten minutes later and he said, "Colonel Elliot is in conference and unable to see you at the moment. But if you will report to No. 2 Reserve Squadron at Brooklands this evening you can start flying." So I did just that.'[4]

John Slessor was another young man who found that resorting to nepotism was the only way to get in. As a seventeen-year-old public schoolboy from Haileybury, left lame in both legs after contracting poliomyelitis at the age of three, he had been rejected by both the army and navy as 'totally unfit for any form of military service'. So he made an appointment at the War Office to see a Lieutenant-Colonel William Warner 'who had been a brother-officer of an uncle of mine in the Indian Cavalry'. Slessor, 'with a beating heart', was ushered into his office, 'past a long waiting queue of regular serving officers of other Arms, all better qualified than I to be received into the then extremely limited ranks of the RFC. In this holy of holies, seated on the edge of a desk gossiping to Colonel Warner, was an officer whom I later knew as Major Ferdy Waldron. Waldron was a Flying Corps pilot.'

Said Willie Warner, 'I don't see why this boy shouldn't perfectly well be able to fly, do you Ferdy?'

'Oh well – I don't know. Yes, I should think he'd fly all right. Let's see you walk across the room!'

Ferdy Waldron's verdict seemed to clinch it. Within five minutes I was down in the street in a lather of apprehension, under orders to get my form of application for a commission signed by my father and the Master of Haileybury and be back in the War Office by 5pm.

Slessor got his signatures. He was given a commission, became a pilot and was to rise to become the head of the Royal Air Force.[5]

Geoffrey Wall had been taken at the age of ten to live in Melbourne, Australia, where his father had become manager of an insurance company. At school there, and at Melbourne University, he established a reputation as an analytical thinker and significant poet and writer. In 1916, Geoffrey made the 12,000-mile sea voyage to London to join the RFC.

Hoping it would increase his chances if he conformed with the uniform of the young Englishmen he met, Wall presented himself at the War Office dressed in a bowler hat and carrying a walking stick and kid gloves. 'The War Office is a terrible place,' he told his mother.

It is the very personification of the hide-bound unreasoning and arrogant stupidity that is going to, or at least, should lose Britain this war. After arguing your way through a small army of policemen and boy scouts, you fill in a form that would furnish material for a biography, and commence to wait in a curved hall with colossal fire places on each side. You wait and wait, and presently a flunky announces in a disinterested voice that 'Captain W——— will see Mr Wall.' Captain W——— did, but he was very little use. He suggested a commission in the artillery, which rather surprised me, but that of course was no good at all.[6]

The captain gave Wall a note of introduction to an officer at the RFC's headquarters at Adastral House on the Victoria Embankment. There he was put on a waiting list and sent to a medical board. Here, although he wouldn't have known it, his temperamental suitability was evaluated in a decidedly rule-of-thumb assessment. A joint RFC/RNAS medical research committee had issued advice to the interviewing doctors. The head of the committee, Major Martin Flack, an army doctor, summed up what to look for. 'There is a type of facial expression one gets well acquainted with carrying out this sort of interview,' he said. 'It consists of a furtive look as if always expecting something unpleasant to happen, in marked contrast with the straight, decided expression of the crack fighter pilot.'[7]

Wall passed, though he was startled by some of the tests.

> The nerve man was rather decent, though he had drastic methods. He put me in a revolving chair, told me to shut my eyes, and spun the thing round till my head reeled. Following this you had to walk along a red line in the carpet, and balance on one leg for a minute. You've no idea how difficult they both are. The last test was the most difficult of the lot. He balanced a tuning fork on a flat box, and told me to lift it till it was at right angles to my body. I raised the thing very cautiously and, just as I got it into position, the doctor, who was standing behind me, let off a big clapper with a noise like a gun. It seemed such an unnecessary thing to do that I put the box down and asked him what he did that for. He laughed for quite a while, and finally said he thought I would do, but I wasn't to smoke while I was in the F.C.
>
> The heart man wanted to know if there had ever been any lunacy in the family. I said not so far. Then he wanted details of the whole family and enquired affectionately after your health. Then he started to worry about my father's people, and I pointed out that I didn't carry the family tree about with me, which seemed to satisfy him. The eyesight test consists principally of matching different coloured wools.[8]

Satisfied that Wall wasn't colour-blind, the Flying Corps accepted him. He was sent away to wait for his call-up.

Although the selection process may have seemed absurdly hit and miss, by 1916 the RFC's flying training system had, in some respects, become a relatively efficient machine, if only in its initial indoctrination into the still-evolving world of aeronautics. For this cadet pilots went first to be smartened up by means of the ruthless discipline and unpleasant procedures of boot camps, where they were bullied and shouted at by drill sergeants seconded from Guards regiments. After this daily assault on their dignity they moved on to an almost completely opposite milieu: Oxford University, where some of the emptied colleges had been temporarily commandeered by the Flying Corps for technical training into the mysteries of the flying machine.

One of the initial square-bashing camps was at rural Denham in Buckinghamshire. It was under heavy snow when Geoffrey Wall arrived there as a cadet pilot in bitter midwinter. He described the event to his mother.

> On Thursday afternoon the train stopped at a little wooden platform in the middle of a Christmas card picture. I got out. The train went on. Just over the rail of the platform was a little group of wooden huts – a couple of long tin sheds, and behind, a snow covered meadow, fringed with trees. I admired the prospect for a while and then looked around and saw about 20 other individuals doing the same. We all regarded each other sheepishly. They were all young chaps and had 'Public School' written in horrible hieroglyphics all over them.[9]

The public schoolboys were to be Wall's companions in a hut of twenty cadets during the rigours of the next two months as, with scarcely a pause, they were painfully knocked into shape.

> Reveille goes at 6.30am and the first parade is at 7.30. It is wonderful fun getting out in the dark and breaking the ice in the water buckets. Trotting round the frosty meadow to the tune of a running fire of sarcasm from a stony hearted sergeant is a wildly hilarious business. Breakfast is at 8.45 and drill starts again at 9.45 & goes on till 12.30. Lunch happens at 1pm & then we are free till 5 o'clock when lectures start. These go on until 7, & dinner is at 7pm. After dinner we are supposed to study – until 9pm. Lights out sounds at 10pm and you turn in. A bed certainly, but no sheets or pillows – only blankets. You just close your eyes and the reveille sounds and the whole routine commences again.
>
> How do I like it? Well frankly I hate it. I was never cut out for a soldier & have no desire to be one longer than I can help. It certainly smartens a fellow up – but I don't want to be smartened up. As soon as I get back into civilians again I'm going to wear my hair long, a bow tie – and a velvet jacket . . . I am pruning my imagination for a couple of months so that it will either die altogether or come out of the ordeal stronger than ever. Either of which might be a good thing. I shall become a mere machine or a useful intellect. After the war a whole army of men will be turned loose who are quite incapable of thinking or acting by themselves.

As an Australian, accustomed to a more egalitarian society, Wall struggled to come to terms with the English class system. The public schoolboys he encountered at Denham never ceased to offend his colonial sensibilities. One of them,

a chap from Richmond, insisted on telling me all about his 'bird' as
he calls her – and produced photos etc today. He considers himself
an awful swell, but didn't seem to know that a lady's name is
never mentioned in decent society. This is a curious feature of these
English Public School johnnies – they have not the elements of
manners in some things ... This only applies to the Public School
type – some RFC mechanics who have been sent up here are perfectly decent fellows.[10]

Had he been able to read some of the letters the public school cadets
were, in turn, sending to their upper- and upper-middle-class families,
Wall's theories would have been sadly reinforced. Arthur Rhys Davids,
an old Etonian, had definite views on the lower orders of society and 'the
coarse and uneducated company' in which he found himself among as a
Flying Corps cadet pilot. 'My darling Ma,' he wrote to his mother, lam-
enting the lack of kindred souls, 'You can't imagine how much I loathe
the army ... Nobody except the little few I have collected around me
understands me in the least: above all nearly everybody is so <u>common</u>
and so sordid – especially after Eton where one did make <u>friends</u>: here
one merely makes acquaintances by the score ... I have found one really
admirable person called Wilcox who has just been married: he is really
artistic, but even he is saturated with a veneer of Cockney common-
sense which just mars the perfect friend.' Few of his colleagues had
any manners. 'There are so few individuals here: nearly all are animal
creatures.'[11]

But the Flying Corps treated them without discrimination. They were
all ordered to have their hair cut. 'The colonel came and planted himself
in front of us and glared at me steelily,' Geoffrey Wall wrote. 'My hair
was flopping over my eyes in a most Byronic fashion ... He remarked:
"What do you think you are? Paderewski! ... Good lord, man, no authority on earth would give a man with hair like that a commission. Have
it all off." I had it all off – and looked like a convict in consequence.'[12]

In a letter to his father Wall reported:

The authorities have to work on the assumption that all men are
idiots and possibly they're largely right. But in their very attempts
after efficiency they waste a lot of energy. For instance the C.O.
informed me that my trouble was that I hadn't learnt to march yet.
Quite true, but then I can get there much more easily and quickly
by not marching. All Australians have a peculiar stride that will take

them twice as far as the little sharp step which the Kings Regulations require . . .

A favourite phrase of Lieut Gerrard's is 'It's not done.' I think it is a sort of religion with him. He applies it to all sorts of things, but the fact that a thing isn't done doesn't mean that it shouldn't be done. For instance, the cross-lacing of boots will reduce him to a state bordering on apoplexy. They must not be cross-laced. 'It isn't done.' What he really means to say is he doesn't do it, nor the men he knows. Gerrard is full of this sort of thing and is consequently hated by everyone. He is second in command and used to be a master at Harrow and that is all one needs say of him.[13]

Wall survived Denham boot camp, 'a sort of Hades composed of mud, weather-board sheds, and red-faced sergeants – a hideous phantasma. Another month of it would have pretty well broken me up.' Now an officer cadet, he was sent on to his aviation technical course at Oxford. For the cadet pilots the change was dramatic. Suddenly, in famous colleges, they were sleeping between sheets in their own bedrooms being treated like undergraduates. And Wall was delighted to tell his father that he'd been allowed to get his hair 'back to a nice floppy length again' and was enjoying the unexpected luxury of a batman. From Jesus College he described the happy transformation in his military life.

Having reduced us all to a becoming state of docility, we were sent on to Oxford to have a little 'swank' and self-respect brought back to us. The change was marvellous. After nine weeks at Denham, we blinked at Oxford like owls brought into daylight. All the cadets are fellows who have been used to the good things of this world. But it was pathetic to see them on the night of our arrival, sitting on the edge of easy chairs in a timorous sort of fashion, waiting for someone to shout 'On parade C Squadron' (I shall hear that shout for years and years in my dreams). Here we have no drills and the discipline is that of any university – lectures all day.[14]

Yet Oxford was not entirely devoid of military discipline. On arrival the pupils were given a pamphlet. It told them that all work would be treated as a 'parade'. They would be marched from the colleges to the lecture rooms, they had to salute an instructor every time they spoke to him, and no cadet was allowed to speak with an air mechanic or NCO while being instructed. They were also 'specifically forbidden to damage maps, spill ink, break pencil points or otherwise waste the resources of war'.[15]

At the Oxford School of Military Aeronautics they were taught how to
rig an aeroplane, transmit Morse code, use a compass and strip down a
machine gun and aircraft engine. The university city also introduced Wall
to some of life's temptations in the shape of the 'ladies of the town' who
waylaid him on the streets every night. He reassured his father: 'You
needn't be alarmed, I can get quite a lot of amusement out of it, without
venturing on the primrose path ... Sodom and Gomorrah are back
numbers compared with any English town after dark.'

While at Oxford Wall had his first experience of flight. An Australian
friend, Harry Rigby, who'd qualified ahead of him, invited him down to
the RFC's Wiltshire training base at Netheravon for an unofficial trip
in an Avro trainer. Rigby subjected him to a dizzy and disorientating
demonstration of violent aerobatics.

> I hung onto the seat while earth and sky reeled round me in con-
> centric circles. First we dropped 300 feet in a vertical nosedive – you
> know what starting in a lift feels like. Then he did a vertical bank.
> The marvel is, how a plane can keep up like that. Once it didn't and
> for a sickening moment we side-slipped and came out of it with a
> long sideways dive.
>
> Quite a number of subs [cadet pilots] came out to see the corpse
> lifted out and were quite disappointed when I climbed out unaided.
> It appears that Harry's prevailing sin is stunting and they send him
> up to put the fear of God into a new and bumptious pilot. I said
> I felt alright. But half an hour later I could hardly stand, and even
> now I feel a bit shaky.[16]

Geoffrey Wall's traumatic baptism into the perils of flight was not one
shared by most students. The Flying Corps introduced them to military
flying a shade less abruptly. But it was none the less a highly risky business.
The schoolboys sent to the flying schools to be groomed for battle with
the Fokkers were as likely as not to be killed or crippled trying to master
dangerous aeroplanes long before they got anywhere near the Western
Front.

Chapter 7
The Instructors Who Stuttered

D eath was the constant companion of the pupil pilots. Of the grand total of military and naval pilots and observers killed in the first air war it is a staggering fact that just over two-thirds lost their lives in training accidents at flying schools. The training squadrons suffered crashes with such regularity they became virtually routine. Three or four at the same airfield on the same day was not uncommon. The sight of colleagues they'd been chatting with a few minutes earlier being carbonised in burning wreckage before their eyes was a horrifyingly and all too regular occurrence for already apprehensive students.

Apart from the English weather, which frequently grounded the training machines, this appalling accident rate had many causes. Although very late in the war it was to improve, the standard of instruction during the first three years of the conflict was so abysmally primitive that pilots were getting their wings before they could safely fly an aeroplane, let alone take it into battle. The instructors, many of them mentally traumatised by aerial combat in France and with no training in the skills of tuition, were simply posted to the schools and expected to begin flying nervous and clumsy pupils round the sky. Having escaped from the front with their lives – if not entirely with their minds – war-shattered pilots were reluctant to now meet their deaths spinning to earth in an aeroplane mishandled by a terrified student. Because many of the instructors refused point-blank to let go of the dual controls their pupils, in the three-dimensional world of flight, rarely felt for themselves the vital consequences of their movements of the control column and rudder. And, to shorten the time their strained nerves were exposed to the flounderings of the fledglings, the instructors often sent off their charges ridiculously early to make solo flights that ended far too frequently in disaster. With such genuine fear did many pilots regard their students they referred to them as 'Huns', considering them more dangerous in the air than the German enemy.

The training machines were as inadequate as the instructors. Some aeroplanes had stalling characteristics that made them downright dangerous for anyone, let alone a student, to fly. Others were structurally unsound: wrongly handled they could break up in the air. Their engines and fuel systems constantly failed at crucial moments. Added to this the training squadrons were usually equipped with such an astonishing range of different aircraft types that the confused pupils never had the chance to perfect the small amount of flying skill they did acquire on any one model. Instructors came and went almost as often as their students crashed, and cadets rarely had the chance to develop a teacher–pupil relationship with a tutor before he was gone.

Some pilots maintained they received so little meaningful dual instruction that they taught themselves by trial and error, flying themselves around the sky. Many, including some who went on to become legendary figures with big tallies of enemy aircraft to their credit, failed ever to master basic aerodrome flying skills. Because they had not been properly taught, they regularly suffered pilot-error take-off and landing accidents throughout their otherwise heroic service.

The pressure of the air war and its high casualty rate drove this imperfect training operation to cut corners. It consumed machines and aviators faster than they could be replaced. It had the factories in such a continuous frenzy of invention and development they poured out a bewildering array of aeroplanes that were all too often technically flawed and obsolete within months. While the race was on to produce an opponent to match the triumphant Fokker the safest aircraft for elementary training had scarcely evolved at all from the primitive flying machines of 1914. The trusty Maurice Farman pusher biplanes didn't look to the pupil pilot a whole lot different from the Wright brothers *Flyer* that had staggered into the air at Kitty Hawk thirteen years earlier.

One thing had advanced. The students no longer sat on the lower wing hugging their instructor as they stretched round him to place their hands on top of his holding the control stick. They now sat one behind the other in separate open cockpits in what looked like a narrow bath in front of the engine. They also had dual controls but, as yet, no intercom. Above the roar of the engine they could hear each other only by briefly throttling back for a few seconds and shouting. Instructors were forced into more basic methods of communication. They scribbled notes or, when the pupils were in front of them, kicked their seats or tapped them smartly on the head.

The French-designed Farmans, the workhorses of the early years of the Flying Corps, came in two versions: Longhorn and Shorthorn. Described by one pilot as 'a sort of aerial joke like a Daddy Longlegs', the

Longhorn was distinguished by what to modern eyes was the uncon-ventional location of its elevator, which sat out in front on a pair of long curved skids intended to prevent the machine from tipping up on its nose on landing. In the Shorthorn the protruding front appendage was chopped off and the elevator positioned more familiarly with the rudder in the tail. It was in this aeroplane, known as the 'Rumpety' for the rumbling noise it made on take-off and landing runs, that hundreds of Flying Corps pilots were taught to fly.

Albert Ball learned privately at Hendon aerodrome in north London. It cost him £75 (around £5,000 today). The son of a Nottingham plumber who had sent him to a minor public school, Ball had been commissioned in the army at the age of eighteen soon after the outbreak of war. He fitted his flying lessons in between his military duties at a nearby London camp. He would get up at 3am, drive through the dawn on his Harley–Davidson to Hendon, have a flying lesson and be back at camp in time for the first parade at 6.45. He hadn't told his father about this covert aviation activity. When he cautiously revealed it he said: 'Please do not be cross with me for flying for it means that if the country is very short of pilots I shall be able to go.'[1]

The accident rate at the Hendon school was as shocking as the toll in the Flying Corps, and Ball witnessed several terrible crashes. 'Well my flying is going on fine,' he wrote to his father, 'but I am very sorry to say that a great many of our men have been killed in the last few weeks. It is rotten to see the smashes. Yesterday a ripping boy had a smash, and when we got up to him he was nearly dead. He had a two-inch piece of wood right through his head and died this morning.'[2]

Ball survived the flying course, got his licence and went up to London to the War Office to offer his services to military aviation. He was accepted, seconded to the RFC from his army unit and sent to Mousehold Heath aerodrome near Norwich to learn to fly all over again. His Flying Corps instructor was not as patient as his civilian tutor. Although brim-ming with confidence and enthusiasm, Ball was not a natural pilot. His landings were often atrocious. After one of them his instructor

came up, told me to get out, and advised me to look out for a good flying school for girls and join it at once. He ended up with saying that he would never let me fly again. I told him that as I had only had 15 mins instruction on the S.H. [Shorthorn] he could not expect me to even fly them, let alone land them. I ended up saying that, if I could not fly and he would not let me use the machines, the best

thing I could do was to get back to [his army unit] for I have got no
time to spend watching other people fly. He at once got another
machine out and told me to get off on it. I did so and made a fine
perfect landing. He was very pleased with me and you bet I was
pleased with myself.[3]

Ball's self-confidence was short-lived. Within days he had a frightening
accident which he described to his father. 'I feel rotten today ... You
know by now about my smash; it was a good one. They say I crashed to
earth at 120 miles an hour, and to look at the undercarriage I should think
that I did ... It was a rum feeling coming down, for I had time to see that
my number was up; however it is not!'[4]

The narrow safety margins made it all too easy for learners to kill
themselves. Few students ever learned the theory of flight – the finely
balanced way in which the machine was delicately supported in the air
by the airflow over the wings that provided the lift to sustain it. If airspeed
wasn't adequately maintained the aeroplane simply ran out of lift and
stalled: its nose would abruptly drop, a wing would roll over and within
seconds the pilot would be hurtling earthwards in a sickening spin from
which he hadn't necessarily been shown how to recover. With some early
aircraft it was impossible to recover anyway.

To avoid the feared stall that killed hundreds of students continuous
adequate airspeed was crucial. The difficulty was that the top speed of
some machines was dangerously close to the stalling speed. To help the
pilot stay within this narrow window of safety there was a primitive
airspeed indicator. Not a digital display or even a helpful needle on a dial
but a sort of flask with a column of red liquid that rose and fell with
fluctuating airspeed. And even this device could bring false comfort to
pupils to whom it hadn't been demonstrated how dramatically speed
would drop with the increased wing loading that occurred whenever they
attempted to turn. Many fatalities were caused by spinning off the basic
manoeuvre of a simple turn. And many more by engine failure on take-
off when panicking pilots broke the cardinal rule that they must force-
land straight ahead. Instead they would instinctively try to turn back.
Having lost the thrust of their engine and their flying speed they would
invariably stall on the turn and spin to the ground.

Ball was sent from Mousehold Heath to the Central Flying School at
Upavon in Wiltshire. Nearly every letter he wrote from there described a
training crash. With seeming routine casualness he reported these disasters in which young men, fresh out of school, were being regularly

killed or grievously injured. 'Two other smashes on Friday but pilots will be right in about six weeks. It has been a month of bad luck for all flights up to now for 12 of our latest machines have been smashed.'[5]

'Flight has just had another crash. Pilot lost his head when up at 1500 feet so you bet it has been a good smash.'[6]

From this cauldron of destruction Albert Ball emerged alive and uninjured to be awarded his RFC wings. His flying logbook has never been found but his quantum of experience as a pilot would have been minimal – probably a mere twenty hours at best. Yet, astonishingly, he was promptly made an instructor and posted to a training squadron to pass on to more sacrificial lambs the skills of which he himself had acquired only the most rudimentary grasp.

Ball took his shaky piloting expertise to the flying school at Gosport in Hampshire. His fellow instructors were equally inexperienced. No one had shown any of them how to teach someone to fly. Instructor training schools turning out specialist flying teachers didn't yet exist. But so desperate was the need, it was just assumed that any pilot with freshly awarded wings was automatically capable of assuming this dangerous task.

To minimise his exposure to pupil handling disasters Ball's style was brisk and brief. In one day, he told his family, 'I took thirty officers up for instruction and got six off solo. On Monday I hope to get eight more off solo. It is good sport instructing, but out of eighteen officers with their wings only three of us instruct, the remainder slack about all day. This is rather rotten for we do not like taking all the risk.'[7]

Geoffrey Wall, who had been sent off solo after just two hours' flying, was also bewildered when, on receiving his wings at the Patchway training base near Bristol, he was expected almost immediately to start instructing. He had begun his flying training only a few weeks earlier at the RFC's lonely, windswept Netheravon base on Salisbury Plain. Here he had been shocked at the battle-damaged state of the instructors who had been sent back from the Western Front 'with one or two Huns to their credit. Some of them have had some pretty tough experiences. They stutter terribly, take aspirins and smoke their own brand of cigarettes – all very decent fellows on the whole.'

Ira Jones was another victim of a battle-damaged instructor. After months of front-line service in France – first as a ground wireless operator, during which he was awarded a Military Medal, then as an aerial observer – Jones, a tiny aggressive Welshman who had suffered from a chronic stutter ever since being rolled down a hill in a barrel as a child,

was sent back to England for pilot training. At London Colney in Hertfordshire for advanced instruction on an Avro, he was immediately
shocked by the poor quality of the teachers. If they weren't suffering from
post-traumatic stress they were unfit for other reasons. Some 'were too
hasty tempered, intimidating the trainees when they should have been
encouraging them ... or rushed their pupils into going solo to claim
credit for having trained the highest number of pilots in a given period.
I had to contend with one of these speed-merchants as soon as I started.'[8]

After three hours' dual flying, 'at the hands of seven instructors', Jones
was ordered to go solo in an Avro on which he'd never been allowed to
work the throttle and which, for some reason, lacked the basic essential
flight instruments. It had no engine revolution-counter, compass or alti-
meter. When he refused to fly it he was immediately reported to the
training squadron commander, 'charged with disobeying orders – one of
the worst offences in the Service'. The charge was dismissed and the
instructor posted elsewhere.

Bill Taylor, an Australian student who would later become one of
aviation's most celebrated trans-oceanic pioneer navigators, was also
brave enough to risk court-martial by refusing to fly before being properly
taught. After less than an hour and a half of elementary instruction on a
Farman he was flabbergasted to be ordered to go off alone without even
being shown how to take off or land.

'The prospect of flying thrilled me,' he wrote. 'The dangerous impli-
cations of becoming a pilot in the RFC and being sent to France made
no impression on me at this stage. The war in France stayed far enough
away not to have to be reckoned with.' Arriving at Netheravon to begin
his ab initio training 'I was suddenly confronted by a morose instructor
who, with few words, launched me abruptly into my first experience of
flight'.

> 'You Taylor?'
>   'Yes, sir.'
>   'Had any instruction yet?'
>   'No, I haven't sir.'
>   'All right, I'll give you some landings.'

With these brief words he walked off towards a Maurice Farman
standing on the tarmac and I followed him in a somewhat confused
state of mind. This wasn't exactly what I had expected. I had pictured
some sort of orderly approach; a talk with the instructor before my
flight, and some idea of the theory behind controlling an aeroplane.

Instead, I climbed up after my instructor into the rear seat of a thing about the size and shape of a bathtub, slung between the wings of a biplane ... A mechanic swung the propeller, the pilot ran up the engine, waved away the chocks, and we were away. My instructor said nothing.[9]

They took off, did one close circuit of the aerodrome, landed, and immediately took off again. The instructor did not speak until he lined up for a second landing. Then, closing the throttle, he shouted, 'You land it!'

Taylor was terrified. He'd never handled the controls. He had never been asked to touch them. In a panic he now seized them for the very first time. As the ground rushed up he pulled back on the control column. He over-corrected the descent and the aeroplane swooped back into the air. The controls were snatched out of his hands and 'a savage shout came back to me from the instructor, "Bloody awful!" '

As the throttle was slammed open and they staggered back into the air not a further word came from the front cockpit. The aircraft did another circuit. Taylor was afraid to touch the controls again.

I just sat there, feeling utterly confused and ineffectual. The grass was coming up again and another landing was upon us. The machine began to flatten out, swept low over the surface and the now familiar clatter of wheels told me we were on the ground once more. Visibly acknowledging my existence for the first time, the instructor turned slightly and announced in a more conciliatory tone, 'That's better.'

'What's better?' I thought. Then his meaning hit me, and with it a surge of fear about the whole mad act. I hadn't touched the controls.

Once more they took off. This time they left the aerodrome and, to Taylor's profound relief, the instructor at long last began to communicate in the air and teach him the elements of straight and level flight. But when the instructor had made the landing back at Netheravon he simply taxied up to the hangar, switched off the engine, jumped to the ground and walked away without a word. 'I sat for a few moments, taking stock,' Taylor said. 'I badly needed some advice.' He was a very junior probationary second lieutenant. His instructor was a captain. He respected his authority and the need to obey orders without question.

That evening Taylor shared his outrage with a fellow Australian student, 'Anzac' Whiteman, a Rhodes scholar. They both decided that the captain was not fit to instruct. Whiteman urged him to have it out with him next day. But when Taylor went back into the air again with his unhappy instructor it still remained unclear which of them, from minute to minute, was meant to be flying the aircraft. Still given no demonstration of the critically delicate techniques of landing and take-off, Taylor once more got a shouted instruction to do the landing. Somehow it turned out to be quite a good one. But Taylor was far from ready to risk it on his own. He was therefore horrified when the instructor climbed out and shouted, 'You can bloody well go solo now.' As the instructor walked away Taylor switched off the engine.

> He turned and came back, shouting at me. His voice was almost hysterical. 'What's the matter with you? Why did you stop the engine?'
>
> I shouted back at him. 'I'm not going solo. I can't fly the aeroplane and I won't attempt to.' I had never done a take-off, nor a landing without interference. I hadn't come all the way from my home in Australia to kill myself at an instructor's orders.
>
> Shaken and worried, I waited for the inevitable blast. I expected to be placed under arrest. But my instructor was completely unpredictable. He called up to me in an almost friendly voice, 'What do you want to do, then?'
>
> 'I want to fly with another instructor,' I said.

To Taylor's surprise his tutor agreed to arrange this. 'I was handed over to a tall genial instructor, Lieutenant Prallé. "I believe you're having trouble with your flying, Taylor."

"Well, not exactly, sir. I just don't know how to fly the aeroplane, that's all."' His new instructor responded with a marvellous suggestion. 'Come on out and we'll start from scratch.'

After two more hours of 'concise and friendly instruction' Taylor was taught not only how to fly, take off and land the Shorthorn, but most importantly about all the vices of the machine that could kill him. Vitally, he was shown the peril of allowing the nose to drop below the angle of glide on the approach from which, he was warned, it was impossible to recover. Prallé taught him how to fly the aeroplane with confidence and safety and, when he was ready, sent him off on a successful solo. For the first time he began, he said, 'to appreciate some slight sense of the freedom of spirit possible in the great ocean of air over Earth'.

Taylor's original instructor, he discovered, had returned from active aerial combat in France as 'a nervous wreck ... his spirit had been broken and he was returned to Home Establishment. There he'd become a victim of the system, posted to Netheravon as an instructor. He was terrified of flying. His one frantic aim was to get his pupils off solo as soon as possible so that he wouldn't have to fly with them.'

A few weeks later Taylor was posted for more advanced pilot training to the Central Flying School at nearby Upavon. He had been there only a few days when he was surprised to be summoned to report to the station commander.

Major Small invited me to sit down. He came to the point imme-diately. 'I'm sorry to tell you, Taylor, that Whiteman was killed this morning on his first solo. Apparently he got his nose down and couldn't pull the machine out ...'

I went back to my tent under the pine trees. That damned, lousy instructor! I knew what had happened. He'd sent Anzac solo before he could fly the aeroplane – just as he'd tried to do with me ... I sat on the edge of the bed, thinking. I was eighteen and Death was a newcomer to my thoughts. But I knew that he would never leave them while the war lasted. Finally I went for a walk, in the cold brilliant darkness over the grassy uplands of Salisbury Plain. I would have to be alone in the war. There might be passing friends, people around, but the only permanent companion would be Death.

The unwilling instructors were, of course, themselves victims of the cavalier training system. In July 1916 the commandant of the Central Flying School had issued some guidance notes, *Hints for Young Instructors on How to Instruct in Flying*. They began by stressing the importance of strict discipline and attention to shaving, dress, punctuality and saluting. Cleaning a dirty oily engine was recommended as a punishment for slackness. 'Any fool can fly,' the note declared, 'but it takes a flier to land.' Banking, turning and 'spiralling' were described along with the golden rule that a pilot should never climb or dive in a turn. As for taking off and landing in cross-winds, forced landing procedure, side-slipping, aerobatics and the true nature of the stall that killed most pupils, they were nowhere mentioned. The notes concluded with a health hint: 'Remember to keep your own liver and that of your pupils in order,' it urged. 'Do so by exercise ... If your pupils are slack, give them drill and see it is carried out vigorously.'[10]

Mastering take-off and landing were only the first of the skills the pupils had to acquire. They also had to learn some rudimentary navigation to be able to leave the familiar surroundings of their home aerodrome and fly accurately for perhaps fifty miles across country. There were no such things as radio direction-finding aids with comforting voices in headsets to help steer them safely to their destination. They had to use their own eyes, map-reading their way from A to B by staying in contact with the ground and steering a course with the assistance of a simple magnetic compass whose sloppily wandering needle made precision impossible. It took enormous skill and concentration to maintain a heading to within five degrees of accuracy, let alone one tiny degree. And all too frequently, because so many of them looked confusingly alike from the air, the profusion of towns, roads, railways, rivers and canals the learner pilots would see rolling by below would fail to match the features on their maps. Sent off on their own to fly across country, the 'Huns' frequently got so completely lost they ran out of fuel.

This happened to Harold Balfour, who did his initial pilot training at Gosport. Balfour, who was later to be credited with nine enemy aircraft, be awarded two Military Crosses, serve as under-secretary of state for air in the Second World War and become Lord Balfour of Inchrye, was sent off in a BE2 to fly the fifty or so miles from Gosport to Upavon. 'I flew and flew and flew until the petrol was getting dangerously low, when I landed more by good luck than good piloting in a sort of municipal park, surrounded by tall trees. I was told I was at Bath.' He was twenty-four miles off course. He had been flying more than 12 degrees too far to the west. 'Luckily,' wrote Balfour, 'I had money with me. I bought some more petrol at a neighbouring garage. I eventually got to Upavon in time for a late lunch, making some excuse for the long time I had taken to come from Gosport. I was determined not to go wrong on my way home, but unfortunately took the wrong river at Salisbury. I found myself over some strange town on the South Coast.'

The town was Bournemouth. This time he was over thirty miles off course. But not until he'd put down on a golf course did he discover this. 'Eventually I made Gosport, crossing the Solent with barely enough petrol to reach the aerodrome. I was so frightened of what would be said of my bad navigation that I never told anyone of this adventure.'[11]

The eighteen- and nineteen-year-old Flying Corps instructors who didn't yet stutter but had been forced into the job long before they themselves were safe to fly didn't enjoy very long lives. If the pupils with whom they trundled about the sky every day didn't kill them the unreliable aeroplanes were just as likely to do so. On a dual-instruction flight from Netheravon Geoffrey Wall and his student were lucky to survive an engine failure at barely 100 feet over a Wiltshire valley cloaked in standing crops. In a letter to his father, Wall described how they crashed into the pastoral peace of a small Wiltshire village.

We hit the ground through 4 feet of wheat and downhill. When I extricated myself from the debris I observed the good Symondson standing on his head in the wheat some distance away. Presently he got up and, after feeling himself very gingerly all over, decided that he was not dead and expressed his intention of immediately applying for leave. That's what I call presence of mind. The bus itself looked rather pathetic. The undercarriage reposed some way up the hill and the rest of the thing lay with her back broken and a crumpled wing and a 'now-I-hope-you're-satisfied' sort of expression in the wheat.

In the fullness of time a Crossley tender came swaying and bumping over the top of the hill. The job was too much for them, so I told Symondson to go and have some breakfast and bring a repair gang back . . . Bye and bye, the local populace began to arrive. First on the scene were two ladies in deshabille who had seen the crash from their window and had come to extricate the corpse. They seemed a bit disappointed and, after giving me gory details of several other mishaps in the locality, they faded away into the morning mist.

My next visitor was the rector of Figheldean. Evidently he had been working up next Sunday's sermon when we wopped over his head. He enquired for the pilot and when I admitted I was the culprit he insisted on shaking hands vigorously and produced some cigarettes. He was really quite a decent chap, a bit of an archaeologist with a lot of interesting information about the old mounds and barrows on the plain. He invited me to tea at the rectory to see the parish records, unbroken for 600 years. I accepted. He might have some nice daughters.

The next character to enter was a bucolic individual who introduced himself as the owner of the field. It appeared that his visit was due more to anxiety about his crops than to brotherly love. He talked loudly of the price of wheat per acre and informed me of the terrible damage I had done. I pointed out that there was a great and terrible War raging and that, had he happened to be born in Belgium, he wouldn't have had any crops at all – nor farm for that matter and yet he was worrying over a paltry £5 worth of wheat.

For a while there was an interval. Then a flock of sheep, escorted by a woolly dog, came along the edge of the field. Behind them was a shepherd who enquired, rather superfluously, if I had had a smash. I told him I was only helping my farmer friend to get his crops in. He seemed to be in no hurry. No-one is in Wiltshire, so he delivered himself of a lot of local gossip and decided that he wouldn't go up in one of them things for a lot. Presently he went into the mist and for a bit things hung fire until Symondson arrived on my motorbike, followed by a lorry. The aeroplane's fuel tank was leaking steadily. So we saved all we could and put it into the bike.

The repair gang sawed the wings up into small sections and packed the remains on their lorry. I went back to the station. The CO was awfully decent. Said the machine didn't matter a damn so long as the occupants were alright. So I had a bath and went to bed till evening. With luck it will rain in the morning. Otherwise I shall have to be up with the idiotic lark.[12]

Six days later at Netheravon twenty-year-old 2nd Lieutenant Geoffrey Wall was killed. He was giving a trainee his first lesson. The pupil died too. The aircraft was seen to spin to the ground from around 500 feet. The machine had not failed. Wall had probably never been taught how to recover from a spin because his instructors hadn't known how to do so, either. In his pocket was a half-finished letter to his mother. And in his room at Netheravon he left a collection of poems he had written about the England he'd arrived in and the war in France he was never to experience.

The dead pupil's father, reflecting the almost universal beliefs of the era, sent a moving letter to Wall's parents in Australia. 'We hope,' Thomas Clark wrote from Scotland, 'the Almighty will sustain you and yours under the heavy burden you have been called upon to bear and that, in your sad bereavement, you will have the consolation of knowing that your dear son died in the performance of his duty while preparing another to take his place in the ranks along with those who have so willingly sacrificed everything, even their young and promising lives in this great and dreadful war for righteousness and true liberty.'[13]

But not everyone in Britain accepted such losses as inevitable, at least not at the rate at which the promising lives of young Flying Corps pilots were now being forfeited in the great cause.

Chapter 8

Unhappiness in Parliament

The loudest voices condemning the scale of the loss of pilots continued to rise from the House of Commons. Noel Pemberton-Billing, whose murder denunciations had led to the judicial inquiry, was on his feet in the chamber week after week. His fixation was the RFC's BE2 reconnaissance biplane, the much-maligned product of the government's Royal Aircraft Factory that was being shot out of the sky by the Fokkers. Pemberton-Billing blamed the Directorate of Aeronautics. 'I say,' he told the House, 'we are guilty of supplying our officers with machines that are inefficient and if they meet their death in consequence . . . it is very difficult to find a word with which to describe the behaviour of those people who are primarily responsible.'[1]

Pemberton-Billing had become a figure in whom the airmen themselves felt able to confide their concerns. The letters from France they wrote privately to him, describing disastrous BE2 incidents in which colleagues had been killed, Billing would read out in the Commons in regular chronicles of human sacrifice. Many spoke of the mechanical failures of the aircraft's Farnborough factory-designed engine.

Lord Hugh Cecil, the pilot of little skill who helped the War Office select candidates for the Flying Corps, was one of the two MPs to represent Oxford University at that time. He tried to inject a rosier, more romantic note into the debate. At the War Office, he told the Commons, he regularly read the aerial combat reports that arrived from the squadrons on the Western Front. He portrayed the pilots as young men doing their best with imperfect equipment. Nothing was more stimulating, he said than to read 'the tales of the aerial combats as they come in . . . You have as much a combat between two individuals as it used to be in the days of knights of old – but all done when flying at 80 or 100 miles an hour thousands of feet above the ground. Nothing in fiction is so inspiring to the imagination as these thrilling dramas of courage and dexterity played without spectators.' Cecil courageously ventured a word, too, in praise of the BE2. 'These machines, if you look at them, are marvels of finish and ingenuity, and marvels of the resources of mechanical ability in dealing with the great difficulties of the air problem ... Taking all considerations into view, our Royal Flying Corps is the best and most efficient in the world.'[2]

Lord Cecil's words were greeted with a great roar of cheers. These were exactly the sentiments the House preferred to hear. They may not have cheered so loudly had they ever been able to read the views of some of the pilots who lived to describe the BE2, known in the squadrons as 'Quirks'. 'We've got too many death traps in service,' Arthur Gould Lee wrote from France to the young wife he'd just married back in England. The son of a Lincolnshire publican, Lee had been injured in a take-off crash in an Avro during training in England. Dreading a repetition of this in the BE2, he was dismayed when, soon after his arrival in France, he had been sent with five other pilots to ferry a batch of them to Candas. Lee was the only one of the six to arrive safely. One crashed en route, three on landing and one went missing and was later found dead in the wreckage. 'I felt,' he told his wife, 'rather a cad not crashing too, because everyone is glad to see death-traps like Quirks written off, especially new ones.'[3] In another letter he declared: 'It's a damn scandal that such dangerous crocks are still being sent to France ... every variation of the BE is like a mangle.' He added how 'darned sorry I feel for the poor devils' who had to take them up against the enemy. 'It's as bad as sentencing every other man to death.'[4] The Australian pilot Bill Taylor described the BE2s he flew as 'underpowered, under armed and unmanoeuvrable'. They were, he wrote, 'probably the most vulnerable aeroplanes ever used in war'.[5]

Yet 3,500 BEs were built. They were designed at a time when the army needed no more than a reliable, stable aircraft to range the guns and photograph the enemy's troop movements. The need for it to be a gunship as well, defending itself with power and manoeuvrability against other aeroplanes, had not been a requirement in the gentle days before the arrival of aerial combat. Superiority, as the Fokker had so devastatingly demonstrated, now belonged to the air force with the most effective fighter aircraft – in the early months of 1916 the British high command was still struggling to find one.

The anguish raging around the BE family of biplanes opened up a much bigger can of worms. It laid bare the fundamental problems at the heart of the entire management of the two rival air arms. Far from functioning in the supply of their equipment and operational roles as one military air force, the Royal Flying Corps and the much smaller Royal

Naval Air Service had remained bitter rivals with astonishingly little co-operation and even less trust between them.

Like the RFC, the Naval Air Service had gone to war in 1914 as a tiny organisation. It had just ninety-three aircraft, six airships, two balloons and around 700 officers and other ranks. Its air bases were scattered round the coasts of Britain and France. Initially its role was the defence of the homeland against air attack, long-range reconnaissance for the navy's Grand Fleet, submarine spotting and attack operations and the bombing of German naval and Zeppelin bases. The era of the aircraft-carrier which could take whole squadrons of aircraft to sea, fly them off long decks and land them back there had yet to dawn. The open-cockpit floatplanes were transported to sea on converted warships and lowered over the side to take off from the water. A few of the seaplanes, with detachable wheels that were jettisoned after take-off, were launched in hair-raising manner from incredibly short platforms built on top of gun turrets. With the ship heading into wind at perhaps 25 knots the aircraft, at full power, would stagger into the air only to sink immediately in a perilous swoop almost down to the waves to pick up safe flying speed and, with luck, slowly climb away without hitting the water. It would land back on the sea on the lee side of the ship and be hoisted on board. Early attempts to land on flight decks patently too short for purpose depended, before the development of arrestor wires, on sailors grabbing them before they hurtled over the side.

Most of the navy's aircraft, however, were shore-based landplanes. The best, with the latest designs, were invariably seized by the Admiralty straight from the drawing boards of private factories. The aviation admirals, spurning the bureaucratically run government factory, obtained their own funds directly from the Treasury. They simply went on buying the cream of the construction industry from whichever manufacturer they chose. Rejecting the inadequate and obsolete BE2 thrust upon the Flying Corps by the War Office, they chose instead the vastly more successful Sopwith Pup. This was the splendidly superior product of a company formed by Tom Sopwith, one of the giants of early British aviation and a celebrated Americas Cup yachtsman. The Pup was just the first of a long line of pedigree, high-performing WWI fighting machines his factory would create.

Having cornered the British production market, the Admiralty also dealt directly with the French to guarantee the Naval Air Service a flow of the infinitely better French aircraft engines at the expense of the Army's less well-financed efforts to compete for the same motors. The competition for the French equipment was so intense at one stage that the competing Paris-based British army and naval officers trying to clinch their separate cloak-and-dagger deals in rival negotiations came to distrust one another so intensely they hardly spoke.

At every turn the Admiralty simply outbid its War Office rival – and there was nobody to step in to stop the wasteful competition. The brilliant Sopwith Pup had actually first been offered to the RFC in February 1916. But it was declined by the Directorate of Military Aeronautics on the advice of the head of the Royal Aircraft Factory, Lieutenant-Colonel Mervyn O'Gorman. An Irish electrical engineer of much drive, wit and charm, he appears to have had the spellbindingly persuasive power to deflect the War Office generals from the more technically advanced offerings of the private sector. O'Gorman had instead pressed upon the Flying Corps a more powerful development of the painfully inadequate BE2: the hated BE12, a pilot-disposal machine Trenchard had to get rid of. It was described by Cecil Lewis, who was unfortunate enough to have to ferry one across the Channel, as a 'cow. The engine rattled like a can of old nails. I was glad to put it down.'[6]

The army and navy were at loggerheads over more than aeroplanes. There was major disagreement, too, about their operational roles. The navy favoured long-range bombing. From bases on the French coast its aeroplanes attacked German Zeppelin sheds at Düsseldorf and Cologne. The Flying Corps, on the other hand, saw its principal purpose as the tactical support of the British Expeditionary Force on the Western Front. Trenchard, the field commander in France, insisted that his aeroplanes were military weapons. He believed that unless the squadrons could dominate the air over the battle lines, the armies could actually lose the war.

The Asquith government of 1916 was reluctant in the middle of a war to cause the upheaval that imposing a merger on the warring factions would entail. Instead it formed a succession of toothless committees and boards of army and navy aeronautical commanders, presided over by peers of the realm assumed to be impartial. None of these bodies was given executive power to exercise authority over the squabbling air forces. One after the other they failed to bring them together. Indeed, the navy often pointedly boycotted the boards' meetings as it went on happily buying its own aeroplanes. When the board protested, the first lord of the Admiralty, Arthur Balfour, bluntly told its latest chairman, Lord Curzon, that 'the Admiralty, not the Air Board, is responsible for the conduct of the Royal Naval Air Service', putting Curzon in his place by reminding him that 'the Admiralty was created some generations before the Air Board'.

In a desperate bid at least to co-ordinate aircraft production, the government turned to the Ministry of Munitions to untangle the chaos. When the ministry, already unable to deliver enough shells for the big guns on the Western Front, tried to sort out the design and supply of aeroplanes as well, it inherited a bewildering scene. It found that the very large scale of production required was hampered by what it called 'the enormous multiplicity of types resulting from too much expert zeal unchecked by practical considerations'.[7] On order for the two air services at the end of 1916 were 9,400 aircraft of no fewer than seventy-six different kinds, in addition to 20,000 engines of nearly sixty varieties. For their part the manufacturers complained that not only was there a shortage of skilled labour and materials, but that as fast as a newly designed aeroplane went into service they were presented with demands for endless modifications to be made to it.

As an RFC pilot daily risking his life over the trenches, Arthur Gould Lee described the tragedy of the air services feud conducted by senior officers, 'none of whom had any experience of air combat'. He spoke of 'the wretched story of the incredible blunders of the air supply organisation . . . the disastrous hasty contracts, the faulty co-ordination of effort, the ill-judged control of material and labour, the mass production of untried, defective engines'.

'Almost the only light,' wrote Lee, 'that shone during the long period of neglect, incompetence and folly in the supply of aircraft to the RFC was the undismayed courage of those sent out every day to face death in aeroplanes that should have been thrown on the scrapheap many months before.'[8]

Lee condemned as a government whitewash the eventual reports of the groups that spent months during 1916 investigating the quality of the aeroplanes and the widely publicised Pemberton-Billing murder accusations against the Flying Corps commanders. The murder claims were dismissed by the Bailhache tribunal as extravagant and without foundation. And, needless to say, its report completely absolved General Henderson. In fact it went to generous lengths to praise the way the Flying Corps chiefs had responded to the enormous unforeseen demands on its services by an army that had initially not wanted it at all. The provocative allegation that the Flying Corps' field commander, General Trenchard, lacked flying experience was also swiftly disposed of in just two words: 'quite unfounded'. There was undoubtedly a degree of truth to the point about Trenchard's relatively small personal solo flying hours. But the RFC field commander who functioned on only one lung was to become so revered for his abilities that the criticism never, at least publicly, resurfaced.

The Burbidge committee that investigated the Royal Aircraft Factory drew attention to the appallingly poor salaries paid to its designers, but finished up merely proposing some tinkering with its organisation. The mammoth Bailhache inquiry, however, had some hard things to say about the factory. The committee blamed bureaucracy at Farnborough for stifling competition from private planemakers producing superior machines. It recommended that the factory get right out of the aircraft-building business and go back to its original purpose of research and development.

There were no aeronautical technical experts among the Bailhache committee's members and some of the most potentially important witnesses, the independent manufacturers, had refused to give evidence, fearing they might be blacklisted from future work. Nor, most relevantly of all, did more than a small handful of front-line pilots come to testify about the horrors of some of the aeroplanes they had been lumbered with. Afraid of being seen by their commanders as disloyal, they demanded to be allowed to tell their stories in confidence.

The principal outcome of the inquiries was that the War Office felt obliged to clip the wings of the beleaguered Farnborough factory. Henderson decided to make a scapegoat of its powerful leader. The charismatic Mervyn O'Gorman was seen as the architect of a web of bureaucracy that frustrated the independent manufacturers and thwarted aircraft development enterprise and it suited the War Office to hold him responsible for many of the RFC's aeroplane problems. Henderson sacked him, bringing in a railway mechanical engineer in his place. But the factory proved an unstoppable force. It went on building aeroplanes of its own design to the end of the war.

The well-intentioned commissions of inquiry, like the succession of co-ordinating committees and air boards, effectively achieved little. The army and navy air service commanders largely ignored their findings. The only obvious cure was a third military service: a single British air force with its own air ministry. But in the dark days of 1916 still no one had the courage to rock the boat and create it. The director of air organisation, Brigadier-General Brancker, in his candid, private correspondence with Trenchard in France, wrote despairingly to the RFC's field commander: 'I get more and more impressed with the rottenness of our system and our institutions and a large portion of our people every day. The Boches will beat us yet unless we can hang our politicians and burn our newspapers and have a dictatorship.'

Trenchard replied gloomily: 'Our institutions badly want revising, and I'm afraid we shall not move until things get worse.'[9]

But things had already got worse. Britain had ceased to be an island. The long-cherished wartime distinction between civilians and soldiers had been shattered. For the first time in the country's history, bombs were falling on English cities.

Chapter 9
Giants Dripping Death

The enemy raids had begun in January 1915 when giant airship bombers, dripping the death that H.G. Wells had so accurately foreseen, arrived silently in the night over the Norfolk coast. To the great shock and surprise of the inhabitants, they proceeded to empty their incendiary and high-explosive cargoes on the towns of Great Yarmouth and King's Lynn, killing four people and injuring sixteen others. More strikes followed. Dover, Ramsgate and Southend were bombed and on the night of 31 May a Zeppelin came to London. The German emperor, the Kaiser, had personally sanctioned the raid, but on condition that no bombs were dropped on the palace of his royal cousin, George V. He instructed that nothing west of Tower Bridge was to be attacked, nor any residential areas. The targets were to be military bases, fuel stores and the docks. In Germany the population was stirred into pride in the airship crews by active propaganda that fed the nation with highly selective accounts of their successes. The mood was captured by a popular song, 'Zeppelin Fly', which schoolchildren were made to sing: 'Zeppelin, fly; help us in war; fly to England; England will be burned; Zeppelin fly!'

Fortunately the Zeppelins, operated separately by both the German navy and army, were far from precision bombers. The great behemoths, more than 150 metres long, propeller-driven by anything from three to six big engines, carried a crude radio navigation system designed to give them bearings from ground stations in Germany. The signals also gave away their position to the British defenders, who began to jam them. But the airships' wireless fixes were in any case often so hopelessly inaccurate that they were forced to rely on dead reckoning – map-reading when they could glimpse landmarks and struggling in the dark to identify targets they frequently never found. Their bombs were scattered over London's eastern suburbs. Two fell on the Shoreditch Empire Music hall, others on Spitalfields market, but most on houses. Seven people were killed, thirty-five injured and around forty fires were started. Compared with the level of death and destruction one night of German bombing would wreak on London twenty-five years later, the outcome was negligible. But these early air raids which, by the end of 1916 had killed nearly 500 people and injured more than 1,000, were just the beginning of regular attacks on English towns that would continue to the end of the war. Despite the Kaiser's urgings to spare the civilian population there would be more strikes on London with bombs falling without warning from out of the night sky on Piccadilly, Charing Cross and Soho, sending frightened crowds rushing for the shelter of underground tube stations.

The main hope of the German high command was that their terror weapons would so sap the resolve of the population Britain would sue for peace. They had the opposite effect. They intensified anti-German feeling, boosted recruitment into the armies in France and brought fresh waves of demands in Parliament for a long-range bomber force to attack cities deep inside Germany.

To keep the Germans in ignorance of the results of their bombing, and to curb national panic that would demoralise the men at the front alarmed for the safety of their loved ones at home, the government gagged the newspapers. There was no wireless to carry emotionally stirring Churchillian calls for pride and defiance from a national leader. When Zeppelins began bombing cities in the Midlands and north of England the reports weren't allowed to name the towns that had been hit. The morning after the first London air raid *The Times* couldn't tell its readers where in the huge city the bombs had fallen. Not a single eyewitness account was published. There was only a short, bland and reassuring official statement reporting the handful of casualties and asserting: 'Adequate police arrangements enabled the situation to be kept thoroughly in hand throughout.'

The Defence of the Realm Act introduced powers by which newspapers could be prosecuted and editors jailed for defying the censors of the army and navy's rigorous press bureaux. 'It is undesirable,' an order to editors warned, 'that too much space should be given to describing Zeppelin raids. 'The actual military damage that has been done is slight. But at the same time so long as the Germans think that the raids have great effect they will be continued, and long accounts tend to produce an impression both in England and Germany that they are of greater importance than they are in reality.'[1]

Though the raids were more psychologically disturbing than materially destructive, the national unease brought loud demands for some visible signs of national air defence which, to most people, appeared non-existent. The attacks had exposed both the country's unpreparedness and the inter-service friction between the War Office and the Admiralty over whose responsibility defence of British airspace actually was. It took twelve months of argument and confusion for agreement to be reached that naval aeroplanes would patrol the Zeppelin air routes over France and Belgium and guard the approaches to the English coast, while the RFC would be left to try to deal with those airships that entered British airspace, which most of them managed to do.

The giant Zeppelins were exceedingly difficult to intercept. To avoid detection they tended to travel on moonless nights. The radar early-warning system that alerted the Spitfire squadrons of Fighter Command a quarter of a century later didn't exist. There was at first only a half-hearted attempt to black out the city. In the absence of air-raid sirens, policemen ringing bells would pedal through the streets on their bicycles with placards announcing 'Police Notice – Take Cover', returning later to display an all-clear sign. In some suburbs warnings were delivered by contingents of Boy Scouts, driven about in cars, blowing bugles. But often the first Londoners would know of an attack would be bombs and frightening showers of incendiaries suddenly exploding around them.

Military observation posts were set up on the East Anglian coast to telephone reports of sightings to London, where mobile anti-aircraft guns and searchlights would be rushed, usually fruitlessly, towards the vaguely assumed course of the incoming bomber. Equipped initially with path-etically small ex-Boer War pom-pom guns, whose puny quick-firing shells could rise barely halfway to their target, the anti-aircraft units for a long time met with little success. The gunners, their searchlights waving uselessly about the sky, frequently couldn't see the Zeppelins. They remained at elusively high altitude, often cruising at between 10,000 and 15,000 feet and above cloud, through which an observer in a hanging gondola would be lowered.

The spy car winched out on the end of a steel cable, could send a crewman down through the cloud as far as 3,000 feet below the mother-ship where, sitting in a wicker chair with a chart table, he would telephone navigation and bomb-aiming directions back to the airship's flight deck. The wandering searchlights rarely picked up these cunning capsules, one of which can today be seen in London's Imperial War Museum. The observation duty was popular among Zeppelin crews because they were allowed to smoke in their cold and lonely eyries as they peered down in the dark, straining to identify exactly where on earth they were over the great confusing sprawl of streetlights and the black spaces of parks, rivers and estuaries. They often mistook reservoirs for the Thames and their task wasn't helped by such defensive deception measures as lights

The 'Rumpety', the Maurice Farman Shorthorn on which thousands of RFC pilots were taught to fly – and many were killed.

The aerial vehicle – this one a BE2 – that was to make their cavalry horses redundant, watched at a 1913 military aviation review on Salisbury Plain by General Sir Horace Smith-Dorrien and his staff.

The ravaged trench engraved landscape upon which the pilots looked down on the Western Front. It stretched for more than 400 miles from the North Sea to the Swiss border.

The nightmarish world of mud and destruction from which many officers escaped to the Flying Corps.

(*Left*) Maurice Baring, the aristocratic intellectual who became Trenchard's personal assistant and amanuensis – as well as a legend among the Flying Corps squadrons for his extraordinary party tricks.

(*Above*) Lieut-General Sir David Henderson, Director-General of Military Aeronautics. His War Office battle to establish the military role of the aeroplane took a big toll on his health.

(*Right*) Major-General Hugh 'Boom' Trenchard, field commander of the RFC in France. For his belief in air power, this lonely, inarticulate martinet remains a legendary figure within the British military air services.

The Fokker Eindecker that fired its gun through the spinning propeller and, in the spring of 1916, dominated the skies over the Western Front.

Empty chairs. The comfortable world swapped for the horror of the trenches often brought an even shorter existence. Research by 45 Squadron historians has identified everyone in this picture, taken at Fossalunga on the northern Italian front in January 1918. Table left-hand side, front to rear: 2nd Lieutenants G.H. Bush, R.J. Brownell, J.P. Huins and W.T.H. Hocking (an equipment officer). Right-hand side, front to rear: 2nd Lieut. J. Cottle, Lieut. M.D.G. Drummond, Lieut. C.K. Attlee (medical officer), 2nd Lieut. R.R. Renahan, Captain Thompson (a visitor), Lieut. D.G. McLean, Lieut. R. Buck (armament officer) and Captain N.C. Jones. In the background, from left: stewards Huband, Ames and Bye.

Cecil Lewis. His memoirs *Sagittarius Rising* remain the most vividly recounted factual record of the ephemeral lives of the pilots among whom he served on the Western Front.

William Rhodes-Moorhouse, whose bravery on a suicidal mission in April 1915 earned him the RFC's first Victoria Cross.

(*Below*) Geoffrey Wall, the Australian pilot and poet, whose acerbic observations of his English public school pilot colleagues and the British military system filled his letters home.

(*Above*) The observer of an FE2b demonstrates the precariously unsecured way he had to operate his gun during the violent manoeuvres of mid-air combat in which some were flung overboard.

(*Left*) Albert Ball, the most publicly revered British ace of the war. His heroic lone-wolf hunting deeds, and 44 credited victories before his inevitable death, brought him fame that inspired hundreds of schoolboys to join the Flying Corps.

Eighteen-year-old Flora Young, whom Ball wanted to marry. They met only six times.

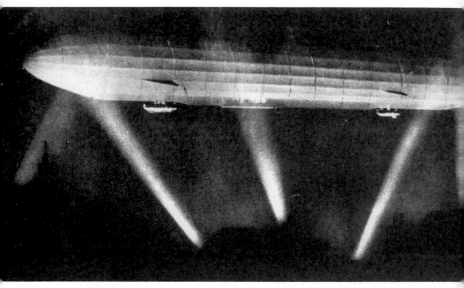

A Zeppelin bomber trapped in searchlights over London. The first to be shot down earned Lieutenant Leefe Robinson (*below, left*) a VC.

(*Above*) Aidan Liddell, the fatally wounded pilot whose skill and bravery in getting his observer safely down in their badly damaged aeroplane earned him a VC.

Manfred von Richthofen, 'the Red Baron'. The most universally remembered ace of WWI, his 80 victories were not matched by any other pilot on either side.

(*Below, left*): The aristocratic Richthofen family. From left: Manfred, his mother Baroness Kunigunde, brother ace pilot Lothar, cavalry major father Albrecht, younger brother Bolko, an army cadet, and sister Ilse, a wartime nurse.

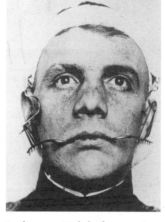

Lothar von Richthofen, a major ace in his own right, spent much of his service recovering from air combat – here a head wound and smashed jaw.

German ace Oswald Boelcke created the classic techniques of aerial combat. He discovered the unknown Manfred von Richthofen, persuading him to join his crack squadron.

Bill Bond and his wife Aimée McHardy. Their passionate love letters were of a rare intensity.

The Honourable Eric Lubbock broke down in tears after he'd shot down his first German pilot. After his death his idolising mother, Lady Avebury, dressed in black for the rest of her life.

hurriedly strung out across Hyde Park to indicate a non-existent thoroughfare.

The Zeppelins were run like naval ships. Some of their commanders had been seagoing captains and the ratings wore traditional sailors' square-rig collars. The engineers, who nursed the big motors that drove enormous wooden propellers on suspended platforms from which machine guns poked, were sometimes called stokers. There were so-called watch officers (non-aviation naval officers in control of the crew), petty officers, navigators, wireless-operators and a sailmaker to repair damaged gas bladders. The control cabin was like a ship's bridge with a large, spoked helm, engine-room telegraph and voice tubes for speaking to crew at remote stations. As well as the helmsman a separate elevator man, with another big wheel, controlled the ship's pitch up and down; he also operated the toggles that dumped water ballast for quick ascent, as well as the gasbag valves that released hydrogen for swift descent. In this big command car there was a navigation room, wireless cabin and an officers' lounge. The latter, in some airships, had wicker chairs, tables with tablecloths, flowers, pictures and a hot plate heated by an engine exhaust to fry eggs and warm soup. Up inside the envelope there were hammocks for crewmen to sleep when off watch during what were often more than 30-hour missions. And from early 1916 these spacious leviathans carried parachutes, though captains would sometimes refuse to take them to save weight.

For the crews the operations were as stressful and frightening as any of those experienced by the men of RAF Bomber Command in WWII raids over Germany. Though the Zeppelin airmen were rarely hit by anti-aircraft fire and initially had nothing to fear from the few defending aeroplanes that ever got near them, they lived in constant dread of a host of other constant risks to their lives. They could be blown up by lightning strikes or explosions of the petrol or bottled gas that fuelled their engines. The engines themselves constantly broke down, threatening their ability to get back to their bases. They could be swept by storms up to heights where the reduced atmospheric pressure led the gasbags to valve off so much hydrogen they would be denied, back at cruising level, enough lift to get home. And they could be forced down by the weight of the tons of ice that would sheathe the entire structure at high altitude.

There was vastly more space in the gondola cabins and the envelope's interior corridors than the Lancaster crews enjoyed, but at least the latter had warmth and oxygen. Despite sheepskin coats and helmets the Zeppelin crews would often find their teeth chattering with the freezing cold. Some suffered from frostbite, others from hypoxia, to the extent that they fell unconscious from lack of oxygen. They could be poisoned by other gases. When one airship arrived back at its base the captain ordered the engines stopped. But the rear motor kept running and the ship crashed. The engineers in the rear-engine gondola hadn't heard the command. They had been rendered unconscious by carbon-monoxide fumes from their engine.

The loss rate of airships and crews was high. Forty per cent never came home. Those that did survive a mission over England often got lost on their return over north-west Europe. Above blankets of winter fog they wouldn't know whether they were over Holland or Germany. Some were reduced to desperate measures. Airship SL12 zig-zagged for hours over a misty landscape that could have been in either country. 'At last we caught sight of a village,' recalled Captain Kölle. 'Helmsman Hüne leant out of the window and yelled like mad through the megaphone: "What's – this – place's – name?" From below we heard a hubbub of children's voices. "Hurrah, Zeppelin!" they shouted up at us. Well, it was an answer of sorts. But at last we found a railway station and read the name on its shield: "Bockhorn".' They weren't far from their base. 'We got home just as darkness was falling. We were all absolutely done up and the ship was down to her last drop of benzine. We had been up for thirty-five hours and fifty-five minutes.'[2]

Navigation problems were worsened by the great distances the airships had to fly to their targets by night, usually through or above cloud, across the North Sea from their bases in north-west Germany and Belgium. The quality long-range radio beams that would guide their Luftwaffe descendants with chilling accuracy to the epicentre of Coventry to reduce much of the city to rubble in the Second World War had not yet come to aerial warfare. On their long, slow journeys the Zeppelins, navigating over the sea by watch and compass and unreliable radio fixes, rarely knew how the winds were affecting their progress. The prevailing westerlies dramatically slowed them, drifting them off course without their knowledge.

On the last day of January 1916 a small swarm of nine airship bombers was sent on a 500-mile mission to attack the industrial heart of Liverpool. They encountered heavy rain and snowstorms. Three of them became so dangerously overweight with ice they had to dump petrol and some of their bombs to stay aloft. Only two of them got even remotely near Liverpool. They didn't know that a 40-mile-an-hour headwind over the North Sea had reduced their groundspeed to a creeping 20mph. When they eventually arrived over a black expanse the two captains mistakenly decided was the Irish Sea and saw the lights of a coastal town they believed it was Liverpool. They were in fact 75 miles short of the city, on the outskirts of Birmingham in the west Midlands. The lights they decided to bomb that foggy, frosty winter night, killing thirty-five people, were shining from a cluster of the nearby towns of Walsall, Tipton, Bradley and Wednesbury.

As the flotilla of nine scattered Zeppelins wandered about the Midlands sky looking for the elusive Liverpool, twenty-two Flying Corps and naval air service BE2c aircraft were ordered into the air from bases all over central and southern England to attack them. None of the pilots succeeded. It was a night of horror for the radio-less defenders. Many of the pilots, unskilled in handling and navigating their aeroplanes in big cloud masses in the dark, struggled to read their flight instruments with torches, got hopelessly lost and finished up force-landing in the pitch black, wrecking their machines. Others crashed either on take-off or landing back at their aerodromes – several of which, when they returned, had disappeared under a blanket of fog. Sixteen aircraft were damaged and two pilots were killed.

As the raid on the English Midlands so starkly illustrated, the airship crews would often arrive back in Germany with not the remotest idea of the name of the English town whose lights they'd chosen to bomb. A Zeppelin captain who survived the war to write a book about his hair-raising fifteen missions over England was a young nobleman, Baron Treusch von Buttlar Brandenfels. One of the Naval Air Service's most illustrious commanders, his exploits earned him Germany's highest military honour, the Pour le Mérite – the Blue Max – a large replica of which he always proudly hung from the nose of his gondola.

Von Buttlar's first operation had been in the spring of 1915, when he set out from Hamburg with two other Zeppelins to night-bomb industrial sites on the Humber in south Yorkshire. He had estimated time of arrival over the English coast at around 11pm. As the hour approached he ordered the ship to be darkened, 'our object being to approach the coast as secretly as possible'. When by 11.30 there was no sight of land they knew they had been slowed down over the North Sea by a strengthening westerly headwind. 'I looked at the clock and was horrified,' von Buttlar wrote.

It was midnight! And still there was no land in sight.

Half-past twelve and still no land! Since we had last ascertained our position near Terschelling [the Dutch Frisian island] a good four hours had elapsed.

I had our fuel gauged; it was terribly reduced.

Should we turn back? We had only enough petrol for another seven hours, and still there was no sign of England!

Having come all that distance, however, and on the very point of reaching the English coast, I was determined to push on at all costs ... I decided to continue on our westward course until one o'clock in the morning – at the very latest.

But 1am came and went with still no sight of land. They had now passed the point of no return to Hamburg. But with luck they might get back to a base in German East Friesland. Had they loaded more fuel they could have pressed on for longer, but that would have reduced their bomb load to zero. 'As it was,' said von Buttlar, 'it seemed rather absurd to carry out a flight of such magnitude just for the sake of dropping three ridiculous bombs on England!'

Further pushing his luck he decided to postpone the retreat just once more. Then 'suddenly a thin shaft of light came into view. The misty arm of a searchlight darted across the sky. It was probably looking for us. We were over England! The flight had not been in vain after all! Then we saw a number of faint lights beneath us ... myriads of them! We must be over some town. Let fly, therefore!'

The bombardier scrambled up the ladder into the envelope's cavernous interior and hurried back along the walkway to the bay where hung the paltry three 50kg bombs. Whatever town this was, it was where they were going to be dropped. The ship climbed to 3,500 feet and as three searchlights suddenly bathed them all in a blinding glare, von Buttlar rang the bell for the bombs to be released. They went down, followed by a cluster of small incendiaries, their pins withdrawn, thrown over the side by hand. As the crew looked down to watch their fires burning they were caught in 'a perfect inferno of gunfire and bursting shells – shrapnel meant for us'.

As Zeppelin L6 set out back across the North Sea the crew tried to work out which Humberside town they had bombed. 'It was quite possible that, with the veering wind, we had drifted ten or twenty miles south or north ... we began to cudgel our brains. But after considering the matter from every point of view we all came to the conclusion that we didn't really know where we had been.' They consoled themselves with the thought that the town they had struck 'was merely a secondary consideration. The point was that we had attacked England.'

The return journey was a nightmare of anxiety over their fuel levels.

When von Buttlar had it checked at 2am 'the report made my hair stand on end. We had only enough fuel for about another four hours.' It wasn't enough to reach even the nearest point of north-east Germany. But von Buttlar was not downhearted. He was convinced that his engine artificer would prudently have kept 'some little reserve up his sleeve'. The engineer had not.

Amazingly, on their dwindling supply they actually made it to within sight of Hamburg. But as the city appeared, still more than 25 miles away on the morning horizon, one of the three engines spluttered and stopped. Presently a second motor also died. In a desperate attempt to keep the one remaining engine running, von Buttlar ordered two men up on to the catwalk to tilt all the petrol tanks to squeeze the last drop from each. These meagre sluicings were fed to the surviving engine. They got them to Hamburg. The Zeppelin landed with less than three litres of petrol.

The airship was hours overdue. It had been assumed they weren't coming back. There was a message for von Buttlar to phone the senior airship commander urgently. Von Buttlar, knowing he would want to know where they'd been, was too embarrassed to call him. But soon the commander was on the phone himself.

> I reported that I had carried out a bombing raid on England. He was highly delighted by the news ... then came the ominous question: 'But where did you actually go?'
>
> With the best will in the world I could not answer his question. I stammered and stuttered into the telephone and declared that opinions were still divided as to the precise spot – but that it must have been one of two places. He asked me what they were.
>
> I thought there was something wrong with the line. I could hardly hear what he was saying – at least so I declared.
>
> Well, the long and the short of it was that he didn't catch the two names which I mumbled into the telephone. I told him I would telegraph them to him.

The commander told him to hurry up as the German Admiralty was demanding the information. Von Buttlar knew his stonewalling had given him only a short respite. He and his watch officer and the helmsman pored yet again over the map of England. They still hadn't a clue where they'd been. With dread von Buttlar wrote out the seven required copies of the mission report, leaving the destination blank. Then, determined to be out of phone contact, he drove to a restaurant for a meal. There a miracle occurred.

A newspaper vendor, shouting 'Airship raid on England!' rushed into the restaurant waving a special edition. Von Buttlar seized a copy. The German Admiralty, he read, had confirmed an airship attack 'on certain fortified places in England'. But for him the best news came in a footnote. A London correspondent reported that 'a German airship carried out a bombing raid at 1.15am today over the English town of Maldon'. How this particular piece of information dodged the strict British censorship to reach the German newspapers is a mystery – but it saved von Buttlar's reputation. He ran to the phone and called the air base. He was just in time. The secretary had almost finished typing his mission reports. He told her to insert 'Maldon' in the blank spaces and send off the documents immediately by express messenger. The newspaper had got him out of a hole. But the identification of the bombed town had exposed the enormity of their navigation error. Maldon, on the Blackwater estuary in Essex in south-east England, was around 130 miles south of the Humber. The wind had drifted them nearly 20 degrees off course to the south. None of the three Zeppelins had arrived anywhere near the Yorkshire coast. Yet von Buttlar's blind raid – which had damaged one house and slightly injured a woman – was to bring him, he wrote, 'recognition and fame!'

'About a fortnight later I received through the usual official channels a communication from the authorities. In it they declared that "the accurate navigation of the airship, and location of the place raided, were worthy of the highest praise".'[3]

Not all Zeppelins were as lucky as von Buttlar's. Some, limping home from England low on fuel, finished up in the North Sea beyond reach of quick rescue. L19, one of the airships that had bombed the Midland towns instead of Liverpool, met this fate in tragic circumstances for her crew. Despite three of his four engines breaking down, the captain, Lieutenant-Commander Udo Loewe, managed to nurse the faltering ship to the Dutch coast. Over Holland, as a military craft entering the airspace of a neutral country, they met with heavy rifle fire, became lost in fog and, on a wind unusually blowing from the east, drifted back out into the middle of the North Sea, where they eventually dropped into the water about 120 miles off the Yorkshire coast.

The crew cut away all the gondolas and climbed on to the long platform on top of the floating envelope, where they erected a shelter. They held out scant hope of rescue, so when, at dawn on the second day, a Grimsby trawler, trailing black coal smoke from her tall funnel, appeared out of the mist the sixteen men on the by now half-submerged airship shouted with joy. The airship captain called in English to the trawler, the *King*

Stephen, asking that they send their small boat across. The Germans' delight was short-lived. The trawler skipper, William Martin, conferred with the mate and the other members of his crew. Although there were nine strong men on his vessel they feared, because they had no weapons on board, they could be taken hostage or overpowered by the Zeppelin crew, finishing up at a German port as prisoners of war. So Martin called through his megaphone: 'No. If I take you on board you will take charge.'

Captain Loewe replied, 'Save us, save us! We will give you plenty of money.'

But the trawler crew didn't trust them. To the horror and disbelief of the men on the sinking airship, the *King Stephen* turned round and steamed away. As she did so, the fishermen heard the Germans shouting angrily 'Gott strafe England!' Did compassion for these enemy airmen, hungry and weak from their ordeal, pleading for their lives, lead skipper Martin to consider taking them on board one by one and tying them up? It appears not. The fishermen had no long-range radio, and by the time they got back to Grimsby, where the Zeppelin crew's plight was reported to the navy, L19 had been slowly sinking for nearly two and a half days. She was never found.

However, her crew shared their desperate final hours with the world. Several bottles washed ashore a few weeks later on the coasts of Sweden and Norway contained heartrending farewell messages written by the doomed Germans as they waited to die.

Of all the poignant letters that bobbed ashore, including a report to his commander-in-chief from Captain Loewe, who added a note to his 'wife and child', the saddest was written by a seaman called Hans.

My dear Ada and Mother,

It is now eleven o'clock on the morning of the 2nd of February. We are all still alive, but we have nothing to eat. This morning an English steam-trawler came up to us, but refused to rescue us. It was the King Stephen from Grimsby. My courage is ebbing away, and the wind is growing fiercer.

Your loving Hans, who will think of you in heaven.

At 12.30 p.m. we all prayed together and bade each other good-bye.

Your Hans

The seemingly callous decision of the *King Stephen*'s crew had some major repercussions. Back in Grimsby the mate, George Denny, was interviewed by reporters. He tried to explain why they'd left the Germans to drown. 'We could see no way of rescuing them without taking too great a risk,' he said. 'We could not trust them. It was not inhumanity but common sense.'

The incident was widely covered by the press and divided British public opinion. But the popular view was that skipper Martin had done the right thing. Supportive letters poured in to him. The Bishop of London was quoted saying: 'Any English sailor would have risked his life to save a human life, but the sad thing was that the chivalry of war had been killed by the Germans, and their word could not be trusted.'

The German newspapers responded with anger, condemning William Martin for his 'brutality and inhumanity'. A Berlin paper declared: 'When Englishmen speak of fair play in future, one will be reminded of the sunken crew of L19.' The German reaction was soon to have some unhappy consequences for the trawler. Commandeered by the British Navy and converted to a Q-ship – a heavily armed anti-U-boat merchant ship with concealed guns – she was seized by a German destroyer, sunk with gunfire and the crew taken prisoner. Recognising the *King Stephen* as the vessel that had left the Zeppelin crew to perish, the Germans threatened to shoot her new captain, a navy lieutenant. Although the trawler had a completely different crew, only a copy of a Grimsby newspaper featuring the story, eventually produced in desperation, convinced the Germans of this and saved the lieutenant from execution. Martin himself never put to sea again. He died a few weeks after his encounter with the stranded Zeppelin. Stricken with guilt and remorse, he had been deeply affected by the awful decision he'd made. People said it had hastened his death.[4]

Although more and more British squadrons were rushed back from the front line in France to defend the homeland against the mounting airship attacks, they only occasionally managed to shoot one down. The unsuitable BE2s took nearly an hour to struggle up to the Zeppelins' altitude and if they were lucky enough to close on an airship they were met with hails of machine-gun fire from its four gunners, three positioned under the belly and one, a tiny figure, perched on the top platform. Drumloads of conventional bullets fired into the skin of the huge sausages had no effect at all. The hydrogen was stored in separate gas bladders within the skeleton of the huge, cathedral-like hull. The shells that did reach them failed to ignite the highly inflammable hydrogen that kept its crews, sometimes more than two dozen of them, at a fever pitch of anxiety throughout their flight. The bullets would simply punch small holes in the gasbags causing them merely to leak, a problem the ship's engineers could repair in flight. What was needed was more destructive ammunition. And, just as importantly, pilots who could fly safely at night.

Chapter 10
Zeppelin Stalkers

F ew British pilots had ever been introduced to the skills of night flying, interpreting the altitude and heading of their aircraft in pitch blackness entirely from their handful of basic instruments. Many were killed even attempting it. Defending London, some of them, to their dismay, were nevertheless ordered into the night sky from Hendon aerodrome. When Lieutenant Arthur Harris reported to the station adjutant he had been asked: 'Can you fly in the dark?'

> I said, 'Well, I can't fly in the daylight – maybe it's easier in the dark!' He said, 'Well, you're the anti-Zeppelin pilot here.' So I said, 'What does that mean?' He told me, 'Well, the station supplies a pilot every other "odd" night. There are two machines up in the end hangar which you have to look after. They are your machines – go to it!'
>
> That very night, in thick, drizzly weather, the station commander, who was also the duty pilot, went up and killed himself before he'd got 100 yards beyond the end flare. The next night it was my turn! I was told to see if I could find an army airship that was going to fly around pretending it was a Zeppelin. Well, by the most astonishing bit of good fortune, both for the airship and myself, I found it by very nearly running into it. It had put its lights on in a panic when it saw me coming. I suppose that was regarded as a bit of skilful scouting navigation on my part whereas all I had done was to fly blindly into the night and hope for the best.[1]

Some of the pilots sent to Hendon to defend London didn't even know how to fly the aeroplane they were expected to do it with. A naval air service officer, Flight Sub-Lieutenant Eric Beauman, was ordered to report to the aerodrome soon after the Zeppelin raids began. The squadron commander at his naval base asked him: 'Can you fly a Caudron?'

'I said, "No!" He said, "Well, you've got to, it's the only one we've got! Do you know the way to Hendon?" I said, "No!"'

'"Well, at dawn tomorrow you will fly in a Caudron to Hendon."'

When he arrived at Hendon, Beauman remembered, 'the fellow in charge of aeroplanes there said, "Now you are the air defence of London – the only one!" I said, "But I've got no guns or observer or anything, what sort of protection can I give against the Germans?" He replied, "I'll leave that to you." So I hoped the Zeppelins wouldn't come over.'²

A weapon capable of striking an airship's Achilles' heel – the highly explosive hydrogen gas that kept it aloft – came at last in the summer of 1916 in the shape of incendiary and explosive bullets. There had been an initial reluctance to use them since they were outlawed by the nineteenth-century Hague Convention rules of war. This prohibited the use of exploding and soft-nosed 'dum-dum' bullets, which expanded on impact, because of the shocking damage they did to the human body. However, the German Army's use of poisonous gas on the Western Front in April 1915 had hardened British resolve to defeat the Zeppelins by any means. A lethal cocktail of destructive ammunition was developed. Its ingredients were three different bullets, each with a name that was to make their deadly purpose both famous and controversial within the Flying Corps for the rest of the war.

The Pomeroy, filled with nitro-glycerine, ignited the hydrogen that escaped from the bullethole when a Zeppelin's gasbags were hit. The Brock (created by a member of the famous fireworks family) exploded in the space between the gasbags and the airship's outer skin. And the Buckingham was a phosphorous incendiary/tracer whose journey to the target could be seen by the pilot. When fired in a cluster into the huge bulk of a Zeppelin, this trio of bullets spelled swift and flaming death for the ship and its crew. To satisfy the Hague Convention it was made clear that the ammunition would be used solely against airships.

Lieutenant Leefe Robinson's Lewis machine-gun drum was loaded with these devastating new missiles on the night 2 September 1916 when he was sent up to intercept an unusually large force of sixteen London-bound airships that had been reported crossing the coast. He took off from Sutton's Farm, a stubble field at what later became Hornchurch, the east London air base from which Spitfires would rise to defend the city again in 1940. But unlike the imperishable Battle of Britain fighter, which could fly at over 360 miles an hour and climb to 10,000 feet in just over three minutes, Robinson's BE2c biplane took fifty-five minutes to reach that height. His mission was to patrol London's eastern approaches over the Thames Estuary.

As his feeble machine struggled up into the cold, cloudy darkness his face was buffeted by the freezing slipstream, his body ached with cold and his alertness began to be dimmed by hypoxia. He had none of the comforts that would be enjoyed by Spitfire pilots – no heater, no cockpit canopy, no oxygen. No ground controller's voice with crisp headings to steer towards the incoming fleet. Instead Robinson, eventually at nearly 13,000 feet, cruised fruitlessly up and down above the river, his brain blurred by lack of oxygen, for more than two hours. Then, around 1am, he saw in the distance the shape of an airship caught in the glare of searchlights near Woolwich. When he turned to pursue it, it disappeared into cloud. It took him nearly an hour to find it again, by which time the ship had travelled north into Hertfordshire. In the grip of more searchlights it looked like a gigantic white cigar. It was now being fired upon by the latest and more accurate anti-aircraft guns whose shells were bursting around it. Robinson dived towards it.

It was not in fact a Zeppelin, but a rival wooden-structured Shutte-Lanz of the German Army. Even with his destructive ammunition, it was not easy to shoot down. Approaching from ahead, Robinson first flew below it, strafing the envelope from bow to stern along the full length of its enormous underbelly, burning up a full drum of his upward-pointing Lewis gun. The fusillade had no effect. So he circled the airship and made another run, firing a second full drum into the ship's side. This, too, brought no visible result.

With his one remaining drum Robinson decided to try attacking from the rear. Slipping below and behind the airship, he pressed the trigger. As the explosive and incendiary stream poured into the envelope a red blush began to appear around the entry point. Within seconds the glow burst into a blazing mass from which he was forced to retreat as fast as he could while burning fragments showered his aeroplane. He was so excited by his triumph – in which his Lewis gun had shot off part of his top wing – that he grabbed his Very pistol and fired off a celebration cluster of red flares, a moment later adding a victory parachute flare for good measure. In a daze of euphoria and exhaustion he watched the awful death throes of SL11 as it sank in flames below him. 'It was a glorious sight!' he later wrote to his parents.

> It literally lit up all the sky all around me ... I saw my machine as in the firelight and sat still, staring at the wonderful sight before me.
>
> My feelings? Can I describe my feelings. I hardly know how I felt. As I watched the huge mass gradually turn on end and slowly sink – one glowing, blazing mass – I gradually realised what I had done and grew wild with excitement. When I had cooled down a bit I did

what I don't think many people would think I would do, and that is I thanked God with all my heart.

You know, darling old mother and father, I'm not what is popularly known as a religious person, but on an occasion such as that one must realise a little how one does trust in providence. I felt an overpowering feeling of thankfulness, so it was strange that I should pause and think for a moment after a first 'blast' of excitement was over and thank, from the bottom of my heart, that supreme power that rules and guides our destinies.[3]

What Robinson didn't know until later was that as the wreckage of the blazing airship fluttered down into a field at Cuffley in southern Hertfordshire, its spectacular death in the night sky north-east of the city had been watched by a huge number of Londoners. A blaring orchestra of ship and locomotive hooters and whistles had brought people everywhere rushing on to the streets in alarm that Sunday morning in their night attire. When they saw what was happening they cheered and danced. 'Thousands, one might say millions, of throats giving vent to thousands of feelings,' he marvelled in his letter to his parents. 'I would have given anything for you dear people to have heard it . . . the gratitude of millions of people – and the cause of it all: little me sitting in my little aeroplane above 13,000 feet of darkness!'

Not everyone had joined in the mass applause. From Harrow, where she was staying with friends, Sybil Morrison had watched the 'awful sight' of the burning airship as it floated down. 'We'd always been told that there was a crew of about sixty people and they were being roasted to death. Of course, you weren't supposed to feel any pity for your enemies; nevertheless I was appalled to see the kind, good-hearted British people dancing round in the streets at the sight of sixty people being burned alive, clapping, singing and cheering.' There were in fact sixteen men aboard the ship, commanded by Captain Wilhelm Schramm. When Sybil expressed her disgust to her hosts 'they said, "But they're Germans, they're the enemies! Not human beings." This is what war did. It created this utter inhumanity in perfectly decent, nice, gentle, kindly people.'[4]

The airship's destruction triggered a bloodlust in many Londoners. People poured out of the city that Sunday morning by train, bicycle, horse-cart and car to visit the Cuffley field and gaze upon the pile of ash and tangled coils of bracing wire amid which the blackened bodies of the crew still lay. They were put in coffins and taken to the local church. Peering through the keyhole, a girl later claimed to have seen several policemen 'playing ball' over the caskets with the dead men's helmets. Scattered in the ash of the burned-out airship were three Iron Cross gallantry medals and a revolver, which was later presented to Leefe Robinson.

Twenty-one-year-old Robinson, the grammar school- and Sandhurst-educated son of an English coffee plantation-owner in India, was said to have been a particularly modest person, embarrassed by the wave of public adulation heaped upon him as the first pilot to destroy an airship over Britain. On landing back at Sutton's Farm after his mission his fellow airmen ran out to meet him and carried him shoulder-high to the mess. Not only was he immediately awarded a Victoria Cross, a consortium of businessmen gave him a handsome reward of £4,000 – today worth more than £1 million. He didn't enjoy being lionised, showered with invitations from the high and the mighty to receptions and dinners in his honour or besieged by people wherever he went. Strangers inundated him with gifts, babies were named after him, poems were published about his great feat, his portrait was painted and he did scores of interviews. He went to Windsor Castle to receive his Victoria Cross and had a long chat with the King. When he entered a box at the Gaiety theatre in London the whole house rose and cheered him like royalty. 'I am recognised wherever I go about town now, whether in uniform or mufti. The city police salute me, the waiters, hall porters and pages of hotels and restaurants bow and scrape, visitors turn round and stare. Oh, it's too thick!'[5]

To escape the adulation Robinson pleaded with the Flying Corps to be allowed to return to flying duties. He went back first to Sutton's Farm and, later, to the Western Front, where he was shot down and taken prisoner. His health was badly affected by captivity and by the especially harsh treatment meted out to him sadistically because of his VC, and died on repatriation in the influenza epidemic of 1918.

The increasing annihilation of airships with explosive ammunition, combined with sharper early-warning systems and more effective anti-aircraft guns, proved a turning point in the first Battle of Britain. In the autumn of 1916, more and more ships were spectacularly brought down in flames. Indeed, this became the fate of almost every Zeppelin that came in range of the killing machines – most of which, ironically, were none other than the widely reviled, long-obsolete BE2c. The devastating new bullets didn't need a high-performance aircraft as a launching plat-form. The Flying Corps improved their success rate further by main-taining continuous night-long patrols over Greater London. The Zeppelin missions were now near-suicidal for their stressed-out crews, who were only too aware that each raid could be their last. Flight engineer Pitt Klein wrote of the cold fear that never left them: 'It is only a question of time before we join the rest. Everyone admits that they feel it. Our nerves are ruined by mistreatment. If anyone should say that he was not haunted by visions of burning airships, then he would be a braggart.'[6]

The airship squadrons produced their own heroes. One of the most famous and publicised commanders was Lieutenant Heinrich Mathy. He was reputed to have dropped more tons of bombs over England than any other Zeppelin captain. But he shared all the anxieties expressed by engineer Klein and, on 1 October 1916, they were tragically realised when his ship was shot down in a flaming mass over Potters Bar. At the last moment Mathy leaped out on to the ground. He survived for a few minutes. When his body was removed hundreds of people came to view and photograph the deep impression his sad, sprawled torso had left in the soft soil.

To unleash their bombs from altitudes beyond the reach of the BE2s the Germans began to send stealth bombers, 'height-climbers' that, unheard on the ground, arrived at 20,000 feet. Up here, four miles high, they were safe from aeroplanes and guns. But not from the devastating effects on their crews and engines of the lack of oxygen and temperatures as low as minus 30 degrees. The height-climbers were a failure. Although occasional attacks on Britain would continue for another two years, the days of the massed airship terror raids had, for the moment, ended. The giant invaders paid a terrible price for their campaign. By the end of the war, of more than 120 German airship bombers built, nearly eighty had, in all theatres of the four-year conflict, been destroyed in accidents, in attacks on their hangars, lost at sea or shot down. Nearly 600 men, a large proportion of their aircrew, had died.

The autumn of 1916 brought, at last, merciful respite for English cities from death and destruction in the night. But the relief would be short-lived. In Germany a substantially more muscular, more menacing aerial vehicle was emerging from the factories in a further attempt to bomb Britain out of the war. However, in the race for superior flying machines the British had been busy, too. Some aircraft had finally begun to arrive on the Western Front that could face the forward-firing Fokker on equal terms.

Chapter 11

The 'Fees' Come to France

The first aeroplanes to stem the Fokker Scourge did so, surprisingly, without machine guns that fired through the propeller. They simply had their guns positioned in front of the spinning blades. Two of them, in fact, were old-technology pusher aircraft that had been around for some time. Their guns and cockpits were already up front. These interim Fokker-beaters were pressed into service on the Western Front while the British air services searched for their own interrupter gear.

First to arrive in squadron service, early in 1916, were two rear-engined biplanes: the FE2 and the DH2. Both these spindly-looking machines, designed by the masterly Geoffrey de Havilland, appear, in pictures, to be the last sort of aircraft one would imagine enjoying great success in aerial battle. The crew sat in front of the engine and wings in what Cecil Lewis described as the shape of 'an old boot; the pilot sat fairly high up in the heel and the observer squatted down in the toe'. The business part of the aircraft was connected to the tail unit by four flimsy-looking little poles. Yet, because the pilot and observer had an unobstructed field of view ahead, both aircraft were immediately successful. Their machine guns, like those of the Fokkers, could happily fire forward in the direction of flight.

In some versions the 'Fees' bristled with guns: the pilot had one and the observer two, one firing forward and the other, mounted on a wobbly telescopic pole, shooting upwards and backwards over the top of the upper wing. The latter called for some frightening airborne gymnastics. To fire it the observer had to stand precariously on his seat and turn around in mid-flight. With his body completely unsecured and pummelled by the freezing 70mph slipstream, he would shoot rearwards at enemy aircraft attacking from above and behind as he clung on to avoid being flung from the cockpit during the violent banking manoeuvres of combat. And while all this was happening he ran the risk of being shot in the heat of battle by the pilot's own gun spitting bullets past him.

One aviator who survived to write about this hazardous business was 2nd Lieutenant Frederick Libby, an American former cowboy, who served with distinction as an observer with the RFC. 'This gun is a nightmare,' he recalled.

> Nothing to hang on to except the gun, sticking up in the air, anchored to a steel rod. A quick sideslip by your pilot would toss you so clear of the machine you would never get back . . . All of you from the knees up was exposed to the elements. Only your grip on the gun and the sides of the nacelle stood between you and eternity. You had nothing to worry about – except being blown out of the aircraft by the blast of air, or tossed out bodily if the pilot made a wrong move. There were no parachutes . . . No wonder they needed observers.[1]

As the Fees got into their stride on the Western Front their tally of Fokkers destroyed rose by the week. Yet it would be months before the tide was effectively turned against the Eindeckers which, upgraded with more guns and more powerful engines, began to face problems of their own. Two or three machine guns firing through the propeller proved too much for the synchronising mechanism to handle. The bullet streams from multiple guns started shooting off the blades. The imbalance this caused created such a violent vibration of the crankshaft that the whole disintegrating engine was liable to break free in a clattering convulsion and drop out of the aeroplane. Max Immelmann experienced it twice in one week, narrowly escaping with his life. As a result the Eindecker's weaponry was reduced to two guns. Although this helped, it didn't entirely eliminate the problem. Synchronising mechanisms were yet to acquire total reliability.

Immelmann had become the special darling of the German public and his name, nearly a century later, is still one of the best remembered of the First War's German aces. His feats had brought him a large collection of medals, knighthoods and bravery awards and daily piles of letters from adoring young women who sent him flowers, rosaries and crucifixes. He appeared in cinema newsreels and the King of Saxony visited his air base especially to meet and take personal snaps of him. Because he often flew patrols over the French city, Flying Corps pilots began to refer to him admiringly as the 'Eagle of Lille'.

Immelmann remained obsessed with his victories. When his victims fell behind German lines he would afterwards drive for miles to seek out the wreckage and proudly have himself photographed beside it. Not only fêted by the German public, he was revered by his fellow pilots. When he was promoted to full lieutenant the squadron marked the event with a celebration dinner, hiring a band to serenade him throughout the meal. Hundreds of soldiers congregated outside to listen and began, Immelmann told his mother, 'shouting enthusiastically: "Immelmann, Hurrah! Hurrah! Hurrah!" After that we sang the airmen's march and "Deutschland Über Alles" [the German national anthem, 'Germany Above All']. When the strains of that died away I called for three cheers for His Majesty, in which hundreds of male voices joined enthusiastically. Altogether it was a happy occasion.'[2]

Immelmann's closest friends were said to have been his huge dog, Tyras, and his doting mother back in Dresden, who kept him copiously supplied with chocolates and with whom he unfailingly shared the details of his dangerous life of spiralling fame. The first to hear of his every victory, Frau Immelmann, a widow plagued by ill health, would hang out a flag on her front gate to proclaim the event to the neighbourhood. Such triumphs were doomed to be finite.

In the fading light of a late summer's evening in June 1916, Immelmann's luck finally ran out in an encounter with a group of FE2s of the Flying Corps' No. 25 Squadron. During the aerial battle between four Fokkers and eight Fees, Immelmann's aircraft was seen to stagger before breaking up and plunging to the ground. He died instantly.

What had happened? Who had slain the Eagle of Lille? Probably no other pilot had. Nor had he shot off his own propeller. When Anthony Fokker was allowed to inspect the two halves of the wreckage, which had landed some distance apart, it was clear that the aeroplane had been accidentally destroyed by German anti-aircraft fire.

Fokker had come to know Immelmann well. The pilot's death, he was aware, was inevitable. The aces were in a contest, wrote Fokker, 'with Time, the cruellest foe in the world. Knowing the accuracy of the machine gun and the aeroplane in the hands of a skilled pilot, calculating the remote chance of surviving any prolonged campaign in the air, I should never have had the courage to face the enemy. Every man who went aloft was marked for death, sooner or later, once his wheels left the ground.'[3]

When news of Immelmann's demise reached the Flying Corps, one of its pilots was sent to drop a wreath as a mark of respect for 'a gallant and chivalrous opponent'. His funeral in Douai was given the pomp of a state occasion. Crown princes and generals followed the coffin on a gun carriage drawn by seven horses while fellow Eindecker pilots flew over to shower the cortège with roses. At Dresden, his home town, an unusual statue was later erected. Stark naked, in startlingly perfect anatomical detail, Immelmann stands in heroic pose with a dagger in one hand and the other arm outstretched, reaching for the sky.

Despite its abundant firepower the FE2 was too sluggish in combat to be an effective fighter. Battling their way back from long reconnaissance missions twenty miles behind the German lines they were easily picked off by waiting Fokkers. 'It's no joke,' said one pilot, 'to be shot up by a dozen machine guns for half an hour, engaged in a running fight in which the enemy can outpace you, outclimb you and out-turn you. It needs a lot of guts and a cool head.'

The single-seater pusher de Havilland DH2 was a much more successful machine. Carrying just one man it was immediately more nimble and manoeuvrable than the Fees and, with its single forward-firing gun, was the first aeroplane capable of at last engaging the Eindeckers on equal terms. It could climb in the then revolutionary time of just fourteen minutes to 7,000 feet, where it was able to fly at the brisk speed of 85mph. It did, however, have some drawbacks. The same sensitivity of its controls that made it formidable in combat initially killed so many pupils, who stalled and crashed while learning to fly it, that it acquired the grim nickname 'the spinning incinerator'. But in experienced hands, when they began to arrive in France in February 1916, the DH2 showed that it could outfight the Fokker. Suddenly the small de Havilland gunships started to take their revenge on the Eindeckers. As the RFC pilots learned how to fly it safely and to kill by aiming their machines rather than their guns at the target, it was the Fokkers that began to fall out of the sky. A 32 Squadron pilot, Gwilym Lewis, delighted by his first victory in a DH2 told his parents that the Flying Corps had at last 'gained the genuine article, supremacy of the air. If a Hun sees a De Hav he runs for his life. They won't come near them.'[4]

This primitive machine, the bare, uncovered skeleton of its fuselage giving it the air of an aeroplane still under construction, belied its rudimentary appearance. It became the first British aircraft to truly merit the description of a single-seat fighter. And it had appeared in time to keep the sky clear of German reconnaissance machines over the lines where the British armies were preparing for one of the biggest, most terrible battles of the war.

Chapter 12

Terror Above the Somme

The Battle of the Somme, launched on 1 July 1916, has become a metaphor for the horror and futility of trench warfare. It saw the sacrifice for little gain of the lives of hundreds of thousands of young British, French and German men who clashed on a twenty-five-mile front of Pas de Calais farmland between the valleys of the Somme and Ancre rivers. A desperate attempt by the Anglo–French commanders to end the stalemate of the trenches and break through the German lines in a titanic infantry assault, it was intended decisively to turn the course of war. The inter-Allied planning had begun in December 1915, but before the great attack could be launched the Germans struck first. Not on the Somme, but 130 miles to the south-east on the other side of France. Here, at the historic old fortress city of Verdun on the river Meuse, they surprised the Allies with a bombardment of exceptional ferocity. Amassing a ring of more than 1,200 big siege guns, their aim was the swift annihilation of the unsuspecting French defenders.

The Germans, who sent a million men into the attack, hadn't, however, reckoned on the force nor the speed with which the French would manage to respond. Verdun developed into a battle that would drag on for ten bitter months. The Germans deployed the horror of flame-throwers; both sides fired gas shells and destroyed each other with bayonets and grenades. They reduced more than a hundred square miles of countryside to yet another cratered lunar landscape. Around 700,000 German and French men were killed, wounded or simply obliterated by shellfire.

The colossal casualties at Verdun had major repercussions for the offensive on the Somme. The French armies were left with insufficient men to spread between the combined Somme operation and the Verdun battle that was, in the midsummer of 1916, still raging in north-eastern France. General Sir Douglas Haig, now the British Expeditionary Force's commander-in-chief, had to provide the lion's share of forces for the assault. Although there was now an enormous supply of them they were largely raw and barely trained, commanded by inexperienced officers. The professional British Army that had gone to France in 1914 had been virtually wiped out. In its place, to fight on the Somme, there had arrived hundreds of thousands of the millions of men who had responded to the war minister Lord Kitchener's legendary 'Your Country Needs You' appeal for recruits. A staggering number of them were to die on the first day of the offensive without firing a single shot.

The front lines of the Somme battlefield, which lay across undulating country astride the poplar-lined old Roman road between Albert and Bapaume, were in some places barely 60 metres apart. All the advantages lay with the Germans. They occupied higher ground and were established in shell-proof bunkers dug deep into the chalk terrain. In the fortified villages they massed in labyrinths of ancient catacombs. On the slopes between the lines they had spread an ocean of impenetrable coils of heavy barbed wire anchored to tall steel poles.

To destroy the deeply bunkered defenders and this forest of wire the attack was preceded by a week-long bombardment that unleashed more than a million and a half shells. The barrage was so intense it could be heard on Hampstead Heath in London, 160 miles away. The hurricane of shellfire was intended to rip apart the wire and punch gaps in the enemy trenches through which the cavalry would lead an immense infantry breakthrough to victory. Tragically for the British foot soldiers ordered to accomplish this task, few of the guns fired high-explosive shells. Most of the ammunition was ineffective shrapnel. The shellfire largely failed to demolish either the wire thickets or the German trenches. Nor did ten gargantuan landmines, exploded at the start of the battle from tunnels driven under the enemy lines, achieve this. When, that morning of 1 July, the British divisions poured 120,000 men, encouraged by whistles, bugles and bagpipes, 'over the top' into no-man's-land, the result was beyond disastrous.

The British volunteers had been reassured that the German lines had been razed by the week-long bombardment: they were told not to charge across, merely to walk confidently in military formation. 'When you go over the top, you can slope arms, light up your pipes and cigarettes and march all the way to Pozières before meeting any live Germans,' the commander of a Yorkshire infantry battalion was said to have told his men. There was no way they could have run anyway. Soldiers in the leading waves were each burdened with around 32kg – 70lb – of equipment. Some were carrying cages of communications pigeons. They were so weighed down they had difficulty even climbing out of their own trenches. As they tried in great bunches to push their way through the few tiny gaps in the wire they were scythed down in a merciless fusillade of fire.

Peering out of their emplacements the German machine-gunners were astonished at the human targets presented to them on the slopes below: lines of men, as if on parade, plodding steadily up towards them. When they sprayed the slowly advancing figures with fire and the German artillery began exploding among the survivors, most of them were sliced down, killed outright or torn to pieces, horribly wounded. By the end of the first day the British divisions had made no significant advance and no-man's-land was littered with dead and dying limbless infantry and disembowelled horses. Hundreds of men lay where they had fallen in shell holes or sprawled like collapsed scarecrows, hanging pitifully on the warren of uncut barbed wire.

Circling overhead the goggled figures of the army's aviators, looking down from their open cockpits, witnessed the bloodbath beneath their wings. Their role was to keep enemy aircraft out of the battle zone and the army commanders in touch with both the progress of their struggling infantry and the locations of the German forces. They contended with lack of sleep, unreliable engines and blizzards of shells in their airspace. But they were spared the awfulness of the ground war. 'When we returned to the aerodrome our war was over. We had a bed, a bath, a mess with good food, and peace until the next patrol . . . Though we lived in the stretch or sag of nerves we were never under any bodily fatigue, never filthy, verminous, or exposed to the long disgusting drudgery of trench warfare.'[1]

The casualty rate on the ground on that first day of July 1916 reached unprecedented levels. By nightfall the eleven British divisions, for minimal gain of enemy-held territory, had lost over 57,000 officers and men of whom nearly 20,000 were dead, mown down in the first hundred metres of their advance. Entire battalions were effectively wiped out. Back in Britain the heavily censored newspapers represented the failed attack in astonishingly encouraging terms. In his joint dispatch to the *Daily Telegraph* and *Daily Chronicle*, the prominent war correspondent Philip Gibbs wrote: 'Our troops, fighting with very splendid valour, have swept across the enemy's front trenches along a great part of the line of attack . . . His dead lie thick in the tracks of our regiments . . . It is a good day for England and France. It is a day of promise in this war in which the blood of brave men is poured out on the sodden fields of Europe.'[2] But the shocking lists of casualties that began to appear daily in the British press told a different story. So did the increasingly regular sight of the hospital trains that were now delivering thousands of grievously wounded men, whose lives would never be the same again, to Charing Cross station.

The Flying Corps crews who had been assigned on the first day of the battle to 'contact patrols' brought the ground commanders a continuous stream of bad news. They had become bird's-eye witnesses to the day-long catastrophe as they watched the swarms of doomed human ants crumpling en masse below. Eighteen-year-old Cecil Lewis, now a Morane Parasol pilot with No. 3 Squadron, wrote that in the bullish briefing for the battle the evening before they had been told 'victory was certain; that the lines would be broken, the cavalry put through, and the Allies sweep on to Berlin'.

The reality, as Lewis, would discover, would prove anything but such a triumph. He and his observer had been flying over the area of the imminent battle every day through the week of the softening-up bombardment. They had taken scores of photographs for the army of the destruction their guns were supposed to be inflicting on the enemy's network of impregnable concrete redoubts. These were terrifying missions.

At two thousand feet we were in the path of the gun trajectories, and as the shells passed, above or below us, the wind eddies made by their motion flung the machine up and down, as if in a gale.

Grimly I kept the machine on its course above the trenches, waiting, tense and numb, for a shell to get us, while Sergeant Hall (who got a DCM and a commission for his work that week) worked the old camera handle, changed the plates, sighted, made his exposures. I envied him having something to do. I could only hold the machine as steady as possible and pray for it to be over. At last, after an hour, I felt a tap on my shoulder. Gratefully I turned for home.

Below, the gloomy earth glittered under the continual scintillation of gun fire. Right round the salient down to the Somme, where the mists backed up the ghostly effect, was this sequinned veil of greenish flashes, quivering. Thousands of guns were spitting high explosive and the invisible projectiles were screaming past us on every side. Though they were our guns, their muzzles were towards us, and suddenly I knew it was at us they were firing ... Of course it was ridiculous, but for about a minute I was in the grip of nightmare terror.

In another minute we were through the danger zone; but the vivid memory haunted me back to the aerodrome. Even there we could hear the thud and rumble of the guns, even back in England they were hearing it ... But I could not forget its blind fury, and pitied the men who for a week lived under that rain. I suppose I was many times nearer death than on that particular evening; but for me it remains none the less, the most fearful moment of the war.'

On the cloudless summer morning the Somme offensive was launched Lewis and his observer were back over the lines at dawn. The preliminary bombardment had reached a crescendo. It was, he said, the greatest bombardment of the war, 'the greatest in the history of the world. The clock hands crept on, the thrumming of the shells took on a higher note. It was now a continuous vibration, as if Wotan, in some paroxysm of rage, were using the hollow world as a drum and under his beat the crust of it was shaking. Nothing could live under that rain of splintering steel.'

Lewis had been warned to keep clear of La Boiselle, a heavily fortified German position. Two huge mines had been placed underneath it in tunnels hewn by Welsh miners out of the chalk beneath no-man's-land. The place was due to be blown up at 7.28am, two minutes before the 7.30 great attack. From a safe distance they watched. The first massive mine to be fired contained 26 tons of ammonal.

The earth heaved and flashed, a tremendous and magnificent column rose up into the sky. There was an ear-splitting roar, drowning all the guns, flinging the machine sideways in the repercussing air. The earthy column rose higher and higher to almost four thousand feet. There it hung, or seemed to hang, for a moment in the air, like the silhouette of some great cypress tree, then fell away in a widening cone of dust and debris . . . A moment later came the second mine.

When the dust settled Lewis saw the white eyes of two enormous craters. One of them, preserved as a tourist attraction to this day, was 100 metres across and 30 metres deep. But the great explosions had not destroyed the heavy machine-gun emplacements. The earth had heaved short of the redoubt. The guns remained intact to pour their murderous fire upon the slow marching lines of British infantry, so pinned down and decimated they ceased to be able to identify themselves to the circling aircraft. In consequence the commanders, directing the assault from their headquarters behind the lines, were largely ignorant of the catastrophic failure of the whole operation. There was no two-way radio to keep them in touch; field telephone lines strung out across no-man's-land were often blown apart as soon as they were laid. Unbelievable as it sounds today, the commanders on the Somme that day were left dependent on runners, flag-waving semaphore signals and, most reliable of all, pigeons, for news from the front line.

Communication between the soldiers and the contact-patrolling aeroplanes in the height of battle was at first equally hit and miss. Some of the infantry had small metal mirrors sewn on to their packs which, with luck, might be seen flashing. But in the inferno of smoke and explosions and hand-to-hand fighting below, pilots and observers frequently had difficulty identifying the troops as friend or foe. They would circle, screeching Morse code requests with their klaxons, calling for identifying red flares which the platoons carried for the purpose but were often too hard-pressed to use. Sometimes just one solitary flare would flicker to reveal a position and enable a scribbled note to be flown back to brigade headquarters and dropped in a bag on to the white groundsheet that was supposed to be, but often wasn't, displayed there. On the first day of the Somme the whole system broke down at both ends.

'I was bitterly disappointed,' Lewis wrote. 'For months we had been preparing, hoping and believing that at last the Air would do something valuable and definite for the wretched men who were carrying forward the line.' Instead 'it was a complete washout, with no co-operation from the very men we were there to help'. The truth was that the hard-pressed infantry, awash with dead and wounded, were afraid to fire the flares for fear they would bring hostile shells and squalls of machine-gun fire raining down on their already tenuous position. The reconnaissance aircraft were forced into swooping dangerously low to check the colour of the uniforms – British khaki or German grey. There was further disappointment in the failure of the artillery batteries to respond to the aeroplanes' wireless messages providing map references of hostile guns to shell. The British gunners were too preoccupied to factor the co-ordinates into their firing operations.

Lewis's dogged observation patrols brought him a Military Cross. He was lucky to survive the Somme. The ground battle was to drag on inconclusively for four and a half months. The much less-remembered air war, fought between heaven and the hell of the killing fields, took the lives of many of his colleagues. It consumed pilots, observers and aeroplanes almost as fast as they could be replaced.

But, in its early weeks, the Somme campaign saw both the end of the Fokker Scourge and a reversal – if only temporarily – of the Flying Corps' fortunes on the Western Front.

Chapter 13

Morale and the Offensive Spirit

On a foggy morning early in April 1916 the sappers of a battalion of the Royal Fusiliers behind the front lines near St Omer were surprised when an aircraft bearing a German black Maltese cross loomed out of the mist and put down nearby. They thought at first it was dropping off, or collecting, a spy. It was a single-seater and it wasn't. The young German pilot had got lost in the haze and run out of fuel. Before he learned the sorry truth about his location and set fire to his aircraft, it was seized and he was taken prisoner. The machine was a Fokker Eindecker, complete with its infamous propeller interrupter mechanism – the first to fall into Allied hands.

The embarrassed, badly frightened pilot, a humble lance-corporal who, before the war, had been a junior clerk in Berlin, was whisked off to Flying Corps headquarters to be interviewed by a brigadier-general. He told the general that if the British copied the Fokker's firing device and he was returned to Germany after the war he would be shot. But there was no longer any need to replicate the mechanism. It had arrived too late to be of any value. Not only had the Flying Corps' forward-firing pusher machines already begun to reverse its fortunes, but a nippy new French aeroplane, the Nieuport Scout, which fired its gun forward over the top of the propeller, had reached the front line. It was closely followed by the first British plane to be fitted with a synchronised gun: Sopwith's oddly named '1½ Strutter' fighter-reconnaissance biplane.

On its own the technical edge the RFC had acquired was not, however, enough to win the air war. The new aerial weapons were only as effective as the way they were deployed. Again the British air services drew on the expertise of the French, whose strategic doctrines had been shaped by painful experience at the Battle of Verdun. There, the French air commander, Commandant Paul du Peuty, had initially yielded to the demands of his army masters to concentrate his squadrons over the front lines to provide the comfort of their visible presence, artillery ranging and reconnaissance support. But hordes of German machines, organised into strike units and spearheaded by Boelcke's Fokker attack group, had quickly begun both to pick off the orbiting French aeroplanes and to shoot up and bomb the French ground defences.

Du Peuty defied the orders of his generals. He reversed the policy, removing his fighters from their sheepdog task protecting the army co-operation machines and switching them from defence to an attacking role. Unleashed for offensive missions far behind the enemy lines, the French fighters had started bombing enemy aerodromes and intercepting the German invaders in the air long before they could reach the front. Despite howls of complaint from the French ground commanders at the loss of their visible fighter cover, they found themselves much less frequently spied upon by enemy observation aeroplanes over the front line. The strategy – in football terms, keeping the opponents permanently in their own half of the field – worked. It gave the French at Verdun a high degree of aerial mastery over the battle front. It was so successful that du Peuty shared the detail of his philosophy with Trenchard, who introduced it to the Flying Corps. The two began to meet frequently to share ideas and became warm friends.

There couldn't have been a greater contrast between the curt, undemonstrative forty-three-year-old Trenchard, a non-flying general, and the charismatically engaging active fighter pilot du Peuty, five years his junior. They spoke very little of each other's language and had to communicate through an interpreter. Curiously commanding the French air service with only the rank of major, this ex-cavalry officer was no stranger to air combat. Not only had he already been shot down and wounded, he continued to inspire his pilots by personally leading high-risk, long-range intruder raids.

This unlikely friendship, through which the two men developed a new approach to the most effective use of air power, led to a joint doctrine that was to dictate the strategies of both air forces for the remainder of the war. For the now twenty-seven-squadron-strong Flying Corps on the Somme, where Trenchard decided to split his aircraft into separate fighter and army co-operation units, the policy in the early months of the battle, revolutionised the fortunes of the Allied squadrons. It kept German aircraft out of the Somme skies, preventing them from photographing the Allied positions and from directing their big guns and strafing the soldiers in their trenches. It delivered despair to the commander of the First German Army on the Somme.

'With the aid of aeroplane observation,' complained General Fritz von Below, 'the hostile artillery neutralised our guns and was able to range with most extreme accuracy on the trenches occupied by our infantry . . .

the enemy's aircraft inspired our troops with a feeling of defencelessness.'[1]
An unfinished letter in the pocket of a dead German soldier read: 'Just a
word about our own aeroplanes. Really one must be almost too ashamed
to write about them, it is simply scandalous. They fly up to this village
but no further, whereas the English are always flying over our lines,
directing artillery shoots, thereby getting all their shells right into our
trenches'.[2]

The 'English' who were bringing terror to the German trenches from
the air were daily facing fears of their own. Enemy fighters, Archie and,
most frightening of all, a new horror: 'flaming onion' incendiary shells,
fired up in alarming fiery strings whose blazing metal set fire to an
aircraft's fabric fuselage. From all these agents of destruction the crews
would all too often return with dead or wounded pilots and observers.
And it wasn't always the pilots who brought the aeroplane back.

Only some two-seater aircraft were fitted with dual controls. The risk
was that duplicate control columns would prevent the observer from
swinging his front machine gun from side to side, and that discarded
ammunition drums could jam the rudder bar. Some two-seaters provided
the observer with a detachable control stick to clip on in an emergency
plus attachable hand-pulled rudder cables. But most RFC machines kept
all the controls in the pilot's cockpit. Which made it all the more incredible
that some observers still managed to land aircraft whose pilots had been
too badly wounded to fly or killed.

One such landing acquired immortal status through the eminence
of the aristocratic pilot. The 8th Baron Lucas of Crudwell joined his
squadron in France with a most untypical *curriculum vitae*. At forty he
was twice the age of most of the squadron pilots and he had only one leg.
In civilian life he had been a Boer War correspondent for *The Times*, a
British Cabinet minister and a privy counsellor. But this significant past
became irrelevant on 22 Squadron, where his title was never used, he was
known as 'Bron', and was regarded as a slightly crazy 'air hog' who
demonstrated an almost excessive need to participate in high-risk
operations.

Unusually for someone of his upper-class background, Lord Lucas was
not a public-school man. He'd been sent to Bedford Grammar going on
to Balliol, where he'd become an Oxford rowing blue. An unenthusiastic
scholar, he had scraped by with a third-class degree in modern history.
Regarded as a mildly eccentric gypsy, he had spent much of his time at
Oxford on private expeditions into the countryside to study wildlife.
Reporting the Boer War in South Africa he was wounded in the foot, the

injury that led to the amputation of his leg below the knee. It had scarcely affected his hunting and steeplechasing lifestyle. His closest friends were Edwardian socialites and intellectuals, among them Raymond Asquith, the eldest son of the British prime minister, a friendship that led to a string of government appointments as a Liberal peer. He had become under-secretary for war; later he had joined the Cabinet as president of the Board of Agriculture. In the middle of 1915 he had turned his back on the corridors of power, on his many inherited estates, his fishing, his horses, his musical supper parties, and joined up.

Astonishing as it may seem, the one-legged Lucas was accepted into the Royal Flying Corps. He became a pilot, then an instructor and was even offered command of a squadron. He refused it, insisting that he should prove himself first as a front-line pilot. In 22 Squadron this rather languid bachelor peer, who gave the impression of being permanently amused and a little puzzled by life, startled his fellow pilots, young enough to be his sons, with the aggression of his offensive spirit. 'He was the oldest in years, but youngest in heart, of all the pilots on his squadron,' wrote the RFC's historian.

In the first week of November 1916 on a grey, stormy day with a turbulent high wind sweeping over northern France, Captain Lucas led a flight of Fees over the lines on a photo-reconnaissance mission. Three of the aircraft were shot down. Lucas was hit in the head and leg, collapsed into unconsciousness and never woke again. Although also wounded, his observer, Lieutenant Anderson, managed to reach back and control the aeroplane. He landed it successfully behind German lines and was taken prisoner. The remarkable Auberon Lucas was buried nearby. News of their fate took a long time to reach the squadron. When it was finally reported a month later, Trenchard's private secretary, another aristocrat, the Honourable Maurice Baring, was moved to write that 'the most fitting crown to the example of his life' was 'the splendour and sacrifice of his death'.[3]

Through the summer of 1916 Flying Corps pilots and observers on the Somme continued to watch the slaughter as men on the ground, often trying to take possession of no more than a small wood or an even smaller village, died in their tens of thousands. From the dominion of the sky it was possible, Cecil Lewis found, to view the horror of this Armageddon with a degree of remoteness.

The war below us was a spectacle. We aided and abetted it, admiring the tenacity of men who fought in verminous filth to take the next trench thirty yards away. But such objectives could not thrill us, who, when we raised our eyes, could see objective after objective receding, fifty, sixty, seventy miles beyond. Indeed, the fearful thing about the war became its horrible futility, the mountainous waste of life and wealth to stake a mile or two of earth. There was so much beyond. Viewed with detachment, it had all the elements of grotesque comedy – a prodigious and complex effort, cunningly contrived and carried out with deadly seriousness, in order to achieve just nothing at all.[4]

To the British infantry, meanwhile, the Flying Corps airmen were a welcome presence as they spotted and destroyed the enemy guns that were hindering their faltering advance. A Captain Whittaker and his observer, circling an embattled brigade trying to take the village of Montauban but pinned down by heavy shellfire, located the German battery and put it out of action, strafing it with their machine guns. They then poured fire into nearby enemy trenches, wiping out enough of the German infantry to allow the brigade to resume its advance, and watched the 16th Manchesters, according to the RFC's historian, 'enter Montauban in splendid formation. They could see, too, that the men of the 18th Division had fared equally well, and were now moving up the ridge to the west of the village. So exhilarated were they with what they saw that they flew low along the ridge, waving their hands to the victorious infantry, on whom their greeting had a heartening effect.'[5]

'My men,' the brigade commander later wrote to Flying Corps headquarters, 'were immensely cheered and delighted on reaching the Montauban ridge when one of your gallant fellows came down very low and exchanged a wave of the hand.'[6]

Many of the pilots knew what it was like to be down there in the thick of the ground battle. Some had endured trench warfare for over a year before joining the RFC. One of them, a 19 Squadron pilot, Lieutenant Ian Henderson, had been rescued from the ghastliness of it all by his father, the RFC commanding general Sir David Henderson. Ian had lived under constant shell and machine-gun fire in the mud and wire of no-man's-land at the Battle of Ypres. In a letter to his mother, Lady Henderson, scribbled in pencil from his dugout, he wrote: 'We have just gone through the most awful time and I have seen some sights I never wish to see again ... I am afraid the regiment has had heavy casualties in the last few days; 500 men or so, and three officers killed and four wounded. I have been lucky and am all right, although the three next men to me were all killed by one shell and I was not touched at all.'[7]

Another letter described how a bomb had exploded among thirty men in a neighbouring trench, burying many of them. The survivors, crawling into Henderson's trench, had been unable to drag out a wounded sergeant.

> This sergeant tried to cross the gap and got it in the back. He shouted out, 'I'm hit, goodbye boys!' and they couldn't get to him. In about ten minutes, after everyone who wasn't wounded or killed, had got safely to our trench, three men came up and volunteered to go and fetch, or at least bandage up, the wounded remaining there. They found the sergeant and were just bandaging him when another one came. They were literally blown away in different directions. But they were unhurt and came and unburied him who had disappeared under the showers of mud. This happened again when another shell burst. They at last got him done up and stayed with him for about 12 hours in the open trench half full of water. Rather wonderful don't you think?[8]

Now Ian Henderson was observing the terrors of his former existence from the detachment of the air. 'It is most awfully interesting to watch,' he told his mother. 'You see all the men running forward and jumping into the German trenches and running after them down the communication trenches.' He went on to describe an extraordinary vignette of ground warfare that unfolded beneath his wings. 'I saw one man (a Canadian I think) catch about 70 prisoners single-handed. I saw all the Germans huddled in their trench and I saw our men advancing towards them. Then one of our men suddenly ran out and into the German trench. I expected to see him shot. No! All the Germans got out of the trench and followed him back to our lines, running as hard as they could.'[9]

Though the Flying Corps might for the moment have swept the Somme front-line air of German intruders, success came at a very high price. 'Archie' could still deliver violent death. It did so devastatingly to Lieutenant Bernard Coller and his observer, 2nd Lieutenant Thomas Scaife. One minute they were orbiting the front line. The next, in full view of the troops with whom they were communicating, their BE2 machine was blown to pieces over the soldiers' heads by a direct hit from an anti-aircraft shell. Trenchard's aggressive new strategy of taking the air war far inside enemy-held territory sent his losses soaring. The long-range bombers attacking German airfields, railway and troop targets were slow, vulnerably overladen BE2s forced, because of their heavy bomb loads, to fly defencelessly without observer-gunners. Despite their fighter escorts they were liable to be pounced upon and shot down, sacrificed to the greater good of the 'offensive spirit', a phrase that had become the RFC's mantra.

Even when the average lifespan of pilots shrank to barely three weeks Trenchard refused to spare his crews. When newly invented British tanks were first sent into action on the Somme the army wanted their assembly parks kept secret from the spying enemy observation balloons that hung like strings of sausages behind the lines. Ahead of a massive tank-led push on the German lines in mid-September, Trenchard was ordered to deal with a cluster of three of these tethered balloons.

He decided to give the urgent task to No. 60 Squadron and to brief the airmen personally. Driving to their aerodrome at Savy at dawn, he told the gathered pilots that the three balloons must be destroyed before the imminent ground attack was launched at its now rapidly approaching zero hour that very morning. 'A deathly pause,' wrote Trenchard's biographer, 'followed his final words: "Now I want three volunteers."'

'Good luck, Gilchrist,' he said to one of them. 'But remember this: it's far more important to get that balloon than to fail and come back.' It was a death knell of a farewell. He repeated it to the others; yet none took the words amiss, perceiving how much it cost him to utter and mean every brutal syllable.

He was watching when the trio took off with Le Prieur rockets fastened beneath the wings of their Nieuport fighters, hoping that their speed might carry them through unscathed, but aware that rockets could not be aimed with any degree of accuracy except in a steep power-dive through the field of fire above the targets. Trenchard was still waiting when, after a short eternity, the telephone rang. Army Headquarters were on the line, reporting that three balloons had just fallen to earth in flames. Presently the miracle happened. All three aircraft returned, badly damaged but intact.[10]

But Trenchard's latest relentless offensive began to come under fire again both within his pilot corps and back in England, where the swelling lists of casualties were watched with growing concern. His ruthless policy, not always fully understood at the time, was driven by the British Army's ever-increasing dependence on air power for their survival. Whereas the German armies, through all the years of the static trench war, occupied the commanding heights of hills and ridges from which, with a wide field of view, they could observe their enemy's activity without danger, the

Allies, from their usually less elevated positions, were compelled to use aeroplanes. And because they were forced to wage endless offensive battles against vastly more fortified German strongholds, their aircraft were obliged to operate constantly in the lion's den at the mercy of often technically superior enemy machines. The enormous losses this brought put such pressure on the training schools that the squadrons' cockpits were more and more routinely being filled with vulnerably inexperienced aircrew. It was a vicious circle, never fully resolved. 'Had they attempted less,' the RAF's historian wrote with post-war pride, 'they would have suffered less.'[11]

British air losses were four times as great as those of the German. 'For the High Command to persist, despite the toll in life and material, in continuously patrolling the lines and in sending obsolescent machines deep into German-held territory, was incomprehensible,' wrote Arthur Gould Lee.[12] No. 1 Squadron's adjutant, Lieutenant Thomas Hughes, also recorded his disillusionment. 'Trenchard,' he noted cynically in his diary, 'follows the good military principle of repeating any tactics that have not been actually disastrous – and often those that have – again and again, regardless of the fact that the enemy will probably think out some very good reply, until they really are so disastrous that they have to be abandoned.'[13] Trenchard, whose carefully guarded feelings seldom betrayed an inner core of compassion, offered 'few concessions to human frailty'. His heart, according to his biographer, 'was hardened against the contagion of doubt spread by the despondent or the waverers'.[14] And he dealt ruthlessly with the waverers.

Among them was one of his wing commanders, Lieutenant-Colonel Hugh Dowding. Dowding had long qualified as a member of the Flying Corps' brigade of singular characters. His career had followed a familiar pattern, from public school to the army, with which he'd enjoyed years of fishing, shooting and polo in India and the Orient. Back in England he'd learned to fly at his own expense, gaining his pilot's certificate after a mere 100 minutes in the air. By the time he joined the RFC he was approaching his mid-thirties and had acquired a reputation as a below-average pilot and a coldly, highly competent but uncompromising, intensely serious character to whom very few ever warmed. He seemed to cast a gloom over the squadrons he commanded. But beneath the surface of this unloved man there was a passionate concern for his aircrew and the rate at which they were being sacrificed. He believed that Trenchard failed to recognise the need for realistically adequate training before pilots were sent into combat they didn't stand a chance of surviving. He told him his insistence on sledgehammer offensive tactics was costing more casualties than the military advantage justified.

Dowding's wing had four squadrons. One of them, No. 60, whose pilots had destroyed the enemy balloons, had suffered such enormous losses that, by early August 1916, half its numbers had been killed or wounded – a casualty rate not helped by the difficulty of flying the squadron's Morane Bullets, another aeroplane feared and detested by almost everyone when they first tried to fly it. By early August 1916, after the loss of a squadron commander and two flight commanders, pilot morale had reached such a low ebb that Dowding urged Trenchard to withdraw the squadron from the line for a few weeks' rest. Trenchard reluctantly agreed. But privately he thought that Dowding's compassion demonstrated weakness. Seeing no place for such a man in his air force, he decided to get rid of him.

His interview with Dowding 'left him uneasy – not so much about the squadron's morale as about Dowding's own. If the self-confidence of the pilots had been shaken, it was unlikely to be restored by a wing commander who gave him the impression of being obsessed by the fear of further casualties. Dowding, he informed Brancker in his next letter home, was a "dismal Jimmy" whom he proposed to replace.'[15] The wing commander was later duly banished from front-line flying operations for the rest of the war, disappearing into a succession of administrative jobs back in England. It was not, however, the last the world would hear of him.

How did the pilot victims of Trenchard's immutable strategy feel as, watching the chairs around them emptying, they waited for their own number to come up? The daily losses affected them all. When Albert Ball joined his first fighter squadron in France in May 1916 he had almost immediately become an ace. Within six weeks he had been credited with seven kills. He was on his way to becoming one of the most famous fighter pilots of all time. Yet even that early, the strain of combat flying was already beginning to sap his ability to continue.

'Yesterday four of my great pals went out and never came back,' Ball wrote to his father in Nottingham. 'I shall be glad when it is all over, for at times I feel very whonkey and run down.'[16] A few days later he told his family he was 'feeling very rotten'. His nerves, he said, were 'poo-poo. Naturally I cannot keep on for ever, so I went to see the CO and asked him if I could have a short rest and not fly for a few days.'[17]

The major was sympathetic, but he needed authority from the general commanding his brigade. He didn't get it. Brigadier-General Higgins was affronted that someone so junior and new to the front should have the temerity to make such a request. He refused it outright. Instead, to keep Ball on the offensive treadmill, he transferred him from his fighter squadron to another that was engaged in reconnaissance and bombing. Far from bringing Ball the relief he so badly needed, the move merely whisked him from the frying pan into the fire. In No. 11 Squadron, flying the fast, conquering new Nieuport Scouts, duelling for his life on a daily basis in dogfights had put his nerves on edge. Now, at No. 8 Squadron, he was reduced to trundling round the sky in a slow, obsolete BE2c with Archie exploding all around him. Every mission still threatened to end in flames.

Ball was deeply upset. 'They don't give you a rest unless you are quite a crock, or too whonkey to do your job. This is thanks after my work and not even the major can stop it,' he wrote home bitterly from his new squadron. 'Three majors have done their best for they all think it a cad's trick. However, here I am. Now I think I shall ask to go back to my regiment. Oh! I am feeling in the dumps.'[18]

On reflection Ball decided to stay with the Flying Corps. He survived his few weeks with 8 Squadron, but only narrowly. On one of his long-range bombing missions he was picked off by two Fokkers ten miles over the lines and only some quite extraordinary evasive manoeuvres saved him from the worst. His nerves were as bad as ever. He couldn't wait to go on leave, he told his parents. 'I shall have to have a rest when I get home for I cannot carry on if I don't.'[19] Nor could he wait to escape from the 'rotten and slow' BE2s to which he'd been relegated. Yet, seemingly perversely in the circumstances, he volunteered for a special operation that, by any standards, was highly dangerous: a mission to drop an agent behind enemy lines at night.

Flying a sluggish aeroplane at low level to land in hostile territory in the dark was not a task a lot of pilots were in a hurry to tackle. For six weeks several of them had attempted the operation and failed. They had all refused to risk it again unless ordered to do so. But Ball, hoping it might help redeem him in the eyes of the general, took it on.

It proved a nerve-wracking experience. In the gathering dusk the unarmed aircraft was intercepted by three Fokkers. Ball only just managed to escape them in the gloom. Then he was spotted by anti-aircraft guns. His BE2 was suddenly illuminated by a blaze of flares and assailed by rockets 'to try and set us on fire. Oh! It was nice, I really did think the end had come.' With enormous luck the aeroplane wasn't hit and Ball found a field in the dark and managed a safe landing – a feat in itself. But now, to his anger, the spy refused to get out. 'The Fokkers had frightened him and he wouldn't risk it. There was nothing to do but get off again before the Huns came along and stopped us – so off we went. I went down three times after this but the rotter refused to do his part. So we had to return. Oh! I was so cross after taking so much risk for nothing.'[20]

But Ball's persistent attempts to deliver the agent brought him the acknowledgement he sought from his demanding brigade commander. Higgins congratulated him, amazed that he had risked four night landings in unlit fields in enemy territory. Ball further impressed him by offering to make yet another attempt. 'But Higgins said he was such a rotter that he would not give him another chance.' Ball asked the general if he could now go back to his old squadron as he felt ready to resume some serious aerial combat. Higgins eventually agreed and in the middle of August 1916 he returned to No. 11 Squadron, where he was allocated his own personal Nieuport. Within hours of arriving he had taken it into the air and shot down a Roland reconnaissance machine. Six days later he destroyed three more Rolands in the space of forty-five minutes on one evening patrol, bringing his tally to eleven.

Albert Ball had for the moment contained his resentment of the unsympathetic response to his plea for a rest. He would not have known that the brigade general was merely observing the hard-hearted policy imposed by his field commander-in-chief. Nor would he have known of the private agonies and ambivalence Trenchard suffered in prosecuting it. But he saw no way to satisfy his military masters other than to hurl every available pilot and machine into an uncompromising onslaught to wipe the enemy squadrons out of the sky. Accustomed to human sacrifice on a vastly greater scale, they expected him to maintain total control of the air over the front lines whatever the cost.

Despite the apparent brutality of his demands on his crews and his policy of packing off back to their army regiments many of the men he believed had lost their nerve too early, Trenchard didn't always enjoy doing it. For those who had demonstrated they were made of sterner stuff he would sometimes, as his anguished correspondence with Sefton Brancker reveals, go to unusual lengths to preserve them before they collapsed.

'I have lost a good many machines lately and a certain number of pilots, but really they have done splendidly,' he had told Brancker in the first week of the Somme. 'A lot of the pilots as you know have to do 5 or 6 hours flying a day and this is going on day after day which is a bit of a strain with so many hostile machines and anti-aircraft guns about. I have lost as you know eight machines at low bombing, and I am afraid some of the pilots are getting a bit rattled and it is not popular. I have put two in for VC's.'[21]

With the return to England of Lieutenant Charles Darwin, who had already fought in the trenches for two years as a Coldstream Guards officer, there went a special plea: 'Dear Brancker, I am sending you Darwin who has done splendidly but is undoubtedly tired and weary. Only today he went on a long bombing raid of 4½ hours and he has been on most of the long bombing raids. I wonder if you can put him into a fighting squadron with some fast scouts – but do not kill him by putting him in the BE12.'[22] The BE12 had been a disastrous failure as a fighting machine, writing off a large number of pilots before Trenchard withdrew it from its combat role. Darwin was kept off this deathtrap and survived to become a squadron leader in WWII.

Sometimes it was Brancker who tried to spare a pilot from breakdown. 'My dear Trenchard, I gather indirectly that Sanday of No. 70 Squadron is nearly worn out ... We are quite prepared to take him if you send him home.'[23] Lieutenant William Sanday was a highly decorated pilot who had shot down five enemy aircraft.

'Dear Brancker,' Trenchard responded. 'I agree with you and I want to get him home. I have to send so many home who are absolutely broken down and I must keep up to strength ... If you can get someone to take his place I will send Sanday home because he must not break down.'[24]

But Trenchard needed more pilots than he was being given to replace the growing numbers succumbing to combat fatigue. 'My dear Brancker, We are fighting a very big battle and the fighting in the air is becoming intense, and will increase I regret to say, not decrease. It is only a question of our keeping it going longer than the Huns. If we cannot do that then we are beaten; if we do it then we win.' Sombrely the letter went on: 'I must warn you now that in the next ten days if we get fine weather I anticipate a very heavy casualty list. There are many more German machines, fast and much better fighters which have suddenly appeared on our front opposite to us than there have been before. I hope you will take this letter very seriously and take stock of how we shall be off for pilots this autumn and the larger number of casualties we are bound to have.'[25]

This ominous news signalled the end of the Flying Corps' short respite from enemy air control of the Western Front. The new German machine that arrived to replace the declining threat of the Fokker was a powerful, sleek, biplane fighter. Its firepower, from twin machine guns shooting through the propeller, enabled it to destroy almost anything it attacked with alarming speed. The balance of technological supremacy had turned again.

Chapter 14
Bloody April

The sensational new German aeroplane, the Albatros, began to appear over the lines in the autumn of 1916. RFC pilots dubbed these squat, pugnacious-looking, highly manoeuvrable biplane fighters 'the Albatri'. No other aircraft then in existence could compete with this superb aerial gun platform. Its big Mercedes engine gave it a top speed of 109mph and the ability to whistle up to over 3,000 feet in five minutes. In one dramatic stride the German Air Service had brought to the Western Front an aeroplane with which no Flying Corps machine, except perhaps the Nieuports, in expert hands, could compete. The DH2 and the Fees were doomed. They could no longer protect the trundling old BE2s, the observation workhorses upon which the army had become so hugely dependent to range its big guns and locate the enemy.

To add to the menace of the 'Albatri', the Germans flew them with a new breed of unusually gifted fighter pilots hand-picked and highly trained in the techniques of aerial combat. They were sent to special new hunting squadrons called *Jagdstaffeln*, soon to be better known as jastas. The first of them, Jasta 2, was commanded by the great Oswald Boelcke, the ace who, with Immelmann, had led the Fokker Scourge. Now with twenty kills to his credit, Boelcke had become such a national treasure that Kaiser Wilhelm had ordered his grounding for a month to ensure that he wasn't lost in combat so soon after Immelmann.

During his enforced month out of the air Boelcke had been sent on a tour of squadrons on the Eastern Front in Russia to look for some super-pilots to join his elite hunting force. Here, in the Ukraine, the German Air Service was fighting a much less dangerous air war than in France. The Russian enemy pilots, most of them hastily trained and flying second-hand, obsolete French aeroplanes, were no match for men who had acquired high combat skills on the Western Front. Their losses in accidents and battle during 1916 had reached a devastating 50 per cent a month. It didn't take German airmen long to become aces out here.

Among them Boelcke, looking for experience and aggression, believed he had found it in two men.

The first, Erwin Böhme, was not on the face of it an obvious recruit for a fighter squadron of dashing young bloods. In his late thirties, he was a worldly, cultivated and much-travelled man, a civil engineer who had lived his life adventurously in Europe and Africa. He had worked in Switzerland, where he used to make solo ascents of the sheer face of the Matterhorn, and in German East Africa, with a timber-milling company helping to build a railway.

Back in Germany, on the outbreak of war Böhme had made two decisions that were to affect the future course of his life. He had gone to meet one of the Tanganyika company's timber customers, Heinrich Brüning, at whose mill near Nuremberg he became a regular guest. And he'd applied to join the German Air Service. Thanks to his maturity and exceptional fitness he had, despite his age, been accepted and passed out top of his training course. While serving as a reconnaissance pilot at the Battle of Verdun he had created a major stir at Brüning's mill by arriving unannounced and accompanied by two other pilots in a big borrowed twin-engined bomber in the middle of a party to celebrate the mill-owner's silver wedding anniversary.

For Böhme the event had an unexpected romantic consequence. At the party he met and was smitten by the family's eldest daughter, Annamarie Brüning, a beautiful, dark-haired twenty-three-year-old nurse working at a military hospital. They began a fervent correspondence in which Böhme began to share with her his life as a war pilot. In one of his earliest letters, written from Kovel, the Ukraine base where Boelcke found him, he wrote of his fears that he was too old to be chosen. Boelcke 'would be selecting from all of the air service', he wrote, 'what appeared to him to be the best qualified people'.

That evening I fell asleep with the thought – too bad that you're such an old boy and not fifteen years younger! Such flying in the latest single-seater; that would be your downfall.

So, imagine my surprise in the morning when Boelcke suddenly walked up beside me and simply asked, 'Do you want to go with me to the Somme?' In my entire life I have not voiced a happier 'yes' . . . Besides myself, Boelcke also selected here a young lieutenant out of the lancers, Richthofen, a splendid person who has already proved at Verdun, and also here, to be a brave and steady pilot.[1]

Manfred von Richthofen was a young ex-cavalry officer and minor Prussian aristocrat, the son of a regular army major. He had already distinguished himself in combat on the Eastern Front. He was ecstatic when Boelcke invited him to join Jasta 2.

> Suddenly in the early morning there was a knock at the door and before me stood the great man with the Pour le Mérite [Blue Max] .... I really did not know what he wanted of me. To be sure I knew him ... but it did not occur to me that he had sought me out to invite me to become a pupil of his. I could have hugged him when he asked me whether I wanted to go to the Somme with him.
>
> Three days later I sat on a train and travelled across Germany to my new field of action. Finally my fondest wish was fulfilled and now the most beautiful time of my life began for me.[2]

Boelcke, Richthofen and Böhme spearheaded Jasta 2, the first, and soon to be the most renowned, of the three new German wolf packs, poised with their freshly acquired Albatros fighters to confront the Flying Corps over the Somme in the early autumn of 1916. Boelcke, still regarded as one of the greatest fighter pilots of all time, wore his fame lightly. His great celebrity was said not to have affected him in the smallest way. 'This unpretentious young man, far from allowing fame to turn his head, exhibits a maturity and detached presence that is straight away incredible,' Böhme wrote to Annamarie. 'I admire him not only as my commander, however strange that may seem since I am 37 and he is 25 years old, but I also look up to him as a man.'[3]

In pictures of Boelcke with his fellow pilots, he is easily identifiable by his uncommonly large cupid-bow lips. He wears a sullen expression yet all who knew him described a warm and attractive personality and a rare knack for making each pilot feel he was a special friend. For his skill as a combat pilot they regarded Boelcke with reverence. The wolf cubs were eager to learn his fighting techniques and the master spelled these out for them in an historic document.

The *Dicta Boelcke* laid down the basic principles and tactics of aerial combat that were to endure through the Battle of Britain in the Second World War and on into the era of jet aerial combat, where homing missiles succeeded the guns of old. It aimed to replace solitary hunters with highly disciplined groups of aircraft flying in close formation, protecting one another and sticking doggedly to their leader. The leader would select the victims and launch the attacks with each pilot then pouncing on his own target. Afterwards the group – or what was left of it – was expected to re-form. Boelcke created eight golden rules:

Always attack in groups of four or six, and avoid two aircraft attacking the same opponent and getting in each other's way.

Secure the upper hand before attacking: surprise the enemy by keeping the sun behind you.

Always persist with an attack you've begun.

Fire only at close range.

Never lose sight of your opponent or be deceived by ruses. (To fool assailants into believing they had been mortally wounded pilots on both sides would put their aircraft into a spin and dive away from a fight they were losing, then recover near the ground and flee. The practice relied on the chivalry of opponents: to carry on hammering a man who was already going down was considered unsportsmanlike. Recognising that too many enemies were escaping to fight another day, Boelcke ended the generous convention.)

Always attack from behind.

If your opponent dives on you don't try to turn away: fly to meet him.

Over enemy-held territory never forget your line of retreat.

    What counted in the aerial battles of World War I were speed, altitude, surprise, numerical superiority and performance knowledge – awareness of the strengths, weaknesses and capabilities of both your own and your enemy's aircraft: who could turn tighter, who was faster, who had the most machines supporting him. Speed was critical. The pilot of the faster machine could perform more elaborate manoeuvres as well as controlling the combat: he had the option to break off and retire since the slower aeroplane could not catch him. Altitude gave a pilot the ability to dive on his opponent, gaining a sizeable speed advantage for a hit-and-run attack. But struggling up to higher levels reduced the airspeed of many machines by half, rendering them acutely vulnerable. Surprise provided the best chance of a kill: most victories were achieved in the first pass. And most, increasingly, were won by pilots operating in groups.

Boelcke and Immelmann had achieved their fame in one-on-one dog-fights, patrolling the skies alone. But although this approach still worked for a handful of especially skilful pilots, Boelcke decided that for the average squadron airman the days of the lone hunter were over. Many young pilots still arrived at the front expecting to dash valiantly into battle as errant knights, but they were more and more likely to be quickly overwhelmed by multiple enemies. Attacking in a group allowed the leader to focus his attention exclusively on his target while his colleagues protected his tail. Teamwork had become the key to success and survival.

At the new squadron's base near Bapaume in the autumn of 1916, Jasta Boelcke received its first batch of the new high-performance fighters. Within hours of the arrival of the Albatros machines they went into action. Boelcke, leading a six-strong formation, was taking his cubs out to find some blooding prey. 'We were all beginners,' Richthofen wrote:

> None of us had previously been credited with a success. Whatever Boelcke told us was taken as gospel. We knew that in the last few days he had shot down at least one Englishman a day, and many times two in a single morning. The morning of the seventeenth of September was a wonderful day. We could rely on brisk English flying activity. Before we took off Boelcke gave us precise instructions and then, for the first time, we flew as a squadron under the leadership of the famous man whom we followed without question.[4]

Over the front Boelcke spotted some tempting victims: a group of slow BE2s returning from a bombing raid. They were invitingly escorted by six FE2s. Richthofen recalled:

> We approached the enemy squadron slowly. But it could no longer escape us. We were between the Front and the enemy ... Each of us strained to stay close behind Boelcke. It was clear to all of us that we had to pass our first examination under the eyes of our revered leader.
>
> Boelcke was the first one to get near the skin of the cursed enemy, but he did not shoot. I was the second. The Englishman near me was a big dark-coloured aircraft. I did not ponder long and took aim at him. He shot and I shot, but we both missed.
>
> My Englishman twisted and turned, crossing my line of fire. There was only the growing thought: 'He must fall, come what may!' Then finally there was a brief but advantageous moment. The enemy had apparently lost sight of me and flew straight ahead. In a

fraction of a second I was sitting on his tail. I gave him a short burst
from my machine gun. I was so close I was afraid I should ram him.
Then, suddenly, his propeller turned no more. Hurrah! I had shot
his engine to pieces.[5]

Richthofen's first credited kill was an FE2 of No. 11 Squadron. Its badly
wounded pilot, 2nd Lieutenant Lionel Morris, managed to land behind
the German lines. Richthofen followed him down. 'I was so excited that
I could not resist coming down ... I landed near the Englishman and
jumped out of my plane. A group of soldiers was already streaming
towards the fallen enemy. The observer had died instantly and the pilot
died while being transported to hospital. Later I erected a gravestone to
the memory of my honourably fallen enemies.' When Richthofen flew
back to the jasta's base at Bertincourt his fellow pilots were having breakfast. Boelcke asked him where he had been. 'I proudly reported for the
first time, "One Englishman shot down!" Everyone rejoiced, for I was
not the only victor. Every one of the beginners had gained his first aerial
victory.' So had Boelcke. It was his twenty-seventh kill.

Jasta Boelcke's devastatingly successful first operation signalled yet
another turning point in the first air war. What made it so remarkable
was the fact that all six German pilots who went out that morning against
seasoned opponents had gained a victory, each flying a sophisticated new
aeroplane he had learned to fly only the day before.

To celebrate their triumph Boelcke held a party that night for all
his pilots and mechanics at which he presented Böhme with a medal,
personally pinning the Iron Cross on his tunic. The other pilots received
commemorative first-victory beer mugs. Richthofen went one better. He
sat down later and wrote to a Berlin jeweller to order a special memento
of his own: a miniature silver cup engraved with the number 1 and the
date and type of the machine he'd shot down. It was the first of scores
he would eventually purchase. Six days later he was buying his second
cup; in less than a month he had presented himself with six. He had
also, rather ghoulishly, started to collect souvenirs from the wreckage
of his victims' aircraft. He would take bits of its equipment, a machine
gun or propeller, and cut off a patch of fabric bearing the plane's serial
number. These he carefully packed up and sent home, where they joined
a spreading mosaic of numerals, like a collection of car number plates,
festooning his bedroom walls. But he also made a point of visiting the
hospitals where his wounded opponents were treated, taking them gifts
and cigarettes.

Manfred von Richthofen had been a hunter from childhood. The walls of his Prussian aristocratic military family home in Silesia were already well adorned with the trophies of wild boar and elk he and his father had shot. Manfred had been given no say in his career. At the age of eleven he had been consigned to a military life, sent to endure the ruthless discipline of an army cadet academy where he was miserably unhappy. By the time war came he was a cavalry officer whose regiment went into action charging with ten-foot long pennant-tipped lances. He was said to have been the very essence of a German regular officer in whom obedience, discipline and duty were inculcated from childhood. The hunting instinct ran in his Prussian blood. In the first weeks of the war during the German invasion of Belgium, before he'd switched to the air service, he had taken in his stride the measures his regiment used to punish civilians who held out against them. In his war memoirs he described how the monks of a 'wonderful monastery' had hosted his unit. 'They gave us as much to eat and drink as we wanted, which we consumed with delight.' Casually, he added: 'It should be noted at the same time that three days later we hanged several of our hosts from lamp posts because they could not resist the urge to take part in the war.'[6]

For the British pilots he had started killing in staggering numbers, Richthofen had more compassion. 'I have long since had nightmares of the first Englishman I saw plummeting down,' he wrote. He admired his Flying Corps opponents. 'The Englishman is a plucky fellow – we must allow him that.' He had never met one 'who would refuse a flight, while the Frenchman prefers to avoid every encounter with the enemy'.

By the middle of October 1916 Jasta Boelcke's Albatros fighters had scored more than fifty victories, losing only five pilots. 'It was a wonderful time for our squadron,' Richthofen said. 'We roamed the skies, happily diminishing our enemies.' But on 28 October tragedy struck. The jasta lost its adored leader. In the middle of a whirling dogfight with some DH2 fighters Boelcke and Erwin Böhme briefly lost sight of each other and collided. It was a very minor collision, just a kiss of Böhme's wheels along the other aircraft's top wing. But for Boelcke it proved fatal.

His Albatros spun out of control. As it spiralled down one of its wings broke off. The aeroplane crashed among shell holes and trenches. Boelcke had taken off in such a hurry he hadn't bothered to fasten the seat strap that might just have saved him, and he was killed instantly. Böhme, whose aircraft suffered only minor damage to the under-carriage, was so distressed it was said he had to be stopped from shooting himself that evening. Wracked with guilt, he lay awake at night for weeks agonising over Boelcke's death. 'In the silent hours my eyes see once again that ghastly moment when I had to watch my friend and master fall from beside me,' he wrote to Annamarie. 'Then the torturing question comes up once more: why was he, the irreplaceable, doomed to be the victim of this blind fate, and why not I?' Böhme added: 'Nothing can be taken away from the sorrow over the loss of this extraordinary human being.'[7]

What is unique about Oswald Boelcke is the sheer intensity of the love he seemed to inspire in his fellow German pilots both as a war pilot and as a person. It was a devotion they were moved to express uninhibitedly in their outpourings of grief at his death. British pilots may have felt a similar deep affection for some of their leaders but rarely was it so passionately declared.

When news of Boelcke's death reached the RFC it sent an aircraft to Jasta 2's aerodrome at Lagnicourt to parachute down a wreath carrying the message: 'To the memory of Captain Boelcke, our brave and chivalrous foe. From the British Royal Flying Corps.' Like his famous colleague Immelmann, Boelcke – credited with forty victories – was given a state funeral, in his case at Cambrai cathedral. It was 'worthy of a reigning prince', Richthofen told his mother. 'In the last six weeks we have lost six of our twelve pilots, killed, and one wounded. Two have suffered complete nervous breakdowns. Yesterday I shot down my seventh, after I had shortly before dispatched my sixth. My nerves have not yet suffered as a result of the others' bad luck.'[8]

Jasta 2 was to have fifteen more leaders. Commanding the squadron was not a very long-term occupation: Boelcke's successor was killed within three weeks. But the unit, soon to have its name permanently changed by royal command to Jasta Boelcke, was to remain an illustrious force. By the end of the war it would have created twenty-five aces and claimed over 330 victories with the loss of only 31 pilots. Boelcke's name has survived in the German Air Force to this day. Its No. 31 fighter-bomber wing, flying supersonic Typhoons, is called the Boelcke Wing.

Meanwhile, as the great Somme battle raged on into the autumn of 1916 the expanding host of Albatri in the growing number of the elite German hunting jasta continued to exact an appalling toll of British airmen. The Albatros squadrons were no longer rooted inflexibly at one aerodrome. They were regularly switched at their army commanders' behest to support different parts of the front. The pilots, constantly on the move, began to live in trains that took them from one temporary airfield to another. They wreaked such havoc on the Flying Corps that Trenchard became alarmed at how acutely the rapidly vacated chairs in his squadron messes was demoralising his crews.

As their numbers shrank by the day they were replaced from a pool of freshly trained, inexperienced pilots and observers who sat at the RFC's St Omer base, nervously waiting to be called to the front. But they weren't being delivered promptly enough for the field commander. He issued his historic order making it an unbreakable rule that casualties must be replaced on the very day machines limped back with dead or wounded crews or failed to return at all. 'A full breakfast table, with no empty chairs,' Trenchard insisted, explaining: 'If as an ordinary pilot you see no vacant places around you, the tendency is to brood less on the fate of friends who have gone for ever. Instead your mind is taken up with buying drinks for the newcomers and making them feel at home.'[9]

Every morning somewhere among the RFC's now nearly forty squadrons there were new faces at breakfast. So many, in fact, that Trenchard, concerned by the attrition rate, his inability to fill the chairs fast enough and the War Office's indifference to his need for more pilots and machines, decided that his voice alone was not loud enough. His appeal needed the weight of his boss, General Haig, the British Army's commander-in-chief in France. The letter, drafted for him by Trenchard, that Haig agreed to send to his superiors at the War Office so eloquently argued the tactically vital role of air power as a component of army ground operations that the Army Council sanctioned a massive expansion of the Flying Corps to 106 service squadrons, to be maintained at that level by ninety-five reserve squadrons. Haig's persuasive letter, one of the first ever succinctly defining the role of air power in war, and still quoted to this day, was not in fact written in its final form by either Haig or Trenchard. It came from the pen of yet another of the RFC's singular characters, Captain the Honourable Maurice Baring.

An exceptionally civilised intellectual of brilliant wit and exquisite manners, Baring, once described as one of the war's 'few agreeable practical jokes',[10] had been a surprising appointment as Trenchard's ADC. He was the complete antithesis of his chief. A scion of the great Baring's Bank dynasty, he had grown up in one of England's huge country manors and had been disconcertingly well educated at Eton and Cambridge. A plump, balding middle-aged man, he already had a distinguished career behind him when he came to the Flying Corps in his early forties. He had served as a diplomatic attaché in Paris, Copenhagen and Rome and as a war correspondent in Manchuria, Russia and the Balkans. He was a published author, playwright and poet. He was close to many of the literary and aristocratic figures of the day and his dearest friend was the prime minister's son, Raymond Asquith. A linguistic genius, he spoke fluent French, German, Russian, Italian and Danish and was accomplished in Latin and Greek. How had he finished up in the seemingly minor and boring role of a general's clerk?

Trenchard had inherited his unlikely aide from his predecessor, General Henderson, with whom Baring had enjoyed a long personal friendship. At the outbreak of war Henderson had had him commissioned into the Flying Corps to go to France with him as his intelligence officer and interpreter. When Trenchard took over from Henderson, Baring viewed with trepidation the prospect of working for the notoriously brusque, demanding and autocratic new commander. Nor, at the outset, had Trenchard wanted to retain this gentle, hopelessly unsoldierly figure who couldn't even wind on his military puttees without help. He had heard enough about Baring's reputation as a writer and linguist, his artistic temperament, impressive social connections and extravagant mannerisms to consider him utterly unsuited to the job. What was more, he hadn't forgotten his first encounter with Baring in November 1914 when, as a colonel, he had arrived in France to take command of the RFC's first wing. Baring had been sent to Boulogne to meet him off the ship and accompany him by car to the St Omer headquarters. When Baring had directed them south instead of east they had become hopelessly lost in the dark and arrived hours late. 'I'm prepared to let you stay for a month,' he told Baring. 'If you're no good you'll have to go.'

'I intended sacking him,' Trenchard remembered. 'Yet in conversation that day I was startled by his unselfishness and the loyalty he showed to Sir David Henderson.' Trenchard soon realised he had misjudged this modest and unpretentious man. Sorry that he had spoken so harshly, he said to Baring: 'I'd also like you to give *me* a trial. I think you'll find I'm not so hard to work for, whatever you've heard to the contrary.'[11] And so this incongruous partnership began. 'Wherever I go, I want you to come with me and take notes,' Trenchard told Baring. His ADC was to remain for four years. With his languages and social and literary skills he became Trenchard's mentor and amanuensis. By car or in separate aeroplanes the pair would be flown on the general's endless inspection tours of his dozens of aerodromes around northern France to hear at first hand about the aircraft and equipment problems his squadrons faced. They would usually arrive unannounced, Baring cutting a slightly comical, shambling figure beside his boss who, 'tall and straight as a ramrod, covering ground quickly with huge strides, forced his shorter aide to move in a quaint kind of turkey-trot at his side, trying to keep up with him.'[12] As they listened to the catalogues of complaints that ranged from the flying deficiencies of aircraft to the shortage of carburettors, magnetos and split pins, Trenchard would turn to Baring, standing beside him, notebook in hand, and utter an instruction that would be widely mimicked throughout the Flying Corps: 'Make a note of that, Baring.'

Back at their headquarters Trenchard was surprised to find that the notes, neatly typed up, would arrive on his desk that very evening. Other accomplishments began to soften his view of his assistant, who spent his evenings writing poetry, reading Homer's *Iliad*, the cantos of Dante and polishing his Pitman's shorthand. When the general wistfully admitted one day to a liking for Oxford marmalade, he found a jar of it sitting beside his plate when he came in for tea next afternoon. His initial prejudices began to fade as he fell under the spell of his engaging aide. Not only did he become utterly dependent on Baring, he came to consider him a friend. And he discovered that his ADC had other surprising talents for which he was in much demand at squadron parties.

'Whenever we heard that Trenchard was going to pay us a visit it was always our hope that Maurice Baring would be with him,' recalled Sholto Douglas. 'Baring had a way all of his own of getting things done. He was a man with a rare charm and such a gay humour.' He was also 'one of the star performers' at mess celebrations. 'One of his turns was to balance a glass of port on his bald head and lie down flat on the floor and get up again, keeping the glass in position without spilling a drop ... On very special occasions he was known to perform his little trick with a bottle of champagne while at the same time proceeding to undress while keeping the bottle balanced on his head.'[13] To this frequently executed act Baring often added a flow of his own witty impromptu doggerel about his host squadron.

One squadron, having acquired a circular saw to cut winter firewood, invited Baring, as ADC to General Trenchard, to make the first slice. To commemorate the event he was asked to cut off the end of a cigar to be mounted in a glass box and displayed in the mess. His task performed to loud cheers, Baring then took off his cap and cut it in half. Encouraged by the applause he removed his tunic, but before it could suffer the same fate the pilots seized him and carried him out of reach of the saw.

Baring was one of the few people with the philosophical nous to understand Trenchard's tyrannical psyche. He knew, 'that Humanity is frail and must perforce be chastised with whips and scorpions of sorts', wrote a squadron adjutant, Thomas Marson, recalling how Baring devised a series of punishments meted out to the general when he had been especially rude to one of his subordinates. The punishments were numbered in order of severity from 1 to 5X. Number 1 consisted of taking away 'Boom's' pipe; 5X, rather drastically, was breaking his car window so that he was obliged to sit in a draught, which he particularly hated.

The aggrieved party, said Marson, was always telephoned and informed: 'The General behaved very badly today. He had Punishment Number 1 all the way home. He almost cried for his pipe; but I was adamant. I had it in my pocket, but said I couldn't think what he had done with it. At dinner he was very penitent, so he was allowed to find his pipe afterwards. I think he is really sorry, and that he will be better now.'[14]

As 1916 drew to a close, early heavy snow heralding a ferociously cold winter, the two great battles of Verdun and the Somme that had raged through the year in northern France finally ground to a halt. Both sides calculated the calamitous casualty statistics, which had reached unprecedented levels. No precise figures exist, but even the most conservative estimates, almost impossible for the mind to comprehend today, make quite numbing reading. Between them the twin mincing machines of shellfire and machine guns in the two battles had resulted in more than a million and a half casualties. They had cost the lives of at least 500,000 young British, French and German men and left well over a million more wounded, large numbers of them permanently damaged. At Verdun, where the battlefield's cratered landscape is today cloaked in forest, the mortal remains of over 100,000 missing combatants are still dispersed underground wherever they fell. On the Somme, where the Allies gained a mere six miles of territory and never even managed to reach their first day's objective, nearly 100,000 British soldiers were killed and a third of a million wounded. The Flying Corps total of around 500 airmen killed, wounded or missing shrank into insignificance beside the enormity of the losses on the ground.

There were casualties, too, through 1916 among the politicians and generals running the war. When the French hung on to Verdun the chief of the German General Staff, General Falkenhayn, paid the price and was replaced by the sixty-six-year-old General Hindenburg, recalled from retirement. For the huge carnage at Verdun over which he'd presided the French commander-in-chief, General Joffre, was also removed in favour of General Nivelle, himself destined to be sacked before long. In Britain

prime minister Asquith had been ousted by a more vigorous and charismatic war leader, David Lloyd George, and the country's great military
hero, the war minister Lord Kitchener, had been drowned at sea aboard
a Royal Navy cruiser sunk by an enemy mine. A 'year of new men', one
historian wrote, 'new situations, new desperation'.[15] The burdens of war
for soldiers and civilians, seen today as the epitome of incompetent
generalship and pointless sacrifice, had created a depressing effect on the
spirits of people everywhere.

Nor, that bitter winter of early 1917, by which stage nearly 50 million
men throughout Europe were under arms, did there seem any hope of
the stalemate and slaughter ending any time soon. The president of
the United States, Woodrow Wilson, had tried to bring 'peace without
victory'. He sent a note to all the warring powers proposing that a means
be found to end the conflict. When Germany demanded the permanent
occupation of much of Belgium the peace talks ended. The war would
go on to kill and cripple millions more. And to prolong the deadlock on
the Western Front the Germans retreated around twenty-five miles and
created a near-impregnable new front. The Hindenburg Line replaced
the trenches with a chain of huge concrete pillboxes, deep bunkers and
tank traps. It looked out over a large newly created desert across which,
in their withdrawal, the German Army had laid waste to the countryside.
Every habitation was trashed or burned, every animal slaughtered, every
well poisoned.

Two Allied attempts in the spring of 1917 to break through the line of
ugly earthworks that snaked, often under clouds of sulphurous smoke,
across Belgium and France to the Swiss border brought another surge of
casualties. Although the British, in the Battle of Arras, managed, in an
historic Canadian infantry victory, to seize a strategic ridge at Vimy, the
separate French attack across the Aisne at the Chemin des Dames near
Soissons ended in such disastrous failure it triggered mutiny in the French
Army that weakened the country's military contribution for the rest of
the war. Between them the two battles accounted for a further melancholy toll of a quarter of a million more Allied casualties. The German
losses were even greater. And still the deadlock remained.

Among the nations at war the wholesale destruction of men, entire
towns, productive farmland and food was beginning to undermine the
resolve of populations to go on fighting. On the Eastern Front the Russian
Army, its casualties approaching 7 million, crumbled as the country
plunged into the revolutions that would create the communist Soviet
Union. On the southern front, where more than a million and a half

more men would eventually lie dead, the Austro–Hungarian empire was heading for collapse and large numbers of soldiers deserting from the Italian Army were simply melting into the countryside. The most hopeful development for the Allies was the United States' declaration of war against Germany. But it would be a year before enough American troops to make a difference would arrive in Europe.

In the air the situation was equally bleak for the Allied forces. Helped by the country's pre-war development of big, powerful engines for airships, the German aircraft maintained their performance edge over most of the machines they faced. In the spring of 1917 the Flying Corps, still waiting for the overwhelmed British aviation industry to deliver aeroplanes capable of matching the Albatros, was suffering its most terrible losses of the war. They far exceeded the toll exacted earlier by the Fokkers. In the month of April, known to this day as 'Bloody April', around 500 aircrew were killed or reported missing and more than 1,000 aeroplanes were destroyed.

'From the last week in March to the last week in May our losses were very severe,' wrote the CO of No. 60 Squadron. 'We lost thirty-five officers during those eight weeks, almost twice the strength of the squadron. One weekend in April was specially unlucky. On Saturday A Flight went out six machines strong and only one returned. On Monday C Flight went out and only one returned. In three days ten out of eighteen pilots were lost and had to be replaced from England by officers who had never flown this type of machine – because there were none in England.'[16]

No fewer than twenty-five of the departed pilots had fallen to the personal guns of Manfred von Richthofen.

Chapter 15
Going 'Mad Dog'

For the enormous tally of his kills and the growing legend of the sheer deadliness of his combat expertise, Manfred von Richthofen was well on his way to becoming the most universally remembered pilot of the First World War. He had been given his own squadron, Jasta 11. His decision to paint his Albatros red earned him his celebrated nickname: the Red Baron. He would frequently dispose of more than one British machine on the same day. On 29 April 1917 he shot down four in one afternoon, an orgy of destruction that took his credited total to fifty-two victories. With every fresh triumph flags would ritually flutter around his home town. Kaiser Wilhelm was so impressed he ordered that his squadron be renamed Jagdstaffel Richthofen and regularly summoned him to grand dinners at the royal palace in Potsdam, where he would be seated among congratulating dukes and princes and the highest generals in the land. And as the German media sang his praises a news agency circulated a story that the British had formed a special squadron of volunteer pilots 'to seek exclusively the annihilation' of Richthofen. 'The flyer who succeeds will receive the Victoria Cross, a promotion, the gift of his own personal aeroplane, £5,000 and a special prize from the manufacturer of the aircraft he uses.'[1] There is no British archival record of any such hit squadron ever being contemplated but in Germany the story added to Richthofen's glamour and fame.

Examining the life of Richthofen, several different characters emerge. There is the reserved and rigid Prussian aristocrat described as having the patience and cunning of the instinctive hunter; the humourless ruthless fighter pilot who wrote: 'When I have shot down an Englishman, my hunting passion is satisfied for a quarter of an hour. Therefore I do not succeed in shooting two Englishmen in succession. If one of them comes down I have the feeling of complete satisfaction. Only much, much later have I overcome my instinct and have become a butcher.'[2] The Englishmen he fought both feared and admired him. They feared the very real threat he and his highly disciplined wolf pack posed to any pilot unlucky enough to encounter them. But as fellow professionals they couldn't fail to admire his conquering style, the stalking patience and tenacity he demonstrated in his aerial battles.

His pilot colleagues, who regarded him with such veneration, provide an alternative view. They called him the Rittmeister, the title he had once enjoyed as a captain in the cavalry. Erwin Böhme described to Annamarie Brüning the 'magnificent spirit' his commander had inspired within the jasta. 'It is amazing to what level he has brought his squadron in such a short time. He has nothing but great young men around him who would jump through fire for him. He is a distinguished, but very down to earth man. It would be good if they soon made him head of the entire Air Service.'[3] Another pilot declared: 'Richthofen was just as good a superior officer as a comrade. When we could not fly he played hockey with us and, in the evenings, often joined in card games. One could go to him with any question and any trouble and find sympathy and help when they were needed.'[4]

At his huge baronial home in Schweidnitz in Silesia, Manfred was a much-loved son. His mother, Baroness Kunigunde von Richthofen, said that her heart froze every time a telegram arrived at the door. In her diary she spoke of the fair-haired son with 'something very fine and joyful in his voice'. She wrote of his sense of humour, his love of practical jokes, his unrestrained laughter. And of a maturity far beyond his twenty-five years. But Manfred didn't always bring her positive news. 'I don't believe we will win this war,' she was shocked to hear him say. 'You've no idea how strong our enemy is . . . In the long run everyone gets it eventually.' He asked her not to mourn him if he were killed. ' "Mama, do not ever put yourself through such torment for me, promise me that." Those were his words. I looked at him astonished. Then Manfred put his arm around me and laughed. A joyous, carefree laugh. It frightened away the disturbing thoughts.'[5]

The Baroness was soon to have added to her anxieties the safety of another son. Lothar, two years younger than Manfred, had been encouraged by his brother to switch from the cavalry to the flying service. His first posting as a pilot, arranged by Manfred, was to Jasta Richthofen where in no time he began to demonstrate a pattern of victories as spectacular as his brother's. Within three weeks of arriving he had made his first kill.

Outgoing, less serious and more sociable than his brother, Lothar was undoubtedly his mother's favourite. She wrote in her diary of his 'tranquillity and singular beauty' and his generosity of spirit. 'He was always the giving one.' She would never tire, she said, 'of looking at his noble, dashing face'. And as the combined total of her sons' kills began to mount towards the magic hundred the Schweidnitz mansion became a Mecca for small crowds hoping for a sight of one of the brothers. Little is recorded about the one love of Manfred's life. We don't know her name. But the Baroness is quoted as saying: 'He had for her the love of an honourable man for the woman he wanted to be the mother of his children. I know that she loved him.' However, Manfred ruled out marriage while his life was at such risk. 'I cannot indulge myself in the right of marriage,' he confided to his mother, 'as long as I am liable to die any day.'[6]

Critics of the Red Baron, the fighter pilot, have claimed that he found many of his kills all too easy, swooping on inferior and obsolete Flying Corps reconnaissance machines that he could pick off almost at will. But the BE2s and Fees were directing devastating British shellfire on to German guns and trenches and were wholly legitimate targets. Richthofen could, with equal facility, deal with adversaries flying better-matched aeroplanes and whose duelling skills equalled his own. The Albatros formations he led, observing the *Dicta Boelcke* commandments, would rarely rush into battle with guns blazing. They would stay, quietly, high in the sun watching their victims and waiting for the best moment to surprise them. If they chose a lone machine then Richthofen, at the head of his formation, would have the privilege of being the first to dive down to the attack, safe in the knowledge that his fellow pilots were guarding his tail. If there were two enemy aircraft, the next senior German pilot might take on the second machine. Only if there was a large formation to intercept would all six jasta pilots split up and fight individually after the first sudden swoop. Richthofen's marksmanship was deadly. He never wasted a round of ammunition. His secret, learned from Boelcke, was to close from above and behind to within just metres of his adversary. When the victim's machine filled his gunsight he would fire a short, destructive burst, all that was necessary at such short range.

As Richthofen's bag of victories mounted he reported each duel in great detail in proud letters to his parents. On one occasion, flying back from a successful dogfight, he couldn't resist diverting to a small town where his father, Albrecht, was serving as garrison commander. Scribbling a triumphant note he dropped it into the middle of the barracks in a tin attached to a streamer of cloth.

Manfred's remarkable success was helped by a permanent advantage enjoyed by all German pilots: the prevailing south-westerly wind that blew across northern France. In aerial combat the confrontation would inevitably drift eastward, often far behind the German lines. Having to fight their way home against often very stiff headwinds, their ground-speeds sometimes reduced to barely 40 miles an hour, put the British machines at constant risk of running out of fuel. The Germans chose mostly to allow the battle to come to them. It gave them the ability to trap the Flying Corps aircraft on the hostile side of the lines. And it meant that jasta pilots forced down could often land to fight another day.

The Richthofen brothers often flew together. Lothar was quick to learn the tricks of the trade from his brother. On one occasion they shot down a British plane apiece in the same dogfight. Lothar proved rather less patient and disciplined than his tutor, who stayed alive by abandoning encounters he saw as too risky. Early in their partnership Manfred had decided that Lothar's combat style was too reckless, once describing him as 'a shooter' rather than 'a hunter'. 'I asked him to fly close behind me in order that he might see exactly how the fighting business was done,' Manfred wrote. 'After the third flight with him I suddenly noticed how he had parted company with me. He rushed at an Englishman and killed him. My heart leapt with joy when I saw it.'[7]

It was Lothar's first victory. The Englishman he had hit, 2nd Lieutenant Alfred Severs, was in fact the observer/gunner of one of three 25 Squadron FE2bs that had been escorting some vulnerable BE2s directing artillery fire on to German positions on Vimy Ridge. In the skirmish between the attacking German fighters and the Flying Corps machines Severs' pilot, 2nd Lieutenant Norman Knight, though wounded in the arm, succeeded in landing the aeroplane behind the German lines and was taken prisoner. Severs, at high risk of falling out, had been standing up, unsecured, firing backwards over the Fee's wing when he'd been shot in the head. His death was just another statistic in the casualty lists of the London news-papers. Lothar Richthofen, jubilant at his first kill, would never have known of the protracted anguish suffered by the parents of the cour-ageous, little-known Severs. It was over two months before Mr and Mrs Severs, whose son had been reported missing, learned that he had died. And many weeks before Mr Knight received word that his son was alive in captivity. In a faded file at the RAF Museum in London one can read the touching correspondence that began to pass between the anxious fathers.

Dear Mr Severs,

I expect you have heard from the War Office that your boy and mine were shot down behind the German lines on Wednesday last. I had a letter from the Major today, and as you may not have heard, I will send you a copy. But it appears they were with two other machines on a patrol when they were attacked by an overwhelming number of enemy planes; our boys went to the assistance of one of their comrades and drew off practically the lot, enabling the two other machines to escape. It is impossible to say whether they landed safely or crashed. If you hear anything, you might let me know, as I will you.

Yours faithfully,
C.S. Knight.[8]

Only when Severs' pilot, the wounded Norman Knight, wrote to Mr and Mrs Severs in Croydon from his German prison camp did they discover at last the heroic way in which Alfred had died.

I had only known your son for a week and in that short time I had come to realise what a fine fellow he was.

He had been with me three or four times over the lines before the day we were brought down ... On the 28th of March we were attacked by hostile machines and were outnumbered by five to one. We fought for over ten minutes and in that time your son's courage and nerve was marvellous. If his courage had had anything to do with it we should have come through. But luck was against him. Even when he was hit he stood up and fired until guns were useless. The bullets pierced his head and he was dead before I reached the ground.

Terrible as it is, you must console yourself with the thought that he died fighting as I never thought possible. It seems to me that things are completely wrong – he it was who suffered whereas it should have been myself. But it is always the case the bravest man suffers, and he who does nothing comes through. I am enquiring where he was buried and will write you again soon. I remain, yours very sincerely, Norman L. Knight.[9]

Twenty-three-year-old Alfred Severs' grave was never found. It was destroyed in subsequent ground fighting in the area. His squadron commander recommended him for the Military Cross. It was never awarded.

The German Albatros were not, however, getting it all their own way. Despite the inferior aeroplanes they were obliged to fly, some British pilots with fighting skills matching those of Manfred von Richthofen were clocking up victories to rival his but their deeds weren't as dramatically publicised. Unlike the German high command, which actively created superstars of its aces, the generals at the innately conservative War Office were emphatically against the creation of flying heroes. They viewed air-battle successes as team efforts and discouraged the promotion of celebrities, preferring to keep them cloaked in anonymity. However the policy broke down when the home-town newspapers of the British aces began to splash them so prominently across their pages that Fleet Street was obliged to follow. When Albert Ball, home on leave, had reluctantly taken part in a solemn civic ceremony in which he was made a freeman of the city of Nottingham, his picture and his exploits were soon being featured in the *Daily Mirror* while the *Daily Mail* printed his portrait next to Boelcke's.

By the end of September 1916 Ball had been credited with thirty-one victories. Showered with medals, he had gone to Buckingham Palace to receive from the King in one investiture a clutch of three DSOs and an MC. Ball was the first of Britain's WWI pilot heroes. His handsome, boyish face now widely recognised, he retained behind the image of a ruthless aerial gladiator not only a modesty and gentleness but a charmingly surprising immaturity. His father, Albert Ball senior – who had transformed himself from a humble plumber into a prosperous property developer and who would later be given a knighthood as well as becoming Lord Mayor of Nottingham – at times treated him like an errant teenager. The correspondence between them reveals Albert senior as a proud, critical and often overbearing man anxious about both his son's safety and, quite excessively, his moral welfare. Their relationship was at times tense, particularly when it came to the numerous girlfriends Albert junior attracted whenever he came home on leave. His father regularly cross-examined him about playing with the feelings of so many different girls. In contrite letters he would pour out extraordinary confessions and resolutions to change his ways.

> You ask me to confide in you so I will just a little. About 3 years ago at Matlock I met a ripping little girl, ever since then I have sent her one letter a week without saying anything to you, also without really having any love for her. But I have gradually got to like her very much, but have not gone mad as in most cases. I have visited her a few times and have met her people very often. Now I look back on the last 2 years and see what a rotter I have been.
>
> I have fooled two girls that you know of and of course I have made heaps of other girls think I liked them that you don't know

of. I really do feel a bit of a rotter, but I really mean to stop now – in fact I will try. All the time I knew Dot Elbourne and Thelma, I was writing to this other girl, but only as an ordinary friend. She is very young and very loving. I shall try and treat this girl in a fair and proper way.[10]

Thelma – one Thelma Starr – he wasn't prepared to give up so easily. Mr Ball so intensely disapproved of her that he tried to stop his son communicating with her. To which Albert responded defiantly: 'As regards me writing to Thelma, you must see that although you do not like the girl, I do. Now Dad please do not let us quarrel again for I am anxious to please you.'[11]

Refusing to end his relationship with Thelma, whom he'd nicknamed 'Pup' and to whom he had daringly begun to send silk underwear from France, he finally convinced his father that not only was he in love with her, but he intended to marry her. 'Pup and I will want a house when I come back,' he told him in a patching-up letter from France, adding, 'Ripping to know that I have a good old man and a ripping girl to return to.'[12]

But at his squadron on the Western Front Albert was seen as a colleague unlikely to survive for long. His approach to aerial fighting verged on the fanatical. It became such a personal crusade to him to shoot enemy machines out of the sky that he would insist on going back into the air again and again on the same day. Unlike von Richthofen, who was protected by rigorously disciplined jasta formations as he pounced on his victims, he preferred to operate as a lone wolf. He had a rare informal roving commission to hunt alone and would take the most enormous risks, aggressively tackling odds that wiser pilots considered suicidal.

Ball's was a bull-headed technique. He called it 'going mad dog'. No flock of enemy aircraft was too big to daunt him. Flying his favourite machine, a Nieuport Scout, whose machine gun didn't even shoot through the propeller, but in a complicated manner, over the top wing, he would simply dive in startling fashion into the very middle of the formation, scattering surprised pilots, pull up behind and underneath one of them, swing his gun upwards on its mounting and destroy it at virtually point-blank range of less than ten metres. He flew so close to enemy aeroplanes that they were unable to fire on him for fear of hitting one of their own. And, having picked off his victim, Ball would make a swift getaway before the German formation could recover. He flew without helmet or goggles and on some days he would go out as frequently as twelve times, often returning with his plane so shot up his mechanics were amazed that it had survived to get him back. Obsessed with a desire to acquire the highest score of any pilot, British, French or German, Ball routinely shot down two or three hostile machines in one day. His colleagues marvelled at his skill and rare luck in staying alive. Ball believed that God protected him.

'I put all my trust in God,' he told his permanently worried parents. 'That is why I feel safe no matter in what mess I get.' His deeply Christian mother would inquire about his daily prayers. 'Oh, don't you trouble about me being afraid to acknowledge God before people,' he reassured her. 'I shall never neglect that duty.'

'You ask me to be sure to come back safely. Oh, yes, if God wishes it, I shall come back safely and oh, I do want to, but I want a few more scraps yet, for one must stick it.'[13]

The robust partying camaraderie of the officers' mess didn't appeal to Ball. He may have been one for the ladies but, unusually for a WWI pilot, he neither smoked nor drank. He spent his time on the ground in a small wooden hut he'd built some distance away, near the hangars, tinkering with his aeroplanes and guns. Here he created a garden in which he planted vegetables and flowers. In the evenings he would play his gramophone as he produced detailed daily reports of his combat adventures for his family and 'Pup'. He also developed a curious nightly ritual in which he would light a red flare outside the hut and walk round it slowly in his pyjamas while playing his violin.

During the day he was conspicuous by his studied disinterest in military smartness. He would go about hatless, displaying his non-regulation heap of long hair, sloppily dressed in a uniform that was frequently streaked in oil. His fellow pilots were never quite able to get the measure of this schoolboy mega-hero in their midst. 'Ball was utterly fearless and uncommunicative,' wrote one of them, Lieutenant William Fry. 'Though he was considered somewhat unfriendly, he was never unpopular ... He was a self-effacing, skilled and dedicated killer with no other motive than to use his machine and armament to shoot down enemy aeroplanes. There was in his attitude none of that sporting element which to a certain extent formed the basis of many scout pilots' approach to air fighting. Ball never made jokes about it.'[14] Cecil Lewis, who served alongside him, said: 'Ball was a quiet, simple little man ... but his example was tremendous.'[15]

Ball himself had accepted that there were limits to his phenomenal endurance and the damage constant air combat was doing to his nerves brought him nightmares. He began to hate the job, suffering from guilt for all the lives he had taken. 'I feel so sorry for the chaps I have killed. Just imagine what their poor people must feel like. I must have sent at least 40 chaps to their death. However it must be done or they would kill me.'[16] In another letter home he wrote: 'But Oh! I do get tired of always living to kill and am really beginning to feel like a murderer Shall be so pleased when I have finished.'[17]

Ball's mental frailty was bolstered in October 1916 by a temporary posting back to England. The interlude brought a dramatic development in his life. He fell in love, in a way he claimed he had never experienced before, with a very beautiful eighteen-year-old, Flora Young, who was doing war work for the Women's Land Army on a farm near the airfield at London Colney in Hertfordshire where Ball, in March 1917, joined a squadron about to be sent to France. On a visit to the aerodrome she'd been introduced to him and, instantly dazzled by her, he had taken her for a flight. Their relationship developed at high speed. In the two weeks before Ball flew back to the Western Front with 56 Squadron they met every day. By the time he left they were informally engaged. Instead of a ring he gave her his small silver identity wrist bracelet. She gave him a book of Robert Louis Stevenson prayers.

Of how his relationship with Thelma Starr came to be replaced by this new one there appears no longer to be any accessible record. But Ball's niece, Paddy Armstrong, the daughter of his brother Cyril, learned from her mother Marie a great deal about the women in the flying hero's short life. 'He had lots of girlfriends,' she recalled. 'Flora just happened to be the latest infatuation before he went back to the Front that time in 1917. They were never formally engaged. He seems to have proposed to an endless succession of girls, giving them all, for engagement rings, one of his silver identity wristlets – he apparently kept quite a supply of them in his drawer at home. He was extremely good-looking and in uniform, the girls just fell for him.'[18]

Ball recorded his astonishing stream of liaisons in his private diary. In one entry, Paddy Armstrong said, he described how he had proposed to a young woman in Skegness.

He did it in the full regalia of his dress uniform, complete with his officer's sword, and wrote that he'd gone down on his knees, declaring how madly in love with her he was, and asking her to marry him. He apparently used to take women to hotels for the night. One of his diary notes said that the Nottingham one he'd used charged 10 shillings for the room. He was certainly a bit of a lad. It used to shock his very proper father. Especially on one occasion, when Albert senior found himself sharing a compartment on a train with a young woman. They began talking and somehow the Flying Corps ace's name came up. The girl, who didn't know who Mr Ball was, utterly shocked him when she proudly told him: 'I've just spent the weekend with Albert Ball.'

Paddy Armstrong's mother told her that on his visits home on leave the normally calm and unruffled Albert would be so battle-stressed and on edge he would explode into rage at the slightest provocation. 'He used to retreat up to his room in the attic and shut the door,' Paddy Armstrong recounts. 'The family became nervous of even calling him down for dinner they were so afraid of the outburst of shouting it would create. He would sometimes remain there, locked away for hours on his own.'

On his last days in England in early 1917, Ball had gone up to Nottingham to say goodbye to his parents fearing he might never see them again. In his bedroom he tidied up his chest of drawers, arranging his clothes and bundles of letters in neat piles upon which he left the instruction: 'Please do not take anything unless asked to do so.' To avoid the distress of parting from his mother he took her to the cinema and slipped away in the darkness. In a farewell letter to his parents he wrote: 'It is an honour to be able to fight and do one's best for such a country and for such dear people. I shall fight for you, and God always looks after me and makes me strong; may He look after you also.'[19] Meanwhile the newspapers had learned about the latest girlfriend to enter his life. The London *Evening Standard* dubbed him 'a modern Romeo', which got him mercilessly teased on the squadron. On his last evening with Flora Young, whom he called 'Bobs', he asked her to sing for him again and again his favourite song 'Thank God for a Garden'.

No. 56 was a brand-new squadron. It had been given the first batch of some powerful new fighters that the designers at the much reviled Royal Aircraft Factory hoped would match the Albatros in combat. The squadron commander, Major Richard Blomfield, was determined to make it a very special, elite unit. He brought together some of the Flying Corps' most experienced, highly decorated and battle-distinguished pilots and chose his flight commanders, among them Albert Ball, from the cream of the crop. He also scoured the RFC for the finest mechanics, poaching those who could play an instrument and join the squadron band he created to keep his pilots' morale pumped up in the evenings.

The single-seater SE5 Scout was another open-cockpit biplane which, at first glance, didn't look vastly different from the long-obsolete BE2. However, it came with an impressive array, for the era, of cockpit instruments and a much more powerful engine, whose big square radiator looked like the front of a lorry. It could none the less generate a healthy 115 miles an hour at 10,000 feet, a height to which it could climb in fifteen minutes. A Romanian inventor, George Constantinescu, had replaced the hit-and-miss through-propeller mechanical systems with an ingenious new device that, esoterically, used 'sonic impulses' transmitted by a column of liquid to trigger the gun.* For good measure a second machine gun fired over the wing top. Behind an enormous windscreen the pilot sat snugly in a cockpit reassuringly protected in a steel-plated armchair. It was a fast, robust manoeuvrable machine and it presented the Albatros with its first serious threat. But it was plagued by a host of teething troubles. When the Flying Corps pilots began to fly it they hated it. And Albert Ball's was the loudest of the protesting voices. He demanded to be put back on to the Nieuports with which he'd built his awesome reputation and sought an interview with the field commander-in-chief who invited him to tea at his headquarters.

Trenchard was already trying to deal with a pilot revolt over another new aeroplane, the RE8, another unpopular product of the government factory built to replace the ancient BE2s. Inexperienced pilots had immediately had problems coping with its flying characteristics. Nicknamed the 'Harry Tate', it spun all too easily and its lack of manoeuvrability saw it frequently shot down in combat. The RE8 had begun to kill its young pilots and observers in such horrifying numbers that there was an outcry in the British newspapers and the familiar public demands for an inquiry.

Under pressure from his masters in London, Trenchard didn't want another pilot rebellion on his hands. He decided to allow Ball a rare concession. He agreed that he could have his own Nieuport Scout as well as a personal SE5. Ball was delighted. He had got his favourite machine back for his solo hunting missions and an SE5 in which, now as a flight commander, to lead his flight's formation operations. To eliminate its undesirable features, he set about modifying his SE5, removing its dangerous windscreen and tinkering with the arrangements of its guns, fuel

---

*The Constantinescu synchroniser was declared top secret. Although they captured some, the Germans, wrongly believing it to be hydraulic technology, never discovered its much more sophisticated 'sonic impulse' principles. The system continued to be used by the RAF until the late 1930s, when the arrival of WWII fighters with wing-mounted guns made propeller synchronisation redundant.

tanks and undercarriage. These modifications left him so satisfied with the faster new aeroplane that it became his main battle plane of choice in spite of his vociferous complaints, from then on. Each victory was proudly described in his daily letters to Flora Young, in which he repeatedly told her she had given him back something he had lost: a powerful reason to live.

'Thank you for your last topping letters. Bobs, they help me so much. In fact they got me my Huns today.' But the determination to stay alive was at odds with his other consuming ambition: to become the highest-scoring fighter pilot on the Allied side. Officially, because Trenchard didn't want to lose the most celebrated and inspiring of all his airmen, Ball was told he would stay in the front line for only a month. Those weeks were to prove so physically draining they interrupted his flow of letters to Flora.

For several days Ball was flying constantly and so exhausted he didn't write. When he resumed again on 7 May 1917 he explained:

Am so very sorry dear that I have been so long in writing again, but I have been having such a poo-poo time. Firstly, a few days ago, my first SE5 had all its controls shot away. It had to be sent to the doctor. I got the Hun that sent me down first. Also I managed to land without crashing. Well, I got a new SE and all went well for a day or two, but then the gun gear went wrong . . . You don't know what a beastly game it is when nothing is going as it should.

You say I am engaged in serious and awful things. Oh!, no, not awful. Serious if you like, but what a pleasure to fight for my Bobs and for my people . . . All I ask is to come back in time to enjoy a good and useful life with you dear. Your little prayer book gives me lots of help. Not only the faith in my machine, but my God, and you, also my dear people give me all the security I shall ever need.

Last night I had a dream. Oh! Such a topper. War was over and we all came home. You met me at the station and we had such a topping time. I often dream about you Bobs and it is so nice for they are always topping dreams. Well it's fine to know that the dream will come true one day and you will meet me, won't you Bobs? Now I must go up again, so dear I must close.[20]

Flora Young would never meet Albert Ball at the station. The day he wrote this letter, his aircraft was seen on the enemy side of the line, diving upside down out of low cloud, its engine apparently stopped. It crashed to the ground, killing one of the most illustrious pilots of the first great air war. The German officers who rushed to the scene in a field near the village of Annoeullin, south of Lille, found Ball lying in the arms of a young Frenchwoman who had pulled him from the wreckage of the SE5. He had opened his eyes briefly before dying on her lap. They found in his pocket a pound note and the book of prayers Flora had given him. She and Ball had met fewer than six times.

Who had at last shot down the man whom the German pilots had begun to call 'the British Richthofen'? It's possible that no one had. Ball had been engaged in a series of sprawling dogfights that had continued into fading light, low cloud heaps and rain. The protracted battles had involved three British squadrons, one of them from the Royal Naval Air Service flying Sopwith triplanes. Among the enemy formations were the Albatros of Jasta 11, led that evening by Lothar von Richthofen who, as dark approached, found himself in a fierce duel with Ball whose guns, or those of one of his fellow 56 Squadron pilots, finally ruptured the German's fuel tank, forcing him to land unharmed. What happened next has been debated by aviation historians for nearly a century. In the gathering gloom and rain, one of Ball's fellow pilots, Captain Cyril Crowe, flying at around 4,000 feet, saw two red flares fired from Ball's aircraft, signalling that he was about to dive into an attack. Almost immediately Ball flew into a cloud. 'I followed him,' Crowe said. 'When I got out of the clouds again I saw Ball diving after an enemy aeroplane which disappeared into another cloud and which was hotly pursued by Ball.'[21] Crowe went after them into the second cloud. When he emerged from it there was no sign of either machine.

Lothar von Richthofen immediately claimed that he had shot Ball down. But he wrongly described his SE5 biplane as a triplane, and none of the British naval triplanes had failed to return that evening. None the less the German Air Service credited Lothar with the victory and he was presented with a machine gun from Ball's aircraft to send back to join the ever-expanding hoard of battle keepsakes he and Manfred maintained in Schweidnitz.

The puzzling feature of Ball's demise was that his body had no bullet wounds. He had died from multiple injuries caused by the crash impact. His aircraft was too badly wrecked for the Germans to establish conclusively whether it had been destroyed by gunfire or anti-aircraft flak, but the officers who had rushed to the scene were convinced that it was neither of these. The most persistent theory is that Ball, exhausted by three hours of punishing combat, had lost control in turbulence within that final cloud and toppled into the fatal spin that ended his life. Upside down his carburettor could have choked and denied him the engine power that might just have saved him.

Whatever happened to his aeroplane, the pilot was certainly not on the top of his form to handle ferocious air combat. For weeks his battle fatigue had been growing steadily more acute. No one knew this better than his younger brother, Cyril, who had also become a Flying Corps pilot, later to be shot down and to spend the rest of the war as a prisoner. 'Albert should never have gone back to France in April 1917,' he said. 'He may have looked all right, but he was mentally and physically spent.'[22] Harold Balfour, who understood what the stress of prolonged combat flying eventually did to human sanity, agreed. 'Those who had so distinguished themselves building a public reputation on the display of their well-won honours should have been forbidden, even had they so desired, as with Ball, to fly for a further tour of duty in France,' he said. The problem was that the burden of that reputation, among both their fellow pilots and the public, put these celebrated figures under such additional immense pressure they began to take even more extreme risks to sustain the image. The outcome, Balfour said, was 'sooner or later, a foregone conclusion'.[23]

Of the eleven 56 Squadron fighters that had gone out that terrible evening only five returned to the aerodrome at Vert Galant. All except Ball and another pilot who was killed were eventually accounted for, unscathed or wounded. Cecil Lewis, one of those who made it back and one of the last to see Ball, remembered: 'The mess was very quiet that night ... All next day a feeling of depression hung over the squadron.' To help restore their spirits Blomfield organised a wake with a sing-song in a nearby barn. The band played brassy music and the pilots and mechanics sang some of the war's favourites – 'There's a Long, Long Trail', 'Swanee River' and 'Pack Up Your Troubles'. Lewis gave a rendition of Stevenson's 'Requiem': 'Under the wide and starry sky, Dig the grave and let me die ...' Ball's death had 'cast a gloom through the whole Flying Corps', Maurice Baring wrote in his diary that night. 'He was not only perhaps the most inspired pilot we have ever had, but the most modest and engaging character. His squadron, and indeed all the squadrons, will feel this terribly.'[24]

At the village of Annoeullin, where the Germans buried the twenty-year-old who had dispatched around forty-four of their aeroplanes, he was honoured with a full military funeral. A month later he was awarded a posthumous Victoria Cross. After the war Mr Ball went to France, erected a stone memorial at the crash site and purchased the field in which it stands to this day, in the middle of a crop of sugar beet. Albert's mother, Harriet, who became Lady Ball, never recovered from the grief. She withdrew from public life and her son's death was never mentioned in her presence. Like many mothers of sons killed in the war she turned to spiritualism in the hope of communicating with Albert. 'She went steadily downhill,' said Paddy Armstrong. 'She was still grieving for him when she died in 1931.'

Chapter 16
An Airman's Wife

Very few war pilots were married. Most were too young, and those who might have gone to the altar in peacetime were often reluctant to commit to permanent relationships while their lives faced doubtful tomorrows. One of the exceptions was Captain William Bond, who married his wife Aimée during the war. Their declarations of longing for each other are documented in his letters and in her heart-wrenching responses, all of which she shared with the world in a book published in 1918.[1]

Bill Bond was a grammar-school boy from Chesterfield in Derbyshire. He had become a journalist and gone to work for the London *Daily Mail* in Paris. Here he met a fellow writer, Amy McHardy, the daughter of a Glasgow clerk. Three years Bill's senior, she was, for her era, an exceptionally liberated feminist. In France she had smartened her name to Aimée and she and Bond had begun a torrid affair of rare intensity, defying Edwardian convention by openly living and travelling around Europe together in the years immediately before the war.

When hostilities began they returned to England, where Bond joined up with the King's Own Yorkshire Light Infantry, serving as a subaltern first at Gallipoli and then in France. On the Western Front in 1916 he was awarded a Military Cross for an act of exceptional bravery. Though himself hit by a grenade, he had gone out and rescued a wounded fellow officer, helping to carry him more than 200 metres across no-man's-land under withering machine-gun fire. Subsequently he transferred to the RFC, becoming, in early 1917, at twenty-seven, a pilot. He trained at Upavon where, now recently married to Aimée, they rented a cottage near the aerodrome. There she had stitched his brand-new wings on his tunic.

In early April 1917, Bond was posted to France to join No. 40 Squadron flying Nieuport 17 Scouts at Treizennes near St Omer. At Charing Cross station, desperate to postpone their parting, Aimée had pleaded with the boat-train officer to allow her to travel with him to the Channel port of Folkestone. She was refused. '"I'm sorry – if you were the wife of a brigadier-general you couldn't," he replied very kindly, adding, "One tried last week, and she was brought back under arrest." I smiled back at him, but I had to bite my lip.' She was allowed to go on to the platform, where she stood by the carriage door. They hardly spoke. 'The whistle blew. "If the boat is delayed I'll wire and you'll come at once, won't you?" he said, and kissed my mouth. I nodded my head: the train moved. "Good-bye, old boy," I managed and smiled. He smiled too. "Good-bye," he said. I don't know if he hung out of the window, for I walked away and never looked round. Outside, although it was springtime, the rain and the snow came down together.'

Aimée went back to her London home in Marylebone. Her maid, Purcell, opened the door. '"Oh, miss, has he gone?" she asked. "Yes," I answered, and ran upstairs as fast as I could.' In her room she put on a gramophone record. It was a ragtime tune she and Bill had once danced to there, 'he in his blue crêpe-de-chine pyjamas and me in a state of undress'.

Aimée and Bill corresponded feverishly, often sending two or three letters on the same day. His communicated on two levels: as well as expressing his love for his wife, he provided long reports about his fellow pilots, the camaraderie of the squadron, their increasingly dangerous patrols, the vacant chairs. Despite the mortal fear he often felt in the air and his regular anguish at the death of colleagues, Bill's correspondence was studiously upbeat: 'I have come to the best of the squadrons in a good part of the line. The machines are things of beauty and the mess is splendid. What more could a flying man want?' Forty Squadron was one of the most distinguished and successful in the Flying Corps. Two dozen aces flew with it during the war. Its commander, described by Bond organising a dawn patrol as 'a tousle-headed youth in pyjamas and a flying coat', was a twenty-two-year-old former Etonian, Major Leonard Tilney.

It was several weeks before Bond saw serious aerial combat. His early letters lamented the scarcity of enemy aircraft. 'Yesterday I was sent up at 6.30 and during an hour and a half we saw one Hun. This morning we didn't see any. I suppose I'll come across swarms at once . . . Last night I lay awake a long time thinking of you. It was so wonderfully sweet. My darling wife, I love you. All yours, Bill.'

'I am so glad I am his wife,' Aimée wrote. 'My heart is full of joy because he is mine. He is like sunshine in my life. I seem to bask in the most glowing memories of him. I think of our wonderful intercourse, and again I read the letter of today.'

In his first real dogfight, Bond's gun failed him at the crucial moment. 'If it hadn't jammed this morning I'd have had one off my own bat.' His report ended: 'Your letters are so sweet. I do love you. It was so perfect to read what you are doing and to know you're so happy. I, too, am very happy – in the knowledge of your love for me and mine for you; it is still quite wonderful; more wonderful, in fact, every day. Darling Aimée, all my wife (I like writing it).'

Aimée had moved out of London to stay with friends in a village near the south coast that she didn't name in her book. It was a community of wives, widows, children and old men: all the young men were away at the war – or dead. From her bedroom window she looked down every morning, waiting for the mail, delivered in a donkey cart by an elderly, ginger-bearded postman. There wouldn't always be any. 'Today no letter has come from my love. I want one. I want him to fly over the edge of the Downs and in at my bedroom window. I want to kiss his mouth.' She told Bill she had been for a swim in the sea. 'I wanted to swim out to where I imagined the coast of France must lie, for then I should have been nearer to you.'

Early in May a triumphant letter told her he'd been credited with his first victory. 'I got a Hun yesterday afternoon. It was a great scrap and I was fearfully pleased ... It was a big bus with polished yellow wooden body and green wings ... One of our patrols which had come over in time to see the scrap says he went down and crashed.'

Three weeks later Bond shot down two Albatros within half an hour. In the next fortnight, as the squadron flew in support of the British armies advancing up the Messines Ridge to seize the high ground before launching the Battle of Passchendaele on the plains to the north-east, he accounted for two more, bringing his total to five to qualify as an ace. He was awarded a second Military Cross. But his luck was running out. He had a narrow escape when, hit by a salvo of Archie, he felt a violent shock on the joystick. His right aileron control rod had been shot away. Unable to bank properly he headed for home and with great skill managed to land without wrecking the aeroplane. 'I have broken parts of the rod,' he told Aimée, 'and the armourer is going to produce some souvenir from it for you.'

The pilots were sometimes encouraged to go up to the lines to see how the other half lived. In the squalor of the trenches and the artillery emplacements behind them they would meet the foot soldiers and gunners whose eyes they had become. Bill told Aimée how he had borrowed a motorbike and spent a day with the army. On his journey to the front he was appalled to see on the ground what the war had done to the countryside. 'The sight cannot be described,' he said. 'It's as if roads and villages and woods and fields suddenly had become liquid like a sea, and had rolled themselves over and over in huge waves.' At the new British front 'I had tea with a General, and supper with a sergeant'. The supper was a bottle of beer and a slice of fruit cake and the sergeant was his twenty-two-year-old younger brother, Alfred, known as Dick. He was an artillery NCO who had already covered himself in glory, having been awarded a Military Medal for maintaining the flow of ammunition wagons to the guns under heavy shellfire.

Amid the awfulness of the conditions suffered by most soldiers in the trenches there were, amazingly, rare pockets of mild luxury in dugouts just behind the lines. Pilot John Slessor (who later became head of the RAF) used, on duty, to visit one of these, 'inhabited by rich, fruity characters who drank good port and smoked good cigars . . . There would be cherry brandy and much talk of fox-hunting and what old so-and-so was doing and how long this damned war would keep them away from the really important things of life.'[2]

Bond stumbled on none of this. Later he watched the progress of the huge assault on Messines Ridge from the air. Launched on 7 June, it was preceded, like the opening of the great Somme battle, by the colossal simultaneous detonation of huge mines tunnelled beneath the German defences. A soldier who saw it in the pre-dawn dark described how 'the earth opened and a large black mass was carried to the sky on pillars of fire'. 'It was as though the fires of hell had risen,' a war reporter wrote. What was to remain the world's largest man-made explosion until the atomic era was felt at 3.10am as a rumbling earthquake in London. At work in his study in Downing Street in the small hours, it startled British prime minister Lloyd George who, dreading a repetition of the holocaust on the Somme, had tried to postpone the attack and had sanctioned Haig's battle plan only with great and nervous reluctance. The nineteen mines had instantly killed or buried alive an estimated 10,000 German soldiers, with thousands more left stunned and dazed. But the blast had enabled the British divisions to seize the ridge in one of the war's few British successes to date.

Two miles up in the sky Bond could see none of this as his flight patrolled the front line hunting for enemy reconnaissance machines spying on the attacking artillery positions for the German gunners. What he could see was the awesome might of the British guns. More than 2,000 of them were deluging Messines Ridge with a storm of high-explosive shells – 'a dancing, pricking, shimmering mass of heat. I flew over this, 12,000 feet above it and thanked some of my gods that I was no longer a landsman in combat.'

Now that he had been on the ground he knew the position of his brother's battery. Identifying it from a gun flash, he flew down low over it at the end of a patrol and exuberantly looped and rolled over the emplacement. 'I chucked a few stunts and waved to Dick,' he said. In the same letter he told Aimée: 'When you write as you do today, when you tell me of your longings and your thoughts, I can hardly bear to stay here. For I want you too, my wonderful lover; and just to want you so intensely and to know you want me is exquisite happiness.'

They were soon to be briefly reunited. When Bond came home on leave they spent seventeen days seeing their families and at a hotel some- where by the sea, where they played golf. Of those 'glorious days together away from the rush of town' Aimée wrote: 'I wonder if those who believe in Heaven could imagine anything more enthralling, more complete.' On 19 July Bond returned to France. He had been asked to fly a new Sopwith Camel across the Channel. It was a terrifying flight. The Camel, despite its fame as one of the greatest fighting aeroplanes of the First World War and its great combat success, was inherently unstable; it was one of the Flying Corps' most perilously unforgiving machines for a novice to fly and had earned a grim reputation for killing pilots. Bill Bond had never set eyes on one before and he was totally unfamiliar with the idiosyncrasies of its rotary engine, in which the crankshaft remained fixed while the cylinders and attached propeller rotated around it. The powerful gyroscopic effect of the rotary, spinning like a big flywheel, continuously pulled the machine to the right. The engine permanently ran disconcertingly at full power, which could only be controlled by blipping the ignition on and off with a thumb switch on the control column. To add to all this, if mishandled, its eccentric fuel–air mixture control would immediately stop the engine. Bond knew nothing of this dangerous catalogue of eccentricities. Nor was he aware that he would be showered by a constant flow of the castor oil that lubricated the engine, blackening his face, staining his uniform and irritating his stomach. Rashly, 'when they asked me if I could fly one I said "yes" promptly'. He was quickly to regret it.

His problems started the moment he got into the cockpit. He couldn't get the air–petrol adjustment right and the engine kept stopping. It took a mechanic half an hour to get it to run properly. Out on the airfield he made eight attempts to take off. On each the engine petered out before he got into the air. 'When I did get off I hardly knew it. I was barely breathing for wondering if the engine would stop for the ninth time when I crawled over the sheds.' He crept nervously up to 5,000 feet, where the revolutions began to drop. As he fiddled with the fuel mixture the engine spluttered and stopped. He was down to 1,500 feet before he coaxed it back to life. Climbing to 7,000 feet he headed out across the Channel. Within a few minutes, over the sea, the engine stopped again. He was looking round for a naval vessel to ditch beside when, at 2,000 feet, the temperamental rotary coughed back into action. 'I can't describe to you the tenseness with which I watched my engine for the next twenty minutes,' he wrote. 'Every two or three minutes it started to fail.'

Only with delicate tweaks of the finely balanced mixture did Bond eventually make it to France. Back at Bruay, near Béthune, the squadron threw a party to welcome him home and celebrate his promotion to captain. In the morning he was back in the air, now a flight commander, resuming his vulnerable occupation over the lines, skirmishing with the Huns of the flying circuses. His precarious future never left Aimée's mind. 'I wonder why I am so confident that he will come back to me? Every day I see the Roll of Honour and am forced to realise that there is no reason why I should be spared a grief that others have to bear just now.'

Aimée moved to Derbyshire to stay with Bond's family until his next leave. She joined his sister for a summer holiday at a spa hotel at Buxton in the Peak District. It was there that the terrible news came.

The phone call to the hotel was taken by Bill's sister Leila, whom Aimée in her book called 'Joan'. She went up to knock on Aimée's door. 'She stood there,' Aimée said. 'Her face was quite grey. I moved aside to allow her to come in, but I couldn't take my eyes from her eyes.

'What is it? . . . Oh, Joan, what is it?' I managed to say at length. Then, as she seemed unable to speak, I caught hold of her hands.

'Joan – tell me what it is!' I cried.

'I can't . . . I can't,' she began, and her voice was all broken up.

'It's not Bill?' I whispered – but of course I knew.

The War Office telegram reporting Bond missing had gone to his parents in Chesterfield. Aimée and Leila immediately abandoned their holiday and went there. Bond's father showed her the telegram. 'It seemed to give us hope. After all, many airmen have gone missing and afterwards have been reported prisoners of war.' At the bereft Bonds' home Aimée and Leila had to share a bed. 'When we lay down she put her arm round me. Somehow she seemed so small and helpless that it made me cry. The tears trickled on to the pillow until it was wet.' Writing to the absent Bill, she described in the first of a stream of unposted letters she poured into her book how they switched the light on and sat up to look through her photo album full of pictures of herself and Bill during their idyllic years travelling through Europe.

Two weeks after the first telegram another arrived. Mrs Bond stood at the door, afraid to open it. She called to Aimée, who rushed downstairs, seized the green envelope and tore it open. It read: 'Home on leave. Arrive tonight – Dick.' She wrote to Bill: 'The tears blinded my eyes. You were so anxious for Dick and me to meet, and now it happens like this!' When Bill's brother, who hadn't been home for two years, arrived, he brought new optimism. 'He whistles and sings ragtime and brings a gust of life to this house. He simply *can't* be downhearted, because he knows you'll come through all right.'

Dick took her by train to the grammar school where Bill had gone. He showed her the spot by the railway where his brother had sat for hours with a notebook logging the numbers of the engines. To try to cheer her up he took her to a song-and-dance revue. She sat in the theatre clutching her favourite memento of Bill, which she now took with her everywhere. 'Your stick, the one made from the broken propeller, with the band of the fragment of aileron control.' As a troupe of girls began a ragtime dance, she claimed she had a vision. 'I saw *you* against the blue morning sky . . . High up against the blue you were! I saw the Archie-bursts around you . . . I saw your machine stagger and begin to spin. I saw it spinning – down – down. And when it reached the ground my heart stopped – for you stood up and, after saying "damn" quietly, just once, you fumbled in your pocket and brought out your pipe and tobacco pouch.'

Bond had died like that – but more swiftly and catastrophically. He had survived barely three days after his return to France. In the hazy dawn of 22 July he had led a flight of five Nieuports across the German lines hunting for targets to attack. Over Lens the formation had, with deadly accuracy, been hit by a salvo of four closely clustered anti-aircraft shells. Bond's aircraft was blown up. One of his fellow pilots, 2nd Lieutenant William MacLanachan, whose machine had been blasted upside down, was shocked, when he regained control, to find that his patrol leader's aircraft had completely disappeared. 'Pieces of aeroplane fabric were whirling crazily in the air amidst the huge black smoke balls of the Archie bursts. Incredulous, I looked round for Bond, but he had gone. All that remained in the air were the stupid, dancing remnants of his planes [wings].'[3]

That night MacLanachan had the awful task of sorting out Bond's belongings, his shaving brush, still wet with the morning's soap, his books, his clothes, the letters that were 'the delicate souvenirs of his happiness with his wife'. All to make room, MacLanachan said, 'for another pilot who might share the same fate within a week or a month'.

William Bond has no grave. His name, carved into the stone column of the Flying Services monument in Arras for missing aviators of the First World War, is his only memorial.*

*Aimée remarried. Her second husband, Philip Stuart, was an author and playwright. He and Aimée collaborated on the writing of a stream of successful London West End plays through the 1920s and early 1930s. When Philip died in 1936 Aimée continued on her own. She lived to around ninety-five. For many years until her death in 1981 she was regularly seen lunching at the exclusive Ivy restaurant, sharing her theatrical wisdom with young writers and actors.

Chapter 17
The Mothers

Arthur Rhys Davids, the old Etonian who had difficulty finding colleagues of equal intellectual calibre among his fellow pilots, had inherited an astonishing mind from remarkable academic parents. His Welsh father was an orientalist who occupied at University College, London, the chair of Professor of Pali, the language in which the Theravada Buddhist scriptures were written. His mother, to whom he was extraordinarily close, was a university fellow who spoke both Pali and Sanskrit and held a doctorate in Indian philosophy. Arthur won a scholarship to Eton where, despite ill health and a chronic nervous stammer, he proved a brilliant classics scholar, became captain of school and gained an exhibition to Balliol College. But in 1916, instead of going up to Oxford, he had joined the Royal Flying Corps and finished up at the exclusive 56 Squadron.

Here, despite the intellectual snobbery revealed in his running commentaries to his mother, his breeding and innate good manners ensured that his fellow pilots never had the slightest inkling of his carefully guarded arrogance. His easy charm made him enormously popular and he was soon admired for his deadly skills as a fighter pilot. Had his colleagues ever glimpsed the contemptuous comments he was making about some of them in his letters, they would have been devastated. As it was, they respected and applauded his fighting aggression and the kills he was adding to the squadron's total. His first combat, in which he was shot down but survived unharmed, was the running battle in which Albert Ball was killed. In the following weeks he took his personal score from one to six in three days, shooting down three enemy aircraft within just an hour on one evening. There was talk of him becoming another Ball.

To his mother and his two sisters, Arthur sent back daily reports of his mounting bag of killings. He was Caroline Rhys Davids' only son and she doted excessively on him. With much of his young life spent beyond her reach at regimented boarding schools she had showered his housemasters with anxious telegrams at the very first whiff of his latest illness.

She was, not surprisingly, greatly alarmed when she learned that, having joined the Flying Corps, he had chosen to become a fighter pilot.

'Dearest Mums,' he wrote to reassure her. 'First of all it is no more dangerous than any other branch of the RFC if done well; secondly, it's twice as much fun, and thirdly, Mums, you know I simply cannot and will not shirk in any way just because I happen to have more brains than some of the people here, in fact that is all the more reason why I should be in a position to use them on the more difficult job.' His letter ended: 'I want to be worthy of my salt and of your name.'[1]

In the corrugated iron Nissen hut in which he lived at Vert Galant, Rhys Davids created a private world where he wrote poetry and adorned the walls with photographs of the old Etonian friends he missed. He read the plays of the classical Greek dramatist Euripides and devoured the little-read verse of the Romantic poet William Blake and the long-forgotten William Henley.* Whenever he flew he carried a small volume of Blake to enjoy should he finish up in captivity. The subject of one of the first of his own poems was his mother. 'I have visions of another poem coming,' he told her. 'It started yesterday in bed I think: anyhow it's about you. I haven't settled the metre yet, but things are simmering.'[2]

The standards of class and intellect he demanded of the colleagues he was prepared to accept as true friends disqualified most. 'I would give anything for a friend worth calling one,' he sighed. Most, though agreeable enough, had fatal flaws and Arthur maintained it was not possible to have anything more than 'pointless conversations' with them.

One of the few who measured up was his flight commander, Captain Cyril Crowe, a pre-war pilot with a formidable accumulation of battle wisdom that had taught him how to survive in the air. 'Crowe's father owns a big iron and steel works in Durham. Except for the fact that he is engaged and rather loose about wine and whisky we have much in common.' He was on good terms, too, with public-school man Richard Maybery. 'He was in the 21st Lancers in India and played rugger for Wellington against Eton about 1911–12. He is a first class tennis, squash, chess and bridge player and a damn fine scrapper and "pukka" gentleman.' So, he later discovered, was Keith Muspratt, probably the closest of the handful of friends he ever made in the Flying Corps. Muspratt had learned to fly while still at Sherborne School. He and Arthur, who were of a

---

*For its message of self-mastery, William Henley's immortal poem 'Invictus' ('Undefeated') was, fifty years later, being read aloud by Nelson Mandela to his fellow detainees in their South African prison.

similar age, temperament and outlook, immediately clicked. Muspratt, Rhys Davids and an automatically embraced old Etonian, Maxwell Coote, became an inseparable trio, known in the squadron as 'the Children'. While their worldlier colleagues were drawn to the bars and brothels of the nearest towns, 'the Children' preferred to take long walks together in the woods where, according to Coote, they would 'talk about every subject under the sun'.

In the air Rhys Davids assumed a more violent persona. Throwing caution to the winds, he took such reckless risks in combat that he had, he told his mother, been ordered to rein in his style. 'I have been an unholy dangerous fool,' he confessed.

> I have taken 4 times the risk I ought to have done and that, by sheer <u>luck</u>, I have come through with a whole skin, a great joy in life and five and a bit Huns brought down to my credit.
>
> In fact I have been going on Ball's lines. But I think I have had enough of that for a time. I started off being ultra cautious, to say the least of it and that riled me; then I began being a mad dog in so much that one evening after a show the CO said, 'You put up a d--- good show and I'm proud of you.' But, after my last and silliest effort, my Flight Commander asked me not to do it again, and the dear old adjutant gave me a fatherly piece of advice and beseeched me not to take undue risks, said it didn't pay.
>
> But, O my old Ma, one can't lay down rules while on mere earth for people on fighting patrol in the air. You are a different man – at least you aren't a man at all, that is I am not – you are a devil incarnate filled with the dazzling thrill of playing the best game God ever created, mad after Huns and just forget everything else but showing the old Hun that there's only one man fit to be in the air and not two.[3]

His letters sent Caroline into paroxysms of anxiety. She knew every hour he was in the air she might lose him. Not only might he be shot to pieces in battle but he could be killed in one of the succession of the mid-air break-ups and engine failures his aircraft almost routinely suffered. One of these forced him to drop down into a field behind the lines. While awaiting rescue he sat down under a haystack and wrote to his sister Nesta. 'So here I am all alone with a gorgeous May sun and a little finicky breeze making things so nice with a lark or two above simply bursting with the joy of life. I can just hear the guns going, but bar that the war seems very far away thank God. It seems such blasphemy to wage war in weather like this.'[4] When Nesta sent the letter on to her mother, Caroline wrote back to her: 'It is interesting and poignantly so to see how the clean sweet message of Spring makes him call out against the whole hideous business and his own mental loneliness.'

Like many of the pilots, he wrote about religion. 'You will find (at least I do),' he told Nesta, who had just been confirmed into the Church of England, 'that you can walk with God much easier in a pinewood than in a church. The one great thing is to think as though you were walking arm in arm with God the whole day. Because he is <u>always</u> there. Best love and please don't be an ordinary Christian.'[5] He corresponded with his mother about Buddhism. 'Tell me – do you think Buddha himself <u>really</u> believed in the Karma doctrine of rebirth? Because it <u>must</u> involve animism of a kind and who or what is the judge of one's life work and consequent rebirth in a higher or lower stage?'[6]

That summer of 1917 Rhys Davids had joined the pantheon of the RFC's great aces. He found himself flying alongside James McCudden, the mechanic who was by now a pilot and was on his way to becoming one of the war's highest-scoring knights, the equal of the Red Baron in conflict. He and Rhys Davids flew against the cream of a German Air Service now confronting them in small armadas of jastas. Manfred von Richthofen's Jasta 11 had joined up with three other squadrons as the first *Jagdgeschwader*, a single massive fighting wing that sometimes put up to eighty aircraft into the air in one great swarm. Commanded by Manfred, it was soon to be dubbed, for the bright-painted colours of its aeroplanes and its use of trains with dining cars and comfortable sleeping compartments to travel from airfield to airfield, his 'Flying Circus'. To avoid Richthofen's machine being picked off in battle most of the aircraft of the *Jagdgeschwader* were now painted red, or red and green. And to confuse the British pilots further, some even began to appear in startlingly unmilitary purples and yellows, while others bore the menacing emblem of a skull and crossbones on their noses. For their records of natural aggression and combat skill the German pilots flying them were each personally hand-picked by Richthofen. Refusing to accept those delivered to him by the replacement pools, he travelled round the squadrons personally selecting his own team.

Richthofen's ability to choose winners was unerring. It was he who found the little-known Ernst Udet and he was so impressed by his devastating abilities in combat he gave him command of his own celebrated Jasta 11 within the circus. Udet's eventual sixty-two victories were to become the second-highest German total of the war. In his autobiography he described one of the consequences of the respect his successes and collection of medals earned him. Back on leave in Munich he and his girlfriend, walking past the King of Bavaria's palace one afternoon, were startled when the sentry, spotting his Blue Max, barked an order to summon the royal guard, who smartly tumbled out to present arms to the couple. Udet's girlfriend was so delighted that she insisted they walk back past the palace and, to his embarrassment, the entire performance was repeated.

In June 1917 the war had moved north into southern Belgium and another of its great clashes at Messines Ridge and Passchendaele. Haig's objective was to continue the grinding pressure on the German people through the attrition of their army and he hoped for a substantial advance that might capture the Belgian ports of Ostend and Zeebrugge used by the U-boats that were threatening the merchant ships bringing raw materials and food to Britain and the first of the American forces to France. The five-month-long battle near Ypres, much of it fought in a porridge of liquefied mud in which men drowned in their hundreds, saw horrors and casualties that rivalled the apocalyptic destruction of the Somme.

The latest killing ground had been made especially ghastly by drenching rain of near-monsoon intensity. Above the front-line quagmire the big guns had turned into lagoons of impassable mud, the British pilots looked down from their cockpits to see men floundering waist-deep in slimy ooze and tanks sunk almost out of sight. Yet again a once-picturesque rural countryside was reduced to a stark, monochromatic grey landscape in which all that remained was an eerie forest of shell-blunted trunks in a swampland of flooded craters. With good reason Passchendaele, known also as the Third Battle of Ypres, has remained not only another byword for the worst horrors of the First World War, but the event that finally prompted the fading of admiration for needless human sacrifice. And although the much-quoted story may be apocryphal, it is not difficult to believe that the British Expeditionary Force's chief of staff, General Sir Launcelot Kiggell, visiting the scene when the battle had ended, might well have shed tears as he exclaimed: 'Good God, did we really send men to fight in this?'

Although nearly a century later wildly different versions of the figures are still being debated by military historians, the consensus puts the total number of British and German casualties at Passchendaele at between half and three-quarters of a million. Once again Haig's armies gained merely a few miles of territory.

Above this latest bloodbath some of the fiercest of the war's air battles blazed. The sky, pungent and hazy with the smell and smoke of the big guns, was more crowded with aeroplanes than ever before. Sometimes there would be nearly a hundred, wheeling and swooping in regular clashes for supremacy in the small slice of airspace over the front line, looking from a distance like clouds of bees circling a hive. Amazingly, these packs of fighting aeroplanes were manoeuvring and attacking with only the crudest means of communication with their leaders. Instructions and warnings came from the waggling of wings and hand signals. 'No section leader called us on the R/T [radio] to take our man or watch our tails,' recalled Cecil Lewis. 'We may have gone down in formation, but we fought alone and I, personally, had this vivid sense of loneliness in every fight I was in. So a man went into combat as if he were going into death – in extreme danger, and alone.'[7]

Both Britain and Germany had now brought to the air war a range of new, more technologically advanced, faster, higher-flying aeroplanes. The Flying Corps had acquired: a formidable Bristol two-seater fighter that could be flown and thrown about the sky like a single-seater scout; the DH4, a two-seater biplane, which, with its big 200-horsepower engine, was the first British machine designed as a day bomber; and the Sopwith Camel – the highly idiosyncratic, inherently unstable single-seat fighter with a reputation both for killing pilots in large numbers and for its stunning success in sympathetic hands.

Triplanes, whose three wings brought faster rates of climb and tighter turning ability in dogfights, had arrived on both sides. Although the British Sopwith version went mainly to the naval squadrons, the Germans had immediately supplied the flying circuses with their Fokker triple-wing. Richthofen flew one. So did one of his squadron commanders, Werner Voss, the second highest-scoring German pilot at that time. With forty-eight victories he was accumulating them faster than the Red Baron, whom he was determined to overtake. But before he could do so he was killed in one of the most celebrated and minutely analysed aerial combats of all time.

The fight, in September 1917, was conspicuous for the sheer reckless bravery of Voss, who found himself hopelessly outnumbered, seven to one, by a group of 56 Squadron SE5s. It was a striking demonstration of the exceptional manoeuvrability of the German triplane handled by a brilliant pilot in a skirmish with a horde of aggressively flown biplanes. And Voss was probably not even on his best form: he was reported to have been still recovering from a hangover from a heavy drinking party the night before to celebrate a colleague's award of a Blue Max. His machine was capable of climbing out of the battle at any time, yet he stayed to the end, his guns inflicting disabling damage on many of his attackers. Inevitably, however, the superior odds decided his fate. He was finally shot down by Rhys Davids.

'As long as I live,' wrote James McCudden, who took part in the fight, 'I shall never forget my admiration for that German pilot who, single-handed, fought seven of us for ten minutes, and also put some bullets through all of our machines. His flying was wonderful, his courage magnificent, and in my opinion he is the bravest German airman whom it has been my privilege to see fight. Rhys Davids came in for a shower of congratulations . . . but as the boy himself said to me, "Oh, if I could only have brought him down alive."'[8] When he landed back at his base Rhys Davids was in such a state of euphoria he was initially quite unable to describe the fight. His room-mate, Hubert Charles, reported: 'He stammered so badly that we couldn't understand him at all – he was so excited.'

Werner Voss was just twenty. 'You will probably have heard from Mother about the German star airman Voss having been brought down,' Rhys Davids wrote to Nesta, describing how he had 'slain a fine fellow'. 'Quite right, yours humbly at it again. How naughty I am . . . My God, he was a brave man, and what is more an absolutely wonderful scrapper. I take off my mental hat to him.'[9] However, his admiration for his famous victim didn't deter him from acquiring some trophies. From the crash site he took possession of Voss's compass and his aeroplane's rudder. Back in England the newspapers seized on his deed, splashing the story of the British flying hero who had stepped into Ball's shoes.

At 56 Squadron the stress of daily air combat was taking a steady toll of the pilots. Flight commander Cyril Crowe had a nervous breakdown. He was sent to hospital in France and then back to England to recover. After six months of it Rhys Davids, now the holder of a DSO and a double MC, was also approaching the end of his tether. His letters home began to grow uncharacteristically terse. As the date for the end of his tour grew closer, Major Blomfield tried to preserve him by limiting his battle flying. But when the mid-September date arrived the squadron had become so desperately short of experienced pilots that Arthur insisted on staying on.

When she heard of this, Caroline wrote on 28 October: 'Oh! My heart, how slowly go these last weeks of your term of war! Come soon! Mother.'

Arthur had been killed the previous day. The manner of his death was not immediately established. He had led a patrol which had encountered some German fighters behind enemy lines in the vicinity of

Passchendaele. The SE5s had split up to duel in individual dogfights. Rhys
Davids was last seen going down steeply in a pursuit dive. When he failed
to return to the squadron's base at Estrée Blanche that evening he was
officially reported missing. The squadron commander wrote to break the
news to Caroline. 'I have no definite information as to what actually
happened to your son, who was last seen by two other members of the
formation fighting with his usual dash and gallantry,' Major Blomfield
said, adding that he hoped the worst that had happened was that he'd
survived to become a prisoner. 'Messages are being dropped today, and
every effort will be made to ascertain his fate and to inform you immediately.'[10] Blomfield concluded by offering to send her Arthur's battle
trophies including the rudder from Voss's machine.

Caroline was far from happy with the letter. She had some hard
questions.

Dear Major Blomfield,

I am sorry my beloved son left the commanding officer, to whom he
was so greatly attached, so terrible a task as that of the letter you sent
us. It was too much like an obituary notice to leave us much room for
hope . . .

I never expected when he wrote to say he was staying beyond his
six months that we should get him safe back. I should be glad if you
can tell me just why he stayed on after mid-September and why he
was allowed to do so.

His was really a most valuable young life, so full of high gifts, firm
pure purposes and a winning personality, that it was worth straining
a point and compelling him to come back to relative safety against his
will. And he was all we had!

Thank you, do not send home rudders of fallen Huns. I could not
bear to see them . . .

Sincerely yours,
Caroline Rhys Davids[11]

Blomfield replied that there was no fixed period for a pilot to serve
overseas and that Arthur had requested he stay on to run his flight while
its flight commander was on leave. 'No one – outside his own family –
feels his loss more than I do.'

Caroline began, through prisoner-of-war channels, to write anguished
letters to her son. One went with blind hope to the prison camp at Wahn,
near Cologne: 'Hallo! Hallo! Are you there? Best Beloved, are you there?

Oh me! Is this telephone any good? Will my voice ever reach? Is there a Beloved Son somewhere at the other side of this miserable world to answer? Shall I ever see another word in his handwriting ... shall I ever see him again. Where, in God's name, is Wahn? Sinister word! It means illusion [in fact "delusion"].'[12]

The letter went on to send him family news and ended again: 'Hallo, hallo! Are you there, boy of my heart? Are you there? Mother.' More beseeching missives followed. But, in the last week of December 1917, the last vestiges of the family's hopes were dashed by a letter from the War Office. It said that a German aeroplane had dropped a message in the British lines advising that Arthur was dead. He was twenty years old.

Yet still Caroline was not satisfied. When, in March 1918, she wrote again to Blomfield, he had been succeeded by a new 56 Squadron commander, a twenty-two-year-old New Zealander, Major Rainsford Balcombe-Brown. The latest distressing letter wanted to know why there was 'no burial place, no relics'. And why 'not a soul of those who were on patrol with him have sent us a single word, either of what they last saw of him, or of sympathy to us or of tribute to their comrade!'.

'Is this usual in the RFC? <u>Think what we have been suffering for over four months</u> – the blind darkness, the silence – has no-one in 56 the least imagination what it has all cost us? In Arthur was centred our happiness ... It makes me think he must in some way, after his swiftly earned fame, have disgraced the squadron at the end. What am I to think?'[13]

Fresh to Caroline Rhys Davids' piteous expressions of her desolation Balcombe-Brown wrote a long, sympathetic and sensitive letter. But, with brutal honesty, he was forced to speak of the sad inevitability of Arthur's end. Far from disgracing the squadron her son had deserved a Victoria Cross. He had died 'gloriously', one of a handful of pilots whom he considered the bravest, 'but unfortunately the most reckless' in the entire Flying Corps. 'The brave and the reckless,' he explained, 'sooner or later when taking on heavy odds "stop a bullet" because it needs superhuman skill to avoid it in the end.'[14]

The detailed circumstances of Arthur Rhys Davids' death remained a mystery for more than fifty years. It was not until a tenacious new generation of WWI aviation historians began, in the 1960s, to search British and German archives for combat reports to try to match the times and places of the air battles that some of the participants were identified. The process revealed that Rhys Davids had probably been shot down by a German ace, Leutnant Karl Gallwitz. Arthur's grave, never found, was almost certainly obliterated by pulverising shellfire in the quagmires of Passchendaele.

His loss haunted Caroline for the rest of her life, bringing bouts of regular black depression. She tried to ease it by turning briefly to spiritualism to communicate with him. Although she put on a brave face, 'the dreadful heartache,' she wrote, 'goes on getting worse.' But she eventually, when the war was over, had second thoughts about Arthur's battle trophies and presented Voss's rudder to London's Imperial War Museum. In October 1920 there arrived unexpectedly, in a small package from the War Office, one final reminder of his life. Through diplomatic channels the Germans had sent back the sparse collection of personal effects found on Rhys Davids' body. It comprised an empty wallet, one French coin, a cheque for five francs and some private letters – probably the last from Caroline pleading with him to come home.

So intense was the love for each other expressed by some mothers and their pilot sons on the Western Front that their correspondence reads like letters between lovers. Among the most remarkable for their expression of the attitudes of the era to duty, patriotism and religion, were those that passed between the Honourable Eric Lubbock and his mother, Alice. She was the widow of the 1st Baron Avebury, an enormously wealthy Victorian banker, politician and biologist, who owned a 2,000-acre estate, High Elms, near Bromley in Kent, two town houses in London, a castle at Broadstairs and sundry other properties scattered around England. Born into the privileged world of this upper-class family Eric, seen in photographs as an angelic child with a mop of curly blond hair, was the cosseted favourite of Alice's three sons. An unusually gentle boy who hated killing things, he preferred roaming the High Elms woodlands studying the flora, the wildlife and the insects to hunting.

A product of Eton and Oxford, Eric was twenty-one when, within days of the declaration of war in 1914, he joined up for active service on the Western Front as a private in the motor transport section of the Army Service Corps, finding himself a conspicuous solitary 'toff' among the ranks of young working-class men whose personal habits and language came as a huge shock. Singled out by NCOs for the dirtiest of tasks, he mucked in, never used his title and was soon accepted by his colleagues. From time to time he met old schoolfriends whose backgrounds had brought them automatic commissions and who were horrified to discover that Lubbock was serving as a common soldier. Yet he didn't lack sponsors in high places. With the help of a letter from the then commander-in-chief of the British Army in France, Sir John French, and the war minister,

Lord Kitchener himself, he was accepted in the summer of 1915 for commissioned service as an observer with the Flying Corps. With some
trepidation, and much economy with the truth, he wrote to break the
news to Lady Avebury.

> My darling Mum,
>
> I am most awfully excited about it – but there's just one fly in the
> ointment, that is, that I'm afraid you'll worry. You needn't Mum as
> there is nothing to worry about and I promise that I won't take to it
> in peacetime. Men who are keen about it in peacetime of course are
> always trying tricks and looping loops and being foolish. One admires
> it and all that but that is 'pas pour moi'. Out here they just go straight
> along and take no risks . . .
>
> Ever your loving son, Eric[15]

Lubbock was posted as an observer to No. 5 Squadron, where he found
himself flying with a well-known London stage actor, Robert Loraine,
yet another of the unlikely larger-than-life characters who seem to have
been magnetically attracted to the Flying Corps. Now approaching forty,
Loraine had run away from school at thirteen to join a touring repertory
company, became a leading romantic actor on the London and New York
stage, had served as a trooper in the South African war, learned to fly in
1910 and bought his own aeroplane in which he had made the first-ever
flight across the Irish Sea – though he'd had to swim the last 400 yards to
shore when his engine failed. But, like so many of the war's most experienced pilots, although he was to earn gallantry decorations for aerial
combat he never quite mastered his take-offs and landings and his flying
career was strewn with crashes. Lubbock was soon to be the victim of
one of them. 'My darling Mum,' he wrote from France, recuperating
from a deep cut in his leg:

> I have promised always to tell you of anything that happens to me.
> I am laid up with a slight cut on my left leg. It is nothing bad, just
> another 'jelly' trick below the knee. We had a take-off smash this
> morning and fell. It took a long run to get off, then we rose to some
> 40ft. The engine stopped. The nose went absolutely straight down.
> I was thrown clear as we hit the ground . . . I landed perfectly upside
> down in very soft plough and got up with my head covered and my
> mouth and nose absolutely full of earth!
>
> I am in a very nice airy room. But I mustn't move my leg as it's

important I should get well quickly. I am on the floor with my blankets quite warm and comfortable and for the moment not sorry to have a rest.[16]

What Lubbock didn't share with his mother was the accident's sober reminder that life in the Flying Corps was essentially finite. Instead he privately recorded the reality in his diary: 'I have always looked on death as a thing of the remote future. Today for the first time I look upon it as a likelihood for the near future. I don't know that the idea appals me, only that I think of Mum. For her it would be too unthinkable. However, I am always lucky so "laissons à Dieu".'[17]

Alice Avebury, whose eldest son had just sailed off to fight in Gallipoli, received the news of the take-off crash with predictable concern: 'A most ghastly accident happened to Eric as his letter of the 18th shows. Thank God he is not seriously hurt. How he escaped death I do not know. It was a most narrow escape. My darling Harold started for the Dardanelles. Just exactly the same date a year ago that Eric went out. I heard of Eric's accident just after I'd said goodbye to Harold.'[18]

Back in the air Eric soon had better news for Alice. Flying with Loraine, he had shot down his first enemy aircraft. When they landed Loraine was astonished to learn that his observer, far from taking pride in the victory, was stricken with remorse. In notes he kept of the characters of the officers with whom he served, Loraine described Lubbock's struggle to harden his emotions.

We shot down a Hun. I was very elated but somewhat shocked to find Lubbock in tears. 'Just think of his mother,' he said. 'I hate this killing business.'

'Think of your mother,' I said 'You can't win wars by weeping over the enemy dead.'

'I don't mind risking my own life,' he replied. 'But I'm sure it's wrong to kill others.'[19]

Lubbock was in awe of the actor-pilot almost old enough to be his father. But he didn't enjoy flying with him. Loraine was a highly emotional, volatile personality with a reputation for being moody, uncommunicative and easily roused to anger. 'He never utters, never speaks to anyone except sometimes the Major and just answers politely in one or two words when spoken to,' Eric told Alice. 'I think it's his tummy or else he may be in love. If he is I wish she would accept him quickly and make him cheer up!'[20]

For his combat victory Lubbock was awarded a Military Cross. 'I sent him a telegram – a thousand congratulations,' Lady Avebury wrote in her diary. 'Oh! My beloved little boy . . . Oh dear! I am a proud mother – but oh, how I wish Eric could now rest on his laurels and have done with it all. Bless him a thousand times.'[21] Next day she recorded anxiously: 'No letter from Eric. There have been great air fights. Five air battles. Whether I want to or not I just can't help it – that sickening, ghastly feeling of fear which is very seldom absent, try as hard as I can to conquer it, so when I don't hear it is worse. I sometimes want to lie down and never think again. Where great love is there must be also great fear.'[22]

When Lubbock's award was announced in the newspapers Alice was inundated with letters of congratulation. They came from masters at Eton, Balliol tutors and friends and they had a common theme:

'How splendid Eric is. Everyone is full of him here at Eton. It is so wonderful to think he is the delicate, beautiful little boy that I remember who has developed into this brave and self-reliant man It seems such a little while since he was a little boy . . .'

'One cannot hope to keep courage and enterprise like Eric's from attempting and doing great things, and I suppose we ought not to want to. It is all part of himself and he would not be what he is if he did not want to do the best and bravest . . .'

'I can hardly realise that the little beautiful curly haired boy has become the dashing, daring soldier and done such wonderful things in such a simple modest way. You must be proud of him . . .'

Lubbock was sent back to England for pilot training at Shoreham-by-Sea in Sussex. The day he got his ticket he wrote in his diary: 'I was awfully bucked at getting it. Then I caught the 5 o'clock train from Brighton and came up to London. I dined with Lady St Helier and danced. I sat next to Lady Cynthia Hamilton who was quite pleasant and I enjoyed the dance most awfully much, in fact I loved it.'[23]

Back in France in April 1916 Lubbock, promoted to captain, was given command of one of the three flights of 45 Squadron. Lady Avebury continued to worry about him: 'Beloved, Great things are required of you. You will be wanted in the future very much. Run no risks, darling, please.'[24]

In January 1917 Eric was briefly back on leave in England. When he arrived at High Elms Alice was shocked by his appearance. 'He is so thin and white and tired looking. I dread his going back now more than ever. One's whole life is a big dread these days . . . Eric is not very sanguine about the end being soon, but perhaps that is because he is so tired and weary of it all.' He was due to fly an aeroplane back to France from Farnborough, but phoned to say his departure had been delayed. Alice prayed he would come back to High Elms for one more night. 'I would give anything to have him here for the night to see his darling face once more – to kiss him again. Oh, my God, how I love him and how frightened I am!'

In the end Eric didn't fly back to France. He went by sea, leaving from Charing Cross station. 'I saw him off. It's a ghastly thing to do. It was bitterly cold. That was the last time I saw him – as the train disappeared – with tender smile. How tender his smile always was. I read in his eyes all he left unsaid. It seems impossible that I may not see that wonderful look again.'[25]

Lubbock had returned to face hopeless odds in the air. His squadron's Sopwith 1½ Strutters were being decimated by the Albatros of the swarming flying circuses. The days of 45 Squadron's pilots were dispiritingly numbered. When Alice pleaded with him that 'there is a limit to human endurance', that he had done his bit and deserved to come home for good before it was too late, he told her there was no way he could abandon his fellow pilots. 'My darling Mum, I am too keen on my flight and too attached to the officers in it. They have shown themselves to be such brave fighters and so determined to do their work splendidly that I admire them and feel it an honour to lead them. They are the finest collection that I ever saw together.'[26]

On 11 March 1917 Lady Avebury wrote the last of her anguished, pleading letters: 'My darling Eric, When are you coming home? You ought to have rest and your poor little Mother ought to have rest. You have done such splendid work. I love you my own so very much. I am so silly to tell you so so often . . . but I like saying it so you must bear with it . . .'

Several days later the letter was returned. Eric had been killed on the day she wrote it. He was buried behind the British lines at Poperinghe in Belgium. His observer had died with him.

Lady Avebury was desolated by grief. 'It seems impossible to believe that Eric has gone out of our lives,' she wrote. 'I have actually to remind myself that he has left this world that sorely needs such men . . . I shall never believe that so keen, original and loving spirit is not living somewhere.'[27]

How did Eric Lubbock die? His wing commander, Colonel George Stopford, told Alice: 'He met his death in an air fight between two German machines and two of ours. Both our machines were brought down, but I know that your son would have preferred that death to any other. He

was known to all the Flying Corps near here for his pluck and gallantry
... Although I only knew him for such a short time I shall never forget
him. He was a boy to be truly proud of.'

When Eric's effects were returned to the family Lady Avebury found
among his papers a letter addressed to her. It must rank among the
most remarkable that any First World War son wrote to his mother.
Exceedingly long, its considered philosophising about death had been
written sixteen months earlier, soon after he'd joined his squadron and
realised how appallingly soon he might die. It revealed that his mother
was not the only one to whom his special love had extended. There was
a girlfriend who'd broken his heart by ending the relationship while he
was in France.

'My darling Mum,' Eric wrote. 'One is here confronted almost daily
with the possibility of Death, and when one looks forward to the next
few months this possibility becomes really a probability. I am therefore
sitting down now to write to you a few words which in the event of my
death I hope may help to comfort and to cheer you.' Although life was
very dear to him he did not fear death, he said. He loved 'this wonderful
and beautiful world' – a place he hoped 'before I go I may be able to make
it in some way (however small) just a bit better than I found it'. His love
for his mother and his family 'makes me long for life because with it
I hope to help you all and add to your happiness'.

To fear or dread death for its own sake is absolutely against all reason
and I want to point out to you that you must not grieve too much
if I die. You my poor Mummy suffer a lot from sleeplessness. But
suppose now that you went off to sleep at 10 one night and woke
up at 8 next morning having had no dreams or consciousness at all
would not that seem to you a blessed 10 hours. Now death at its
very worst is that, absolute blank, and therefore why fear it?

But I do not believe that death is that. I believe it is something
very different ... If this world is the final end, this imperfect world
with all its sorrows and griefs, if this is the best we can attain to then
the Great Giver of Life is but a torturer. That death should be the
end is inconceivable. I believe the world is our nursery and that we
are being trained by it to make us fit for another better life.

Of course I know that this is not going to relieve you of the first
pangs of parting. But Mummy if you love me try not to let it be too
great a blow to you, try and conquer your own sorrow and live
cheerfully ...

To one great friend particularly, Winifred, whom I have always loved. I tried hard not to love her, and even though I found I couldn't help it, for some time I did not admit it to myself. Now I do, and I know what it is to love. God bless her and keep her always happy.

So with all my love my darling Mum I now say goodbye – just in case. Try to forget my faults and to remember me only as your very loving little son

Eric Lubbock[28]

Some months later Eric had added a sad postscript. 'This was written some time ago. Now I have again suffered the most awful pain a man can suffer – that of losing the girl he loves. I know that in your heart you fear that it may make me reckless. It will not. You must trust me that I have strength enough not to let it. But Mummy could you see her for my sake and tell her that to the end I loved her. Be kind to her.'

Who was Winifred? And how did he lose her? Eric had known the aristocratic Winifred Martin Smith since his schooldays at Eton, when she would sometimes visit him for a very proper afternoon tea in his room. She was sometimes a guest at High Elms, where the formidable Alice Avebury took a deep dislike to her for no other reason, it was said, than the threat Winifred represented to her obsessive relationship with her son. She went to unusual lengths to terminate the friendship. Eric was nevertheless determined to marry her if he survived the war but he had been reluctant to formalise an engagement while his existence was in daily doubt. Winifred had turned to another man, a Coldstream Guards officer, with no such reservations about wartime marriage. Captain Olaf Hambro was a member of the wealthy banking family. He and Winifred had married just three weeks before Eric's death.*

Alice Avebury, whose eldest son, Harold, was also killed in action, dressed in black for the rest of her life. At High Elms she had an unusual monument to Eric built – a big concrete replica of an RFC aeroplane. She also privately published a lengthy memoir in which she reproduced many of the affectionate letters she and Eric had exchanged, along with extracts from both their diaries. But even within this loving chronicle of his life she demonstrated to the bitter end her antagonism towards

---

*The marriage had a tragic ending. In August 1932 Winifred was drowned in Loch Ness in Scotland after the speedboat in which she and Olaf, their three children and their nanny were cruising caught fire. They all, except the elderly nanny, jumped into the water and all but Winifred made it to shore. Her body was never found.

Winifred, pointedly deleting every mention of her name from her son's published letters.

For the Flying Corps, overwhelmed by Albatros hordes capable of wiping out an entire squadron in less than four weeks, Eric's death was just another sad statistic. The RFC's daily operations communiqué didn't even mention the loss of the two aeroplanes that left four empty chairs in 45 Squadron's mess that night.

Chapter 18

The 'Bloody Wonderful Drunks'

F or many of the pilots the worst agony was the anticipation of the dawn patrol from which they might not return. If not on tomorrow's mission, perhaps the one after. Or the one after that. The dread the night before kept many of them sleepless. It preyed most acutely on the minds of the new and inexperienced pilots, still struggling to master their aeroplanes and unsure of their ability to handle the tactics and violent manoeuvres of aerial combat that would decide whether they lived or died.

As a young pilot who had not even been taught the vital defensive steep turn so essential to his longevity, Harold Balfour, freshly arrived on the Western Front with 60 Squadron, described the pre-dawn horrors of his imagination. The aircrew were billeted in a farmhouse where he shared a bedroom with a fellow airman. While their minds raced, neither could rest. 'Each of us lay awake in the darkness, not telling the other that sleep would not come, listening to the incessant roar of the guns, and thinking of the dawn patrol next morning. At last we could bear it no longer and, calling out to each other, admitted a mutual feeling of terror and foreboding. We lit the candles in the dark and, after that, felt better and somehow got through the night as we had to get through the next day.'

Balfour confessed that in those early weeks on the squadron, when he was at his most vulnerable – the phase in which many new arrivals lasted only a few days – he was so terrified in the air that on one occasion he fled the scene of battle. Badly unnerved at watching his mortally wounded squadron commander, Major 'Ferdy' Waldron, go down, he was stricken with guilt.

I felt I might have done more and kept worrying and questioning myself as to what I should have done other than that which I did.

So much did this disturb my mental balance that I found myself hesitating on entering a fight, which hesitation rapidly developed into nothing short of a dislike to standing up to the enemy, and a strong inclination to turn tail with a dive homewards. One day I did this when out on patrol with another Morane. We were attacked by two Fokkers and my opponent could obviously out-manoeuvre me in every way. So I acted the complete funk and turned my nose downwards and in the direction of our lines.

My companion was fighting about two miles south of me. I told myself that it was up to me to look after myself and up to him to look after himself and, with those temporarily comforting sentiments, I regained safety. My companion never returned, and when I looked back from the sanctuary of our lines I saw a small streak of flame falling earthwards, which I knew must have been his Morane – on fire, defeated by the attacking Fokker.

It would be false to gloss over or deny incidents such as this, or the possession of feelings of panic and fear which I had, and which I am convinced were shared by many of my companions.[1]

Something that could postpone the awful dawn patrol, at least for a few hours, was the weather. Pilots often prayed they would be woken in the dark by their batman to hear the wonderful sound of heavy rain pattering on the roof. Declared Lieutenant Stanton Waltho:

The greatest joy I know is to be wakened after an all-too-short sleep by: 'It's six o'clock, sir, but I don't think there'll be any flying.' When a pilot starts his day thus, he manages to murmur: 'Is Captain Dash up?' The batman goes to ascertain, and returns with: 'No, sir, the patrol's a wash-out.' A still tired head falls back on to a pillow, and a pleased airman mutters something about '9.30' and 'waking' ... Everyone is late for breakfast and arrives in some garb which consists usually of brilliant pyjamas, bright scarf, flying boots and a grease-ruined tunic.[2]

The night-time fears that haunted Balfour were fully shared, whether they dared openly admit it or not, by almost every one of his fellow pilots. In an era when men, especially those from public schools, had been taught that the exhibition of emotion suggested character weakness, many forced themselves to bottle up their terrors. They were nonetheless, despite successful containment, often as badly psychologically trau-matised as their openly less controlled colleagues. The daily nerve-stret-ching experience of aerial combat, in which a single bullet in the petrol tank could convert your aeroplane in seconds into a flaming human incinerator, was the private dread of them all. Alcohol helped, if only for a few hours, to dull the tension and anxiety. At the end of the day's flying there would be a few drinks in the mess bar punctuated by laconic conversations whose discursive fragments Duncan Grinnell-Milne tried to recapture:

'Where's that Mess-Corporal? Corporal, a round of drinks for these officers . . .'

'Mine's a double whisky, hot – getting cold in the air these days . . .'

'Gin and Italian for me, and don't forget the gin . . .'

'What happened to you this afternoon? Got a Hun in flames, did you? Good for you . . .'

'Any further news of Jimmy? He's been missing for two days now . . .'

'Pulled his wings off in a dive, you say? Poor bastard . . .'

'Well, he's dead enough – dived from eighteen thousand – must have made a big hole in the ground – probably came out in China . . .'

'Better luck than his friend K – burnt to a crisp . . .'

'Well, chaps, Dawn Patrol tomorrow – going up high, got to get some more Huns . . .'

'And for God's sake, Skipper, don't lead us under a bunch of Fokkers like you did last time – enough to make one's hair turn white . . .'

'How about having the band in tonight? Haven't had it for the last few days, what with fellows "going west" and all that . . .'

'Passed through Doullens on my way back from leave. There's a peach of a girl at the Bon Air – Marguerite's her name . . .'

'Where's poor old P— buried? We ought to stick a propeller cross over his grave. A damn good fellow . . .'

'Corporal, another round of drinks. And hurry up for the love of Mike – Dawn Patrol tomorrow – don't want me to die thirsty, do you.'[3]

It didn't always end with a couple of drinks. Some of the squadrons' full-blown mess parties were legendary not only for the staggering amount of alcohol consumed, but for the violence of the drunken games and the wholesale destruction of property. Some squadrons were never short of excuses for a celebration. A flurry of victories in aerial combat, the promotion of a lieutenant pilot to captaincy and flight commander, fare-wells to men posted back to England, the award of yet another gallantry medal – all of these, sometimes merely a sudden whim of the CO's, could launch a full-blown party.

One of the most startling accounts of the excesses of a squadron binge was recorded by Cecil Lewis.

One evening the Major came back from Amiens with a case of whisky, a case of champagne, and a large bath sponge. 'Tonight,' he said, 'A Flight will throw a drunk, and B and C Flights are invited.'

After dinner the drunk was thrown. The long trestle table stood diagonally across the room ... The gramophone was wheezing ('*Where the Black-eyed Susans grow*') ...

A row of young men bent their heads over the table. The Major was mixing neat whisky with champagne in a tin basin. The sponge! It came in handy that sponge! It mixed them well.

'Shampoos,' shouted the Major. 'Who's for shampoos?'

He dolloped the sponge on the head of the nearest victim, who raised a dripping head, eagerly licking the liquor streaming down his face. The Mess screamed applause. 'Now me! Now me! Now me!'

'Siphons, Orderly! Siphons!'

'Yes, sir.'

'Sides, take sides! A Flight versus B and C Flights. Action all!'

Over went the table. Siphons appeared by magic. The offensive was launched.

Squirt! Scream! Scream! Squirt! 'Oh you ... Got him! Right in the ... More! More! In the mouth! Give me another! Orderly! More siphons! Yes, sir. God, I'm wet! God, what a life!'

They collapsed, chairs dripping, tunics soaking, walls running, laughing, shouting, swearing, on to the puddled floor.

Cecil Lewis staggered back to his room in a local farmhouse. There he was dismayed to find his pillow black, his bed black, his chairs, table, ceiling all covered with a film of soot. For hours the oil lamp had been smoking. In his account he describes himself as merely one of the pilots and writes in the third person.

'Can't shleep here. Goddam batman. Everything shooty.' A bright idea struck into his reeling mind: 'Shleep with Mam'sel! Shleep with Mam'sel!'

She was a heavy peasant girl, clogged and shawled, fruity with the rank odours of the farmyard. Her room lay through his. He lurched over and opened it.

'Mam'sel,' he announced, 'I – je ... dormez ... vous ... Savey?'

'*Oui, oui, venez,*' said a stupid voice in the darkness. He groped in the stuffy, feather-bedded darkness, found her in the darkness ... God, what a drunk! What a bloody wonderful drunk![4]

'"The bloody wonderful drunk" was the welcome relief that some found from the sterner reality ... and the nervous tension that it caused in so many,'[5] wrote Sholto Douglas, whose father was secretary of the Church of England Temperance Society and who had been brought up in an abstemious home. When he became a squadron commander he saw the necessity for parties as a safety valve. 'I used to organise them myself from time to time so that my pilots could let off steam.' But, he added, he had to limit their frequency because he quickly discovered that 'we could not indulge in heavy drinking and fighting in the air at the same time'.

All too often the parties were a forced antidote to the death of a colleague. The pilots, according to Ira Jones, didn't do grief, or at least, not public expressions of it. 'Air fighting,' he wrote,

was generally looked upon as a game by most pilots – just like rugger. If one of the team in rugger is seriously hurt, he is carried sympathetically off the field, but the game carries on just the same.

This spirit of 'carry on' found its counterpart only to a greater degree in the RFC spirit. This aggressively offensive spirit could not tolerate sorrow, for sorrow was liable to lower the morale. Though it might hide in the bosom of the pilot, it was only permitted to exude in the secret seclusion of his sleeping quarters. In the mess it was an unwritten law for pilots to forget the sorrow and assume a cheerfulness which gave the impression to the casual visitor of 'living for the day'.

Thus was morale maintained at an unusually high level ... Without such a tradition the strongest of spirits would soon break under the excessive nervous strain of terrifying combats and personal losses.[6]

Some of the mess binges to bury grief became the most violent. Reporting one of these to his wife, Arthur Gould Lee described the fearsomely potent cocktail known as 'Health and Strength' that became 46 Squadron's standard pre-dinner drink on party nights. 'Everyone has to like it whether he does or not. It's made of eggs, brandy, port and several kinds of liquor. We drink it at the dinner table, one foot on the chair, the other on the table, to the toast, "Cheerio, Forty-Six", yelled very, very ear-splittingly.'[7]

Billy Bishop, the Canadian who had signed up as an observer and had become a pilot with more than twenty kills to his credit, was said to have once performed in front of General Trenchard, no less, a drunken tap dance on top of 60 Squadron's piano. The commander-in-chief had been persuaded to attend one of the pilots' parties. 'Mellowed by a generous amount of the squadron's best champagne, Trenchard watched benignly as Bishop, equally thoroughly lubricated', climbed up on to the piano and clattered away. As he danced he sang (to the tune of the 'Tarpaulin Jacket') a version of one of the Flying Corps' most celebrated ballads, 'The Dying Airman':

> Oh, the bold aviator was dying
> And as 'neath the wreckage he lay, he lay,
> To the sobbing mechanics about him
> These last parting words did he say:
>
> Two valves you'll find in my stomach
> Three sparkplugs are safe in my lung, my lung,
> The prop is in splinters inside me,
> To my fingers the joystick has clung.
>
> And get you six brandies and sodas
> And lay them all out in a row,
> And get you six other good airmen
> To drink to this pilot below.
>
> Take the cylinders out of my kidneys
> The connecting rod out of my brain, my brain,
> From the small of my back take the crankshaft
> And assemble the engine again.*

Since Bishop couldn't sing, his drunken rendering of the Flying Corps' hymn was less than impressive. He was 'roundly booed for his performance. And General Trenchard himself advised him, "My boy, stick to flying." Bishop blamed the pianist . . . who, in turn, blamed the piano. It was, he complained, "dried out".

---

* In its scores of lyric versions, the 'Dying Airman' song refuses to die. It was regularly sung in officers' messes during WWII and endures within the RAF to this day.

'"We can't have a dry piano in *this* mess," said Bishop, and poured a quart of champagne into the instrument. It was three o'clock in the morning before the weary, happy celebrants made their way to bed for a few hours' sleep before dawn patrol.'[8]

When the aircrew drank to numb their tensions, the copious quantities of often neat alcohol released inhibitions in a euphoric flood. Amid whoops of laughter from their colleagues, individuals would be seized and debagged for their genitalia to be inspected. Some would have their moustaches clipped off. Other victims had their shoes and socks removed and the soles of their feet anointed with soot before being hoisted up to plant their footprints for permanent exhibition on the ceiling. A variant of this procedure would leave a bare buttock-print on high. Scottish officers who had transferred to the RFC from Highland regiments were particularly vulnerable to mess indignities. They would be turned upside down to reveal what they wore, if anything, under their kilts. They took it good-naturedly, as did squadron commanders when, the distances of rank abandoned for the evening, they found themselves in this closely bonded male community being rolled about on the floor by their junior officers. 'To play his part to the uttermost,' said Harold Balfour, 'a Commanding Officer must be able to be a boy among boys.'

These drunken party games regularly hospitalised participants. Furniture would be smashed up and windows, along with legs and arms, broken in rugby matches with forceful scrummaging, using a cushion as the ball. Even more damaging to human limb was a notorious game known as High Cockalorum. In this destructive physical contest, two teams, each about a dozen strong, would line up in the mess anteroom facing each other, the defenders bent over, locked together in a long, single-row scrum. One after the other the attackers would charge across the room and leap on to their backs. 'Not,' wrote one pilot, 'a recommended sporting activity to suffer 12 stone, snorting, alcohol fuelled monsters landing one after the other on your back in a fashion likely to result in catastrophic failure of the middle vertebra.' To win the game the defenders had to survive the enormous load of sweating humanity for ten seconds without collapsing.* A puzzled American pilot attached to No. 85 Squadron commented: 'These Englishmen sure have a funny idea of a party. They want to smash everything.'

---

*High Cockalorum endured as a popular mess game in the RFC and RAF for nearly forty years until it was finally banned in the 1950s because of the high number of injuries it was causing.

The revelry stoked the obsession for practical jokes that had arrived in the squadrons from the public schools, a culture in which pranks – called 'japes' – played an essential part. Within the squadrons, where life for most would be tragically short, the japes acquired excessive and imaginative new dimensions in which animals from nearby farmyards played a popular role. Cows, pigs and chickens would be dragged back to the mess and pushed into the bedrooms of sleeping colleagues due to go on dawn patrol in a few hours.

Second Lieutenant George Coles, an observer with a bomber squadron whose officers were quartered in tents, described to his girlfriend, Connie, back in Preston, a violent apple fight staged by the aircrew in a nearby orchard. He'd finished up with a badly bruised face and black eye. When Connie expressed her shock at the escapade he wrote back:

> Yes, I think it quite a good job you are not in the Army dearie.
>
> We have to tolerate and laugh at quite a lot of things which we don't like – such as frequent drunks. The day before we left our last camp all the boys got drunk, smashed up all the mess crockery and furniture, pulled all of us sober ones out of bed, and let down every single tent to the ground. By 2am things quietened down and we all got back into our beds out in the open. About 2.30am it just commenced to pour down with rain and of course both we and all our kit got soaked.
>
> Although much can be said against such ramsammies, the boys enjoy them, and they certainly clear the air for any extra hard work which is in store.[9]

At some aerodromes there were inter-squadron raids which, at their most harmless, saw sacks of oranges showered on to rival mess buildings and, at their most dangerous, flaming signal flares fired down chimneys. Fire, without the help of the antics of inebriated pilots, was an ever-present danger. Harold Balfour described a devastating blaze that broke out one night at Treizennes aerodrome in one of the hangars of 40 Squadron, whose CO was the theatrical Robert Loraine, now a major. 'The petrol tanks had gone up, the doped wings were burning furiously, the dried wood of the hangar likewise, while machine-gun ammunition went off with continuous pops . . . There was nothing to be done except to form a semicircle around the blaze and let the fire burn itself out.' Suddenly, out of the dark, Loraine appeared. 'With a bound', he pulled aside a sergeant struggling to save some tools from the conflagration, shouting, 'in a voice of ringing tones which carried right across the aerodrome, "Away! If this is anybody's place it is mine."' Loraine, Balfour said, then 'strode to the middle of the arena and there, in the full glare of the light, performed a perfectly natural function in front of the admiring eyes of the assembled officers and mechanics'.[10]

The fire emergency that night had temporarily united officers and men, two groups who for the most part led parallel lives, divided by rank and class. Only the pilots and observers, most of whom were commissioned, enjoyed the comforts and privileges of the officers' mess; the mechanics lived in their own separate world on the same aerodrome. Between these domains there moved a small anomalous group of non-commissioned aircrew: the sergeant pilots and observers. Denied the society of their flying colleagues, yet having little in common with the mechanics whose mess they shared, their lot was not always a happy one.

Chapter 19
They Also Served

The pilots whose inferior rank required them to live apart from their commissioned colleagues in the sergeants' mess led a hybrid life. On two-seater reconnaissance squadrons they found themselves, as a lesser breed, serving as taxi drivers for their officer observers. 'I knew what time I was going up, but I didn't even know what job I was on until the observer came out,' recalled Sergeant George Eddington of No. 6 Squadron. 'I said, "Good morning, Sir" and we got on with our job. When we came down he got out and went to make his report. He did all the reporting – what he'd found, what he'd seen, what he'd photographed. I went to the sergeants' mess and we had no further contact.'

In the sergeants' mess Eddington, conspicuous by the wings on his tunic, was a solitary figure. He was not able to socialise or indulge in flying talk with his fellow pilots in the camaraderie of their club. His companions were mechanics, who spoke another language. 'I couldn't make friends. In the sergeants' mess they were all fitters and riggers – I wasn't in their world any more than they were in mine. It was dreadfully lonely.'[1] Not only was it lonely, but Eddington, as a sergeant, was paid less than a commissioned pilot for doing the same job, exposed to the same huge risks. The truth was that the War Office was never able satisfactorily to resolve this vexed two-class issue of inequality among its aviators.

From its birth the Flying Corps had insisted its aeroplanes be flown by officers. It was felt that 'a good pilot needed to possess much the same personal qualities as those traditionally associated with a commission'.[2] But, by the middle of 1917, as the RFC continued to expand and its aircrew losses mounted, there was competition for its officers. Front-line infantry regiments, suffering enormous daily casualties among their subalterns and lieutenants, were short of them. To try to solve the problem the War Office proposed a major increase in the numbers of the Flying Corps' non-commissioned pilots. The director of air organisation, the outspoken Brigadier-General Sefton Brancker, was dismayed at the suggestion, about which the military aviation generals had not been consulted. In one of his customary frank letters to Trenchard in France, he ridiculed the idea, saying it would have a disastrous effect on pilot recruitment. Potentially good people would simply not apply. The great point about giving a pilot a commission, he said, was that 'it raised his social status and brought him into the officers' mess, with the result that his morale was higher and he was more dependable than if he had been left without a commission'. Employing non-commissioned officers was a false economy. Its only result would be 'that the general average of efficiency would go down'.[3] Even stronger opposition came from some of the squadron commanders fighting the air war. One of them, Major C.T. Maclaren at 103 Squadron, complained that mixed-rank bomber crews never functioned as effectively as a two-man commissioned one The former performed 'indifferently', he said, 'because there is not the complete understanding of two Officers'.

At No. 48 Squadron the CO, Major Keith Park, a New Zealander who was later to head Fighter Command's imperishable 11 Group in the Battle of Britain, was sent nine sergeant pilots. He immediately had four of them posted home for further training and recommended that a fifth be consigned to the trenches. The three who survived his assessment, he said, had been the equal of officer pilots. 'If a man is of the right type and good enough to be a fighting pilot in a fighting unit, he should be commissioned.'[4]

More than a strong whiff of the class-ridden English society of the time, of course, overhung the whole issue. While many of the sergeant pilots were exceptionally competent military flyers, few were the products of public schools. It seems extraordinary today to read that one of the greatest British fighter pilots of the war, James McCudden, was rejected as a possible CO by the pilots of 85 Squadron because of his working-class origins.

'The general came over and had tea with us and asked who we wanted for CO,' wrote an American pilot attached to the squadron. 'He wanted to send us McCudden but we don't want him. He gets Huns himself but he doesn't give anybody else a chance at them. The rest of the squadron objected because he was once a Tommy [a private soldier] and his father was a sergeant-major in the old army. I couldn't see that was anything against him but these English have great ideas of caste.'[5] There was possibly an additional reason behind the spurning of McCudden. The squadron had a reputation for partying hard and some of its pilots had a prodigious capacity for alcohol. McCudden, a serious man who hated the wild binges, was uncomfortable with the boisterous knockabout shenanigans of the mess party and believed that excessive drinking undermined a squadron's effectiveness in the air. There was little doubt within

85 Squadron that as CO he would have firmly curtailed the revelry.

Even more of a separate breed than the sergeant pilots were the squadrons' large workforces of mechanics. The pilots had little direct contact with these unglorified heroes of the air war who maintained their frequently battle-damaged aeroplanes and the engines that were sometimes tortured to near-destruction in the heat of combat. The class barrier between gentlemen and tradesmen was rigidly maintained. Pilots dealt with the supervising NCOs and rarely visited the hangars. The prodigies of devoted maintenance and massive repairs, performed round the clock, were mostly taken for granted by stressed-out aircrew. Yet, 'upon their careful tuning of engines, their skilful adjustment of rigging wires, their accurate sighting of machine guns, many lives had long depended'. A squadron's successes were 'theirs to share with the boldest of those pilots whose names still head the honours board'.[6]

Emotionally involved every day in the fate of the men whose machines they cared for, the mechanics, who might work eighteen-hour shifts from 3am to 9pm and were lucky to get two full nights' sleep a week, would wait anxiously for their safe return – by no means a guaranteed event. 'Mechanics are human beings, very human sometimes,' Corporal William Dalton, of 32 Squadron, wrote to one of his pilots, Lieutenant Gwilym Lewis, who was in hospital. 'It is awful for them to see these men, good and true gentlemen in the true sense of the word, going off with a "Cheerio" never to return. My nerve was as steady as a rock until I saw Lieutenant Bentley killed at Vert Galant – I held him down in his death agony – and since then it has not been worth a damn.'[7]

The diffident letters sent by some of the mechanics to the pilots to whom they'd become attached reflected their awareness of where they belonged in the pecking order of military life. 'May I congratulate you on your well earned promotion,' one of them wrote to a pilot who'd just been appointed a flight commander. 'Perhaps I am not quite in order here as there is such a vast gap between an ordinary corporal and a captain, but in civilian life, I believe we are not so far apart ... You have been a sport and a gentleman to me since I first had the honour to be your mechanic.' The corporal, expressing the hope that the officer wouldn't feel he was being 'too familiar', ended: 'Jolly good luck, I remain your faithful mechanic.'[8]

Popular pilots were given emotional farewells by the ground staff. When the Australian Bill Taylor at 66 Squadron was posted back to England he went to the hangars to say goodbye to the men who'd looked after his favourite Sopwith Scout, No. 7309.

Flight Sergeant Ramsay had them standing to attention to receive me with the clap of his heels and his hand quivering at the traditional salute, which I returned. I said a few words to acknowledge his soldierly manners. Then we all sat down on the grass and talked for a while of all that had happened in the months we had known each other.

It was difficult to know what to say. There was so much, that to say anything seemed almost an affront to their loyalty and their understanding.

I thought back to the day I had come in with severed control wires trailing in the grass and Ellins had told, simply, how he had duplicated them a few days before.

I knew how McFall and the others had repeatedly worked all night to get new engines in for me as the Le Rhones chewed themselves to pieces under the stresses of the unmerciful treatment we had to give them.

I remembered how the armourers had checked every round before loading the clips for the Vickers to give me the best chance of firing with a minimum of stoppages.

I saw these patient, skilful, decent men: friends whose unsung work had kept me in the air and had had a big part in bringing me back from more than a hundred patrols – and I knew that anything I could say would be inadequate.

When Taylor's Crossley tender arrived to take him to the train the mechanics leaped to their feet and lined up in a row. 'I shook hands all round and went down over the hill, and away.'[9]

From time to time officers and other ranks came together to stage concerts and occasionally, more ambitiously, full-length plays. When actor Robert Loraine arrived at Treizennes to command No. 40 Squadron he commandeered a hut and converted it into a theatre. One of the first plays produced was Bernard Shaw's as yet unpublished *The Inca of Perusalem*. It was put on in honour of the great playwright, who happened to be visiting the squadron on a tour of the Western Front. One of the pilots, Frederick Powell, was astonished at Shaw's reaction to the performance. He roared with such continuous laughter throughout that he had to keep wiping his eyes. 'It struck me at the time that it was extremely bad form for a playwright to laugh at his own comedy until he cried,' wrote Powell. 'When it was finished I said, "I'm so glad, sir, that you appreciated our poor efforts at your play." He turned round, still wiping his eyes, and he said, "Do you know, if I had thought it was going to be anything like that I wouldn't have written it." [10]

A vital stratum of the lower orders of squadron life for the commissioned pilot was his personal servant. The batmen, or orderlies, were men too old or unfit for more active military service. Unlike their more rugged infantry counterparts, who lived amid the terror and squalor of the trenches, expected, fully armed, to accompany their officers over the top in bayonet charges across no-man's-land, the Flying Corps servants functioned in a less dangerous milieu, more like butlers. They laid out their officers' clothes, cleaned their shoes, polished their buttons, made their beds. In the dark before dawn, they would wake the pilots due on patrol with cups of tea.

'I have exchanged the saintly Ball for a very martial and clicking batman rejoicing in the name of West,' the Australian pilot Geoffrey Wall told his mother on his arrival at a new aerodrome. 'He is much more of a soldier than I would be in a lifetime and clicks and jumps about in a most annoying manner. Started unpacking my kit on Wednesday – dragging the unfortunate golliwog out of the bottom of my kitbag, remarking with never a smile, "And where will you have this, sir?" '[11]

At the front-line squadrons the pilots' servants found they weren't serving the same young officer for long. On arrival at 46 Squadron at La Gorgue, Arthur Gould Lee went to his hut to unpack. To his surprise he discovered it had already been done for him by a batman called Watt. 'He said he'd been batman to Mr Gunnery, and what a nice gentleman he was, and how he was the second gentleman he, Watt, had had killed, and how very depressing it was the way they went off in the morning, bright and hearty, and just never came back. I sympathised and said I hoped I wouldn't ever give him cause for further depression.'[12]

Because many of the young men they served would be gone in a few weeks, the batmen pampered them. A pilot newly arrived in France was amazed to hear one of the officers issuing instructions to his man.

'Is that you, Dowsing?'

'Yes, sir.'

'I'm off for a raid. Fill my hot water bottle about a quarter to nine and put it right at the bottom of the bed. If you think the fire too hot, move my pyjamas back.'

'Good luck, sir.'[13]

It wasn't only the mechanics and batmen who watched anxiously for the return of their pilots. Their dogs did too, some of them developing an uncanny ability to identify, among a dozen returning aeroplanes, their master's own machine, which they would joyfully run out to meet. Canadian 2nd Lieutenant MacLeod at 46 Squadron had been chosen by a stray 'melancholy-eyed mongrel' he called Sandy. It slept on his bed and hung around the hangars when MacLeod was flying, waiting for him to come back.

'On the day Mac crashed, Sandy stayed up at the hangar until it was closed, when the flight sergeant brought him down to our mess,' Arthur Gould Lee told his wife. 'For days he's been wandering round the huts and cubicles, refusing food, just looking for Mac. He avoided anybody who tried to stroke him, including me, and has just sickened away. This morning we found him lying outside Mac's old cubicle, almost unable to move. We knew he had to be put out of his misery, but nobody had the heart to do it. At last Robeson took him away into the orchard and put a bullet through his poor little head.'[14]

To minister to the spiritual needs and 'moral welfare' of the flying crews army chaplains were attached to the front-line air bases. Many of them had left peaceful vicarages in England to risk their lives amid the mud, death and destruction of the trenches. Here, transplanted from their safe and gentle pulpits into hell on earth, they were liable to find themselves under heavy fire, administering the last rites to mortally wounded men or tending the grievously wounded, often limbless and disembowelled, lying in muddy shell holes out in no-man's-land. The padres were a special caste in the military machine. Many were killed or wounded, some earned gallantry medals and no fewer than three were awarded the Victoria Cross for carrying wounded men under heavy fire to the safety of a trench.

The British Expeditionary Force's deeply religious commander, General Haig, infused his armies with the belief they were fighting a just and righteous cause in which God was emphatically on the Allied side. The German army claimed exactly the same, issuing uniform buckles stamped 'Gott mit uns' (God with us). 'I know quite well,' Haig wrote in 1916, 'that I am being used as a tool in the hands of the Divine Power.'

Under Haig's patronage the army's corps of chaplains, predominantly Church of England and armed only with prayer books, took the word of God on to the front line, encouraging soldiers to maintain their faith in the face of the horrors that constantly threatened it. In the Flying Corps squadrons, beyond the range of ground fire, their role was less arduous. In military uniform in the rank of captain, most wearing their clerical collars, they lived in the officers' mess, many becoming emotionally involved in the operational lives of the flying crews. Some would rise before dawn to give pilots going on patrol their blessing, and would be out on the airfield to await their return. They wrote letters to the families of airmen who didn't, conducted burial services for those killed on the Allied side of the lines, comforted pilots near the end of their tether and held regular services distinguished by their informality and absence of ritual. One much-published photograph shows a padre, prayer book in hand, using as his pulpit the cockpit of an aeroplane in which he is standing, surrounded by a large group of pilots and ground staff sitting on the grass.

But as was the case with the growing numbers of ground troops whose faith was being tested, the brutality of the air war led a few pilots into a deep cynicism summed up by a mock prayer: 'O God, if there is a God, save my soul, if I have a soul.' 'Why should God grant me any special favour?' Arthur Gould Lee responded to his wife, who had asked why he didn't pray before a mission. 'The Hun I'm fighting may be calling on Him too. It isn't as though I have any great faith in religion, but even if I had, would it divert a bullet? Anyway, how can anybody who has to fight believe in God, with all the mass killings, and with the British, French and German priests all shouting that God is on their side? How can I call on God to help me shoot down a man in flames?'[15]

The rival claims for the Almighty's support were poetically described by an anonymous French pilot who witnessed the strange sight of opposing troops in the process of worshipping the same God.

I was flying over the firing-line. Between our first lines and their first lines – it's not very far; sometimes forty yards, sometimes sixty. To me it looked about a stride, at the great height where I was planing. And behold I could make out two crowds, one among the Boches, and one of ours, in these parallel lines that seemed to touch each other ... So I went down several turns to investigate.

Then I understood. It was Sunday, and there were two religious services being held under my eyes – the altar, the padre, and all the crowd of chaps. The more I went down the more I could see that the two things were alike – so exactly alike that it looked silly. One of the services – whichever you like – was a reflection of the other, and I wondered if I was seeing double. I went down lower; they didn't fire at me ... I heard one murmur. One only. I could only gather a single prayer that came up to me en bloc, the sound of a single chant that passed by me on its way to heaven ... they were blended together up in the heights of the sky where I was floating.

I got some shrapnel just at the moment when, very low down, I made out the two voices from the earth that made up the one – 'Gott mit uns!' and 'God is with us!' – and I flew away. What must the good God think about it all? . . . He won't know what to make of it.[16]

Most of the British pilots maintained a dogged belief in the deity, fatalistically convinced that their fate lay entirely in His hands. 'Out here we don't know creeds or anything else,' a 74 Squadron Canadian pilot, Leonard Richardson, told his mother. 'It's just having God to fall back on and to know, whether we win our scrap or go under, that it's just what He wanted. We can't remember that all the time; it seems there are times when we forget it. But we always know.'[17] And when an aunt of the 56 Squadron ace Arthur Rhys Davids wrote to him a few months before his death, saying she knew that God was looking after him, he replied: 'I love what you say about the Great Presence always helping me. But I am quite happy to think that if I am going to do any good in this place the good God will see me through, and if not, well I do not mind going to rest at once.'[18]

Very little has ever been written about the army chaplains who served with the Flying Corps. But, in the little that has, the name of one emerges as someone rather special. Padre Bernard Keymer, a product of both Oxford and Cambridge, the vicar of Eastleigh in Hampshire, was not your conventional Anglican clergyman. When, in February 1917, in his early forties, having been mentioned twice in dispatches for dragging wounded men through barbed wire to safety in the trenches, he joined the Flying Corps' 40 Squadron at Bruay, and arrived as a gust of clerical fresh air. Refusing to wear a dog collar, he opened in a Nissen hut a church he named St Michael, in which he preached a muscular brand of Christianity often laced with earthy humour and instantly became one of the boys. Fondly known as 'the Old Man', he gently integrated himself into the pilot force. To many he was a wonderfully trusted friend and confidant. Many letters home speak of the uplifting effect on their morale of this balding, pipe-smoking father figure, referring to him with admiration and affection.

'He is a wonder parson, a raconteur, a sportsman and a tomboy.' Captain Bill Bond frequently wrote to his wife Aimée about Keymer, whom he jokingly dubbed 'The Odd Man'. 'Just now he is working hard trying to level the ground in the middle of our huts to make a tennis court.' Bond described one of the padre's Sunday night services. It was held, he said, in the anteroom of the squadron mess where the walls were decorated with an array of pin-ups of the sexually provocative 'Kirchner Girls'.* 'Before the service could start we had to cut off George Robey – in the middle of a doubtful song – on the gramophone. The Odd Man explained that he wanted to make it a meeting rather than a service; therefore after prayers and a few hymns he proposed we should smoke while he gave us an address. It stimulated thought, he said.'[19]

Bond described the padre's affinity with the pilots and his fatherly concerns for their safety.

> It is worth a good deal to see him on the aerodrome when any big stunt is going forward. He was down there to watch us start for the balloon strafe. He was fearfully grave and just walked round the machines – hardly saying a word. I don't think he expected any of us to return.
>
> I was the second to get back. I lost my engine on landing and stopped on the far side. The Odd Man sprinted out, beating the Ack Emmas [air mechanics] by yards.
>
> 'Any luck?' he shouted. He was fearfully excited.
>
> 'Yes, it's alright,' I said.
>
> 'Oh, damn good!' he exclaimed. 'Damn good ... Absolutely topping!'
>
> The others came in at intervals, and he beat the CO and everybody in welcoming them. He ran from pilot to pilot, saying 'Damn good! ... How completely splendid!'
>
> The CO joined him in a duet of jubilation and supplemented his 'damn good' with extracts from the new vocabulary.[20]

Increasingly Padre Keymer found himself called upon to comfort pilots at the edge of their nervous endurance. The psychological balm he dispensed worked because he was seen as much as a concerned friend as a military parson. A lot of his quiet counselling, pilots recalled, was given on the tennis court he created for them and on which they were impressed to discover he could easily trounce most of them. Unusually for a padre, he insisted on joining them in their off-duty escapades, during which they were staggered by his astonishingly youthful stamina and exuberance.

'The squadron did a thrilling exploit last night,' Bill Bond wrote.

---

*The work of the Austrian artist Raphael Kirchner, the erotic posters of Parisian girls in various states of undress were wildly popular on the Western Front, pinned up everywhere from the trenches to officers' messes.

It went bathing at midnight. The Odd Man, of course, was the leader.

Some miles away there is a most topping valley occupied by a chateau and its grounds. A river runs through it and about a week ago the CO and the Odd Man got permission to dam the stream. The squadron did the work and it was finished yesterday. After dinner the CO suggested that we should all go and bathe in the pool.

We had a tender and fifteen of us went – some of us armed with pocket lamps and all attired in pyjamas, towels and flying coats.

The water was beautifully deep and clean; it was eerie to see the naked bodies scrambling about the barrier of tree trunks.

The Odd Man was the noisiest of the crowd. He did high dives into the black pool, shouting and splashing like a water baby.[21]

Keymer's liberal attitude to the excesses of squadron life also endeared him to the pilots. Gwilym Lewis was amazed to hear him urging them to let their hair down on Christmas, of all days. 'Our padre,' he told his parents, 'says he sees no reason why everyone should not get thoroughly tight! He is a splendid fellow.'[22] When the pilots repaired to the cafés and restaurants of nearby towns for a change from mess food, to carouse and to seek the company of women, the padre would go, too, matching them drink for drink and in the process witnessing from time to time the efforts of some to seek transitory relief from their battle stress in the arms of French girls.

The finer details of the padre's lively involvement with the off-duty lives of his young pilot colleagues was evidently not something he fully shared with his wife, Ellen, back in England. After his death in 1925 Ellen, in a letter to one of her daughters speaking of how he 'gave his life to God', described a rather stricter, more conventional military priest, one who, far from encouraging indulgence in wine and women, she wrote proudly, saved a 'number of boys and men he had salvaged as regards drink, fornication and this and that'[23] during his war service.*

---

*Bernard Keymer served as padre with a number of RFC squadrons and was twice mentioned in dispatches. His name is often confused with that of his elder brother, the Reverend Basil Nathaniel Keymer, who was also a military chaplain with the BEF in France. After the war Bernard was given a permanent commission and became the RAF's deputy chaplain-in-chief. When he died of pleurisy in 1925 at the early age of forty-nine he was vicar at St Mark's Church, South Farnborough, Hampshire. Two of his sons were killed in WWII serving as RAF pilots.

The fornication referred to by Padre Keymer's widow was extensively practised. Licensed brothels, established by the French Army, were always within reach. They brought brisk British military business as well. Photographs show long lines of men in uniform in a bombed-out landscape, waiting for the door of a small cottage to open. The poet Robert Graves described a queue outside a busy establishment in Béthune.

> The Red Lamp, the army brothel, was around the corner in the main street. I had seen a queue of a hundred and fifty men waiting outside the door, each to have his short turn with one of the three women in the house. My servant, who had stood in the queue, told me that the charge was ten francs a man – about eight shillings at that time. Each woman served nearly a battalion of men every week for as long as she lasted. According to the assistant provost-marshal, three weeks was the usual limit: 'after which she retired on her earnings, pale but proud'.[24]

Safer sex was available for a select few. In Channel ports British girls, WAACs and FANYs, were to be found. Although under orders never to be alone with a man, some members of the Women's Army Auxiliary Corps and the First Aid Nursing Yeomanry would, in a little-known Boulogne restaurant, arrange clandestine meetings with staff officers. However, most officers had to be content with the run-of-the-mill military brothels reserved for them and advertised by their blue lamps. Here a reputedly rather better class of French prostitute worked. 'I was always being teased,' Graves said, 'because I would not sleep even with the nicer girls; and I excused myself, not on moral grounds or on grounds of fastidiousness, but in the only way that they could understand: I said that I didn't want a dose.'

The risk of venereal disease was perilously high. Condoms, yet to arrive in general use, were in any case discouraged as encouraging 'vice'. The only form of prophylaxis to be had was a post-coital calomel ointment. The official British line was abstinence. The army, while recognising 'that during war the sexual instinct is stimulated in both sexes, and . . . there is a tendency towards slackening of moral principles', was concerned by the increasingly large number of men lost to its fighting battalions with venereal disease and treated it unsympathetically as a self-inflicted wound. Viewing it as a wholly avoidable, moral issue, the Royal Army Medical Corps neatly created three categories of men based on their vulnerability to temptation: 'the man who, by nature or training is endowed to resist incontinence; the man who falls to temptation; and the man who deliberately sets out to gratify his sexual appetite'.[25] On the orders of Lord Kitchener, leaflets had been issued advising servicemen 'to avoid strong drink and to respect womankind; to be chaste and to be temperate'. The advice was widely ignored.

Not all Flying Corps pilots were as cautious as Robert Graves. Lieutenant William Earl Johns of 55 Squadron, later (writing under the name Captain W.E. Johns) to become celebrated as the creator of the immortal pilot adventurer James Bigglesworth, the hero of more than a hundred Biggles books for boys, found himself in hospital in France suffering from both syphilis and gonorrhoea.[26] The cure, if one was possible, was unpleasant. Before the arrival of antibiotics, treatment might involve the oral or intravenous administration of poisonous arsenic or mercury-based drugs and sometimes a notorious, much-dreaded and painfully brisk scraping of the patient's urinary tract. To be shipped back to Britain with venereal disease was the ultimate disgrace in a prudish society that preferred to veil the unspeakable subject with silence. None the less young men, determined to lose their virginity before they died, threw caution to the winds.

Cecil Lewis was one of many. Avoiding the risky pleasures of the blue lamp he had, some weeks before he had drunkenly invited himself into the peasant girl's bed, been introduced in Amiens by a French-Canadian fellow pilot to the young mistress of a French army officer who happened to be away in Paris. As with his description of his encounter with the farmer's daughter Lewis, in his book, disguises himself as 'a young man' new to 'the world of cocottes and demi-mondes'.

The girl, who looked at first, he said, to be no more than a child, led him that night through a maze of deserted cobbled streets to her small first-floor room, which was almost entirely occupied by a large double bed.

She took off her hat and coat and shook out her bobbed hair ... Conversation was going to be difficult. He sat on the bed.

'*Quel ... âge ... avez ... vous?*' he began.

She dropped on to his knee unconcernedly and put an arm round his neck.

'*Dix-huit*! Eighteen!' She giggled. 'I do not speak English very good.'

With a good deal of gesticulation and laughter he managed to understand that she did not have friends to see her usually. She had one particular friend, but he had been away a long time now and she was bored.

She stood up and went to the fire. '*Tu veux rester?*' she said, as if she were quite prepared to hear that he did not want to, as if she were not sure whether her charms were sufficient to make anyone want to stay.

'Yes,' he said, and took off his greatcoat. She saw the wings on his tunic.

'*Ah! Tu es pilote! Que j'aime les pilotes!*'

'Yes?'

'Yais! Yais!' she imitated, deftly catching a handful of his hair and tugging at it '*Tu es beau, tu sais.*' She was on his knee again, and under her open blouse the hollow of her young shoulder seemed infinite in its promise . . .

He stayed with her for an age, for a moment, for some period incalculable by the dreary turning of clocks, and at last was ready to go.

At the door the girl clung to him and exacted a promise. That if he ever saw her again in Amiens he would not attempt to speak to her. '"Mon ami," she said, "he kill me if he know. I when I see you, I not know you." (And, indeed, when he saw her again, weeks later, in the same café, with a French officer at her side, she looked at him blankly as one looks at an undesirable stranger.)'

Lewis stole out of the house and found his way back through the blackness of the city to the square. The French-Canadian and another pilot were waiting there for him. They, too, had spent the evening with French girls. The squadron tender hadn't waited for them. So they went to a hotel to fortify themselves with large brandies and sodas before setting off to walk the many miles back to the aerodrome in the moonlight. 'Curiously, they were all three silent about the later part of the evening. Too ordinary a thing? Too shameful a thing? It would be hard to say.' Instead they linked arms as the French-Canadian, who had arranged the evening's pleasures, began to sing 'Alouette, gentille alouette . . .'[27]

This demonstration of brotherhood was bred by what Arthur Gould Lee called 'a tight squadron spirit'.

We pilots live in a world of our own . . . so wrapped up in our daily routine of patrols, and the excitements of scraps, that we're not interested in what goes on outside . . . We seldom talk to each other about our private affairs. You seldom get to know much about a fellow's background . . . The only thing that counts is whether a chap has guts and can shoot straight. You share the same risks every day. Some get shot down the other side, and that's the last you hear of them. Some go home, and probably that's the last you hear of them, too. Yet, here in France, we're a sort of brotherhood. It's a rum life.[28]

Chapter 20
The Majors

The majors who commanded the Flying Corps squadrons set their tone, morale and the measure of their fighting spirit. They were supposed to be carefully chosen. Commanding groups of highly individualistic, frequently outspoken pilots, all of whom had their own views on how the squadron should operate in the air, called, one historian wrote, 'for a form of democratic dictatorship, a formulation of majority opinion, a leadership of equals ... Spit-and-polish majors, or majors unable to argue and convince or unbend and play, were quickly sent home to training squadrons, where such rigidity did less immediate damage.' But there still arrived at squadrons COs who lacked the essential touch. Hugh Dowding, the wing commander who had clashed with Trenchard over his concern to preserve the lives of his exhausted pilots had, despite his core of humanity, earlier been a remote and unpopular failure at No. 16 Squadron. There, his developing abilities as a great air warfare commander notwithstanding, he had been a reserved and aloof figure who came to preside over a unit of unhappy pilots who used to refer to him as 'old starched shirt', a tag that morphed into the lifelong nickname 'Stuffy'. His shyness and distance somehow cast a shadow over the entire squadron and, as the nervous, nineteen-year-old Duncan Grinnell-Milne found on being posted there with a tiny number of flying hours, created a band of unusually subdued pilots and distinctly unfriendly flight commanders.

The squadron mess was on a floating barge on the river Lys, near enough to the front line for the voice of the guns to sound like thunder. 'There were very few officers about,' wrote Grinnell-Milne, 'and the one or two I met were strangely distant, offhand, unwilling or unable to speak. Near the river I met one who so far broke the ice as to ask me to which Flight I had been posted. I told him. He nodded down the river bank to a line of canvas hangars. "There's your Flight Commander," he said.'

> Glad to know of someone to whom I had a legitimate right to speak, I hurried off.

'Come from Gosport, have you?' he remarked when I had explained my presence. 'H'm – how much flying have you done?'

'Thirty-three and a half hours.'

'How much?' he exclaimed, but he meant, 'how little'. And he went on to declare violently that it was a disgrace to send pilots to a squadron on active service who did not have fifty, no, a hundred hours to their credit. What types had I flown? Longhorn? Of course, but that was no damn use! Caudron? Good Lord – that was worse than nothing. Ah, so I had flown a BE, had I? What sort of a BE? Not the latest type, with the new undercarriage and the 90 horsepower engine? No? Well then – no good. A Shorthorn? So I had actually had the goodness to fly a Shorthorn. Well, I should fly more of them here.

'And stand to attention when I'm speaking to you,' he concluded sharply. 'And salute when you wish to address me, and call me "sir", and put your cap on straight!'

I slunk wretchedly away, wishing myself dead and decently buried. No wonder people spoke of the horrors of war, this Flight Commander must be one of them.

Grinnell-Milne later discovered that the unpleasant captain, whom he discreetly avoided naming in his memoirs, referring to him only as 'Growl', was 'not such a bad fellow as he made himself out to be'. Although 'addicted to raving and ranting ... he could be quite amusing and his heart, deeply buried, was in the right place. But at the time I was thoroughly crestfallen; joining this squadron was worse than being a new boy at school. Boarding the barge, I went to hide my shame in the little cabin which had been allotted to me.'[2]

At dinner that night there was so little conversation among the pilots Grinnell-Milne wondered if he had not 'by some chance strayed into a colony of Trappists'. Almost everyone 'seemed afflicted with unnatural reserve'. The dominant sound was that of the nearby guns, their incessant firing flickering the horizon with continuous orange and green flashes. 'Alone the two flight commanders spoke with any freedom, seated one on either side of an empty chair in which, I supposed, the squadron commander would presently take his place. Only one other pilot spoke much above a whisper, and he was a man who had recently been awarded a Military Cross for bringing down a German machine ... I would have liked to talk with him, to listen to his account of the fight. But he was very sullen, with a perpetual scowl on his face. He spoke only to the

senior flight commander, who gave him a patronising smile every now
and then.'

It wasn't until halfway through the meal that Major Dowding arrived
to take the empty chair, 'murmuring faintly, "Don't get up, don't get up,"
as everyone rose to his feet'.

When we were all seated again, Growl, my flight commander,
suddenly remembered me and I had to walk round the table to
shake hands while the entire company stared in open-mouthed
silence as if I were some newly discovered disease. The major gave
me a limp hand together with a tired smile, and if I had not been so
nervous myself I should have seen at once that, amongst other
things, he was cursed with shyness.

After I had returned to my place dead silence reigned which he
attempted to break by speaking to everyone in turn. But it was
always with that same tired little smile ... He seemed satisfied at
rarely eliciting anything more than a 'Yes, sir', or 'No, sir', by way
of response. Conversation dwindled gradually to a sort of timid
squeaking of mice in the wainscot when the cat is near. It was plain
that he was not popular in the squadron.

And yet, Grinnell-Milne said, it was apparent that Dowding

was in many ways a good man. In the long run I came to esteem
him as much as any member of that peculiar squadron. He was
efficient, strict and calm; he had a sense of duty. But he was too
reserved and aloof from his juniors; he cared too much for his own
job, too little for theirs ... The flight commanders could hardly be
inspired by his leadership. Joy was not the only thing lacking. The
very life seemed, to my first ignorant glance, to be ebbing from the
mess in the barge as though we were the doomed crew of a derelict
ship.

Towards the end of dinner my neighbour at table jogged my
elbow.

'Pass the bread, please,' he said in a hoarse whisper.

I had been spoken to.[3]

Despite his pathetically few flying hours, not enough even to get him
a private pilot's licence today, Grinnell-Milne came to terms with his
initially dispiriting existence at 16 Squadron. He went on to distinguish
himself as a Flying Corps pilot and highly decorated ace.

At the other end of the spectrum of popularity from the dour Hugh

Dowding there existed a very different style of squadron commander – as a Flying Corps brigadier-general discovered one day when, with a posse of his staff officers, he descended before breakfast upon No. 60 Squadron at Filescamp aerodrome for a surprise tour of inspection. As the group arrived the squadron's CO had just landed back from a dawn patrol, on which, unusually for a squadron commander, he regularly flew and fought, leading his pilots into battle. As the Nieuport Scout taxied in, the general was astonished to see that its occupant, who had to be lifted out of the cockpit by his mechanics and handed a pair of walking sticks, had been flying in his pyjamas and dressing gown. Major Jack Scott, who hobbled across to greet him, had been semi-crippled for life in a crash during his flying training that had left him with two broken legs. He could walk properly only with the aid of sticks.

Not only for his courage but for his agreeable and sympathetic style of command, Scott had become within the Flying Corps a legend among the legendaries. Born in New Zealand, he had grown up in England, gone to Oxford and become a barrister in civilian life. He was also a personal friend of Winston Churchill, whose flying instructor he had been. Now in his mid-thirties, he was fifteen years older than most of the pilots he led. But they had come to like and admire this inspirational, openly eccentric CO, so permanently cheerful, who treated them with unfailing charm and good humour. And although described by Sholto Douglas, under whom he had served as a flight commander at another squadron, as 'a ham-fisted pilot', Scott, despite his disability, had become an ace credited with five victories. His pugnacious fighting tactics were as reckless as Albert Ball's. Outnumbered by big enemy formations he would dive without hesitation into their midst and only luck had saved him in an encounter with a deadly German ace, Karl Allmenröder.

'At first,' wrote Douglas, 'I felt rather awkward about giving orders to this thirty-five-year-old who was obviously a man of the world. I felt that such orders coming from a whipper-snapper of just twenty-three might be resented. But Jack Scott was to teach me a very good lesson, both in the balance of maturity and the handling of men.'[4] If anything, Scott's niceness led him sometimes to generosities that may not have been justified – especially when it came to pilots' unwitnessed victory claims. 'His one fault was that, being such a gentlemanly sort of chap, he thought the best of everybody. He may have been a little tolerant in accepting combat claims from almost everyone when perhaps there was some doubt.'[5]

Some cases were subsequently to create a great deal more than doubt. One in particular was to become a *cause célèbre* that would still be reverberating nearly seventy years later.

Chapter 21

The Raid That Never Was

In the dawn twilight, a few minutes before four o'clock on the morning of 2 June 1917, a lone Nieuport Scout took off in low cloud and drizzle from 60 Squadron's base at Filescamp Farm near Arras. Its pilot was the Canadian Billy Bishop who, in little more than two months, had been credited with a phenomenally large harvest of twenty-two victories. He was headed, on this solitary mission of his own planning, to make a low-level attack on an enemy aerodrome around seventeen miles over the lines near the French city of Cambrai. About an hour and forty minutes later he returned, jubilantly firing Very flares from the cockpit as he approached to land at 5.40am. Back in the mess he had a fantastic story to tell. He claimed to have attacked an enemy aerodrome and to have destroyed three German aircraft, two of them as they took off to intercept him, and one in the air.

Bishop's 60 Squadron commander, Major Scott, to whom he handed his combat report, was so impressed by this audacious and dangerous raid he decided to recommend Bishop for an immediate gallantry medal. Although there were no witnesses, or any other corroboration of the assault, and Bishop didn't even know for sure the name of the target airfield, he was, to many people's surprise, given the huge honour of a Victoria Cross. It was to prove the most controversial award in the history of Britain's most prestigious military gallantry medal and air historians were still heatedly questioning its validity into the twenty-first century.

What precisely did Bishop claim he had done that day? The fullest account he ever provided of the mission is contained in his own war memoir, published in 1918. For a report of an attack that may not actually have happened it is remarkable for its length and vividly descriptive detail. It also, with undisguised candour, reveals that the principal purpose of the raid was simply to add a large bunch of victories to his total in one swift strike. 'I saw I had a rare chance of really getting a lot before going on my next leave,' he explained. 'I had carefully thought it out, and came to the conclusion that if one could get to an aerodrome when there were machines on the ground, and none in the air, it would be an easy matter to shoot them down the moment they would attempt to come up.'

The previous evening Bishop had written his name on the mess black-board to be called at three o'clock 'and sat down, for the last time, to consider exactly if the job was worth the risk. However, as nothing like it had been done before, I knew that I would strike the Huns by surprise, and, considering that, I decided the risk was not nearly as great as it seemed, and that I might be able to get four or five more machines to my credit in one great swoop.'

When he was woken Bishop roused two fellow pilots whom he'd earlier invited to join him, but both declined. One of them told him a solitary attack deep in German airspace likely to be stiff with enemy fighters was suicidal. So, as the first streaks of dawn began to appear in a misty, drizzling sky, Bishop took off from Filescamp in his Nieuport Scout alone and flew east towards the lines. As he crossed into hostile territory and headed for his chosen aerodrome the weather improved. Strangely, given the import-ance of his destination, he didn't name it. It seemed that any enemy airfield would do. Whichever aerodrome it was, when he got there there were no aeroplanes to attack. 'There was nothing on the ground. Everyone must have been either dead or asleep, or else the station was absolutely deserted. Greatly disappointed, I decided I would try the same stunt some other day on another aerodrome.' He flew on eastward for a few more minutes and was about to turn back when the sheds of another airfield appeared ahead. He was now dangerously deep behind the lines and, flying low, no longer knew where he was. He debated whether to risk finding himself alone in a dogfight so far from home. But the temptation was too great. From 300 feet he looked down to see seven German aircraft.

Some of them actually had their engines running. Mechanics were standing about in groups.

I pointed my nose towards the ground and opened fire with my gun, scattering the bullets all around the machines and coming down to fifty feet in doing so. I do not know how many men I hit, or what damage was done, except that one man, at least, fell, and several others ran to pick him up.

Then, clearing off to one side, I watched the fun. I had forgotten by this time that they would, of course, have machine guns on the aerodrome, and as I was laughing to myself as they tore around in every direction on the ground, like people going mad, or rabbits scurrying about, I heard the old familiar rattle of the quick firers on me.

At this moment Bishop noticed that one of the Albatros fighters was attempting to take off.

> I immediately tore down after it. I managed to get close on its tail when it was just above the ground, and opened fire from dead behind it.
>
> There was no chance of missing, and I was as cool as could be. Just fifteen rounds, and it side-slipped to one side, then crashed on the aerodrome underneath. I was now keyed up to the fight and, turning quickly, saw another machine just off the ground. Taking careful aim at it, I fired from longer range than before ... The Hun saw I was catching up with him and pushed his nose down; then, gazing over his shoulder ... he crashed into some trees as my tracers were then going in an accurate line.
>
> I again turned towards the aerodrome. This time my heart sank. Two machines were taking off at the same time and in slightly different directions ... It was the one thing I had dreaded.

Deciding it was time to escape Bishop began to climb away. But one of the two Albatros was now in pursuit. 'I saw that he was catching me, so turned on him and opened fire. We made about two circuits round each other, neither getting a very good shot. But in the end I managed to get in a short burst of fire and his machine went crashing to the ground.'

Bishop recounted how a fourth Albatros took off to attack him. But as he was now out of ammunition he fled back to his base.

The mechanics crowded round his aeroplane. 'Everywhere it was shot about, bullet holes being in almost every part of it, although none luckily within two feet of where I sat. Parts of the machine were so badly damaged as to take a lot of repairing ... I personally congratulated the man who had charge of my gun, suddenly realising that if it had jammed at a critical moment, what a tight corner I would have been in.'[1]

To his fiancée, Margaret Burden, in Canada, Bishop had written picturesquely: 'My sweetheart, I had a very busy day. I rose at 3am and flew over to a Hun aerodrome where I did very cunning battle in the way of shooting many wee folks. I opened fire at seven machines on the ground and killed one or two men on the aerodrome.' He described his exploit exactly as he had reported it to his CO, telling Margaret how he had arrived back with his aeroplane full of holes from a machine gun on the ground.

Overnight Bishop became a Flying Corps hero. 'I find I am quite famous ... I must get busy and get some more Huns soon though, or my reputation will fade away. Darling, you are the inspiration of it all. Everything I try to win is just to make you proud of me. I'd gladly die to make you that sweetheart.'[2]

Bishop had certainly arrived back at Filescamp with a wounded aeroplane. Two sections of the trailing edge of the lower wing had been damaged and machine-gun fire had punctured the rear fuselage near the elevators. But how had it been caused? As pilots joined the mechanics inspecting the apparently battle-scarred Nieuport that morning some of them were puzzled by the groupings of the bullet holes. They appeared not to fit Bishop's account of the enemy fire he had received in his skirmish over the German airfield. Among the sceptics was Bishop's deputy flight commander, Lieutenant William Fry, who shared a hut with him. Fry was one of the pilots who'd declined to join him – he'd had a headache from a mess party the night before and was due to lead an early patrol. His first surprise was that, given the close combat Bishop had reported, the mechanics had found no damage to the engine, petrol tank 'or any other vital part'. He was further mystified by the unusual neatness of the bullet holes near the elevator. They were 'in a circle of about five inches diameter and, what is more, the edge of each bullet hole was circled with the black mark of cordite from the gun which had fired it'.

Fry came to the appalling conclusion 'that the burst could only have been fired by someone holding a machine gun on the ground and from the distance of a yard or two. No hostile aircraft could have got near enough to fire such a group, much less for the bullets to leave cordite marks . . . If, as Bishop said, the holes were fired by an attacking machine, they would have carried on and out through the fairing of the fuselage – in which there was neither a bullet hole nor a mark. In any case a hostile pilot would have been mad to attack at that angle at such close quarters.' Fry said it was the mechanics who had drawn his attention to these apparent anomalies, adding that, at the time, 'we took care to keep it to ourselves'.[3]

There were other worrying details, some of which he didn't make public until many years later, that Fry learned about the purported raid. Bishop told him that after the dogfight that had used up the last of his ammunition he had thrown his Lewis gun overboard to save weight. He also revealed that he'd got lost on his way home and, once back over the lines, 'had landed in open country, got out, leaving his engine running, and asked a farm labourer where he was. Having ascertained his approximate location, he took off again and returned home.'

Two months after the event, it was announced that Bishop had been awarded the Victoria Cross. Fry was flabbergasted. He was convinced that Major Scott's unquestioning belief in the dramatic authenticity of the mission so realistically described to him had overpowered his judgement. Scott's warm report to his wing commander had praised an 'extremely brilliant individual attack' from which Bishop had returned with 'his machine full of holes caused by machine guns with which the aerodrome was armed'. When his recommendation for a VC, on its long journey up the chain of command from the squadron to the War Office, reached the headquarters of 13th Wing, a query had gone back to 60 Squadron seeking some corroboration. As Scott was away the acting squadron commander, a New Zealand captain, Keith Caldwell, had to supply the lame response: 'Personal evidence only.' Answering a second question – the name of the German air base attacked – presented Caldwell with a further difficulty. All he could reply, vaguely, was 'Aerodrome S. of Cambrai'. These inadequate responses should have stopped the recommendation for any award dead in its tracks. But they didn't. And to suggest why, Fry had a not totally implausible conspiracy theory. He believed that Scott had tried to nudge the scrutiny system, using his personal connections with influential people in high places.

Fry's suspicions had been aroused when, after the raid, he learned that Scott had made a point of phoning his close friend Lord Dalmeny with the news. Dalmeny, more formally Albert Edward Harry Meyer Archibald Primrose, 6th Earl of Rosebery and 2nd Earl of Midlothian, whose father, Lord Rosebery, was a former British prime minister, was a captain serving as military secretary to the BEF's 3rd Army commander, General Allenby, under whose command 60 Squadron operated. Dalmeny was so impressed he had immediately asked Scott to bring Bishop to meet the general. Fry was convinced that this meeting, at which Bishop recounted his story to a deeply impressed Allenby, had helped the award recommendation survive its uncorroborated credentials.

Meanwhile, unwise enough to declare his growing cynicism about the truth of the raid to other pilots within the squadron, Fry found himself at odds with his medal-generous CO. When Scott asked him to apologise to Bishop for voicing his doubts, Fry refused. As a result, he said, Scott, 'alarmed at the spread of rising belief in the squadron that Bishop's claims were untrue and himself beginning to doubt the veracity of the mission, had decided that his only possible course was to go with Bishop's story and to get rid of me'. Fry was not alone in his suspicions, but he was the only officer in the squadron to have openly expressed them.

Scott, according to Fry, cancelled his imminent promised promotion to flight commander and posted him back to England. Fry never forgot what he saw as the injustice of his CO's action. Towards the end of his life, over fifty years later, when once-confidential WWI military files were made publicly accessible, he went to the Public Record Office in London to discover if Scott's request for his transfer was there. It was. He read that his former squadron commander had recommended him for repatriation because 'his nerves are now in a shaky state'.[4]

Lieutenant Fry had another reason to question the truth of Bishop's claim. Around a month earlier he and Bishop had been ordered to intercept a German two-seater reconnaissance machine spotted photographing the 3rd Army trenches. They rushed from the lunch table to their aeroplanes and took off together. Over the lines they saw the spying aircraft directly ahead of them at a slightly higher altitude.

> It turned away as we approached and we both let fly at him at long range, too far away to have any chance of hitting him.
>
> Having driven him off we turned for home. On landing, Bishop came up to me and to my surprise said, 'We got him alright, did you see him go down and crash' or something like that. Now I had not seen a German machine go down. But such was Bishop's reputation in the squadron that I thought he must have attacked and brought down another, closer, machine which I had not seen. I was certainly not going to contradict him. I was young and unsure of myself and was not going to jeopardise my place in the squadron.[5]

Bishop filled out the combat report, claiming a kill. He shared it with Fry, to whose own total it was also credited. Fry didn't have the courage to challenge it.

When he'd arrived at 60 Squadron Fry was puzzled to discover that Bishop, its C Flight commander, was leading few of his flight's patrols into action. Already awarded a Military Cross and recommended for a DSO, 'he was very much a lone hunter and off by himself, in which he was encouraged by the CO. It is difficult to imagine who, amongst previous COs, would have tolerated the male equivalent of a prima donna in one of their flights.'

Prima donna though he may have been, Bishop, known as 'Bish', was by all accounts a popular member of the squadron, known for his delight in attaching the garters and stockings of his French girlfriends to his aircraft's struts, and for the excessive zest with which he entered into the most destructive of the party games. He was seen as a rumbustious colonial rascal, a mischievous scamp, a loner in the air who appeared to take huge personal risks building up the tally of victories which, for a long time, were never questioned by his colleagues. He was, said Fry, 'good natured, good company, an extrovert ready for any fun or jaunt'.[6]

Yet very little was known on the squadron about Bishop's less than virtuous earlier life back in Canada. The son of a lawyer at Owen Sound in rural Ontario, he had grown up in the 1890s in an elegant three-storey family home that is today a museum honouring his exploits. His schooldays were unhappy. His academic hopelessness kept him at the bottom of the class in which, conspicuously dressed by his mother in suit, collar and tie, he was viewed as a sissy, constantly bullied and daily involved in scraps in which he acquired a reputation as a vicious fighter. Misery at school drove him into truancy during which he would go shooting squirrels or disappear into the town's billiard parlours. At seventeen he had fled from Owen Sound and somehow gained admission to Canada's Royal Military College, where he again struggled academically and earned a reputation as the college's most successful philanderer. He was regularly in trouble and in May 1914, facing the threat of expulsion for cheating in his final exams, left, before he could be kicked out, to join a Toronto militia cavalry regiment. It was so short of officers that, despite his dodgy, undisciplined background, he was given the commissioned rank he had later taken into the Flying Corps in France, first as an observer, then as a pilot at 60 Squadron, where he had soon made a name for himself for his swiftly mounting string of apparent victories.

The handsome, blond-haired Bishop had powerful connections in London where, on leave, he had been taken under the wing of a prominent high-society hostess, the sixty-eight-year-old Lady St Helier, at whose famous parties guests could find themselves dining with the author Thomas Hardy, Winston Churchill and various princesses. As a decorated war pilot back from the Western Front he revelled in the fuss made of him at these soirées. When his VC had been gazetted he went to Buckingham Palace to receive it. George V simultaneously pinned on the DSO and Military Cross awarded to him earlier, remarking, according to Bishop, that his trinity of medals had just made investiture history.

Bishop had developed an extraordinary obsession with becoming the highest-scoring Allied pilot, determined to beat his then nearest rival, the French ace Georges Guynemer. 'I'm catching up with him,' he wrote to Margaret. Four days later he reported: 'He had 35 when I had none.'[7]

'My dearest, tonight I got two more Huns, one in flames and the other burst into flames when it fell and crashed, so I'm much pleased. That makes 30 for me. Seventeen more and I will beat Guynemer – then one and I'll lead the Allies.'[8]* He was not only desperate for victories, he was hungry for celebrity. 'I hope to be famous throughout the whole Army.'[9]

Bishop went on to notch up numerous further claimed victories, ending the war with a frequently quoted seventy-two. Back in Canada, he had helped create the Royal Canadian Air Force in which, in the Second World War, he served again, though no longer as a pilot. When he died in 1956, aged sixty-two, he was mourned as one of his country's greatest-ever military heroes. It would be another quarter of a century before this image would be challenged and the authenticity of the VC-winning raid sixty-five years earlier publicly questioned.

The man who had the temerity to open Pandora's Box was a Canadian film producer, Paul Cowan, who discovered that there was no German record of such a raid on 2 June 1917. Cowan, who worked for the country's National Film Board, made a dramatised documentary, *The Kid Who Couldn't Miss*, which, sensationally, set out to challenge the famous aviator's integrity, suggesting that he had actually faked the attack that had immortalised him as one of his country's greatest warriors. Damagingly for the long dead Bishop's reputation, the film, with the help of some of the Canadian ace's elderly surviving fellow former pilots, clinically demolished the legend of the heroic mission, highlighting the flaws in Bishop's story and inconsistencies that for decades had privately bothered some of them. Now their doubting voices were heard at last. The programme also drew extensively on excerpts from a long-running highly successful Canadian stage musical, *Billy Bishop Goes to War*, in which Bishop was portrayed as an egotistical, hugely ambitious and distinctly unlikeable person who had cheated in his exams at military college. Although the show, still being performed more than thirty years later in 2011, gently glossed over the questions about the June 1917 attack, it left the impression that the famed pilot was indeed someone quite capable of perpetrating such an outrageous fraud.

When the television film was screened in 1982 it brought such howls of rage from elderly veterans of the Second World War that the Canadian Senate decided to investigate its allegations. Paul Cowan was hauled before a veterans' affairs subcommittee. Thrown to the lions, he was cross-examined with an aggression that bordered on inquisition as the incensed committee took evidence from a clutch of witnesses sympathetic

---

*With 53 confirmed victories at the time he was shot down and killed in September 1917 Captain Georges Guynemer was the second-highest scoring French ace after Captain René Fonck, who survived the war credited with 75, making him the Allies' highest.

to Bishop. The angry senators accused Cowan and the National Film Board of deliberately and irresponsibly setting out to besmirch Bishop's reputation, distorting the thrust of the film to that end. On the contrary, Cowan responded: he'd begun his research, like most Canadians, fully believing the legend and had been shocked to discover that it was fatally flawed. The senators weren't having any of this. One after the other they poured bullying scorn upon the film's producer. One of them, Senator David Walker, a former Canadian crown prosecutor, told him: 'Having heard how honest Billy Bishop was and how his friends believed in him right across the board, how can you come here today with the pip-squeak amount of evidence that you have, evidence from nonentities, and try and defend the film that was made, a film that was trying to make a fool and a liar and a scoundrel out of Bishop? Aren't you ashamed of yourself?'

'Absolutely not,' Cowan replied defiantly.[10]

Unfortunately for the committee, despite the lengthy hearings that ground on for months, the conclusions it was forced to reach in its 1986 report left the central question of the truth of the attack unsatisfactorily unresolved.[11] The report had to devote its strictures almost entirely to criticism of the docu-drama techniques Cowan had used, according to the committee, to blacken Bishop's image. It failed to produce any primary evidence to authenticate the VC exploit. The aviation 'nonentities', historians who had spent decades painstakingly searching in vain for that evidence, and who had shared their discoveries with Cowan, were not invited to present their unpopular findings to the committee.

Had they done so they would have further shocked the senators with embarrassing support for the theory that the contentious raid was by no means the only mission for which Bishop had been credited with uncorroborated victories on his word alone. There were in fact, it was sadly alleged, almost certainly dozens more.

The historians, acknowledged for the professionalism and sheer doggedness of their First World Air War research, had since the early 1960s, with the help of British and German air service records in the two countries' military archives, been engaged in verifying the outcomes of the thousands of aerial combats over the Western Front in the four years of the war. They set out, with great success, to match places, dates, times, pilots' names, squadrons and the outcome of the encounters. However, the hard facts they uncovered didn't always concur with the claims of the pilots or with the victories credited at the time. One of the most tenacious of these historians was a retired Canadian air force wing commander, Philip Markham.

When, using German Air Service records, Markham attempted to match Bishop's claims with the Luftstreitkräfte reports of the attacks and the losses of aircraft and pilots he had claimed, he discovered that no aerodrome had been raided or any aircraft shot down on that part of the Western Front, within the range of Bishop's aircraft, on the morning of 2 June 1917.

In his combat report Bishop had recorded the name of the airfield as 'either Esnes aerodrome or Awoignt'. The German records showed, to Markham's surprise, that both were in fact unoccupied at the time. There were no aeroplanes or pilots there. Scott, in his own report to his wing commander, had caused further confusion by naming yet a third airfield, Anneux, as Bishop's destination. But this, too, Markham learned, had been deserted, abandoned earlier in the year by the constantly moving jasta. Perhaps, he wondered, Bishop had attacked another aerodrome elsewhere. He widened his search to include the casualty records left by the German area command headquarters. No losses had been recorded by the air force squadrons of the German 2nd or 6th Armies that occupied the Cambrai locality on that date.[12]

If Markham needed further confirmation of the awful truth, it came in his discovery of a blunt November 1917 official German denunciation of Bishop's claim. Reacting to the worldwide publicity given to the Canadian's deed, it stated that none of its aircraft in the relevant area had been shot down that day, adding: 'Since Bishop was alone during the attack, the details of this fictitious incident could only have come from him.'[13]

With great reluctance, Markham was forced to the shattering conclusion that 'Bishop was a fake'; that there was not a shred of evidence from either British or German sources to support the claims.[14] It was as if proof had just surfaced that Edmund Hillary and Sherpa Tenzing had not actually reached the summit of Everest. It was inconceivable. Yet another WWI aviation researcher, Ed Ferko, an American with an unrivalled knowledge of German Air Service records, was unfortunately compelled to agree with Markham. He had collected every relevant particle of the German documentation that recorded daily the operations of squadrons based within range of the RFC's No. 60 Squadron. He found no record of an attack on the crucial June day. However: 'I left the matter in limbo,' he said. 'Few people derive pleasure from destroying myths.'[15]

Markham had delved further. He had tried to find the records of the British authorities that had sanctioned the VC before passing it to the King. Since its inception by Queen Victoria in 1856 the issue of the VC had been governed by strict rules. They demanded the evidence of witnesses, in the absence of which 'never without conclusive proofs of the performance of the act of bravery for which the claim is made'. Despite months of searching in the mid-1980s by Defence Ministry officials in London, the Bishop file was never found. It may possibly have been destroyed when the building was bombed during the Second World War.

Had the vital file been unearthed it might have laid to rest a popular theory that the War Office, in a rare disregard of the enshrined conditions, had quietly decided to break the corroboration rule. That it was anxious to create a new pilot hero to succeed the recently killed Albert Ball and to acknowledge the disproportionately large contribution of the Canadians, who represented around a third of its pilot corps in the RFC. If this highly unlikely scenario is true, unfortunately, the world will never know.

The shadow the television programme cast over the image of Canada's hallowed aviation idol has never lifted. And in 2002 it was further darkened when a prominent Canadian military historian, Brereton Greenhous, published a book in which he claimed that many of Bishop's seventy-two victories 'were the product of an ambitious imagination that was encouraged by the authorities. Billy Bishop was a brave flyer – and a consummate, bold liar.'[16] Sadly for the Bishop legend, Greenhous also exposed the deceitful claim in Bishop's war memoirs that he had fought a fierce air battle with the Red Baron on 30 April 1917. The truth, Greenhous had discovered, was that the Baron had not flown at all that day.

He produced a table listing every one of Bishop's 207 sorties during his Western Front service. The list was compiled from his combat reports and his logbooks for the entire period of his active service on the Western Front. It shows the dates, locations, fates of enemy aircraft claimed, whether he was hunting alone or on a patrol with fellow pilots and whether the encounter was witnessed.

The most striking feature of this table is the high concentration of victims Bishop recorded in late May and early June 1918, when he was in such a hurry to become the Flying Corps' top scorer. On 19 June he was credited with no fewer than five victories within the space of a few minutes. Yet two of the aircraft he claimed to have shot down that morning had actually collided and destroyed each other.

Twenty of the kills credited to Bishop were made on patrols with other pilots. In the heat and confusion of the air battles, pilots' victims weren't always seen to go down by the victor's colleagues; yet for the kill to be registered, confirmation was required that army units had observed the fate of the German machine – whether its wreckage had been found or that its pilot had managed to land behind the Allied lines. Taking everything into account, Greenhous calculated that around twenty-seven – a little more than a third of Bishop's tally – were probably genuine kills.

No one ever doubted Bishop's courage and aggression in his many aerial battles. And if his true record was something in the region of twenty-seven enemy aircraft this is no mean score and would still have ranked him among the elite of the war's aces. But even at the time Bishop's fellow pilots had begun privately to question the sheer volume of his claimed wave of destruction. 'How do people do it?' Arthur Gould Lee wrote to his wife, marvelling at how Bishop, who had arrived in France only two months ahead of him, could already have shot down forty-five planes.[17] Keith Caldwell, one of the two pilots who'd declined to join Bishop on his notorious raid, was still commenting on it sixty years later when, as a retired air commodore back in his native New Zealand, he refused to endorse a Bishop VC commemorative envelope being issued in 1977 by the RAF Museum in London. 'I cannot,' he wrote to tell William Fry, 'do what they wish: sign and endorse the picture of Bishop doing his VC act when I have to doubt its authenticity.'

Although Bishop's VC was to become an embarrassing *cause célèbre* he was not alone in claiming questionable successes. What exactly constituted a 'victory' was imprecise. There were difficulties with accurate corroboration, and some squadron commanders and their superior officers were excessively anxious to demonstrate Flying Corps triumphs to offset their huge and demoralising losses in the spring and summer of 1917. Added to which there was the constant eagerness of pilots to prove themselves by constantly increasing their scores. All of this made a mockery, many believed, of the whole scoreboard system of credited victories of aircraft shot down or observation balloons destroyed, which also counted.

Even apparent kills witnessed in the thick of battle by fellow pilots could prove false. Was an aircraft suddenly spinning down out of combat in fact fatally crippled and heading for a fiery crash? Not necessarily. When things got too hot the practice of flicking into a controlled spin, spiralling down into the clouds below and, once safely beneath them, resuming normal flight to escape home never ceased on either side.

The definitions of victories, and who was credited, remained, then, a muddy and constantly evolving area. They were not always represented by the dramatic image of popular belief: the stricken, blazing machine plunging out of the sky, trailing black smoke. Aircraft could be destroyed without bursting into flames. Damaged by gunfire they could be sent down out of control to a fatal crash or a forced landing. They could be driven down intact, only to crash or be compelled to land behind the Allied lines and taken prisoner. Duplicated claims were rife. Two pilots from the same squadron might both be entitled to a slice of the award: So might a pilot and his gunner-observer who, with their separate guns, between them brought down an enemy aircraft. When pilots of more than one squadron were among the mass of machines fighting in the same battle there tended to be a particularly marked doubling of claims to the same German aeroplane. How these were resolved was an equally untidy area. A squadron commander would accept a claim only to have it disallowed by his wing commander, then restored by the brigade commander. There was no centralised co-ordination or review system. When, much later, it was possible to compare Flying Corps' credited victories with the records of German losses, it was clear that many of the huge totals attached so spectacularly to the names of some celebrated British aces were in truth much smaller.

The tallies awarded to German pilots were essentially more accurate. Confirmation was easier because most of the combat took place behind the German lines as a result of the sustained policy pursued by the British commanders of offensive action across the front and because the prevailing westerly wind tended to delay the return of the Allied aircraft to safety. Most of the German squadrons' victims finished up, for verification, in German-held territory. And this is where the evidential wreckage and bodies of Bishop's defeated opponents should have been found.

There remains a reluctance among the probing historians to publicise the apparent enormity of the Bishop fraud beyond the realm of their aviation societies. Canada's history books prefer to steer clear of this sensitive subject. It has created a dilemma for the Owen Sound Billy Bishop museum which preserves the record of his life and deeds. However, on the advice of an historian at the Royal Military College of Canada – who believed there was insufficient evidence that the raid had not taken place, and that there probably really had been transiting German aircraft temporarily at the field Bishop claimed to have attacked – the museum decided that its public exhibition would ignore the embarrassing allegations and present the controversial VC raid as fact, and exactly as Bishop described it.

Whatever the truth of his WWI exploits they guaranteed Billy Bishop's fame for the rest of his life during which, in Canada, he was treated almost like royalty. Some of his former Flying Corps colleagues wondered if he was ever troubled by the grand deception. There is no evidence that, if indeed he felt any trace of unease, he ever betrayed an inkling of it. Modern psychologists, studying his larger-than-life background, believe that Bishop's personality displayed strong narcissistic traits that gave him an over-inflated sense of his own importance. This would have created a constant need for attention and admiration which bred fantasies of success and achievement that were sometimes realised by the elaboration of real-life events. The lone flight over deserted German aerodromes would have presented Bishop with the opportunity to construct one such heroic fantasy. The false memory he built up became, with subsequent continual repetition, firm fact in his own mind, where the truth resided in a remote compartment beyond the reach of even a flicker of guilt.

Once the airfield raid and the huge honour it brought him were permanently embodied in his image there could be no retreat to the truth. The shocking revelations of the accusers that could have rocked the foundations of his reputation were tactfully kept out of the public domain during his lifetime. Indeed, his legend remained so well preserved that, back in Canada, the Second World War brought him further great distinction. As an honorary air marshal responsible for recruiting in the Royal Canadian Air Force, his stature as his country's greatest military aviator was only reinforced.

Air Marshal Bishop's VC will remain attached to his name. But the doubts about its validity will never die and what he actually did during those 103 minutes in June 1917 we shall never now know. In 1966, Keith Caldwell shared his views with another of the then few surviving 60 Squadron pilots in a letter to one of them. 'All references to poor Billy Bishop,' he told Air Vice-Marshal Geoffrey Pidcock, 'do raise a problem because some of us know that many of B's claims were unreal, including his VC job when no German aircraft were reported lost – it's all very sad, but he is dead.'[18]

Chapter 22
Gothas

Nineteen seventeen took the heaviest annual toll of the war on the Flying Corps as, in the eye of the endless battles, it photographed, bombed, strafed enemy trenches, pursued intruding German aircraft and struggled to re-equip with the new technically advanced combat machines that were arriving in only a frustrating trickle. They came in the shape of the Bristol Fighter, the Sopwith Camel, the formidable SE5 and the machine that was the favourite of the French aces, the SPAD. But although the new generation of aircraft had begun by the summer of 1917 to stem the huge losses of the spring and 'Bloody April', the squadrons' mess chairs were still emptying with depressing frequency. Replacement pilots, fresh to the lethal skies, were continuing to die within weeks of arrival. And when their keen, youthful faces failed to reappear at the dining table their fellow pilots didn't always know exactly what had become of them or where, dead or alive, they might be.

When, on 28 March a Nieuport Scout pilot, 2nd Lieutenant Hugh 'Toby' Welch of No. 1 Squadron, had failed to return to his base at Bailleul none of the other six pilots in his reconnaissance formation knew what had happened to him during their skirmish with enemy Albatros fighters over Lille. 'It was a very cloudy day,' Welch's CO, Major de Dombasle, recounted as he wrote to break the news to Welch's father in England, 'and in the general confusion no one paid very much attention to the others, and no one appears to have seen him go down. It is thought that he must have had his engine hit and been forced to come down, as if he had been hit his machine going down out of control would certainly have attracted some notice. He was a very gallant officer and cheery companion beloved by us all.'[1]

The hope was that Welch had survived and was alive somewhere behind the German lines. But within days this optimism was dashed. A German Albatros pilot, Leutnant Flintz, driven down and taken prisoner, was able to confirm in unhappily accurate detail that he had shot down Welch's Nieuport and watched it disintegrate and crash. Later, one of the other Flying Corps pilots who had been on the fatal patrol, got in touch while on leave in London with Mr Welch. Lionel Mars had known his son from their public-school days at Merchant Taylors' School and had shared a hut with him at Bailleul. He revealed the specially brave act that had led to his death that day.

> I was awfully sorry to see that poor old Toby was killed as I thought he might have a good chance. But I bet he got one Hun at least before they got Toby.
>
> He was at the back of the formation. When we got to Lille five Huns came up, but they very quickly disappeared. I'm sure they were not the cause of Toby's death.
>
> After the scrap the weather became rotten and everybody got lost and went home as best they could. A report came round that a Nieuport by itself went to the assistance of a BE2c which was being attacked by two Huns and we thought in the squadron that this must have been Toby. When he did not come back at once no one thought much about it because three other fellows had landed miles away from the aerodrome. But when two days passed then, of course, we knew something had happened. He was a simply top-hole fellow.[2]

Welch's parents had only their son's letters to console them. In one of his last, to his mother, he had written: 'Mumsie darling, I've got nothing on earth to say 'cos I only wrote a couple of days ago and I've done practically nothing since then, except a few Hun chases with no effect. Weather's dud, anyhow. Can't write – the hut is half full of damfools who <u>will</u> talk and dance and play the gramophone. Cheeryoh, old thing, and lots of love, Toby.'[3]

It would be two years before, from an unexpected quarter, the family learned exactly how Toby had been killed and buried, with much love, by the people of a village near Lille. His death had been witnessed by the parish priest of Sainghin-en-Melantois, a Monsieur Derycke, who was traced by Mr Welch early in 1919 with the help of the war graves department of the War Office. In July Mr Welch received a letter from M. Derycke.

> It is true that your son fell in the parish of Sainghin, about two kilometres of the church, a few hundred metres from the historic fountain where Philippe Auguste [a twelfth-century king] quenched his thirst before going to battle, and a few hundred metres also from the plateau where there used to be the old chapel in which the King

of France prayed. He therefore fell on ground glorious with the deeds of past centuries. His fall was equally glorious.

I plainly saw from my house, as did many of the villagers, the fall of your brave boy's machine. It had been struck in an aerial combat by a German aviator. I seem yet to see as upon the day of the accident whole pieces of the fuselage fluttering in the air just like pieces of paper, and the remainder of the machine, together with the body of your regretted son, fall to the ground in a few seconds.

The village doctor, who was just then passing, could but verify the fact of the death of your son on approaching the debris of the machine. Some difficulty was experienced in extricating your son. The whole was buried in the ground more than 18 inches deep. But all was done decently by the Germans.

The body was taken to an inn near by and the people of the house prepared a bed and a room to place him in. Many people came that day and the next to pray by his body to show their sympathy for the brave and courageous Lieutenant Hugh. We wanted to have an elaborate funeral but the Germans, fearing that there might be too patriotic a demonstration by the people, opposed it.[4]

The priest described the brief German military funeral, which the villagers were forbidden even to watch, as Welch, in a coffin of solid oak, was buried in the local cemetery. 'The next day,' he wrote, 'as a mark of protestation, nearly all the inhabitants marched past the grave of your son and placed wreaths and flowers on it.' And every year, on the anniversary of his death, the floral tributes would be repeated.

In the spring of 1917, already fighting for their very survival over the front lines against superior German aeroplanes, the Flying Corps was handed yet another task. There was now an urgent need to attack enemy aerodromes near Ghent in Belgium from which a brand-new terror had been launched upon the cities of Britain. Far more devastating deliverers of destruction than the failed Zeppelins, the big Gotha bomber aeroplanes had begun to arrive in huge numbers in daylight.

It was in the lazy spring warmth of the late afternoon of 25 May 1917, to now largely undefended English cities made complacent by the virtual defeat of the airships, that the blitz returned. It came in more terrifying fashion than the civilian world had ever seen when a fleet of long-range bombers struck. They came first to Folkestone on the Channel coast. The thrumming drone of a large force of aeroplanes brought people out into the streets to gaze up in fascination at the cluster of white shapes they assumed were British. 'I stopped to watch their graceful antics pirouetting over my head and thought to myself at last we are up and doing, fondly imagining they were our own machines practising,' a woman later wrote. An American clergyman told the *New York Times*: 'I saw two aeroplanes, not Zeppelins, emerging from the disc of the sun almost overhead. Then four more, or five in a line and others, all light bright silver insects hovering against the blue of the sky . . . There was about a score in all, and we were charmed with the beauty of the sight. I am sure few of us thought seriously of danger.'[5]

Suddenly the insects began to discharge their cargoes. In Tontine Street in the town centre, crowded with Whitsun weekend shoppers, the bombs hit. 'Ear-splitting explosions smashed shop windows, splintered beams and sent bricks and rubble cascading into the roadway. "I saw," said the town's chief constable, "an appalling sight which I shall never forget. Dead and injured persons were lying on the ground. Three or four horses were lying dead between the shafts, and fire had broken out."'[6] When the casualties were counted ninety-five people had been killed and nearly 200 injured.

Folkestone had not been the bombers' primary target. London was. But bad weather over the Thames estuary had forced them to abandon the attack; the Gotha squadron commander had decided instead to attack the Channel ports on the way home. They had met virtually no resistance. The anti-aircraft guns had failed to hit a single one of the twenty-one invaders and the seventy-four British aircraft that 'rose to the defence' also failed to intercept any of them.

The audacious raid unleashed a storm of fury in Parliament. But the truth was that demands for special home-based fighting squadrons had been competing with equally urgent calls from Haig and Trenchard for more pilots and aircraft to support the hard-pressed armies on the Western Front. Here British ground casualties, exceeding often 2,500 a day, made the Folkestone toll seem almost trivial. The case for dedicated home defence squadrons just couldn't compete.

The Gothas soon came to their prime target. They first struck London on the morning of 13 July 1917. Again, 'as the sky over the Thames resounded with the distinctive throb of the Mercedes engines', people couldn't believe what was happening. As they ran into streets and gardens to look at the diamond-shaped formation of seventeen machines flying three miles up, few realised, in the absence of any proper warning, that they were German. Unlike the huge airships that had cruised over as elusive shapes in the dark, the Gothas arrived as if in a flypast at an air display. There were no air-raid warnings, the buses kept running, and 'men and women stood watching, vastly interested, a little excited, but not in the least frightened'.

The Gothas were bound for Liverpool Street station. Within two minutes seventy-two bombs had crashed down on to its great arched roof and into surrounding streets. One scored a direct hit on a train filled with passengers. Another, killing fifteen people, blasted Soho, where the cafés were filled with office workers having lunch. At Poplar in the East End over forty children were killed or appallingly wounded by exploding glass from a strike on a school. The anger surrounding their slaughter prompted mobs of shouting women to rampage through East London ransacking and looting the shops of every trader they could find with a German name.

There were nearly 600 casualties from the raid, which killed more than 160 Londoners. None of the Gothas was destroyed and of the scrambled ninety-two defending machines sent up the only one to get anywhere near them was itself shot down. All seventeen bombers returned safely to their Belgian base where the raid commander, Captain Ernst Brandenburg, was immediately decorated by the Kaiser with a Blue Max and his crew celebrated with a boisterous party. The official German communiqué announced triumphantly: 'Today our airmen dropped bombs on the Fortress of London.'7

The resoundingly onomatopoeic Grosskampfflugzeug, the Gotha was a revolutionary development of the military flying machine. The huge two-engined strategic bomber had been created as a more precise means than the night-flying airship to attack in daylight, with the aim of forcing England out of the war by destroying morale and crushing people's will to fight. They were intended to disrupt Britain's war industry, its railway system and ports, hindering the supply of war materials to the Western Front and compelling large-scale diversion of British squadrons and guns back home from France. The elite unit formed to do it was named the England Squadron and, so importantly was it regarded that it received its orders direct from the German High Command in Berlin.

Built by a pre-war German railway-carriage manufacturer, the Gotha was a biplane with three open cockpits. Its vast wingspan of nearly 78 feet – around 24 metres – was greater than that of any of the Luftwaffe's Heinkels and Dorniers that bombed London in the Second World War. Although it flew at only around 80mph it was exceedingly well protected from attack by three machine guns, and from its 15,000-foot bombing height – around 4,600 metres – it was beyond quick reach of the British fighters.

The Gothas were commanded by a navigator-bombardier who sat out in the open in front of the pilot in the aircraft's box-like nose with a machine gun and a bulky but sophisticated telescopic sighting device for aiming his bombs. The rear gunner occupied the third cockpit, defending the tail with two machine guns, one of which, to the surprise of opposing fighters traditionally accustomed to approaching from below and behind, could pour a hail of fire back down on to them through a tunnel in the bottom of the rear fuselage.

Unlike the Zeppelins, the Gothas couldn't afford the weight of radio. They steered across the North Sea by dead reckoning and celestial navigation and sent messages back to their base with pigeons kept in a cage in the front cockpit. They had no intercom, communicating between the three cockpits with arm signals. Setting course from the Belgian coast, the navigator would stand up and point an outstretched arm in the correct direction. When the pilot had banked on to the right heading he would drop his arm. Because of the height at which they flew the crew were supplied with cylinders of compressed oxygen, which they inhaled through a mouthpiece, sucking it in as if they were smoking a hookah. To protect them from the freezing cold they wore heavy fur-lined coats and gloves, thigh-high boots and leather helmets. Some of the pilots were still wearing the uniforms of the army regiments from which they'd come (one of them, a nineteen-year-old ex-cavalry officer, always flew with his spurs). Their departures from their Belgian bases were spectacular affairs. Up to two dozen of the large aeroplanes would line up, one behind the other, as a controller with a red flag waved them off in succession like racing cars.

To terrorise the English it had been planned to send on each raid a giant cluster of at least forty bombers. But this was never regularly achieved, and on the one mission that managed to dispatch thirty-eight, ten failed to reach the target. And like the Zeppelins, the Gothas were plagued by engine failure, navigation problems and, most frightening of all, by the incredible difficulty of landing the leviathans safely. They were so notoriously nose-heavy that even the most experienced pilots were liable to crash them disastrously on touching down back at their base. They often ran out of fuel on the way home, crash-landing where they could. Straying into neutral Holland, some were shot down by Dutch gunners and the crews interned.

London was as helpless to defend itself against the latest onslaught from the sky, as it had been with the Zeppelins. The shells of the mobile anti-aircraft guns destroyed more houses and killed more people on the ground than the Gothas and their crews. The city's early-warning system was still pathetically inadequate: policemen still cycled through the streets with their noticeboards and truckloads of Boy Scouts still bugled. To these primitive alarms red signal flares were added in some places, which were helpful when the bombers started coming at night, but they were silent. Mostly the Gothas heralded their own arrival. Their unsynchronised twin engines created a distinctive sonorous double hum that earned them the name 'wong-wongs'. This repetitive *wonga-wonga* beat travelled so far ahead of them that a concave sonic dish installed on the Dover cliffs could detect them twenty miles out over the sea. Inland, guns and searchlights were alerted by crude mobile sound-locators – a sort of ear trumpet connected to a stethoscope. Across London's eastern approaches balloons tethered at up to 10,000 feet were hoisted to support an apron of dangling steel wires. The Gothas simply flew over the top. The scores of British Flying Corps and naval aircraft that went up to meet the invading formations hardly ever hit one.

As the bombers continued to rattle British nerves through the summer of 1917 the British War Cabinet, presided over by the prime minister, was forced to decide between the priorities of the defence of the realm and the wider aims of the war to defeat Germany in France. Lloyd George summoned Trenchard to London. The Flying Corps commander was pressed to send home urgently two of his fighter squadrons to bolster the capital's defences. He was also urged to launch immediate reprisal bombing raids, within range of his aircraft, against Germany, starting with the factories of Mannheim on the Rhine. Trenchard was strongly opposed to measures merely 'to slake the popular thirst for revenge'. He told the War Cabinet that long-range strategic bombing of Germany would only hasten its military defeat if it could be decisively sustained, and that would require a bomber fleet he didn't yet have.

For Britain the Gothas had brought the air war to another crossroads. When it created the elite England Squadron the German High Command could never have conceived of the monumental consequences it would have within the warring British military aviation establishment. To Trenchard's considerable astonishment, the Cabinet suddenly approved a massive expansion of the Royal Flying Corps, virtually doubling it to 200 squadrons, of which forty would consist of long-range bombers. Even more sweepingly, it decided at long last to bite the bullet and begin the process of forcing the RFC and the Royal Naval Air Service into one united air force. Meanwhile, protesting that by doing so would be immediately removing the eyes he was providing for the army in its Passchendaele offensive, Trenchard reluctantly spared two of his best squadrons for three weeks to try to deal with the Gothas. One went to Calais; the other, No. 56, with its new SE5s, to Bekesbourne, near Canterbury in Kent. The nerve-stretched pilots of the latter couldn't believe their good luck. After the Western Front it promised to be a blessed holiday.

'Agitation in the press! Scandalous neglect of the defence of dear old England,' wrote Cecil Lewis sardonically. 'Questions in the House! Panic among the politicians! Lloyd George acting quickly! Result: a crack squadron to be recalled for the defence of London . . . and twelve elated pilots of 56 packing a week's kit into our cockpits. God bless the good old Gotha!' He added: 'To fight Hun bombers over London would have been a picnic for us after a month of gruelling offensive patrols. Good old Jerry! Good old Lloyd George!'[8]

Shortly before they'd come back to England, Lewis, on a homesick impulse, had unofficially sneaked over Kent from France. Sent up to test one of the new SE5s, he had climbed high into the sky over the Pas de Calais on a calm, cloud-free evening to check the aircraft's ceiling. From around 17,000 feet he looked longingly across the Channel to see southern England laid out as if on the map. 'Oh, to be home again! Just to be over England, even if one could not land on it. After all, why not? I turned north.' He flew across the sea and high over Kent. Below him 'my countrymen were walking, talking, going about their daily business in the peaceful lanes . . . The faintest drift of blue smoke from the chimneys of some country house. There would be the scent of a wood-fire down there, far, far below.' He didn't know that, within days, he would himself be savouring that sweet wood smoke.

At their temporary base at Bekesbourne the 56 Squadron pilots quickly established their priorities. 'The defence of London,' Lewis said, 'was quite a secondary affair. The things of real importance were squadron dances.' They erected a large marquee and laid down planking. 'Very soon there was a regular Savoy dancing floor. Visits were paid to Canterbury to enrol the fair sex. Those lightning two or three day acquaintanceships began to ripen.' During the squadron's welcome sojourn back in England not a single Gotha came to London. They filled their long summer days, during which wives and girlfriends moved into Bekesbourne, with parties, picnics, air displays to entertain their stream of visitors and nightly visits to London. 'The squadron,' Lewis wrote, 'stood by gloriously idle. It was a grand war.' But back in France Trenchard had been counting the days he had agreed to part with his two squadrons. The moment their three weeks was up they were promptly recalled to a much grimmer life back on the front line. The latest ground offensives around Ypres had brought a further round of huge air battles and, in daily savage duels, the squadron suffered some of its biggest losses of the war. By the middle of July, of the full complement of pilots who had flown out to France only three months earlier, only four remained.

Back in England the Gothas were still coming. And, early in September, they were joined by a mammoth new aeroplane. The Staaken Giant biplane was an astonishing machine for its era. With its 138-foot (42-metre) wingspan, and in every other dimension, it was bigger than the Lancaster bomber of WWII. Dwarfing the size and destructive capacity of the Gothas, its engine power and great spread of wings enabled it to bring to London the war's first one-ton aerial bombs. It was not only enormous but also remarkably sophisticated. For the first time most of the flight crew enjoyed the comfort of a closed cockpit. Some even had electrically heated flying suits, all with oxygen and, revolutionary for a WWI war machine, all had access to parachutes. Photographs of this little-known and rarely seen strategic jumbo, with its array of eighteen wheels, show it towering above the fifty ground crew required to operate it.

The Giant was the creation of the Zeppelin airship company. Its design engineers included Claudius Dornier and Hugo Junkers, whose bombers would ravage English cities during the Second World War. A confusingly large family of these great bomb-carriers was built, powered by anything from three to six engines. The crew sizes ranged from seven to ten or eleven men, depending on the number of full-time machine-gunners carried. The Staakens sent to England were manned by two pilots in the cabin, behind which sat the commander, who was also the navigator and bombardier, and the wireless-operator, who got position fixes from radio beacons back in Belgium. In addition there was a fuel attendant whose job, minute by minute, was the transfer of petrol between the ten tanks to maintain the machine's critical flight trim. There were also two mechanics who sat in pods beside the engines and communicated with the flight deck using a code of flashing light signals. The Staaken was heavily defended. It could carry as many as six machine guns handled by a small team of gunners who, on some of the aircraft, had to make a dangerous climb in the 80mph slipstream up a vertical ladder to a firing platform on top of the upper wing. The Giants' pilots faced an unusually advanced display of instruments which, rare for the period, included an artificial horizon and a gyro-compass. Also unique was a pneumatic tube message system that whisked notes between six of the manned stations.

In theory these German superbombers, embodying the most advanced of aeronautical technology and flown by dedicated squadrons, could have brought great destruction to London. But in practice, on their few operations, their 13-foot, one-ton bombs rarely hit any of the mainline railway stations, docks or military barracks they targeted. They came over on moonlit nights as solitary raiders, usually in groups of no more than two or three; lone wolves adding their bombs to those of larger fleets of Gothas. On the ground people rarely saw the Staakens and they never existed in great enough numbers to make any serious contribution to the bombardment of English cities. Fewer than thirty were ever built and they flew to England only eleven times. Even the Gothas, which generated the most fear, made only twenty-two raids during the twelve months of their operations. Between them the Gothas and Giants claimed fewer than 3,000 civilian casualties. Even adding the toll taken by the Zeppelins, combined German aeroplane and airship attacks in the course of the entire war were to kill fewer than 1,500 people. It was a minuscule fraction of the human losses on the Western Front, where up to 20,000 men could perish on one day. Small, too, compared with the more horrifying blitz that would come to England just twenty-three years later, when German bombs would kill 40,000 people, half of them in London, where more than a million houses were damaged or razed to the ground.

The German bomber aeroplanes themselves suffered badly on their missions. Although the Staaken squadrons lost no aircraft on the few operations they accomplished, the Gotha losses of sixty aeroplanes on the England raids were beyond disastrous. In one bad week for the England Squadron, of ninety-two machines sent out, only fifty-five managed to cross the English coast and a mere twenty reached London. Twenty-four were shot down or disappeared over the sea; thirty-six more were wrecked in the ceaseless crashes to which they were so prone. Yet if the death and destruction the Gothas and Giants sprinkled on England was minimal, the psychological effect on the jittery nation of daily fear and constant anticipation of the next unheralded explosion was enormous. And although the reprisal attacks on Germany that Parliament and the newspapers continued loudly to demand would not seriously begin for many months, Trenchard was compelled, in the meantime, at least to be seen attacking the bombers' Belgium bases. Joined by naval aircraft of the RNAS from their Channel port aerodromes in France, in September

1917 the Flying Corps launched their own blitz on all the Gotha and
Staaken airfields near Ghent.

Some of the night-bomber squadrons ordered to undertake this task
were pathetically equipped only with obsolete FE2 pusher biplanes. Still
with their rickety-looking uncovered wooden fuselage stringers and
carrying bomb-loads of barely 350lbs (160kg), these quaint machines contrasted curiously with the sophisticated monsters they were expected to
destroy in their lairs in Belgium.

Trenchard, stung by the sustained demands of the British press for
retaliation, put inordinate pressure on his night-bomber commanders to
mount and press home these raids even in the face of dangerously bad
weather. But not all of his squadron leaders were prepared to sacrifice
their pilots by ordering them out in such conditions. One of those who
fiercely resisted was Major Harold Wyllie, CO of the newly formed 102
Squadron based at Treizennes, south-east of St Omer. Thirty-seven-year-
old Wyllie was not someone to be messed with. A cultivated, artistic man
of the world, he'd served in the Boer War and, back in England, become
a distinguished marine artist. Before training as a Flying Corps pilot he
had been an observer, valued for the realistic detail of the sketches he
brought back from reconnaissance flights over enemy positions. As a
squadron commander with a fatherly concern for his young pilots he
refused to accept orders that guaranteed needless death on impossible
missions. The firm stand he took over Trenchard's harassment of the
squadron, conveyed down through its wing commander, during a long
spell of appalling weather early in November 1917 he recorded angrily in
his diary.

In the middle of the night of 1 November, when northern France was
being buffeted by a storm that had lowered the cloud base almost to
ground level and brought winds too high for the Fees even to attempt
night take-offs, Wyllie was roused from sleep by an urgent phone call
from his colonel at wing headquarters. He was calling

> to strafe me. 'Boom' had been raising Cain and the colonel seemed
> to think we hadn't done enough – or at least he'd been told to say
> so by 'Boom'.
>
> Apparently the Huns had been bombing London and therefore,
> in the official mind, if the weather was fit for the Hun it must be fit
> for us. I told the colonel I never left the aerodrome in impossible
> weather. Also that I had been at this job for over a year and wondered
> if the Flying Corps in the field was now run by the Daily Mail.

The colonel said he would come over and see the weather conditions himself as he thought we <u>had</u> tried our best. I am furious to
think that it should be thought necessary for the wing commander
to come and sit on my aerodrome to see if I can run this show
properly.[9]

Two nights later, with the weather still atrocious, Wyllie sent up one
of his aircraft to check the visibility for a raid on a Gotha base. The pilot
reported cloud so low he lost sight of the flarepath at 500 feet. Wyllie,
fearful of more challenges to his judgement from his superiors, decided
to spend the night out on the aerodrome to watch the weather minute
by minute. At 3am he was called to the phone. It was the colonel demanding to know if the squadron was going up. Wyllie said it wasn't. The local
weather had become even thicker. 'He appeared very much annoyed and
said, "Well, what's the matter with it now: it ought to be clear on the
ground – it's blowing like the dickens here." I was furious. Here was an
absolutely hopeless night and, because a Hun had laid eggs on Dunkirk
during a clear patch, I was supposed to push my people into thick mist
to break their necks – or arrange with the bon Dieu for a patch of clear
sky.'[10]

For a few nights conditions improved sufficiently for the squadron to
resume bombing. Then more low rain cloud, gales and snow swept
northern France. In the middle of this latest spate of unflyable weather
Wyllie was told that Trenchard expected his squadron to operate in the
thick of it regardless. Over at 9th Wing headquarters at Boisdinghem,
where it was blowing a gale and the cloud was down almost to treetop
height, he found his colonel 'looking rather blue'. He had just heard that
two of the wing's aircraft, attempting at the general's behest to attack an
enemy target, had 'crashed to earth'. While they were still absorbing this
news, Wyllie and the colonel, looking out at the scudding, almost ground-
level cloud heaps rolling past, were horrified to see a DH4 bomber suddenly burst out of it in a violent spin and plunge into the ground in front
of them, killing the pilot and observer. Even as the crash happened there
was a phone call from Flying Corps headquarters at St Omer. 'It was
"Boom". Why hadn't machines gone up? "You've let me down. Shall
I come and send up the machines myself?"

'At last the colonel said, "I wish you would come and send up the
machines yourself, sir" and the "booming" ceased. It wasn't pretty. It was
uncommonly like red murder.'[11]

But Trenchard's tetchy voice, rumbling down the telephone, would not be bullying his flying commanders for much longer. He was destined, in the New Year of 1918, back in London, for bigger things.

The carnage of Passchendaele through the summer and autumn of 1917 had not seen the end of the futile slaughter on the ground. Despite the growing nervousness of his prime minister, Lloyd George, Sir Douglas Haig, now a field marshal, decided to order a brand-new attack on the seemingly impregnable concrete-bunkered Hindenburg Line. He launched it on 20 November at Cambrai, fifty miles south-east of Ypres aiming to punch a hole in the enemy defences through which the cavalry would charge and finally turn the tide of the war. The Germans, taken by complete surprise, were overrun by four miles. So great was the excitement back in England that church bells were rung throughout the land to celebrate the victory. The rejoicing was premature. Ten days later the Germans counter-attacked. They retook every yard of ground they had lost. And with it, as one WWI historian wrote, 'Haig lost his last vestige of credit with his political masters. Lloyd George took over the strategic conduct of the war.'[12] He also removed Haig's greatest ally at the War Office, the chief of the imperial general staff, General Sir William Robertson. He was replaced by the prime minister's protégé, General Sir Henry Wilson.

In France military operations were also taken out of the hands of the generals. The prime minister, Georges Clemenceau, and Lloyd George set up an Allied Supreme War Council on which political leaders of both countries, with their military advisers, henceforth dictated the strategy of a war that was now entirely in civilian hands.

Meanwhile, as the winter of 1917 spread its icy blanket over the stalemate of the Western Front and both sides counted the dead of the fruitless battles of Passchendaele and Cambrai, the German High Command was busy planning a gigantic spring attack it saw as the last hope to win the war before the American armies landed.

Some Americans had in fact already arrived. Attached to squadrons of the French and British air forces, they had been making a name for themselves in the air – and often, sometimes scandalously, on the ground.

Chapter 23
America Comes to London

When, in April 1917, the United States, prompted by mounting losses of its shipping to German submarines, had finally joined the bitter war soon to enter its fourth year, it was unprepared for the decisive military contribution urgently expected of it. Its army stood at less than 100,000 men and with barely 140 obsolete aeroplanes and a tiny force of just twenty-six pilots, not one of them experienced in aerial combat, its military air service scarcely deserved the name. It would be another year before an adequately sized army and an air force big enough to influence the outcome of the war would arrive on the Western Front.

Meanwhile, a small trickle of pilot hopefuls had already made their own way to Europe to enlist as volunteers with the French Air Service. A special squadron had been formed for them called Lafayette Escadrille, in which they fought alongside French pilots. Other Americans joined the British Flying Corps and the Royal Naval Air Service. Conspicuous by their accents and uniforms, some with odd-looking lemon-squeezer felt hats, by their relative wealth and by their uninhibited approach to life, they brought a highly informal style of their own to the conventions of life on the squadrons. They brought, too, an awesome reputation for unleashing reckless flying pranks on the civilian population and for their bacchanalian off-duty excesses, which involved regular fist fights and women in prodigious measure.

Their antics were graphically recorded by one of their number, Elliott White Springs, the son of a wealthy South Carolina cotton mill-owner. A philosophy graduate of Princeton University, Springs came to England in the autumn of 1917 with two friends: another graduate, Lawrence Callahan, from a well-to-do Kentucky family, and a rather less privileged young Arkansas farmer, John MacGavock Grider, who had wed at seventeen, a short-lived marriage that none the less produced two children. Labelled by their fellow pilots the 'Three Musketeers', the trio of Southerners had forged a close bond. In what became an instant bestseller, Springs later documented their wartime flying lives, the terror they encountered in the skies over the Western Front and the riotous conduct in which they indulged on their leaves in London during their pilot training in England. Springs disguised his authorship by issuing the book as the anonymous diary of 'an unknown aviator', using the real names of some of his colleagues and referring to himself in the third person – a device that sixty years later was still causing confusion among reissuing publishers and aviation historians.*

The 210 young Americans with whom Springs arrived in England in October 1917 were treated like Flying Corps cadets. They were sent to Oxford for ground training and taught to fly on Farman Shorthorns before those who weren't killed in the process joined front-line squadrons. Springs, Grider and Callahan went to the newly formed No. 85 Squadron at Hounslow Heath west of London. Its commander was Major Billy Bishop, soon to add to his record the final twenty-five victories that would bring his total claims to the much-challenged seventy-two. With his Victoria Cross and phenomenal bag of professed kills, Bishop was at the pinnacle of his fame, mobbed wherever he went in London and treated like the royalty with whom he now so comfortably mixed. When the Three Musketeers signed up with his squadron at Hounslow he became a regular guest, participating in the drunken revelry at the almost daily parties the young Americans began to throw at a stately town house, complete with butler and cook, they had rented from an English lord for £10 a week in exclusive Berkeley Square. Over one of the bedrooms they hung a sign: 'Ladies' Room'. The house-warming, which Bishop attended, was memorable more for the paralysing potency of its cocktails than for the food. Springs wrote:

> We got around the food problem easily. All we had cooked was soup and fish. Then we made a big tub full of egg nog and a couple of big pitchers of mint julep. To make sure that no one got beyond the fish

---

*Elliott Springs' book, *War Birds: Diary of an Unknown Aviator*, first appeared anonymously as a serial in the weekly magazine *Liberty*. It was published as a book, again anonymously, in New York in 1926. It attracted rave reviews and was regarded at the time as a classic of its genre. Curiosity inevitably surrounded the name of the unknown aviator and the true identity of the author of the diaries. Publishers of subsequent reprints, attempting to throw some light on this, unfortunately credited the authorship to John MacGavock Grider, saying that the diary had been edited, after his death in combat in June 1918, by his pilot friend Springs. In fact, apart from a few sentences, nothing remains of the brief three weeks that Grider's journal matter-of-factly recorded. Although he never allowed his name to be attached to the book, its racy, moving and powerful narrative is entirely Springs' work: his personal air war autobiography drawn from his own diaries, logbooks and letters home.

course, we shook up cocktails too. Our guests arrived about six and we started bottoms up in rotation. It was a riot. Springs was at the head of the table and served. Everybody had a bottle of port and a bottle of champagne. The butler brought in a big platter of fish and Springs served them up by the tail, tossing one to each guest as if they were seals. At the end of the fish course, I was alone at the table. The rest were chasing each other all over the place.[1]

The house-warming was just the beginning. Page after page of Springs' diary proudly recorded the Americans' subsequent off-duty lives of frenzied indulgence in a wartime London filled with men in uniform and a surplus of women captivated by their extrovert, uninhibited style and engaging slow, Southern drawls. Most of the women had never met an American before and weren't used to being addressed as 'M'am'. They were like moths to a flame. 'Twelve of us,' wrote Springs, 'were up in our suite at the Court having dinner last night and we decided we ought to have some girls. So after dinner we all went out in different directions to round up the girls after the theatre. As we needed so many we thought that everybody should get as many as possible in case the others had no success. By twelve o'clock we had twenty-two girls in the suite.'

Convinced he would never return from France, Springs was determined to live life to the full while he could. In a sobering lecture a Flying Corps major warned them what lay ahead. 'It's a war of men – strong determined men, and weaklings have no part in it,' he said. 'You'll be frightened many times, but most of you will be able to conquer your fear and carry on.' Springs declared: 'I haven't lived very well, but I am determined to die well . . . Thank God I am going to have the opportunity to die as every brave man should – fighting – and fighting for my country.' Later, he wrote: 'I just hope I can stick it through. I know I'm not afraid to die. I'm pretty young to be ready for it – and I'm not. Why, I'm just beginning to live!' He and the other Musketeers did so in a more or less continuous alcoholic haze. It enveloped their parties, their nightclub dancing, their regular fights and their stream of sexual encounters. 'These London women,' wrote Springs, 'are in a class by themselves. They are good sports, good looking, good dancers, well educated, act like ladies and they don't sit around and worry about their honour all the time . . . Virtue over here isn't even its own reward.'

At the RFC Club in Bruton Street they were regular visitors to the bar. 'By the time Springs got there they were well oiled. He ordered a round of double brandies. Then Kelly ordered triple whiskies. Then Bird called

for some port and they started a round again. We had to put Springs in a
cold tub before he could call the roll for dinner . . .

'There was a big party last night and we went to a dance at the Elysee
Gardens. The whole Flying Corps was there and all as tight as a nun's
corset . . . Cecil gave a dinner party in honour of Peggy and the Doll the
same evening. This is a new Peggy – the third. This one came as a present
in Murray's [a nightclub] the other night.' At the same party 'the Doll
was dancing with some Englishman and Springs and I went out to get
her . . . Her partner got very nasty about it and told us to run along and
gave me a gentle push. I saw red and took a long swing. Springs saw me
swing and jumped in the way. I knocked him flat and then Cal grabbed
me. That's three times they've jumped on me in a fight.'

Springs' memoir reflects his almost automatic response to perceived
insults when drunk: to use his fists. In a bar at a Maidenhead riverside
hotel he heard two British Guards officers 'taking cracks at the American
Army'.

> One of them, a long, tall bird, said, 'I've been reading in the papers
> until I'm bloody well sick of it, about the number of American
> troops that have come over. But what I can't understand is why
> none of them will fight. Paris is full of them, London is full of them,
> but they all jolly well stay away from the front. None of them will
> fight.'
>
> 'Well,'says Springs, 'here is one of them that will.' And with that,
> he hauls off and stretches the long, tall bird on the floor. The other
> one makes a pass at him, but he ducks and beats it out and jumps
> in his boat and shoves off.

Next in the procession of women was Lily. 'She's a cute little kid and a
good dancer. She's been living with one of the boys for a couple of
months. He's nutty about her. She has a sort of past that wouldn't sound
well at home, but doesn't seem to make much difference over here. At
home every woman that isn't a virgin has a past.' When Lily's American
boyfriend was killed in a crash she came to the Musketeers claiming she
was pregnant. They gave her some money and quickly passed her on to
a colleague. Lily was followed by a more sensational young woman.

> Last night we had another choice assortment of callers . . . one of
> them, oh la, la, what a knockout! Her name is Billy Carlton [actually
> Billie Carleton]. She and I got on like Antony and Cleopatra. How
> that woman can dance! Well, she ought to be able to, seeing as how

she is leading lady in a musical show . . . She sure is witty. She kept us laughing all evening. She had a general in tow who wasn't at all friendly to me.

I took her home and the general wasn't very mad! It's getting to be a disgrace the way we welcome our friends and then put them out and keep their girls . . . She has a gorgeous flat and there was a supper waiting for us when we got there and a maid to serve it. She slipped on a negligee and looked like a million dollars.

Meanwhile his lordship's town house had to all intents and purposes become a nightclub for the entire American contingent. The place would jump until the small hours with their ceaseless drunken parties, their thumping piano, the loud choruses of their singing, their fights, and the constant traffic of women, some providing their services commercially. The airmen taught the women the latest American dance steps – the 'giant swing' and the foxtrot. The nightly uproar began to attract complaints from the Berkeley Square neighbours.

The pilots' shenanigans weren't confined to wild parties. There were outcries from terrorised victims of their low-flying missions along the river Thames. On one occasion four of them took their fighter aircraft in a noisy line-astern formation from Hounslow to Maidenhead.

We ground-strafed the place and chased everybody off the terrace at Skindles. Then we steeplechased all the way back down the river and kept our wheels just out of the water. Nigger dipped his once. Cal missed hitting a bridge by inches and Springs landed with about two hundred feet of telephone wire dragging on his undercarriage . . . At one long open stretch there was a punt in front of us right in the middle of the river. A man in a bright blazer was standing up in the stern punting and a girl was sitting in the bow with a big pink parasol. As we dove on them the man fell overboard and the girl lost her parasol. I looked back to see it floating down the river and the man in the blazer floundering about in a regular whirlpool.

Late in May 1918 the Americans' London idyll ended. No. 85 Squadron at last flew to the war. Its SE5 fighters were waved off at Hounslow by a small flock of young women, fascinated by the silk-stocking skullcaps the pilots wore under their fur helmets. One of Springs' girlfriends, Dora, 'wanted to know whose stocking mine was made from'. Among those who came to say goodbye was Billy Bishop's wife, Margaret Burden, whom he'd married the previous year. Margaret, swept up into the stratospheric levels of London society in which he now dwelled, had brought along Princess Marie Louise, a granddaughter of Queen Victoria, who wished them godspeed on behalf of the King. Bishop led the squadron into the air in a massed formation take-off. The nineteen machines made a wide circuit then turned back to swoop thunderously low over the heads of the farewell party, blowing off the women's hats in a shower of dust.

When the Americans landed that day at Petite Synthe near Dunkirk they swapped their carefree, dissolute London lives for the terrors of the Western Front. Within two days the squadron was in combat. Springs had exchanged his nights with a woman in his arms for nights now stalked by the first of his air-war nightmares.

Chapter 24

Operation Michael

When the Americans landed in France that day they were no longer serving with the Royal Flying Corps. The previous month, on 1 April 1918, the RFC had finally been merged with the Royal Naval Air Service to form the Royal Air Force. The rival air forces that had so unremittingly and wastefully fought each other for money and resources throughout the war had in the end been given no option. An Afrikaner soldier, General Jan Smuts, who had fought the British in the Boer War and would later become South Africa's prime minister, had been asked by Lloyd George to investigate the entire organisation of British air power, including its ability to defend Britain and respond to the Gotha raids with sustained bombing of German cities. Smuts, who came with no entrenched loyalty to either flying service, not only quickly identified the glaringly obvious root of the problems seething within the divided kingdoms but produced his commendably brief reports within a few weeks. The most sweeping one declared that aviation had become 'a powerful means of waging war in its own right . . . There is absolutely no limit to the scale of its future independent war use. The day may not be far off when aerial operations with their devastation of enemy lands and destruction of industrial and populous centres on a vast scale may become the principal operations of war, to which the older forms of military and naval operations may become secondary and subordinate.'[1]

Smuts saw no room for two competing air forces. He recommended the creation of an Air Ministry to form a third British military arm. The proposal was almost immediately accepted by the War Cabinet. The first air minister was the newspaper baron Lord Rothermere, who immediately appointed Trenchard the new Royal Air Force's first chief of air staff. Unfortunately the two men vehemently disagreed almost immediately over the way air power should best be used. The clash of personalities was total and irreconcilable. Trenchard resented his civilian boss while Rothermere found Trenchard 'an intolerant know-it-all of dull, unimaginative mind'.[2] Both men resigned. Trenchard, who had been succeeded as field commander in France by another aviation general, was replaced as chief of air staff by an officer he had for years actively distrusted and despised as secretive and over-cautiously ineffective, Major-General Frederick Sykes, a much less daunting and dominating figure but a more intelligent man than 'Boom'. When the replacement air minister, a Scottish industrialist, Sir William Weir, arrived on the scene the prime minister told him to find a new job for Trenchard. As 'Boom' was unwilling to work under Sykes it proved a far from easy task.

Offered the post of commander-in-chief of a brand-new bombing force, established to appease public opinion by raiding German cities, Trenchard turned it down. For weeks in the spring of 1918, the unhappy and suddenly jobless former head of Britain's air operations in France retreated into a sulking wilderness of his own making. From his bachelor flat in Mayfair he would go to Green Park for hours every day to ruminate while reading his newspaper on a bench. One morning, sitting anonymously there, bowler-hatted in his civilian suit perusing *The Times*, he famously overheard the conversation of two passing senior naval officers. To his utter shock they were discussing him. Moreover, they were loudly criticising his resignation as head of the new air force. 'It's an outrage,' one of them apparently said. 'I don't know why the government should pander to a man who threw in his hand at the height of a battle. If I'd my way with Trenchard I'd have him shot.'[3]

Stung by this crushing view of him from two complete strangers Trenchard realised it might be a judgement shared by others. His resignation in a time of war was being discussed in Parliament. Rumours of a court-martial circulated within political and military circles but it was questionable what charges could have been brought against such a powerful personality.[4] However, Trenchard had been so shaken by the comments he'd overheard that he left his park bench and went straight back to his flat where, swallowing his pride, he sat down to write to Air Minister Weir accepting the command of what would become the Independent Air Force. Weir was said to have been so relieved to have found a job for this formidable figure who had helped create from a tiny battalion the world's biggest most powerful air force that he allowed him to bypass Sykes and report directly to him.

Trenchard wasn't the only casualty of the birth of the single air force. His boss, Sir David Henderson, now a lieutenant-general, had, as director-general of military aeronautics, done more than any other man to shape the development of British air power, and he had hoped to become chief of the new service himself. When the job went to Sykes, whom he, too, disliked, Henderson resigned as well, citing his desire to escape from 'an atmosphere of falsehood and intrigue which has enveloped the Air Ministry'. He went back to France to serve in the army. It was there, in June 1918, that the tragic news reached him of the death of his son, Captain Ian Henderson, killed in Scotland in a flying accident.

Meanwhile, the now knighted Sir Hugh Trenchard had donned his major-general's uniform and gone to eastern France to take command of the new bomber group at its headquarters near Nancy. It was a small outfit, scarcely justifying his high rank and towering experience as field commander of an entire air force. The great armada of aeroplanes General Smuts had so confidently foreseen would break Germany's spirit and bomb her into submission never came. The overwhelmed British factories couldn't produce enough engines and the Independent Air Force was never to acquire more than nine squadrons. Although its small night-bomber wing was equipped with the RAF's answer to the Gotha – a twin-engined biplane, the Handley-Page 0/400, whose eight-hour endurance could take it to Frankfurt, Stuttgart and Cologne – the big machines didn't arrive in sufficient numbers to make any difference to the course of a war that, in the spring of 1918, had begun to go very badly for the Allies.

With the defeat of Russia on the Eastern Front the German High Command, faced with swelling demands within the country for peace, riots of hungry civilians spreading and mutinies erupting within its navy, was more desperate than ever for urgent victory before the Americans, still not arriving in decisive numbers, could significantly reinforce the flagging British and French armies. General Ludendorff transferred forty-four divisions from the east to the Western Front. On 21 March, in one of the most massive attacks of the war, he had struck.

With crushing numerical superiority 'Operation Michael' had hit the British first. At 4.40am in dark and dense fog, using great clouds of concealing smoke mixed with waves of choking gas, fifty-two German divisions spearheaded the attack with highly mobile assault units. These 'stormtroops' swept across the lines on a forty-mile front from the Somme to Cambrai, ending the stalemate of three years of trench warfare.

Within four days they had driven an enormous wedge forty miles deep into the British positions, threatening to break the Allied lines, seize the Channel ports and capture Paris. It was like the 1914 great retreat from Mons all over again. And it led Haig (now under French General Ferdinand Foch, who'd been made supreme commander, of the Allied Armies) to issue one of the war's most famous edicts. His Order of the Day on 11 April declared: 'Victory will belong to the side that holds out longest. There is no other course open to us but to fight it out. Every position must be held to the last man. There must be no retirement. With our backs to the wall and believing in the justice of our cause each one of us must fight on to the end.'[5]

Above this latest inferno which, even more rapidly than on the Somme and Passchendaele, would add a staggering 3 million more Allied and German men to the war's casualties, the new Royal Air Force's pilots and observers began to suffer yet another surge of losses that would eclipse those of the dreadful days of the previous year's 'Bloody April'. The seemingly unstoppable rush of the German divisions forced the British squadrons to begin a series of retreats to new airfields behind the daily shifting line of the enemy advance, which was to sweep as far south as the earlier battlefield of the Marne and see German guns shelling Paris. In the face of the sudden, appalling possibility of defeat for the Allies, the RAF was forced into a new offensive spasm, ordered into low-level strafing of German troops and attacking the aerodromes and railways that were sustaining Ludendorff's advancing divisions. They were met with a ferocious response from the German air service. As the British and French squadrons clashed with the biggest flying circuses they had ever encountered, more of the war's great aces began to fall.

Erwin Böhme, who had never ceased to blame himself for the death of the German titan Boelcke in their mid-air collision, and who had fallen in love with nurse Annamarie Brüning, had already gone. From the day he and Annamarie had first met they had exchanged letters with great frequency, his eventually being dispatched from the elite Boelcke squadron, Jasta 2, which he had come to command; hers from the military hospital in Hamburg. The correspondence, in which they addressed each other with strict formality – 'Dear Miss Annamarie' and 'Dear Mr Böhme' – was surprisingly devoid of expressions of affection. His letters focused instead on his life and the satisfactions of doing battle in his Albatros with his Flying Corps opponents.

'With us,' he told Annamarie, 'each dogfight is like a joust . . . a sporting duel. I have nothing against the single man with whom I fight. I only want to put him and his aircraft out of commission so that he will harm us no more.' But on neither side were the airmen really fighting for themselves, the thirty-eight-year-old Böhme explained. 'We are fighting for our colours. Every victory which I achieve is counted not only for me, but also for my squadron and in its service we strive to achieve successes. It is called Esprit de Corps . . . It may indeed seem strange that I, an old character, have been so set on fire – but it is a holy flame.'[6]

Few of Annamarie's letters have survived. One began with the startling declaration: 'Dear Mr Böhme, Do you know from where I am writing you? Without blushing I say it: in the bath!' She was sharing it, 'tightly packed together', with no fewer than four other nurses. When the Hamburg hospital's central heating system ran out of coal, they'd decided it was the only way, in the freezing weather, to keep warm off duty. To add to this scene of sisterly decadence they were drowning their sorrows with glasses of wine from a crateful sent to one of them by her family, sipping as they wrote letters on an ironing board balanced athwart the tub.

When her fellow nurses discovered that Annamarie was writing to one of their country's prominent fighter aces they all insisted on adding their names to the letter. 'The wine shall not fail to warm us from inward out,' she told him, adding: 'And so we take our glasses, clink them together, and shout with enthusiasm: health and victory to our brave German fighter pilots!'[7]

But as Erwin Böhme's victories mounted he became increasingly disillusioned at the pointlessness of it all. An innately solitary man who enjoyed his own company, he went on leave alone to the Bavarian Alps for some skiing. 'My God, the world is so beautiful,' he wrote to Annamarie.

Here, with the war far removed, in the heavenly peace of the mountains, the thought came to me: is not this mutual slaughter without ending insanity?

Amongst our enemies there are many men of worth whose unfinished life work is destroyed by a stupid fluke hit! What kind of gallant foes do I find amongst the English with whom we do battle? What decent fellows have I got to know amongst those we have taken prisoner? But I have to shoot at them as if they were fair game.

When I am back again in the field I will no longer be able to understand this course of thinking. However, today these thoughts occurred to me and I wanted to confide them in you.[8]

In late October 1917, by which time a bullet had destroyed the tendon in his vital right trigger finger, Böhme was ordered to attend a ceremony at the Dessau grave of Oswald Boelcke on the anniversary of his death. On the way back to his squadron, now in Belgium, he diverted on an urgent personal mission to Hamburg. The train schedules allowed him just eleven hours in the city, during which he proposed to Annamarie. 'I now have a fiancée!' he wrote elatedly to tell his younger brother Gerhard, a horse veterinary officer with the German artillery.

You, my dear brother, should hear of such tidings immediately ...
For me it was love at first sight and, as she recently admitted to me,
also the same for her.

Each of us tried in our letters not to reveal our true emotions –
she because of her womanly modesty, and I because of my reserved
style. We both were tormented with the uncertainty of how the
other felt in his or her heart ... Boy! I would never have believed
that an old man who life had made so serious and stern could once
more be so happy. Rejoice, Gerhard, for your old but rejuvenated
brother.[9]

The few remaining letters that passed between them were suddenly
warmly intimate. Böhme began to enclose flowers he'd picked for her in
the woods or saved from the dinner table in the mess – it was the
squadron's custom to place blooms around the plates of pilots who had
scored that day. 'You, my dear Annamarie! First a long, quite long kiss,
and then throw in a quick short kiss, too! My love, what a rich man am
I!'

He began to address her as 'my sweetheart', telling her:

I was not able to conceal my happiness from my staffel mates. There
was great rejoicing ... What a fool I was not to seek my greatest
happiness long, long ago, and not to direct the big question to you
weeks ago! ... The fear of a 'no' answer gripped me by the throat.
I knew that your rejection would so rock my emotional balance
that I would no longer be capable of performing my duties and
responsibilities at the front ... It is my prayer that we can soon find
a way that we can always be with each other. Please send me some
pictures of yourself and kiss each of them a couple of times. Until
morning my darling, Your Erwin.[10]

Less than four weeks after Böhme wrote that letter, he was killed,
dying in agony, shot down on 29 November 1917 in a flaming Albatros
over the devastated Passchendaele battlefield by the crew of a Flying
Corps two-seat reconnaissance plane. 'I sent a two-second burst of Vickers
fire into him,' the No. 10 Squadron pilot, Lieutenant John Pattern, recalled
in his nineties. 'His aircraft seemed to flutter, then slid out of sight below
my starboard wing ... When I caught sight of the Albatros again it was
burning like a torch and sideslipping toward the ground trailing a streamer
of smoke. For an instant I saw the German pilot looking down over the
side of the cockpit. Then the smoke and flames enveloped him.'[11]

Böhme's partly charred body was recovered from the wreckage. It had fallen just inside the British lines. He was given a full military funeral, but his grave was later obliterated by shellfire. Earlier that day he had claimed his twenty-fourth victory and back on his squadron desk was an unopened envelope. It contained the notification of the award of a Blue Max. On Böhme's body there was a letter he'd just received from Annamarie. They had not met again since his hurried proposal between trains in Hamburg a month earlier.

Ten days before he was killed Böhme, on his way back from a patrol, had diverted to Richthofen's airfield. He'd told Annamarie he'd gone to have a chat with his old friend, and 'to have a cup of coffee – they always have such fine pastries there'. When news of his death reached Richthofen he wrote to Böhme's brother Gerhard: 'In war one becomes hard and cold. However his death has touched me very deeply – you yourself know how close a friend your brother was to me.

'On the last afternoon before his death, he was here visiting me – full of joy over the development of our dear old Boelcke squadron, which he had led solely and single-handedly to its old heights. Now they are both united in Valhalla: your splendid brother and his great master, who of us all was closest to him.'[12]*

All too soon the Baron would be joining them there.

---

*In 1922 Annamarie Brüning married a languages professor by whom she had three daughters. She died in 1955.

Chapter 25
Death of the Red Baron

As the conflict on the Western Front was exploding into its latest spate of violence in the spring of 1918, 600 miles away, in her mansion at Schweidnitz in Silesia, Baroness Kunigunde von Richthofen went to her desk every day to write up her war diary. It recorded the growing hardship the German population at home was suffering. In Schweidnitz there was no coal; people were freezing in their houses. The markets had no fruit or vegetables. Potatoes were rationed to a handful per week. Coffee was made from acorns, sausages from fish, flour from potatoes. Paper dresses and stockings that would survive only three washes had begun to replace cotton ones. Because the shops had run out of leather shoes people were making them from old carpets. Many were walking about barefoot. 'The people's mood is very irritable,' Kunigunde wrote. 'I wouldn't know how to live either if we didn't have our garden. It keeps us from hunger.'[1]

Beside her as she wrote stood portraits of the five most important people in her life, all away at the war: her bearded husband, Major Albrecht von Richthofen, a Prussian nobleman with his regiment in France; her daughter Ilse, serving as a Red Cross nurse; her youngest son, fourteen-year-old Bolko, a cadet at a military academy; and her two hugely famous pilot sons. The main content of her diary was Manfred's and Lothar's letters, her daily expressed concerns for their safety and the rising totals of their victories. Miraculously, by the spring of 1918 both sons had survived, though not unscathed.

Every time the phone rang or there was a knock on the door the Baroness's heart would 'thud'. It had regularly quickened as news had come of the succession of wounds sustained by the hot-headed, reckless Lothar. He had spent months at a time grounded in hospitals recovering from awful battle injuries. That he was to fly on just seventy-seven days of combat duty in the entire war would make his final forty victories remarkable. In May 1917 anti-aircraft shrapnel had shattered his hip so badly he was out of action for five months. Then, in March 1918, forced down by a British pilot, he had flown into a power line. Lucky not to lose an eye – it haemorrhaged for days – he'd been thrown from the wreckage with a broken nose and fractured jaw and had nearly bled to death. Again he was out of action for weeks, during which photographs show him with his head locked into a crude frame. His jaw is clamped tightly around a metal rod jammed into his mouth, lending him a more than passing resemblance to the muzzled monster Hannibal Lecter in the film *The Silence of the Lambs*. Recovered and back in the air, he was next hospitalised with a burst eardrum. Later he was shot in the thigh by a Camel pilot, a wound that finally ended his wartime flying career.*

Nor had Manfred escaped serious injury. Kunigunde would marvel at 'how wonderful it was that Manfred up to now hadn't caught it. He seemed immune to bullets; once a round went through his fur boot, another time through his flying scarf; once again through a fur and leather jacket – but never scratched his skin.'² But on 6 July 1917, in an encounter with a flight of British FE2 pushers near Ypres, at last one did. A bullet struck him on the top of his head and, temporarily blinded by concussion, his arms and legs briefly paralysed, he spun down from 13,000 feet, out of control. When his vision began to return, only 2,000 feet from the ground, he managed to level the Albatros and make a forced landing in a field of tall grass. The bullet had cut a four-inch-long slice along his skull, exposing the bone. The wound and concussion grounded him for three weeks and he spent months with his head bulkily bandaged.

The head injury marked a turning point in the Red Baron's life. Although he had written to his mother from hospital: 'It is certainly a good thing if one has a thick head in life,' the trauma his brain had suffered was permanently to change his personality.

Long before he was medically fit, Manfred insisted on going back into the air. He had been allowed to pay earlier, non-flying, visits to the squadron only as long as he was accompanied by his nurse, Katie Ottersdorf, who strictly guarded him from visitors in the Courtrai hospital. Richthofen was said to have been acutely embarrassed at having to meet his pilots with a nurse by his side. Photographs show him with his bandaged head standing by the attractive Katie. Perhaps inevitably, rumours of a romantic relationship began to circulate but she was soon to fade from his life when, three weeks after being wounded, he was

---

*At the price of a multitude of crippling wounds Lothar von Richthofen survived the war with his forty victories. He married a German countess who gave him two children. But his restless unhappiness told on the marriage. As it began to break up in 1922 he went back to flying, taking a job with a small airline operating between Berlin and Hamburg. A few weeks after his divorce he was killed in a landing accident at Hamburg.

discharged and back in the air, claiming his fifty-eighth victory.

But Richthofen was far from recovered. When, in September 1917, he made a flying visit to Schweidnitz, landing his red Albatros on a playing field near his home, Kunigunde was shocked by both his appearance and his altogether altered character.

To my horror I found that Manfred's head wound is still far from healed. The bone still lies exposed. Every other day he goes to a local hospital to have the bandage changed. He looks ill and irritable. Until now, he seemed to me like young Siegfried, the invulnerable. His elasticity, the light way with which he described his air battles, had deluded me a little about the frightful danger of his profession. But one after another the brilliant young flying heroes had fallen. They have all been adept fellows, and of unexampled bravery. Now fate has risked itself against Manfred.

When his mother, reminding him of his phenomenal number of victories, pleaded with him, 'Have done with flying Manfred,' he responded angrily. 'Would it please you if I brought myself to safety now and rested on my laurels?'

'No – it didn't matter,' she wrote. 'Manfred would fight again until—until— the war came to an end.'[3]

Normally amiable and patient with the crowds who surrounded the house during his visits in awed and deeply respectful groups, Manfred was now curt and unsmiling. Beset by blinding headaches and increasingly displaying obvious symptoms of traumatic stress, he spent much of his time resting on his bed. Woken up to greet a group of wellwishers at the front door he stood there resentfully with a dour face. 'He was almost unfriendly,' Kunigunde reported. 'He was scarcely able to conceal his foul mood.' After a few days Manfred left Schweidnitz to seek isolation with a noble family on their remote estate in East Prussia, where he could make lone elk hunts into the forests.

The German Air Service had a term for his condition: *abgeflogen* – 'flown out'. Affected pilots were usually sent on recuperation leave or as happened in the RFC, transferred to training schools as instructors. But there was no way the Baron, ill as he was, was prepared to contemplate any such option. There was only one place he wanted to be and that was with his squadron. However, back in France he faced some major problems. A new fighter aircraft, the latest of Anthony Fokker's products, was arriving – a triplane to rival the British Sopwith. It would 'climb like an ape', Manfred told his pilots. But although it could do just that it also started to kill them when its top wings began collapsing in flight. The triplanes had to be grounded and returned to the factory for structural strengthening. While this was going on, in the winter of 1917–18, Richthofen, unwell but now a national treasure of worldwide fame, was ordered out of service to tour as a war hero for propaganda purposes. He was taken to the Eastern Front to add prestige to the German delegation at the Russian–German peace conference and to munitions factories to exhort workers striking in protest at harsh conditions, and the cold and hunger created by nearly four years of war, to return to work.

At the end of January 1918 Richthofen went home to Schweidnitz. It was to be his last visit. His head wound was finally healing, but his mother was shocked to find him in an even more wretched emotional state. 'Although he looked healthier and fresher than on his leave in the fall, the high spirits, the light heartedness, the playfulness, were lacking in his character. He was taciturn, aloof, almost unapproachable. His words seemed to come from an unknown distance . . . I think he has seen death too often . . . I had never before seen Manfred so.'[4]

When his sister Ilse took him to the station to bid him goodbye she is believed to have said, holding his hand through the window as the train began to move: 'Do be a little bit careful, please. We want to see each other again.'

The telegram came on 22 April. The Baroness was being served her afternoon tea when the maid brought it in. 'Not without a thudding heart I open it.' The telegram came from Major Richthofen, her husband, in France. An urgent message had been sent to him by Richthofen's squadron that their leader was missing. 'Manfred is in English captivity,' Kunigunde read. 'My hands shake. For a moment the room seems to spin. How would his reception by the English have been? The restless creative spirit now condemned to a long inactivity. Then another voice spoke inside me. We will see each other after the war. He survives for us.'[5]

Next day the telephone rang incessantly. Friends and complete strangers demanded to know if the rumour of Manfred's capture was true. She told them all it was. But that evening, as she walked in the garden, a young boy called to her through the fence: 'Is it true, Frau Baroness, that the Herr Rittmeister has fallen?' He had seen the news in a bulletin on the town's war information kiosk where the daily casualty lists were posted.

Kundigunde rushed inside to the telephone. Frantically she attempted to ring the town's newspaper. It had closed for the day. She tried the post office. Had there been a fresh telegram? There hadn't. In desperation she called the mayor.

'And now I learn the horrible truth. It was painful for him to give me.' The newspaper had brought out a late edition reporting Manfred's death. As she stood holding the receiver, numbed, someone handed her a copy of the paper. The headline read: RITTMEISTER FREIHERR VON RICHTHOFEN DEAD. He had been killed two days earlier.

No single air battle has been as minutely researched, dissected or voluminously written about as has that over the Somme valley on 21 April 1918 in which the Red Baron died, his end witnessed by many. But who actually killed him is still a matter of debate.

The previous evening at their base east of Amiens, the pilots of Richthofen's squadron, Jasta 11, had thrown a party to celebrate their leader's eightieth victory that day. He had in fact shot down two Camels in flames within three minutes. The squadron, constantly moving on to keep up with Ludendorff's fast-rolling westward advance, had only just hurriedly created its latest temporary landing ground in a field near Cappy on the Somme river. At the party Lieutenant Karl Bodenschatz, the adjutant of Richthofen's four-squadron 'flying circus' group, had tried to persuade him that the time had come for him to rest on his laurels. The commanders of the German Air Service had already attempted to do so, without success. When he refused a prestigious high-level post at Air Service headquarters, they had turned to his adjutant to see if he'd fare any better. He didn't. That night Richthofen dismissed the idea out of hand. 'A paper-shuffler? No! I'm staying at the front,' he insisted.

Bodenschatz described in his diary the unusually buoyant mood that pervaded the squadron next morning as the pilots prepared for another day of combat in their now wing-strengthened Fokker triplanes. 'Again and again their laughter sweeps across the airfield. They have every reason to be in a good mood: the splendid successes of recent days, the unreserved appreciation of their superiors, their speedy triplanes which have proven to be first-rate.'[6] Dressed in their flying clothes, waiting for early morning fog to clear, they indulged in horseplay. Richthofen started it when he walked over to one of his pilots, who was snoozing on a stretcher on the ground, and tipped him out of it. 'As soon as another tired, equally unsuspecting human lies down for a nap on the vacant stretcher, the Rittmeister tips this youngster into the spring mud as well.' In response the pilots seized Richthofen's Great Dane, Moritz, and tied a wheel chock to his tail, 'leaving the poor, aggrieved creature utterly dejected'. Richthofen joined in the laughter. The pilots had 'seldom seen him so downright, openly delighted. They know that this hunter is actually extremely pleased about his eightieth kill – even though he says little about it.' The hunter said even less about the blinding headaches that still never left him. Or spoke of the frazzled state of his nerves.

Around 11.30am, as the fog began to lift, the squadron phone rang. Some British aircraft of the newly created Royal Air Force were approaching. The two flights of Jasta 11 were scrambled, one of them led into the air by Richthofen, who had also ordered the machines of another of his wing's squadrons, Staffel 5, flying Albatros fighters, to join them. Through a telescope Bodenschatz watched them disappear into the distance as they headed west up the Somme valley to the front eight miles away, its lines no longer static but rolling back and forth. Here, high above the temporary trenches, the legendary air battle began.

It was a complex affair, involving three separate groups of aeroplanes. Richthofen's two fighter squadrons, two Australian reconnaissance machines and a Sopwith Camel squadron. The Camels of No. 209, flown by former British naval pilots whose unit had just been absorbed into the RAF, were, from their base at Bertangles, on an offensive patrol at around 15,000 feet. They had arrived over the lines at about the same time as the German circus. Far below them two slow and unprotected two-seater RE8s from an Australian Flying Corps squadron were going about the dangerous business of photographing the enemy positions when two of the triplanes dived down to try to pick them off. The Australians, who responded with withering fire of their own, escaped into the safety of a cloud. Above them, there now began a furious battle between the opposing fighters in which more than forty aeroplanes, in a heaving, wheeling, and diving swarm of blasting guns, filled the sky with the sound of their fury.

Unusually for the Western Front an easterly wind was blowing that day. Unhelpfully for the German circus, it steadily wafted the great mêlée of aeroplanes westward over the British lines. Most of the participants were seasoned pilots, many with impressive records. The Camel flight commander, Canadian Captain Roy Brown, had nine kills to his credit, four of which had earned him a naval Distinguished Service Cross. But on both sides there were also unblooded novices nervously facing their first dogfights. The Baron was shepherding a young cousin, Wolfram von Richthofen. Brown was anxiously mentoring a friend with whom he'd gone to school back in Canada, Lieutenant Wilfred May, known for some reason as 'Wop'.

Brown had instructed May to avoid combat and confine himself to observing the way it was conducted. But he found the battle too tempting. After a few minutes, spotting what looked like an easy kill, a triplane apparently unengaged in the fight, May banked his Camel and dived on to it with both guns firing. He failed to hit the German machine and, as his guns had jammed, he decided to quit the fight and head home. Unfortunately, May had chosen Wolfram's aeroplane to attack. The inexperienced German pilot had, like himself, been given orders to watch and not fight. For his huge error of judgement, May was soon to reap the whirlwind. As he dived away, to his great shock, his aircraft was suddenly hosed with bullets that seemed to come from nowhere. Looking round, he saw that a red triplane was sitting on his tail. May recounted later:

> If I'd realised it was Richthofen I would have probably passed out on the spot. We came over the German lines. Troops fired at us as we went over – also the case coming over the British lines. I got on the Somme river at a very low altitude ... I went around a curve just near Corbie, but Richthofen beat me to it and came over the hill. At that point I was a sitting duck. I was too low down between the banks to make a turn away from him. I felt that he had me cold and I was in such a state of mind by this time that I had to restrain myself from pushing my stick forward and nosing into the river.[7]

At that point something astonishing happened. As the terrified May glanced over his shoulder he claimed to have seen the pursuing triplane suddenly wobble before curving down in a wide turn to crash-land in a field of crops. What he didn't discover until he got back to his Bertangles base was that, during the last moments of his desperate zig-zagging flight along the Somme, another Camel had joined the pursuit. His flight commander, Roy Brown, spotting his predicament, had dived down out of the dogfight to fire on the triple-winged Fokker. As the three aircraft, weaving one behind the other, had hurtled west barely feet above the river, they had flown over the position of an Australian machine-gun company on the north bank. Several of the gunners had fired at the red triplane before it flopped down close to their temporary trenches.

When Australian soldiers reached the aircraft they found Richthofen sitting dead in the cockpit. Although his head and face were bruised and his jaw had been broken when, unharnessed, he'd been thrown against his guns, the fatal wound had come from a single bullet that had pierced his heart. The largely intact aeroplane didn't remain that way for long. As Richthofen's body, clad in black silk pyjamas under his flying clothes, was removed and later taken by truck to a canvas hangar at

Bertangles aerodrome, the triplane was so comprehensively demolished by souvenir-hunters that by the time it followed him to the air base it was hardly recognisable as an aeroplane any more. A cameraman on the front line shot some revealing footage that shows Australian pilots picking through the wreckage at Bertangles. One of them is holding one of the Baron's machine guns up to the camera. Even more appalling than the degree to which the triplane was torn apart, Manfred's cockpit was not only emptied of its instruments, but his body was stripped of his flying helmet, scarf, personally monogrammed handkerchief, goggles and fur-lined boots. His revolver was taken and almost every square foot of fabric was cut off the machine in dozens of souvenir pieces.

The medical officers who examined Richthofen to try to confirm the cause of death found that the fatal bullet had entered beneath his right armpit, passed through his chest and exited near his left nipple. They could not have imagined that these simple forensic details would remain at the centre of the debate over the manner of his death almost a century later.

In the Bertangles hangar Richthofen was laid out, almost as if in state, on a small raised platform. A constant stream of people came that evening to gaze upon his body. 'It was a curious experience, after all we had heard about him, to see him lying there,' wrote Major Sholto Douglas, now commander of 84 Squadron, whose hangar it was. Roy Brown, who hadn't known when he landed and made out his combat report that the pilot he was sure he had shot down was Richthofen, also went to see him. 'He appeared so small, so delicate,' he wrote to tell his parents back in Canada.

> He looked so friendly. Blond, silk-soft hair, like that of a child, fell from the broad high forehead. His face, particularly peaceful, had an expression of gentleness and goodness, of refinement.
>
> Suddenly I felt miserable, desperately unhappy, as if I had committed an injustice. With a feeling of shame, a kind of anger against myself moved in my thoughts that I had forced him to lay there . . . If I could I would gladly have brought him back to life . . . I could no longer look him in the face. I went away. I didn't feel like a victor. There was a lump in my throat. If he had been my dearest friend, I could not have felt greater sorrow.[8]

A British aircraft flew over Cappy and dropped a canister with the sad tidings. If proof were needed, it was provided by the accompanying photograph of Richthofen's body.

Baron Manfred von Richthofen was given a full military funeral by the Australian Flying Corps' No. 3 Squadron. Something of the sadness of the occasion survives in the scratched and jerky images of a newsreel film that poignantly recorded the whole event: the solemn padre in his cassock, prayer book in hand; the Australian pilots serving as the pallbearers lowering with ropes the coffin into the grave. The firing party discharging the final salute.

If the Kaiser had died Germany couldn't have gone into deeper mourning. Across the country flags flew for days at half mast. Black-bordered obituaries and tributes filled the newspapers as Manfred, just eleven days short of his twenty-sixth birthday, was hailed as a martyred warrior hero. His eighty credited victories, almost all of them corroborated, were never to be exceeded by any other pilot in the first air war. The Royal Air Force accepted that Roy Brown had shot him down and he was awarded a second Distinguished Service Cross in recognition of his giant-killing feat. There were, however, several other claimants to the scalp of the Red Baron.

At least three Australian machine-gunners were convinced that the fatal bullet was one of theirs. Rarely can the physical cause of death of a man in battle, and the identity of the serviceman responsible, have attracted more post-mortem argument, or such a wealth of published material, than the demise of Richthofen.

The debate centres on the gruesome pathological and ballistic details of the superficial post-mortem that probed his chest wounds but without opening up his body. The separate reports of the doctors who examined him make macabre reading.

First to inspect the body was a British Fourth Army surgeon, Colonel Sinclair. Lacking a surgical probe, he set out to trace the route of the bullet from right armpit to left nipple by the extraordinarily crude means of a length of fencing wire, which he pushed along the track of the wound. This bizarre, imprecise procedure convinced him that the bullet, fired upwards, had struck the spinal column, which would have deflected it through the heart. Two other Royal Army Medical Corps doctors who were with Colonel Sinclair disagreed that the bullet had hit the vertebra but neither did they believe it came from ground fire. To confuse matters further, a second team, headed by a senior Australian doctor, Colonel George Barber, added another view. 'I used the same bit of wire for the same purpose,' Barber wrote. 'The bullet hole in the side of the aeroplane coincided with the wound through the chest. I'm <u>sure</u> he was shot from <u>below</u> while banking.'[9]

Of the Australian anti-aircraft gunners who had fired at the red triplane that morning three were convinced they'd delivered the burst that shot it down. As the trio of hedge-hopping aeroplanes in ragged line-astern formation had come roaring overhead, they passed directly over a circle of gun emplacements from which, one of them said, 'A rain of death bespattered him.' The aircraft were so close together that the gunners, swivelling their pole-mounted weapons, had difficulty getting a safe sighting on the German machine. When Gunner Robert Buie's officer shouted at him: 'Fire on that plane, Buie!' he couldn't at first do so without hitting May. 'Snowy Evans, manning the other gun on the opposite flank, got first clearance. He opened up at a range of slightly more than 300 yards.' But the triplane flew steadily on. 'I was at the ready with my finger on the trigger, waiting the clearance. I can still remember seeing Richthofen clearly. He was hunched in the cockpit aiming his guns at the lead plane.' When Buie was able to fire safely he knew his bullets were striking their target when he saw fragments flying off the German's machine.

A kilometre away Sergeant Cedric Popkin, a Queensland carpenter before enlisting, was also firing. His Lewis gun hit 'the Fritz', he claimed, from not much more than a hundred yards, shortly after which he saw Richthofen lose control and go down. Moreover, Popkin fired from the right as the triplane was travelling away from him, a trajectory consistent with the entry wound from a bullet striking from below and behind. Roy Brown's bullets, fired from behind and above, were unlikely to have caused the wound. Nor, if they had done, would Richthofen, with his perforated heart, have remained alive for the full minute it took his aeroplane to make a wide turn and descend, under some degree of control, to the ground. An Australian officer who clearly witnessed the aerial chase and the triplane's final moments reported that it continued to be flown for at least that long after Brown had ceased shooting and turned away. Popkin's burst of fire, later than Buie's, had been the last to hit the German machine.

Most historians now give the credit to Sergeant Popkin. However, Roy Brown remained equally certain that the *coup de grâce* had been his. He dismissed the claims of those on the ground. 'It was rather funny about Richthofen being shot down,' the Canadian pilot told his family. 'They had a medical examination on the body. It is a terrible thing when you think of it that they should examine a body to see who should have the credit of killing him. What I saw that day shook me up quite a lot as it was the first time I have seen a man whom I know I had killed. But if you don't shoot them they will shoot you, so it has to be done.'[10]

Why, through the long minutes of the aerial steeplechase along the Somme valley, the great Richthofen hadn't managed to shoot down the floundering, panic-stricken Wilfred May puzzled many of those watching it all from the ground. A possible explanation came to light when RAF armourers at Bertangles examined his two guns. One was jammed by a damaged cartridge casing; the other was found to have a mechanical fault that drastically reduced its rate of fire.

However, his inability to shoot properly doesn't answer the question of how the Baron, given his notorious caution in combat, allowed himself to be killed. Despite his great skill and deadly close-range accuracy, he had never hesitated to steer clear of or pull out of a scrap if he thought the odds against him were too great. He had studiously avoided following opponents down into the reach of heavy ground fire. His own credo, issued as a combat operations manual to the entire German Air Service, formally stated that pilots should 'never obstinately stay with an opponent one has been unable to shoot down'. Yet that is what he did. A likely reason for his uncharacteristic recklessness is that his once masterly judgement had been impaired by the brain damage he had suffered, compounded by the stress that had reduced him to the condition that had so shocked his family. This could easily have led him to make wrong and risky decisions in the air. And to the day he died Richthofen had endured more or less continuous pain from his permanently unhealed head wound, a trauma modern doctors say could have been caused by osteomyelitis, a chronic infection of the bone that could today be arrested by antibiotics.

The psychologically battered state that had hastened his death was by no means unique to Manfred. Indeed, the pilot who claimed to have shot him down was exhibiting even greater symptoms of combat distress. Roy Brown, with a small string of victories to his credit, was himself that morning approaching the end of his own tether.

Chapter 26
The Spent Capital of Courage

People who met Roy Brown at the time of his encounter with the Red Baron were shocked by his appearance. Another pilot, Raymond Collishaw, one of the great Canadian aces who was eventually credited with a war total of sixty victories, was surprised that, in his visible state of nervous exhaustion, he was still being allowed to fly. 'He had lost 25lbs (11kg), his eyes were bloodshot and sunken and his hair was quickly greying,' Collishaw said. Brown told him how ill he felt; how, to counter nausea and vomiting caused by ingesting the castor oil spewed into his face by his Camel's rotary engine, which had painfully inflamed his stomach lining, he'd been consuming large quantities of brandy and milk. 'Brown was definitely in a bad way, both mentally and physically,' Collishaw wrote to a friend. 'He was both nervous and had lost his nerve.'[1] Brown's debility was exacerbated by the increasingly wretched conditions of squadron life imposed by the constant Allied retreat from the unstoppable German *blitzkrieg*. The bitterly cold tented camp hastily established at Bertangles was 209 Squadron's sixth base in less than three weeks, and it was as bleak and transient as all the rest.

Within days of his skirmish with Richthofen, things finally caught up with Brown. His gastritis became so acute he reported to the squadron's medical officer, as he wrote to tell his parents. 'I feel just about all done in today the way things have gone. My stomach has been very bad recently and the doctor says if I keep on I shall have a nervous breakdown and has ordered me to stop active service flying.'[2]

Brown was reluctant to comply. 'I have just got the flight going beautifully and I have all good chaps with me. What is more we have been doing very good work ... we fought Baron von Richthofen's "Circus" ... There were eleven of us and twenty-two of them. It was the most terrible fight I have ever seen in the air. We shot down three of their triplanes which were seen to crash. Among them was the Baron whom I shot down on our side of the lines. We didn't lose anyone in that fight.'[3] He appealed against the doctor's edict and his protest was referred upwards to the brigade general, who insisted he be grounded forthwith and sent on immediate leave. Instead he finished up at the military hospital at Etaples on the Channel coast, too ill even to make the journey back to England.

At No. 24 General Hospital near Le Touquet, where he was treated for stomach pains and battle stress, Brown was joined within days by another combat-fatigued Canadian ace from his squadron. He and Stearne Edwards were exceptionally close friends. They had been buddies at school, trained as pilots together at a civilian flying school, joined the Royal Naval Air Service together, served often in the same squadron, fought in the air alongside one another and sometimes even shared a kill. A specially warm, brotherly bond had grown between them. Their nerves had been equally affected by the terrors of air-to-air fighting.

When the doctors decided Brown was fit enough to be sent on leave to England he was prematurely discharged, still far from well. On arriving in London he felt so emotionally churned up he went to see an RAF doctor, who immediately sent him to a Hampstead hospital which, unusually for the time, specialised in the treatment of psychiatric patients. From there he wrote to sing its praises to his father. 'They do a lot of research work here into the different kinds of troubles which are peculiar to flying people. It is purely for RAF officers so they get lots of material to work on. It is a very good idea having a hospital like this as in an ordinary hospital they do not know how to treat the troubles of flying people. What they will have me do I do not know, but I am certainly not nearly as fit as I thought I was and shall not be able to go back to France for an indefinite time ... All that is really the matter is I am just tired out.'[4]

But Brown was more than tired out. He was suffering from acute war neurosis, then blandly labelled neurasthenia, a version of the shellshock that had immobilised hundreds of thousands of foot soldiers on both sides. The stress of months of ceaseless aerial fighting, every dawn possibly his last, had finally proved too much. His stomach distress had more to do with his anxiety than castor oil. He'd become jumpy, lost his appetite and his sleep was haunted by nightmares of air combat.

The army medical corps doctors attached to the air service had never been trained to deal with casualties of the mind. Most were totally outside their area of competence. Those who had served on the ground on the Western Front had daily faced the awful conflict between their humanitarian duty to their patients and sustained pressure from the military high command to get damaged men quickly back to the trenches. In consequence the treatment given to soldiers for shellshock was often short, sometimes brutal. If they weren't dumped in lunatic asylums, some desperately ill men rendered mute by their experiences found themselves subjected to cruel electric-shock therapy in a vain attempt to bring their speech back. Forcibly administered by means of electrodes clamped to the lower back and throat, the current delivered was sometimes so excessive it burned their bodies. Afterwards, many were simply declared officially cured and shipped back, still ill, to France where, amid the familiar horrors of the battle front, they would promptly collapse again.

In the minds of the First World War generals a man was either honourably physically wounded and deserving of the best of care, or he was a malingering coward. For wounds to the human spirit there was no place. The prevailing philosophy was that men who broke in battle were innately weak. 'Military authorities, especially those traditionalists who believed that courage was a function of background and breeding, were inclined to accept the characterisation. Men of strength and character were judged immune from emotional disorder.'[5] For soldiers driven by extreme fear and horror to desert the front line there remained until the end of hostilities court-martial with the risk of dawn execution by firing squad. Close to 350 men of the British Army paid this price for their fragility. A lesser penalty, imposed on exhausted men for falling asleep on sentry duty, was known as Field Punishment No. 1 or 'crucifixion'. Handcuffed and fettered soldiers would be humiliatingly strapped to gun wheels for up to two hours a day for a whole month, out in the open, where they were sometimes exposed to shellfire.

In the flying services combat-traumatised aircrew could not be treated in such draconian fashion. Pilots and observers so affected by fatigue and stress they were no longer reliable enough to fly became a danger to their colleagues and were quietly grounded for everybody's sake. They would be sent to hospital, or on leave, and many would later join the ranks of the twitchy instructors who scared their pupils at the flying schools. Not until very late in the war did military doctors begin to acquire knowledge of the true causes of the battle shock that daily incapacitated alarming numbers of fighting men at the front line.

Meanwhile combat stress awaited men of every background. Lord Moran, Churchill's Second World War doctor who served in the trenches in the First War, would assert in 1945: 'Courage is will-power, whereof no man has an unlimited stock; and when in war it is used up, he is finished. A man's courage is his capital and he is always spending.'[6]

Just as, on the battlefields of Flanders, shellshock was for a long time attributed simply to the physical concussive effect of exploding shells, in the air the effect of harsh operating conditions on the body was seen as the sole cause of 'flying sickness'. But minds housed in physically intact, undamaged brains were cracking on the ground and in the air for a quite different reason, unconnected to explosive blasts, and on a scale equal to any seen in the recent history of warfare.

The huge losses of shellshocked men from the front line finally prompted extensive medical investigations. The findings that emerged, which helped to establish the foundations of modern psychiatry, forced army doctors to recognise that a major component of shellshock and its aerial counterpart was in fact psychological. In the trenches men didn't have to be physically wounded. They didn't even need to have gone over the top. It was enough merely to be on the front line, trapped within its inescapable horror. There was a limit to how much of this any human being's mind could endure. A new breed of army doctors finally set out to introduce psychiatry into the treatment of battle-damaged patients, replacing the brutal electrical therapy with the kinder, previously untried techniques of psychotherapy. Prominent among them was a remarkable army captain in his mid-fifties, Dr William Rivers.

An unusually shy man with a chronic stammer, Rivers was a gentle, deeply private figure, seen in photographs wearing spectacles and a large, bushy moustache. A neurologist and anthropologist, he pioneered the revolutionary new treatment methods.

Rivers told his patients that, given the traumatic nature of their experiences, their condition was perfectly normal. That any otherwise normal human being could have been affected in exactly the same way. Most of his patients, many of whom arrived with terrible stutters, or having lost their speech altogether, were unwilling or unable to talk about the sickening events that had brought them to him. The military culture had taught them to suppress the memory of the ghastly scenes feeding the nightmares that woke them, screaming, in lathers of sweat. But when, often over slow months, Rivers, with near-saintly patience, sometimes aided by hypnotherapy, gradually succeeded in persuading them to share with him the details of the horrors they'd experienced, he was able in protracted discussions to soften the dreaded memories. Drawing out such information in tiny morsels, he said, was like pulling teeth. But he found that not only could terrible recollections fade from the dreams he analysed for them, their nervous condition improved remarkably, too.

The most vulnerable to anxiety neurosis, Rivers observed, were ex-public schoolboys conditioned to display self-control and repress fear. At

Craiglockhart hospital for combat-shocked officers in Edinburgh, which had become one of the most successful of the military psychiatric centres, Rivers is remembered for his much-publicised slow and endlessly indulgent use of his technique to help heal two prominent shellshocked First World War poets, Siegfried Sassoon and Wilfred Owen.

When, in late 1917, Rivers was posted to the RAF's Hampstead hospital as its chief psychologist he had introduced his revolutionary healing to the treatment of mentally ill aircrew. Within this enlightened regime Roy Brown found a refreshingly understanding approach to his chronic misery. In the Hampstead incarnation of Craiglockhart he entered a world 'oppressive with saturations of war experience' with which Sassoon was well acquainted. 'One lay awake and listened to feet padding along passages which smelt of stale cigarette smoke . . . One became conscious that the place was full of men whose slumbers were morbid and terrifying – men muttering uneasily or suddenly crying out in their sleep. Around me was that underworld of dreams haunted by submerged memories of warfare and its intolerable shocks and self-lacerating failures to achieve the impossible.'[7]

What Brown found so therapeutically positive was that Rivers and his team understood the special dangers and strains of war flying, which were not the same as those faced by the troops who fought the horrendous ground battles. Although, off-duty, the airmen lived well, in their flying machines they encountered the quite different psychological burdens of their aerial calling. It was a reality far removed from the romantic adventure many had believed they were about to enjoy.

They found themselves in combat in the harsh environment of ever-increasing altitudes, operating at flight levels undreamed of by the Wright brothers less than a decade earlier. Flying in unheated, open cockpits with inadequate clothing as high as 24,000 feet in winter temperatures approaching minus 50 degrees Centigrade, made worse by propeller-driven wind chill, they suffered such intense cold that the foul-smelling whale oil they smeared on their faces couldn't prevent icicles forming on their noses or frostbite from peeling skin off their cheeks. They carried no oxygen and at high levels their blood pressure soared dangerously. They experienced all the drastic performance-reducing symptoms of hypoxia familiar to mountaineers, but without the climbers' ability to ascend in gentle stages and acclimatise. They took off and returned to dangerously small aerodromes hastily converted from crop fields perilously lined by obstructing tall trees and ditches. They flew aeroplanes whose noise and vibration levels could deafen them; aeroplanes that showered them with noxious fumes and could break up under the structural stresses of combat. In the frenzied manoeuvres of dogfighting they were subjected to extraordinarily high G-forces that caused them to black out and sometimes burst blood vessels in their eyes. They got ruptured eardrums from the abrupt pressure changes in swooping dives of thousands of feet. They were afflicted by vertigo and airsickness that had them vomiting in the cockpits; by agonising gas-filled bowels that could be relieved only by releasing copious blasts of wind. On the ground most of them lived unhealthy, largely sedentary lives and, unsurprisingly, they drank and smoked heavily. Twenty-four-year-old pilots often began to look forty.

Yet this was only the physical price of their short-lived service. The psychological toll was equally damaging. For airmen breakdowns were eventually precipitated by stress and extreme fear, dominated by the gnawing, ever-present dread of dying in flames. The horror of seeing men they'd sat with at breakfast go down in a fiery blaze of petrol. The constant fear of engine stoppage and structural failure. The revulsion and guilt at having killed other, equally frightened young men with whom they had no personal quarrel. All of these things slowly undermined their peace of mind.

They had been draining Roy Brown's mental health long before his encounter with the Red Baron. There is no longer any record of the outcome of his treatment at the Hampstead hospital, but his stay there in May 1918 was short. He was discharged the following month and he and Stearne Edwards, back in England after treatment for his own breakdown, went on leave together. They hired a canoe and spent a leisurely week soothing their nerves paddling up the Thames to Reading and back. It was 'a dandy trip', he told his father. 'Certainly made me feel a lot better than I was.'

Brown's respite from flying was brief. In July he and Edwards were posted as instructors to an air-combat school at Marske in Yorkshire. Within days of arriving there Brown had a disastrous flying accident. At barely 200 feet on take-off, his engine failed. With his Camel heading for trees and telephone wires he made the unwise decision to turn back to the aerodrome, stalled and dived into the ground. Edwards, who watched it happen, ran to the wreckage, convinced that Brown couldn't have survived. He was alive, but only just.

Edwards described his friend's extensive injuries in a letter to Brown's father in Canada. Roy had been extricated from underneath the Camel's engine, which had flipped on top of him.

Both collar bones are broken, four ribs I think, one of which has pierced his lung. His jaw may be broken. There is a cut, or rather a hole, in the inside upper corner of his eye which they thought at first had pierced the brain. But it hadn't and won't be serious. There is also a cut on his forehead and of course many smaller cuts and bruises on his face and body ... I hope you will forgive me for not having cabled you immediately, but I could not do it up till two days ago as they expected every minute to be his last and I could not bring myself to send you news of that sort.[8]

The RAF station doctor considered Brown beyond saving. Edwards took matters into his own hands. He called in a consultant. When the specialist saw the extent of the injuries he, too, concluded there was little hope. For days Brown hovered between life and death. But slowly he turned the corner and began the long process of recovery.

Roy Brown was in various hospitals for five months. But although his crushed body began to mend, his combat stress, now aggravated by the crash, refused to lift. It grew worse. At an officers' hospital in Staines beside the Thames he sank into depression and the small amount of sleep he did get was invaded by nightmares. In sad letters to his mother, he began to pour his heart out.

I feel as blue as blue today. Last night for the first time in my life I lost control of myself. I couldn't sleep till four o'clock. The nurse came in and I didn't hear her till she was quite close to my bed. When I heard her I jumped and was as frightened as a baby. After that every little noise of any kind made me jump and frightened me the same. My head was pretty bad all the time. Please excuse me writing and telling you all this. I must unburden myself some time. Last night I found myself telling nurse I was so tired of being in pain all the time I could not bear it any longer.[9]

Brown was still in hospital when peace was declared on 11 November 1918. He had been moved from Staines to one in Epsom and it was here, on the day after Armistice Day, that he received the terrible news that his closest buddy had been critically injured in an air accident. Stearne Edwards, a worn-out ace with sixteen credited victories and two Distinguished Service Cross medals had, back at the Yorkshire air-combat school, crashed badly in a Sopwith Pup. He died ten days later. Brown was utterly devastated. He wrote to tell his mother he had lost the person he'd loved most deeply in the world.

Dear Mother,

This has been the hardest day I have ever spent in my life and I don't expect I shall ever spend such another again. I cannot write how I feel at all as words are too feeble.

Stearne has been so much to me since coming over here more than anyone ever has been before or will be again. I could, and did, always tell him everything, a thing I can never do with anyone before or again, no matter, even you mother, much as I love you, nor dad who has treated me so square.

All day since I have heard I have wished to be with him wherever he is now . . . I wish it had been me in place of Stearne. It is so easy to die and so hard to live. That is a selfish wish I know, but I cannot help it.

He was the best friend I shall ever have and one of the best men that ever was on this earth.[10]

Brown told everyone he owed his life to Edwards; that had Edwards not brought in the expertise of the civilian consultant when the RAF doctor had washed his hands of him after the Yorkshire crash, he would most certainly have died.

At the Epsom hospital where Brown was still recovering from his crash injuries he had ceased to be treated for the psychological wounds he still carried from his combat flying. His grief at the loss of his dearest friend was now woven into the stress disorder that still tortured him and intensified it, something his latest doctors weren't qualified to treat. 'The medical services are very good at patching up wounds – but mine are different. They don't seem to take the same interest in a case of my nature as they do with bullet and shrapnel wounds . . . It is not a very cheerful state to be in.'[11]

Roy Brown's suffering remained with him for the rest of his life. Back in Canada after the war he moved restlessly from one venture to another. He worked as an accountant, founded a small, short-lived airline in the north of the country, edited an aviation magazine and stood unsuccessfully for the Ontario Parliament. He married and became the father of two daughters. But he never forgot Stearne Edwards. In the town of Carleton Place near Ottawa where they had first known each other he had a plaque in Edwards' memory placed in the Presbyterian church. Brown lived only to the age of fifty. He died in 1944, engaged in his final enterprise, as a farmer.

Brown would probably never have seen Canada again at all had illness not ended his combat flying. What finally killed so many of the great aces on both sides was the nervous stress that bred recklessness and a fatalistic acceptance of the inevitability of death. Heroic reputations and huge bags of victories were no guarantee of survival.

Dr Rivers and his fellow psychologists brought enlightenment to the treatment of battle fatigue. Painfully slowly, their techniques would eventually create within the RAF a more sympathetic, understanding regime. Recruitment procedures for flying staff became highly selective and by the twenty-first century, in war zones like Iraq and Afghanistan, the RAF would have aircrew stress neuroses detected early, nipped in the bud and sensitively handled by specialist Air Force field mental-health teams. But in 1918 all this was a long way in the future. The doctors in the field continued to believe that, however devastating mental illness had become, all it needed was a short rest out of the front line. They even created their own name for it – 'Flying Sickness – D'. Victor Yeates, whose autobiographical novel *Winged Victory* remains, despite its fictional format, one of the greatest, most authentic accounts of the awfulness of the first air war, described the light-hearted way in which 'FSD' was diagnosed:

'How do you feel?' asked the doctor.

This was not an easy question.

'Tired?' the doctor prompted.

'Yes, tired. Not sleeping.'

'I see. Lost enthusiasm for war flying?'

The doctor made a note that he felt tired and had lost enthusiasm for war flying. Then he sounded and tapped him, and finally wrote down F.S.D.

'Flying sickness D,' he said.

'D for drink?' asked Tom.

'No. Debility. It's the usual phrase applicable to people in your state. Too much war flying. You'll soon get over it.'

'That's good.'

'Of course you will. A month's sick leave and H.E. [*Home Establishment*]. You'll be evacuated tomorrow morning. And while you're on leave, relax. Forget about the war and flying.'

'Forget?'

'So far as you can. Have a good time. Take your girl out – or girls, is it? Enjoy yourself. Finest thing for you so long as you don't overdo it.'[12]

Yeates, a Camel pilot credited with five victories, was, like his character Tom, invalided back to England. He was already suffering not only from war neurosis but from the tuberculosis that would kill him at the age of thirty-seven.

Chapter 27

The Working-Class Heroes

The nervous conditions pilots struggled to suppress and conceal from their colleagues found an outlet in their private letters home and were visible in the distressed state in which they often returned on leave. One of those whose wretched descent into mental illness is unusually painfully documented was Edward Mannock, a largely self-educated half-Irish Catholic of conspicuously working-class origin who became one of the first air war's most revered and highest-scoring pilots. Yet unlike the much-glorified and publicised Ball and Bishop he remained scarcely known to the world for more than fifteen years after the war. Few had ever even heard his name until the middle of the 1930s, when one of his former Flying Corps mates wrote a book to praise and commemorate his little-known deeds.[1]

'Mick' Mannock's arrival on No. 40 Squadron in France in April 1917 was a culture shock for its largely upper-middle-class, public-school pilots unused to the accents and manners of the working classes in their midst. Not only was Mannock from the lower orders of society and ten years older than most of them, he was also brash, outspoken and, worse, a committed socialist and teetotaller – and he had the temerity to tell them how the air war should be fought and taunt them about their privileged backgrounds.

Lieutenant Edward Mannock brought to the squadron a background of poverty, insecurity and family violence beyond the experience of his fellow pilots, most of whom had wanted for nothing in their early lives. He was born in Brighton in 1887, the son of an English Catholic corporal in the Royal Scots Greys and his Irish wife, whose parents were servants on an estate in County Cork. When Corporal Mannock later joined the 5th Dragoon Guards and his regiment was posted to India, he took his wife and their four children with him. Edward got most of his education at a Jesuit school. In the eight years or so that he lived in India he suffered a serious infection of his left eye that was to create a myth, perpetuated by several of his biographers, that he remained blind in that eye for the rest of his life. Within months of returning to England around 1902, to a depot in Canterbury, Corporal Mannock was said to have become addicted to drink, terrifying his wife and children with his physical violence, left the army and deserted them, leaving them in penury. Helping himself to every penny of their small savings, he bigamously married another woman. At fourteen Edward was forced to leave school and find work, first as a greengrocer's delivery boy, then as a barber's assistant, and later as a clerk with a telephone company, during which time he joined the local territorial company of the Royal Army Medical Corps, where he learned to ride and handle horses.

In 1911 Mannock, now twenty-four, had been transferred by his company to a rugged new existence as a linesman in Wellingborough in Northamptonshire, a job that had him working outside in all weathers, climbing poles and repairing phone wires. Wellingborough became a watershed in his life. He lodged at the home of a foundry-owner, Jim Eyles, the zealous branch secretary of the Labour Party, under whose influence he embraced socialism. A strong and affectionate friendship developed between them. With Eyles and his wife, Mannock experienced for the first time the warmth of a loving, functional family. They held musical evenings, encouraging him to play his violin and sing Irish songs. Their heated political debates would go on into the small hours.

Mannock grew bored with climbing poles and, early in 1914, worked his passage on a tramp steamer to Turkey and a cable-laying job with an English telephone contractor. But within months Britain had declared war on Turkey and he was interned in appalling conditions in a Constantinople prison camp, where he acquired a reputation as a troublemaker and was thrown into solitary confinement. Emaciated by hunger and dysentery, he wasn't released until the spring of 1915 when, back in England, he rejoined the medical corps as an NCO with a field ambulance unit. Transferring to the Signals Corps of the Royal Engineers, where his technical skills had him commissioned as a subaltern, Mannock found himself rubbing shoulders for the first time with young men from a very different background. The environment of the officers' mess had him permanently on edge. 'He came across as aloof and aggressive. The jollity and junior common room chit-chat irritated him intensely. He saw his fellow officers as languid drones, with little serious interest in the war other than how it directly impacted upon them. Too often his annoyance manifested itself in tirades against the English class system – which made him even more unpopular. He was seen as a stereotype of the ill-educated labouring classes.'[2]

His colleagues were relieved to see the last of Mannock when, inspired by the feats of Albert Ball, he applied to join the Flying Corps as a pilot. At the age of twenty-eight he was accepted, the doctors examining him finding nothing wrong with the vision in his left eye. 'Now for the Bosche!' he wrote in his diary. 'I'm going to become a scout pilot like Ball. Watch me. I wonder what fate has in store?'

Although he would have permanent difficulty with his landings, Mannock proved to be a natural fighter pilot. At a school of aerial fighting at Joyce Green near Dartford in Kent, the pupils were introduced to the violent manoeuvres of dogfighting, first in a dual-controlled machine, then sent up solo to engage in mock combat with their instructor. One of them was the recently commissioned Lieutenant James McCudden, the former air mechanic who was on his way to becoming one of the war's greatest fighter pilots. At that time he had just qualified as an ace with his fifth victory in France.

McCudden was another pilot of humble background. Like Mannock, he was the son of an army NCO, half-Irish, in his case on his father's side, and had spent much of his spartan early life in military barracks. Unlike Mannock, his home had been a happy one, but after his father left the army the family had such difficulty making ends meet that McCudden had been sent out to work at fourteen as a post office telegram boy. He had faced the same problems as Mannock on becoming a 'temporary gentleman' in the class-ridden commissioned world of the Flying Corps. 'I always wish I had had the advantage of a public school,' he once said. 'After I joined the officers' mess I often felt ill at ease when chaps were talking about things I didn't understand.'³ With so much in common, McCudden and Mannock quickly became friends.

Mannock went from Joyce Green to join 40 Squadron, then based at an aerodrome in the Béthune coalfields. He arrived to the sound of the continuous thunder of the nearby British guns beginning the Battle of Arras and the attack on Vimy Ridge. It was the height of 1917's 'Bloody April', in which the Flying Corps was taking the most terrible beating of its existence. Their wrecked aircraft littered the Western Front and inexperienced new pilots, desperately trying to handle unfamiliar aeroplanes let alone the risks of combat, were lucky to survive for more than a few weeks. The average life expectancy of a subaltern had shrunk to eleven days.

With colleagues disappearing more rapidly than ever before, 40 Squadron's surviving pilots didn't know what to make of the latest lamb to the slaughter. 'From the moment he sat down in the chair of a squadron favourite killed that day, Mannock was a marked man. Although both his flight commander and his room-mate found him shy and unassuming, others found him just the opposite. Intrusive questions on his first day and ill-informed statements on how to fight the Germans were rightly deemed crass and insensitive. Not only that, the brash new arrival talked with a slight Irish accent and displayed scant respect for mess manners and conventions.'[4]

'His manner, speech and familiarity were not liked,' recalled Lieutenant Lionel Blaxland of the unhappy collision of class and culture.

> He seemed too cocky for his experience, which was nil. His arrival at the unit was not the best way to start. New men took their time and listened to the more experienced hands; Mannock was the complete opposite. He offered ideas about everything: how the war was going, how it should be fought, the role of scout pilots, what was wrong with our machines. Most men in his position, by that I mean a man from his background and with his lack of fighting experience, would have shut up and earned their place in the mess.[5]

Working class, semi-educated and tactless he may have been, but the truth was that Mannock was more mature and worldly-wise than the young men into whose public-school common room he had arrived. He might not have been familiar with *The Iliad* or the poems of William Blake but this annoying Irishman was an imaginative, intelligent, complex individual with an inquiring mind who thrived on political debate and could, all too uncomfortably, articulate the inequalities he saw reflected in them that gnawed, in his view, at the heart of wartime British society. This tall, good-looking, forceful and self-assured character, with his shock of unruly hair, was impossible to ignore, though his unpopular views soon had some of his colleagues trying to avoid him. They were further incensed when he befriended another Irish pilot and the pair of them took to 'blowing off steam' with noisy boxing contests around the mess. In his opponent he found more than a physical sparring partner. He and Lieutenant de Burgh were soul mates. 'We were both Irishmen, and we dearly loved an argument,' de Burgh wrote. 'He was the only man in the mess who would talk beneath the surface.' Arguing fiercely about politics, socialism, religion, 'he usually won the argument . . . He would have made a marvellous politician. He had all the Celtic fire to move multitudes.'[6]

For Mannock his early weeks in action with 40 Squadron were unnerving beyond his imagination. 'Over the lines today engine cut out three times,' he wrote. 'Wind up. Now I can understand what a tremendous strain to the nervous system active service flying is. However cool a man may be there must always be more or less of a tension on the nerves. When it is considered that seven out of ten forced landings are practically "write-offs", and 50 per cent are cases where the pilot is injured, one can quite understand the strain of the whole business.'[7]

He was lucky not to have been killed in his first week. Diving on a ground practice target, his entire bottom right wing suddenly peeled off in mid-air and fell away. Only thanks to enormous skill with the controls did he prevent the aeroplane from plummeting to the ground as he crash-landed in a ploughed field. Sent on patrol over the front line as the Canadian divisions below him were storming up Vimy Ridge, he found his first exposure to anti-aircraft fire and aerial combat petrifying. He was so screwed up he lost all ability to control his machine and as aircraft of both sides whirled around him he was horrified to find himself firing at fellow British pilots. Nor could he see himself surviving very long in his Nieuport, with its single gun that fired awkwardly over the top wing, against Albatros with twice the firepower from twin guns blazing through their propellers. Caught on his own, suddenly surrounded by three Alba-tros intent on picking him off, he was convinced his last moment had come. 'A very disagreeable experience,' he wrote in his diary. 'My gun jammed, Aldis [the telescopic gun-sight] oiled up, and the engine failed at the crucial moment. I thought all was up ... I landed with my knees shaking and my nerves all torn to bits. All my courage seems to have gone.[8]

Though terrified every time he went into the air Mannock was deter-mined to conquer his fear and stay alive. He was shocked at how the grim reality of air-to-air combat had unexpectedly affected his nerves and by what he saw as the unnecessary speed with which new pilots around him were being shot down in what seemed like chaotically and suicidally undisciplined battles. At nearby 60 Squadron, 'They've lost four young-sters in five days. All the young men seem to go first,' he said. Instead of sacrificing himself, he decided to try to discover what it was that was going wrong. 'Air fighting is a science,' he told a fellow pilot. 'I want to master the tactics first. The present bald-headed ones should be replaced by well thought-out ones.'

In the course of his study Mannock became so cautious on patrol that, although he survived forty hours over the lines in his first three weeks, he made not a single kill – something his critics weren't slow to note. When he withdrew one morning from a dogfight with a jammed gun, they didn't believe him. Word spread that the unpopular Irishman had cold feet, that he was yellow. And the conviction grew when he embarked on a private routine of target practice, flying off on his own for hours to an aerial gunnery range to improve his marksmanship. No one had done this quite so obsessively before. Nor had they insisted on so fussily adjusting the sighting of their machine guns. Or inspecting every bullet in their ammunition drums to remove the faulty ones that seized up the guns.

They weren't impressed, either, with the Irishman's permanently dishevelled appearance. His uncombed mop of hair was permanently awry, his uniform crumpled, his tunic faded and oil-stained. They noticed, too, that for some reason he always walked with a strangely awkward, slightly jerky gait. Mannock was well aware of the hostility towards him. 'But,' wrote Ira Jones, himself from a poor, working-class family in Wales, 'he fought the difficult battle almost in secret and alone. He kept the agony of combat to himself – a big mistake – thus prolonging the struggle.' In fact, by the standards of the first air war, and given that he was now thirty, Mannock's adjustment to the terrors of aerial combat was by no means protracted. Many young pilots took months to get their first victory. Some never shot down a single enemy aircraft. The scorn that was heaped upon him had much more to do with his seriously unsettling, opinionated, working-class presence in the mess. Mannock's private battle with his nerves was never to be won, but it was only four weeks before, in a hazardous attack on some German observation balloons five miles behind the lines, he suddenly covered himself in glory by spectacularly shooting one of them down.

Balloon attack missions remained the most terrifying of all. That day the seven Nieuports sent out, flying at hedge-hopping low level, had encountered merciless ground fire. Their flight commander had been shot down and the other six had been nearly blown to pieces. 'I was the only one to return properly to the aerodrome and made a perfect landing,' Mannock wrote. 'My fuselage had bullet holes in it, one very near my head, and the wings were more or less riddled. I don't want to go through such an experience again.'[9]

In a letter to Jim Eyles back in Wellingborough he warned: 'I have an idea that my nerves won't stand very much of it. It's beyond a joke now.'[10] His diary logged the daily emotional toll of the losses of fellow pilots:

'Rastus missing. Went out yesterday morning on 2nd patrol, lost the leader in clouds and hasn't been seen or heard of since. I feel awfully miserable about it. My special chum. His loss is felt throughout the squadron. Everyone liked him . . .

'Another big bombing stunt on today at 10.30am. I expect I shall be on it. More nerves . . .

'Old MacKenzie goes away on leave today. 14 days. He is in need of it. If ever a lad is cracked up, Mac is. I wonder if I shall ever get like that! And what my friends will think of me if I do. Old Paddy the "devil-may-care" with nerves. I feel nervous about it already.'[11]

Mannock's balloon success had helped to redeem him in the eyes of his critical colleagues, but it took a second victory to demonstrate his true mettle. This came a month later when, at last, he shot down his first enemy aircraft, an Albatros. 'A beautifully coloured insect he was red, blue, green and yellow. I saw him go spinning and slipping down from fourteen thousand. Rough luck, but it's war and they're Huns.'[12]

Shooting down his first Hun brought little balm to his nerves, as his diary began to record: 'Feeling nervy and ill during the last week. Afraid I am breaking up,' he wrote in the middle of June. Observing the state he was in his flight commander 'let me off some flying for today. I think I'll take a book and wander into the woods this afternoon. O! for a fortnight in the country at home!'[13]

Mannock's wish was fulfilled sooner than he anticipated. Recovering from several painful operations to remove some grit from his eye, he was left so washed out that he was sent home to England on leave. He had intended to stay with his mother, Julia, who had moved to Birmingham, but when he got there he was shocked to find she'd become a virtual alcoholic, so whisky-sodden it was difficult to hold a conversation with her. Nor was there any happier news of his sisters, Jessie and Nora, both of whose marriages, he learned, were on the rocks. It was rumoured that Jessie had dabbled in prostitution to make ends meet. Within a few days he had fled Birmingham to spend the remainder of his leave in Wellingborough with the man who'd become his surrogate father, Jim Eyles, and his wife. Eyles recalled how Mannock demonstrated for them the air fighting tactics he was evolving. Using a lamp as the sun, he leaped up on tables and chairs simulating manoeuvres with his hands. 'Watch me bowl them over when I return,' he told them.

Back in France in mid-July 1917, Mannock began to prove that he could, shooting down a big DFW two-seater reconnaissance plane.

The bus crashed south of Avion. I hurried out at the first opportunity and found the observer being tended by the local M.O. and I gathered a few souvenirs, although the infantry had the first pick. The machine was completely smashed and rather interesting also was the little black and tan terrier – dead – in the observer's seat. I felt exactly like a murderer. The journey to the trenches was rather nauseating – dead men's legs sticking through the sides with puttees and boots still on – bits of bones and skulls with the hair peeling off. This sort of thing, together with the strong graveyard stench and the dead and mangled body of the pilot (an NCO) combined to upset me for days.[14]

Among the souvenirs he sent to Eyles was a strip of the aircraft's fabric and the pilot's boots. There was also a rather macabre item: a bayonet. He told Eyles he'd 'pulled it out of the body of a dead Hun who was lying near the crashed bus. It is one of our own bayonets. I had to crawl out on my stomach to get it as there was not much cover.'

When Mannock was awarded a Military Cross it wasn't universally applauded in the mess. Some of the pilots openly resented Major Tilney's gesture in recommending the honour for such a relative newcomer with such a small handful of victories. And they were even angrier when, only a few weeks later, Mannock was made a flight commander and promoted over their heads to captain. But Leonard Tilney, 40 Squadron's exceptionally young commanding officer – the 'tousle-headed youth' described by Bill Bond – had recognised in the temperamental Irishman a rare talent to be cherished. Whether his pilots liked it or not, he saw that Mannock brought charisma, courage and leadership in unique combination to the squadron. Not only did Tilney's faith prove well placed, but in the weeks that followed through the summer of 1917 Mannock started to surprise and silence even his bitterest critics with a terrific succession of aggressive victories. By the end of September he had been credited with fifteen. And, in a mocking gesture to his detractors, he had the nose of his aeroplane, its propeller boss, painted bright yellow.

The change in attitude towards Mannock on the squadron was nothing short of extraordinary. After some early missions on which he frightened his formation pilots with his recklessness, he began to demonstrate the more cautious battle tactics that were to shape his reputation. There was nothing revolutionary about his much-quoted mantra – 'Gentlemen, always above; seldom on the same level; never underneath' – nor his insistence that strikes should always be made with clear numerical advantage and from a superior position, with the pilots staying in formation until the leader signalled the attack. The German ace Boelcke had preached the same methods and Richthofen had adopted them, too. They not only worked but helped minimise losses. And, like the great German aces, Mannock took enormous care to encourage and protect the vulnerable new and frightened pilots in the pack, impressing on them the imperative to fling the aircraft into an immediate tight turn when attacked, warning that to dive away was to invite the quick death that came to so many in their first week. He also urged them to conserve their ammunition, not spray it wastefully at long range. Aimed straight and close up, a burst of twenty was as good as a burst of 200, he told them. Once they'd used up all their bullets they were defenceless. 'Beware the Hun who fires in short bursts. If he's firing in long bursts, you can bet your bottom dollar that he's windy, and probably a beginner. Fight him like hell. He should be easy meat.'[15] Mannock was also generous with his own victories. He often shared them, or gave them completely to new pilots to bolster their confidence.

A pilot who studied Mannock's remarkable ability to destroy enemy aircraft explained: 'His successes were largely due to his tactical approach to a fight and his extraordinarily fine deflection shooting once he was engaged. In an air fight most people try to get behind the other man to get an easier shot and where, fighter versus fighter, you cannot be shot at, Mannock was able to hit them at an angle ... When he landed back after a successful show he was always in tremendous form, shouting out to the other pilots about incidents in the fights.'[16]

Off duty he became one of the boys, helped by the gregarious padre, Bernard Keymer, with whom he became close friends. Keymer encouraged him to stop brooding and go out and get drunk with the others. Mannock at last abandoned abstinence and did so. With huge gusto he also began to join in the drunken furniture-smashing mess parties and would lead the chorus singing when concert parties came visiting. And although there is no record of any serious relationships with women in his life, he started to take an interest in the French girls in the estaminets who were strongly attracted to him. But Mannock, who, during his time in the English community in Turkey had worn a wedding ring to fend off the women who pursued him there, sought no more than light-hearted flirtation.

Most of the pilots now revered the once-despised Irishman and were keen to fly and fight under his protective eye and to socialise with him on the ground. The squadron's pariah had become its most popular figure and was recognised as a genuinely special phenomenon. 'I came under his spell,' said Ira Jones who was to fly with Mannock the following year. 'He had a dominating personality which radiated itself on all those around. Whatever he did or said compelled attention. It was obvious that he was a born leader of men.'[17]

By the autumn of 1917 the tempo of aerial combat had dramatically declined as the German Air Service withdrew pilots to train others for its forthcoming great spring offensive of 1918. For 40 Squadron, now equipped with more powerful SE5s, there were few victories for the rest of the year. In the last week of December Mannock was posted back to England for leave and reassignment. The night before his departure he was given a farewell dinner. He was the only pilot to have survived his nine months with the squadron. All the other faces had changed. Lieutenant William Douglas, who was present, recalled years later that Mannock, responding to the toasts, 'rose and entertained us to one of his marvellous speeches . . . He was idolised by all who came into intimate contact with him. For me he was the outstanding personality of the war.'[18]

Gwilym Lewis, who had joined 40 Squadron, was so taken with Mannock he pressed him to visit his parents at their Hampstead home. 'I told him to be sure to call on you,' he wrote to his mother and father. 'He is one of the finest personalities I have ever met – a regular hero in this squadron. He was jolly good to me when I first arrived . . . by his being nice to me everyone was. I know you would like him if for no other reason than he is a most arrogant socialist!'

Mannock's departure from Bruay was an unusually sentimental event. As he was driven off, another pilot who was in the vehicle remembered, 'the car was loudly cheered by the officers outside the mess and we found the road lined with cheering mechanics. I then realised Mannock's influence over the men. He was one of the most loveable I have ever known, always cheery, witty, courteous, daring brave and resourceful. On the way to Boulogne we stopped at a hospital as there was an Irish sister named Murphy who wanted to say au revoir to Mick. His popularity in this sister's mess staggered us as much as it embarrassed him.'[19] In 40 Squadron's diary Leonard Tilney wrote: 'His leadership and general ability will never be forgotten by those who had the good fortune to serve under him.'[20]

It was not the last the front-line squadrons would see of Mick Mannock.

Chapter 28

Flamerinoes

When he boarded the leave boat at Boulogne, Mannock assumed he was going back to England for a short break. He didn't know that, on Tilney's recommendation, he was to be rested out of the front line for at least three months. To his disgust he found himself posted to the gentle and boring role of flying an ancient FE2 at a wireless experimental station at Biggin Hill. Accosting General Henderson at the RFC Club in London, he demanded to be returned to France, to active service and to the comradeship of squadron life he was missing. The general succumbed to his pleading and arranged for him to be sent as a flight commander to a fighter squadron preparing for operations on the Western Front.

At the newly formed unit taking shape in Hertfordshire in February 1918, Mannock walked into a very different officers' mess from the public-school society that had greeted him so resentfully in France. At London Colney 74 Squadron rang more with the accents of North America and the Commonwealth than the tones of Eton and Oxbridge. Its commander, a big, swarthy, extremely tough-looking New Zealander, said to have had an insatiable appetite for aggressive aerial combat, was Major Keith Caldwell. 'All the patrols he leads are nightmares,' one of his pilots commented. 'He frightens us as much as we frighten the Huns.'[1]

Known as 'Grid' for his description of every aeroplane – his country's slang for bicycles – Caldwell had flown with Billy Bishop at 60 Squadron and was known for his view that the Canadian had faked his VC raid. Himself famed for his own rising total of victories, relaxed Antipodean view of discipline, casual manner of dressing and his extrovert personal style, his character was so similar to Mannock's that they bonded immediately. Their close friendship would define the squadron's spirit and inspire its pilots in remarkable degree as the two aces lectured them on fighting techniques that would help to prolong their lives and 'knock hell out of the Huns'.

The squadron flew its SE5s to France in formation at the end of March. 'Everyone is keyed up and itching for a fight,' Ira Jones wrote in his diary. 'We want to show "Grid" what we are made of. I often wonder, as I look

Ex-Etonian ace, Arthur Rhys Davids, who wrote love poems to his mother to whom he described aerial fighting as 'the best game God ever created'. On his death Caroline Rhys Davids (*above, right*) entered into angry grief-stricken correspondence with his squadron commander.

Arthur Gould Lee spent months conducting a private investigation into the failure of the War Office to give pilots parachutes.

Fighter pilot Duncan Grinnell-Milne. His life was saved by a two-and-a-half year interlude as a prisoner of war in Germany. He survived to fly bombers in WWII.

Good friend and confidante of the pilots, Padre Bernard Keymer comforted many at the limit of their nervous endurance.

(*Below*) A cluster of 'wonga-wongas' line up for a raid on England. This Gotha bomber squadron was based near Ostend in the spring of 1917.

Canadian hero Billy Bishop, whose Victoria Cross many fellow pilots and war historians believe was awarded for an uncorroborated solo raid that never happened.

Elliott Springs, the American ace whose bestselling book shockingly recounted his London wartime life, distinguished by terrifying flying pranks, drunkenness, fighting and womanising.

Roy Brown, the Canadian pilot who mistakenly believed he'd shot down the Red Baron, never recovered from the traumas of aerial combat.

Dr William Rivers introduced psychiatry to the healing of nerve-shattered pilots.

(*Above*) The death that haunted the flying crews' nightmares: a plunge to earth, roasting alive in a flaming parachuteless cockpit (*below*). The dreams of one of the Irish working-class aces, Mick Mannock (*below, left*), were nightly filled with these horrors. He called them 'flamerinoes'. One eventually claimed him.

King George V meets Ira Jones, a tiny aggressive Welshman credited with 37 victories, who survived the war to fly Spitfires in WWII.

85 Squadron pilots with their assortment of pets seen at St Omer with their SE5 fighters in June 1918.

A hundred aeroplanes sometimes tangled at close quarters in a single swarming air
battle. An RFC pilot captured this moment in mid-combat. He claimed the German
machine in the foreground was about to drop in flames from a burst of fire, seconds
earlier, that had ignited its fuel tank.

Everard Calthrop, the embittered inventor whose safely functioning 'Guardian Angel' parachute (seen on a 1917 test drop from Tower Bridge, *right*) was never fitted to a single operational warplane.

The giant Handley Page V/1500 super-bomber. Intended to bomb Berlin, it arrived in 1918 too late ever to do it.

round the mess, which of us will be the first to be killed. One of us must be, but no one shows any visible signs of caring. I hope it isn't Roxburgh-Smith or Stuart-Smith, as they are both married with families.'² The latter, a young Canadian who wrote poetry, was to be shot down in flames within weeks.

From the more permanent aerodrome they would occupy at Clair-marais, 74 Squadron went into battle with the triplanes and Albatros of the flying circuses at what was by now the height of the German spring offensive. On their first patrol Mannock destroyed two Albatros. Jones was lucky to survive. Separated from his formation he found himself at the mercy of ten triplanes. As its leader tried to pick him off Jones went into a defensive vertical turn. 'I had no desire to have a burning bullet roasting my intestines, especially before breakfast!' he wrote. 'Round and round we waltzed in what my opponent must have thought was a waltz of death – for me.' Jones could clearly see the German. 'He was an old hand at the game. He was flying superbly. He had a small, square face, a puggish little nose.' Jones kept his head and eventually escaped to rejoin his flight. As he did so, 'suddenly reaction set in. I started getting hot and cold all over and momentarily lost control of myself. I decided I was no use as an airman, that I could never cross the lines again, and that I would inform Grid of the fact as soon as I landed . . . I felt convinced that I was a rank coward.' Jones said he was so frightened that the thought of meeting the triplanes again 'nearly made me desert my formation – a coward. Thank God, I overcame the temptation.'

It was as well for Jones that he conquered his terror. For he was soon to witness at first hand what happened to pilots of 74 who 'funked it'. While Mannock was renowned for the patient and caring way he pro-tected and taught new pilots, those who ignored his advice and drifted away in fear from his formation were liable to receive a startling warning: Mannock would turn on them and direct a burst of gunfire over their top wing. Those who continued to show fear of combat he quickly got rid of. Newly arrived 2nd Lieutenant Sifton had been with the squadron only three days when, according to Ira Jones, he 'turned yellow. He went sobbing to Grid that he couldn't do the job. That he had nerves. And he has not even been over the lines! Grid and Mick were speechless. Mick had the fellow's wings torn from his tunic.' Sifton was sent back to England the same day. 'Why the hell he wasn't sent to the trenches or shot, I don't know,' Jones commented – with a strange lack of sympathy, given how close he himself had come to giving up.

But for his Welsh grit Jones, too, might not have lasted beyond his first patrols that sparked off the horrific dreams that were to plague his sleep for the rest of his time on the Western Front. They were sometimes so real that his terrified reactions disrupted the sleep of his hut mates.

Had a terrible nightmare last night. Jumped out of bed eleven times even though I tried to stop myself by tying my pyjama strings to the bed. Each time I jumped out there was a devil of a row. Poor old Giles got fed up to the teeth as I kept waking him up.

It was the usual old business of being shot down in flames and jumping out of my plane. One of the nightmares took a new line. I was forced down and crashed on top of a wood. I slid down a tree and ran to hide in a bush. But the Hun kept on chasing me and shooting me up, wounding me every time. At last he landed in a clearing and chased me with a revolver until he caught and killed me. Lovely dream! Feel very weary today.[3]

Mannock betrayed none of his own anxiety to the young pilots he led into battle several times a day. He masked it with an unnatural, almost euphoric, cheerfulness exemplified by his famous greeting on entering the mess: 'All tickets, please. Move right down inside the car.' Mannock and Caldwell let their hair down by leading violent High Cockalorum contests between 'the British Islanders' and the 'colonials', conspiring in pranks to pour water on late-sleeping colleagues and mounting raids on rival squadrons to shower their messes with bombloads of oranges.

But the strain became evident after one monumental clash at dusk on 26 May. Thirty aircraft from two British squadrons fought around forty German fighters in what Jones described as 'a hair-raising affair'. Machines, 'friend and foe, were so close to one another that pilots had to concentrate on avoiding collision rather than on firing'. According to Jones, it was after this fight that Mannock 'first displayed signs of nerves' over what was to become a deeply embedded obsession that he would die a fiery death. 'He kept on referring to a Hun who had passed close to him going down in flames and saying, "God, I'll blow my brains out rather than go down roasting."' Jones wrote:

A burning machine is a glorious and yet a most revolting sight to the victor. To watch a machine burst into flames after its petrol tanks have been pierced by incendiary bullets is a ghastly, hypnotising sight. At first a tiny flame peeps out of the tank ... then it gets bigger and bigger as it licks its way along the length and breadth of the machine. And finally all that can be seen is a large ball of fire enveloping, in a terrifying embrace, what was a few minutes before a beautiful bird of wood and metal flown by a probably virtuous youth who loved flying and life.[4]

The fear began to affect Mannock's flying, increasing the frequency of his crash-landings – 'a sure sign of impending cracking up of the nervous system,' said Jones.[5] Mannock shared some of his anxiety in his correspondence. 'I'm well,' he told Jim Eyles, 'but feeling the strain slightly.'[6] To his sister Jess he was much more frank in a letter his idolising pilots would have been shocked to read: 'Things are getting a bit intense just lately and I don't quite know how long my nerves will last out. I am rather old now, as airmen go, for fighting . . . These times are so horrible that occasionally I feel that life is not worth hanging on to myself – but "hope springs eternal in the human breast". I had thoughts of getting married but . . .?'[7]

He also wrote to Gwilym Lewis's sister, Mary, a student at the University of North Wales, whom he had met with the Lewis family when he was on leave in London. The two had begun to correspond and to debate what the war was doing to the human race. Trying to persuade her that 'strife and bloodshed and mental anguish are all good, gloriously wonderfully beneficial things', Mannock had written: 'These boys out here fighting are tempted at every moment of their day to run away from the ghastly (externally) Hell created by their Maker. But they resist the temptation (Heaven only knows how strong it is) and die for it, or become fitter & better for it, or because of it.'[8]

Somehow Mannock managed to go on performing with clinical ruthlessness in the air. He was now openly pursuing victories to compete with other great aces. 'My total is now 41,' he told Eyles. 'They have given me the DSO. If I've any luck I think I may beat old Mac [James McCudden]. Then I shall try and oust old Richthofen.' At the mess party to celebrate the first of three DSOs, he gave the most impressive of many drunken speeches which, Jones recalled, he ended by declaring, '"Gentlemen, the sky must be cleared of Huns. And we are the boys to do it." Thunderous applause, with cat-calls, whoopings and rattling of crockery. Several members slid exhausted under the table!' After dinner they had a sing-song and, 'with great pathos', Mannock sang 'Mother Machree'.

As Mannock's victories rose into the fifties, the faces at the dinner table continued to disappear. On one occasion the squadron lost three pilots in twenty-four hours. One of them was Lieutenant Henry Dolan, an exartillery officer who'd joined the Flying Corps with a Military Cross. Dolan was a special protégé of Mannock's who believed he had the fearlessness and aggression to become another Albert Ball. Mannock was so upset by his death that he retired to his hut and wept. According to Jones, his sobs could be heard at intervals throughout the night.

Dolan's death had a profound effect on Mannock. His colleagues were struck by the change in his personality. He became increasingly irascible, losing his cool more than ever with pilots who broke his formation rules. One terrified new arrival who began to avoid combat was given the same treatment as the faltering Sifton – not only were his wings torn off, they were humiliatingly replaced with a yellow patch. Mannock became more ruthless in his treatment of enemy pilots and his hatred of the Germans intensified. His outbursts of gallows humour grew more frequent and he struggled to control his emotions as the daily stress steadily corroded his reason.

'Mick, who gets most of his Huns in flames, is getting very peculiar over the business,' Ira Jones wrote. 'Whenever he sends one down in flames he comes dancing into the mess, whooping and halloing: "Flamerinoes, boys! Sizzle, sizzle, wonk!" Then at great length he tries to describe the feelings of the poor old Hun by going into the minutest details. Having finished in a frenzy of fiendish glee, he will turn to one of us and say, laughing: "That's what will happen to you on the next patrol, my lad." And we all roar with laughter.'[9]

But the laughter was forced. Everyone knew this was the way they were most likely to die. Mannock started checking the reactions of new pilots to the fate that awaited so many of them. 'Mick has been testing their offensive spirit by relating gruesome stories of Huns going down in flames. If they laugh heartily, or appear to get a kick out of the story, he decides they are all right. If they assume a slightly sickly appearance when they smile, he's suspicious.'[10]

Caldwell noticed that the hate Mannock now increasingly expressed for the German pilots was being reflected in the cruelty with which he dealt with them in combat. On a patrol he flew with his Irish flight commander he was appalled to see an example of this new ruthlessness. As 'a Hun two-seater was beetling back toward the lines', Mannock shot it down.

The Hun crashed, but not badly, and most people would have been content with this – but not Mick Mannock, who dived half a dozen times at the machine, spraying bullets at the pilot and the observer who were still showing signs of life. I witnessed this business and flew alongside of Mick, yelling at the top of my voice (which was rather useless), and warning him to stop. On being questioned as to his wild behaviour after we had landed, he heatedly replied, 'The swines are better dead – no prisoners for me'!'[11]

Most of the numerous biographies of Mick Mannock have relied for their descriptions of his state of mind on his fellow working-class pilot Ira Jones. Jones regarded Mannock as such a unique phenomenon that he regularly logged admiring observations of his hero in his personal war diary and later wrote exhaustively about him in two books. Perhaps because of the humble backgrounds they shared Jones was one of the few colleagues in whom Mannock felt able to confide his shattered emotions and premonitions of his end. In Jones he found a sympathetic friend whose own tattered nerves were regularly reducing his speech to an incoherent stammer, and who recognised all too clearly the classic signs. 'It is easy to spot when a pilot is getting nervy. He becomes very talkative and restless. When I arrived in the mess this morning, Mick's greeting was: "Are you ready to die for your country, Taffy? Will you have it in flames or in pieces?"'[12]

Caldwell, whose responsibility it was to spot the mental collapse of his pilots, was deceived by Mannock's bravado. When, in mid-June 1918, Caldwell was told by his wing commander that Mick had been chosen to replace Billy Bishop as CO of No. 85 Squadron, it seems he had no idea he was about to hand over a man who might not be in a fit state to do the job. Mannock had never revealed the extent of his condition to Caldwell, who insisted later that he had never 'sensed any signs of him cracking up'.

When, on his next leave, Mannock went to stay with Eyles and his wife in Wellingborough they were distressed at the state in which he arrived. In the bosom of the Eyles family, he felt able to drop all pretence. They were probably the only people in his life who were to witness Mannock's suffering in its rawest, most pitiful form. 'Gone was the old sparkle we knew so well, gone was the incessant wit,' Eyles recalled.[13] They scarcely knew how to deal with it. Day after day Mannock broke down in front of them in bouts of trembling and uncontrollable weeping, muttering unintelligibly.

Recalling Mannock's departure, his health worsened by a bout of the influenza that was sweeping the country, Eyles said: 'He was in no condition to return to France. But in those days such things were not taken into consideration. That last leave had something very final about it all ... I do feel that he knew he was saying goodbye.' The truth was Mannock was by now a quivering wreck and classic candidate for the therapeutic treatment of Dr Rivers at the RAF's Hampstead hospital. But no one suggested he go there. And Mannock was determined not to give up.

In the first week of July 1918 Mannock assumed command of 85 Squadron at St Omer. 'There is no doubt,' Ira Jones said, 'that from a flying point of view he was a very sick man when he boarded the leave boat' for Boulogne. Mannock broke his journey to spend a night back with the pilots of 74 Squadron at their airfield nearby. It was an emotional evening. His old comrades demonstrated such affection and sadness at losing him that Mannock broke down and wept in front of them. Next day, when he arrived at 85 Squadron, he was given a warm reception. The pilots who, curiously, had earlier rejected McCudden for his working-class background, welcomed with open arms this rival ace of similarly humble origin and limited education. His reputation had travelled ahead of him. The squadron's morale had been badly affected by the indifferent leadership of the departed Billy Bishop, who had proved a disappointing commander. The famous Canadian had spent little time with them on patrol, preferring to roam the sky on his notorious lone-wolf missions to add to his huge and eventually disputed score of personal victories. Mannock set about changing things on his first day. He told them that henceforth they would be flying as a team. 'He certainly is keen,' said the American pilot Elliott Springs, by now an ace at 85 Squadron. 'He got us all together in the office and outlined his plans and told each one what he expected of them. He's going to lead one flight and act as a decoy ... We ought to be able to pay back these Fokkers a little we owe them.'[14]

Within two days Mannock was leading them into the air to a succession of victories. As a squadron commander he wasn't expected to fly – but that wasn't Mannock's style. According to the venerating Ira Jones, 'the pilots found in him a leader who could be trusted and the mechanics discovered a strict but kindly master'.

But on 9 July, only four days after he'd arrived at St Omer, Mannock's apparent equilibrium was blown apart by the news of the death of James McCudden. The shock was made even greater because his fellow Irishman, who had acquired a reputation for the cool and calculating way he fought, had been killed not in combat, but in a take-off accident. Since they had met the previous year at Joyce Green, McCudden had become a top-scoring ace with whom Mannock had begun to compete. Unlike

Mannock, known and applauded only within the air service, McCudden had been propelled into the limelight by his successes, many of them enemy observation aircraft shot down at dangerously high altitudes. Almost all of the fifty-seven victories with which he was credited had been unimpeachably verified and when he was awarded the Victoria Cross, the newspapers had turned this innately modest and low-key man into a reluctant celebrity.

McCudden had been flying his SE5a from England to assume command of No. 60 Squadron at Boffles, between Boulogne and Amiens. As he approached his destination in a summer haze he got lost and landed at another nearby air base, Auxi-le-Château, to ask the way. He taxied in to the hangars where a couple of mechanics, neither of whom recognised him in his flying helmet and goggles, gave him the direction to Boffles, less than five miles away. McCudden immediately taxied away and took off again. On his steep climb out his engine was heard to falter. People on the ground were stunned to see the aircraft suddenly make a deep turn and dive into the woods flanking the aerodrome. McCudden was found lying unconscious in the wreckage. Only then, by his VC ribbon, was he recognised. His skull was fractured and he died that evening.

It was McCudden's habit to zoom-climb after take-off and bank into a turn. It is believed that on this occasion the manoeuvre caused moment-ary fuel starvation and, in the temporary loss of power, he had stalled and crashed.

The revered James McCudden was buried in a small military cemetery nearby after a hastily arranged ceremony that angered some of the pilots who attended. 'It made my blood boil,' wrote Paul Winslow, an American with 56 Squadron. 'All in Latin, mumbled ... Nothing human in it at all ... Richthofen – an enemy – had a far better funeral, and if anyone deserved a real memorial, it was McCudden.'[15]*

Although McCudden hadn't died at German hands, Mannock's grief is said to have intensified his hatred of the enemy into an insatiable desire for revenge. 'He began taking enormous risks in combat, going down after enemy machines to spray their already dead crews with yet more bullets. After placing his men in a position that would ensure their success in an attack, he would head off on his own, charging at every German

---

*McCudden's younger brother, Anthony, another fighter pilot, with eight credited vic-tories, had been shot down and killed in a fight with a Richthofen Circus pilot four months earlier, in March 1918. Trying to emulate his famous brother, Anthony had become dangerously impetuous and aggressive in his combat flying.

machine in sight.'[16] However, according to Ira Jones, there was another reason for Mannock's orgy of destruction. 'His nerves were getting into such an unhealthy state that the excitement was intoxicating him,' he said. 'Every patrol and fight had become a narcotic; he was doping himself with the bloodlust . . . Mannock had reached the alarming stage of nerves which could have but one end in one imbued with his unquenchable spirit.'[17] Yet somehow, it seems, he still managed, with what must have been superhuman self-control, to conceal his shattered state from the pilots so grateful to be under his command. It is largely thanks to the testimony of Jones, who remained Mannock's only confidant, that any record of his final days exists. Jones, still with 74 Squadron, only a few miles away, kept in touch with his idol by telephone and on regular visits. He continued to log approximations of their many conversations in his diary. Increasingly, they returned to the same theme. 'July 25, 1918. Had lunch, tea and dinner with Mick. He keeps bringing up his pet subject of being shot down in flames. I told him I'd got a two-seater in flames on patrol this morning before breakfast. "Could you hear the sod scream?" he asked with a sour smile. "One day they'll get you like that, my lad . . . Don't forget to blow your brains out." Everyone roared with laughter.'[18]

At tea that afternoon he and Mannock had been joined by two army nurses from a nearby military hospital. Some writers have taken the liberty of naming one of them as an Irish ward sister, a Miss Flanagan, perpetuating the myth that Mannock intended to marry her after the war. There is no evidence that Sister Flanagan even existed, let alone of any serious romantic relationship between Mannock and any army nurse.

Whoever the nurses were, they were privy to a conversation Jones recorded between Mannock and a new pilot who had yet to make his first kill. 'Have you got a Hun yet, Kiwi?' Mannock asked him. 'No, sir,' was the 'shy and almost ashamed reply'.

Mannock responded with a famously quoted invitation: 'Well, come on out and we'll get one.'

New Zealander Donald Inglis was in fact a twenty-five-year-old battle-hardened veteran of the Gallipoli campaign where, as an artillery gunner, he had earned a Distinguished Conduct Medal. He jumped at Mannock's offer. Mannock asked the nurses to excuse him 'for a few minutes' as he and Inglis walked out and climbed into their aeroplanes. Mannock took off, but Inglis, finding that his elevator control was jammed, was unable to accompany him. Mannock had decided to go off and look for an enemy aircraft on his own, promising Inglis on his return that they'd try again in the morning.

That evening Mannock invited Jones to his hut. 'Once inside,' Jones said, 'I asked him how he felt. He then frankly told me he thought that he would not last much longer. Suddenly he put his arms upon my shoulders and, looking me straight in the eyes, with a suggestion of a tear in his, he said in a broken voice: "Old lad, if I am killed I shall be in good company. I feel I have done my duty."' As they walked back to the mess Jones described how Mannock linked arms with him and began 'singing "Rule Britannia" at the top of his voice'.[19]

At dawn next morning, flying under low cloud at almost ground level, hugging the contours, Mannock and Inglis went out to the front line in search of an enemy aircraft for the New Zealander to bag. They found one a few miles north of Béthune. It was a solitary two-seat DFW reconnaissance machine and its crew, spotting the pair, fled eastward back over the German lines. With Inglis closely following him, Mannock climbed above the DFW and, diving on it, killed the gunner. 'When he pulled away,' said Inglis, 'I got in a good burst at very close range ... Looking back I saw my first Hun going down in a mass of flames.'

Mannock and Inglis briefly circled the blazing wreckage before heading west towards the safety of the British lines. Flying at only 200 feet, both aircraft were peppered from the ground with enemy machine-gun fire. Inglis suddenly saw a small flame beginning to flicker along the side of Mannock's aeroplane. A few seconds later, it 'went into a slow right-hand turn, the flame growing in intensity and, as it hit the ground, it burst into a mass of flame. I circled at about 20 feet hoping for the best – but Mannock had made his last flight.'[20]

Inglis's aircraft was also hit. As a bullet punctured his fuel tank over no-man's-land he was sprayed with petrol and his engine stopped. He was flying too low to glide very far across the British line but survived a crash-landing just five yards in front of trenches held by Welsh troops, who went out to bring him in. Inglis was hysterical. In the safety of the trenches, he later told Ira Jones, all he could say, as he burst into tears, was: 'The bloody bastards have shot my major down in flames.'

In the 85 Squadron mess at St Omer that night its officers were joined by pilots from other nearby squadrons. Prominent among them were Mannock's former colleagues from 74 Squadron, more affected, Ira Jones said, than those of his more recently joined at 85. There was no party spirit. 'The thought of Mick's charred body not many miles away haunted us. There was more drinking than usual on these occasions, the Decca [gramophone] worked overtime; we tried to sing, but it was painfully obvious that it was false.' In his diary he wrote: 'Mick is dead. Everyone is stunned. No one can believe it. I can write no more today. It is too terrible.'[21]

Equally terrible to many was that Mannock had been killed doing the very thing he had so constantly lectured against: remaining low over the site of his victim's crash. He was not alone in this. Many experienced fighter pilots, fully aware of the risk and momentarily succumbing to the same temptation, had paid the price with their lives – among them, indeed, the great Richthofen himself.

Mannock had proclaimed so often that he would shoot himself rather than die a hideous death in a flaming cockpit, but there is no evidence that he did so. A British infantryman who saw the burning machine go down said that it made several turns, suggesting it was under control until very near the ground. In fact, when the Germans removed him from the wreckage and buried him, his body had not been consumed by the fire. When, after the war, some of his effects were returned by the Red Cross to his family, they were surprised to see that his tunic, notebook, and ID discs, though slightly charred, were not seriously damaged. Some authors have claimed that Mannock's revolver was found in the wreckage but, if it was, there is no longer any record of what happened to it. And, despite persistent investigations by his friend Jim Eyles and subsequently by extraordinarily dedicated aviation historians, some of them still searching around Pacault Wood between Merville and Béthune as recently as 2008, Mannock's grave has never been found.

Because Mannock was scarcely known outside the air force his death attracted little coverage in the newspapers. The tributes came almost entirely in private letters from those who'd loved and revered him in the squadrons. Padre Keymer was one. 'We were very close friends and I shall miss him more than words can say,' he told Mannock's brother Patrick. 'I know him not only for the most dashing brave and clever pilot that the RFC has ever produced, but also for "one of the very best", and that is saying a good deal where the RFC is concerned ... He was always so keenly interested in my work and used to attend my services very regularly. How we shall miss his kindly ways and irrepressible humour, but I trust we shall meet him again, and at least he has gone into wonderfully good company.'[22]

The squadron's adjutant, Lieutenant Cushing, described the extraordinary love his thirty-one-year-old dead commander had so universally inspired. 'There was no man or officer in the squadron but loved him for his bravery, for his cheerfulness, for his skill, for his patience in teaching others, and for his personality, which made him at once the most efficient and most popular Commanding Officer in France. He was a friend to us all.'[23] No one spoke of the personal battle Mannock had fought against class prejudice, which had once prompted him to tell another pilot: 'You fellers were born with silver spoons in your mouths. I had an iron shovel.'[24] His bewitching personality and bravery had triumphed over the class divide.

Ira Jones felt so strongly that Mannock's achievements deserved greater recognition that he launched a campaign to have him awarded a post-humous Victoria Cross. He led a petition from the RAF Club. It was joined by another from Wellingborough, organised by Jim Eyles, and a third from the dignitaries of Canterbury, where Mannock had lived as a child. When the petitions reached Air Minister Winston Churchill he was sufficiently moved to order an inquiry into the dead pilot's war service record and the number of enemy aircraft he had accounted for. The response convinced him that a VC was merited and, almost a year after Mannock's death, in July 1919, it was gazetted. The citation took an excessively conservative view of his victories, conceding him only fifty – a figure aviation historians were subsequently to elevate to a positive sixty-one, noting that, given his generosity in attributing many of his kills to new pilots, the true figure was unquestionably much higher.

The medal, together with his hitherto unpresented three DSOs and two MCs, was bestowed in one glittering array by the King to Mannock's father. Retired Corporal Edward Mannock, who had abandoned his family twenty years earlier and bigamously married another woman, had reappeared from out of the blue. When he read of the award he wrote to the Air Ministry with unashamed cheek to inquire whether his son had left a military service will. He also asked what steps he should take to claim the 'Victoria Cross and 'tother decorations'. Mannock senior was not to know that his son had so loathed him he had gone to the trouble of stipulating in his will that he should receive nothing from his estate. Corporal Mannock was, however, invited to Buckingham Palace to receive the clutch of medals. When, some years later, Mannock's brother Patrick tried to trace the priceless collection, he discovered it was in the possession of the woman his father had illegally married. It turned out he had later deserted her, too. Patrick bought the lot for £5.[*]

Despite notching up impressive numbers of victories, very few of the

---

[*]In 1992 a descendant of Patrick Mannock sold the collection at Sotheby's for a reputed £120,000 to Lord Ashcroft, who loaned them to the Imperial War Museum, where they are on display.

falling aces were acquiring enduring fame as, one after the other, they died over northern France. Names that had never featured in the newspapers were soon forgotten by all except their loved ones and friends. By the summer of 1918, however, many of these deaths, together with those of hundreds of other pilots who would never achieve ace status, were preventable. A means of avoiding the ghastly incineration they all so dreaded had actually arrived. But the life-saving device was being made available only to enemy pilots.

One day in the autumn of 1918 an eighteen-year-old Sopwith Dolphin pilot, Captain Donald Hardman, was caught up in a big air battle in which he shot down two enemy attackers. As one of the aircraft burst into flames he saw something that flabbergasted him. 'To my absolute astonishment, a parachute came out of it. I couldn't believe it. There was a man coming down in a parachute.'

Hardman, who survived the war to become an air chief marshal, said, 'It never occurred to us that it was possible to have a parachute in a small aeroplane. We were used to seeing them come down from a balloon, of course, because balloons were shot down a good deal and you would see them coming out in parachutes – but never from aeroplanes.'[25]

As pilots began to see a steady flow of Germans leaping out of their blazing aircraft to float safely to earth beneath a white canopy, more and more of them were asking: 'Why can't we have them too?'

Chapter 29
Waning of the Spirit

The fear of an agonising death in a furnace of blazing petrol did not haunt the Boer War-generation generals now denying pilots parachutes from the safety of their offices back in London, Arthur Gould Lee complained angrily. 'What the hell is wrong with those callous dolts at home that they won't give them to us?' he wrote to his wife. Lee had just watched another aircraft in his 46 Squadron formation, flown by Canadian Captain Robert Ferrie, begin to break up in flight after a dogfight.

His right wing suddenly folded back, then the other, and the wreck plunged vertically down. A bullet must have gone through a main spar during the fight.

The others went after him and steered close to him in vertical dives. They could see him struggling to get clear of his harness, then half standing up. They said it was horrible to watch him trying to decide whether to jump. He didn't, and the machine and he were smashed to nothingness.

I can't believe it. Little Ferrie, with his cheerful grin, one of the finest chaps in the squadron. God, imagine his last moments, seeing the ground rushing up at him, knowing he was a dead man, unable to move, unable to do anything but wait for it. A parachute could have saved him, there's no doubt about that.[1]

Ira Jones witnessed the death in inferno of one of his 74 Squadron colleagues, twenty-year-old Lieutenant Hamilton Begbie, who had been commissioned at seventeen and had earlier fought with the army on the Somme. 'Suddenly there was a blaze in the sky nearby. I looked. It was Begbie's S.E. A sudden feeling of sickness, of vomiting, overcame me. Poor old Begbie, I thought. How terrible! . . . He had to leave us without a farewell wave. One by one the Huns left the fight. Giles and I flew towards Begbie's machine which was floating, enveloped in flames. It was a terrible sight. I hope he followed Mannock's advice and blew his brains out as soon as he realised he was on fire . . . Why have we no parachutes, like balloon observers?'[2]

The pilots of doomed machines had three options: stay and die in the flames, shoot themselves or jump out. Watching those who chose to jump, said Ira Jones, 'chilled the blood of friend and foe alike. The victims, with arms and legs spread-eagled, would drop away, twisting and turning, as they hurtled towards certain death.'

Another 74 Squadron pilot, Canadian Leonard Richardson, who had told his mother his fate would always be 'what God wanted', heard a new pilot asking their down-to-earth commander, Keith Caldwell, why they carried revolvers. '"Grid" told the pilot to use his own "bloody imagination",' Richardson wrote in his diary. 'Since we don't have parachutes and perhaps it would be quite hot coming down in flames, we have the revolver to shoot ourselves in case we can't stand the heat!'[3]

Parachutes had existed since the end of the eighteenth century. For more than a hundred years they had been used with growing reliability by exhibition jumpers descending from balloons. By 1912 successful jumps were being made from aeroplanes and during the war parachutes were routinely issued to airship and kite balloon observers on the battle fronts. The latter were at permanent risk of being shot down by enemy aircraft, and because of the time and expense involved in training them, they were considered a human asset it was important to preserve when their big, hydrogen-filled sausages were regularly set ablaze above them. German balloon observers wore their chutes in backpacks while the British and French had theirs packed in containers attached to the observation basket and linked to the occupants' body harnesses by a static line. In an emergency all they had to do was leap out. As they fell the line would tighten and pull the canopy out of the container. The German aeroplane chute, worn on the pilots' backs, was likewise attached to the aircraft by a cord which, when the pilot jumped, deployed the canopy. The same method is used by paratroopers to this day.

With both systems the force of the parachute opening broke a link in the cord to free the chute from the plane or observation basket. Failure of the British balloon chutes to open was fairly rare, fewer than one in a hundred jumps. Throughout the war they saved the lives of hundreds of Allied and German observers.

Why, then, were parachutes never fitted to British military aeroplanes as they were – eventually – to their German counterparts? The technology existed in two proven forms: a version produced by the Spencer company for use by airship and balloon crews, and another, called the Guardian

Angel, for escape from aeroplanes, invented by a former railway engineer, Everard Calthrop. Romantic legends surround the creators of both versions of the life-saving device.

The Spencers were a long-established dynasty. Glamorously known as aeronauts, generations of the family had been developing man-carrying balloons and parachutes since the early nineteenth century. They engaged balloon pilots and teams of men and women parachutists who travelled Britain like aerial circuses making demonstration jumps. In 1914 Henry Spencer, who was then running the company, so impressed the British military authorities with a descent he made from a balloon at a naval air station that Spencer parachutes were ordered for both naval and Flying Corps observation balloons.

However, the Spencer parachute was not designed to work from the cockpit of an aeroplane moving at 100 miles an hour. There would have been a high risk of the rigging lines tangling with the machine's tailplane. Calthrop's Guardian Angel was designed to overcome this problem. Unlike the Spencers, Calthrop had arrived on the scene with no parachute expertise at all. His long career had been spent building railways around the world. In the summer of 1910, he had gone to an air show in Bournemouth with a close friend, the Honourable Charles Rolls, co-founder of the Rolls-Royce motor company. Rolls had bought one of the Wright brothers' celebrated but difficult-to-fly aeroplanes. While he was demonstrating it that day the elevator collapsed and Calthrop watched him crash to his death. The event so affected him he decided to devote his retirement to the development of a special aeroplane parachute he believed would have saved Rolls. He worked on the project at his country estate in Essex, where he bred Arabian horses. Their companionship, he wrote, had provided him with the tranquillity he'd needed while his mind was wrestling with parachute aerodynamics. 'There was no occasion more favourable for thinking out the more abstruse problems than when I was able to lie out under the stars on a summer's night, with one warm pony stretched out for a back rest, and the others lying close around me ... My taming of horses and ponies has most certainly helped me to tame that most uncanny beast, the parachute.'[4]

The Guardian Angel born in this idyllic environment was a lighter and technically more sophisticated parachute than the Spencer. Its silk canopy was packed between metal discs stowed in a canvas container attached to the aircraft. The chute, with its cluster of rigging lines, was linked to the pilot's harness by a long cord and its deployment was controlled by a series of break-ties to prevent the pilot from tangling with anything when he jumped. It was a great technical success. Early in 1917, a New Zealand pilot, Captain Clive Collett, made an historic test jump with it from a BE2c for the Flying Corps. Calthrop hoped the British air services would adopt his invention and fit it to all its fighting aircraft. But although the Guardian Angel was repeatedly tested by the Royal Aircraft Factory at Farnborough and found to function faultlessly the War Office generals were, for reasons still not fully understood, in no hurry to acquire it.

Who were the 'callous dolts' so angrily blamed by Arthur Gould Lee? Over almost a hundred years since, aviation historians searching the War Office files at the National Archives in London have failed to identify them. Nor have they succeeded in tracking down a monstrous and still frequently quoted statement, attributed by many authors to the Air Board, that parachutes would encourage cowardice. The notorious minute allegedly declared that it was 'the opinion of the Board that the presence of such an apparatus might impair the fighting spirit of pilots and cause them to abandon machines which might otherwise be capable of returning to base for repair'.[5] There appears to be no record, either, of the pilots' assertions that the very opposite was the case: that the comfort of a parachute would increase their fighting aggression and the risks they would take in battle. Or that an aeroplane was cheaper to replace than an expensively trained airman.

The precise form of words expressing the harsh view that aircrew whose machines were on fire should go down like a captain with his ship were probably recorded somewhere. Possibly in late 1915, at the time Calthrop was dealing directly with the Royal Aircraft Factory at Farnborough where modifications were being made to a BE2 aeroplane, so that it could be used for test jumps. The superintendent at that stage, Mervyn O'Gorman, excited by the invention and by its huge life-saving potential, had fitted the capsule containing the chute to the underside of the aircraft. But to Calthrop's astonishment the jumps were suddenly cancelled. 'Everything was ready for the tests,' he wrote, 'when peremptory orders came from the War Office that they were not to be made.'[6] Instead, he offered his parachute to the rival naval air service whose commanders expressed an immediate interest and arranged for demonstrations.

From where in the War Office had the cancellation order come? Arthur Gould Lee, who had survived more than 120 patrols over the lines, engaged in around sixty combats and been reported missing four times, was determined to discover why the RFC pilots had been denied parachutes. More than thirty years later, on his retirement as an air vice-marshal after the Second World War, he spent several weeks at the Public Record Office at Kew combing through the WWI War Office aeronautical records. His search was finally rewarded by the discovery in a yellowing file of a scribbled note. Written by the general officer commanding the Flying Corps, General Henderson, its three words were to have him demonised as the instigator of a no-parachutes policy. Lee found it on a minute to Henderson from Mervyn O'Gorman, who was about to start the Guardian Angel trials using dummies. 'Do you wish experiments of this nature to be proceeded with?' O'Gorman had asked. According to Lee, the response, in Henderson's handwriting, read: 'No, certainly not!'

General Henderson, himself a pilot, was an exceedingly caring man. Although he may have been obliged to decline the experimental funds at that moment the overall British air services parachute policy had not been solely his to make. It was the responsibility of the higher authority of the Air Board, the 'sheer ignorance' of whose members so appalled Lee. Few had ever flown or fought in combat. The soldiering days of the sixty-nine-year-old Lord Sydenham, for example, 'had ended over twenty years earlier, and his two previous public appointments had been Super-intendent of the Royal Carriage Factory and Chairman of the Royal Commission on Contagious Diseases' – code for venereal diseases. As he scoured the records, Lee was amazed to read some of the absurd objec-tions that had apparently been raised in all seriousness. 'Smashed aircraft generally fall with such velocity that there would hardly be time to think about the parachute,' one member was recorded as saying. Another insisted that 'a falling airman would lose consciousness'. A third suggested that, for economy, pilot and observer could share one chute.

Despite the evidence of Henderson's test cancellation note, Lee found no record that the succession of committees, boards and councils that presided over the affairs of the Flying Corps and Naval Air Service ever formally vetoed parachutes. Nor was he able to attach any ban to General Trenchard, often wrongly blamed for withholding chutes from his squadrons. Nowhere, Lee said, did he find 'any specific statement by any officer or official on which could be pinned the calumny that parachutes would encourage unnecessary abandonment of aircraft'.[7] On the contrary, it had become such a burning issue that, under pressure from the media and Parliament, the Air Board was forced, in late 1917, to form a parachute subcommittee charged with developing a reliable one that could be fitted to aircraft without its extra weight and bulk impeding either the occupants or the performance of the machine. The committee's ponderous investigations proceeded unhurriedly and the high standard of design perfection it demanded was painfully slow to be satisfied.

While these deliberations bumbled on, Everard Calthrop was not silent. An abrasive character, which did little to help his dealings with the authorities, he bombarded the War Office with letters pressing for the adoption of his parachute and publicly accused it of needlessly sacrificing the lives of thousands of young pilots and observers his device could have saved. He accepted that the training death toll from accidents occurring too low for anyone to bale out would not be much reduced but claimed that combat fatalities in France would be halved. To galvanise public opinion he continued to make spectacular demonstrations of the Guardian Angel. In one of the first, in November 1917, a balloon officer, Major Thomas Orde-Lees, proved from just how low down escapes could be made by jumping off the top of Tower Bridge into the Thames.* Calthrop went on to advertise his parachute in the newspapers and, to the consternation of the Air Board, began to offer to sell it directly to the military pilots. One of several who seized upon it was the American Elliott Springs at 85 Squadron. He went to meet Calthrop and offered him $2,000 to make him a bespoke chute to install in his SE5 fighter. To his disappointment, 'Calthrop said he couldn't do it as the War Office wouldn't let him work for individuals'. So he 'tried to get permission from the US Headquarters to go ahead with it, but they said nothing doing'.[8]

By the summer of 1918 the spectacle of parachutes regularly blossoming from burning German aeroplanes on the Western Front brought a fresh burst of questions in Parliament. They were answered by the parliamentary secretary to the Air Board, Major John Baird. An old Etonian, the future Viscount Stonehaven and governor-general of Australia, who, earlier in the war, had earned a DSO with his infantry regiment, Baird had a foot in both camps. He was both an MP and a member of the board and had become adept at dismissing awkward questions about pilot casualties. Pilots did not desire parachutes for aeroplanes, he had once, to Lee's disbelief, told the House. 'Another stock attitude,' Lee said, 'was that the Guardian Angel was not efficient enough ... But the active-service flier did not want to wait for perfection. He wanted something quickly. Even if the parachute were not infallible it would offer a sporting chance, which was better than a death that was certain.' There were 'few

---

*A newsreel showing Orde-Lees' brief 140-foot descent into the river can still be watched on YouTube.

fliers with any experience of air fighting who were not obsessed to some degree, though usually secretly, with the thought of being shot down in flames'.[9]

The Germans hadn't waited for perfection. Nor had the Austro–Hungarians. The German Air Service had begun issuing parachutes to pilots and observers in the spring of 1918. Very soon they were proving their worth. The first to jump using one was Leutnant Helmut Steinbrecher, who successfully baled out of his burning Jasta 46 Albatros after it was set on fire in an encounter with a British Camel near Amiens on the evening of 27 June. He was so grateful that he wrote to thank the Schroeder company, which manufactured the Heinecke chutes in Berlin. 'The thing functioned very well. I congratulate you on the splendid success of your parachute. I am carrying it ever since that flight and do not want to fly without it any more. As far as I know this was the first time that a parachute was used under actual wartime conditions and that it was used for a jump from a single-seater to boot. Congratulations once again on your excellent parachute.'[10]

In his combat report Steinbrecher wrote: 'Up to that time I had been a Doubting Thomas in the matter of parachutes. I had been under the impression that baling out with a parachute from a single-seater would be only rarely successful. And I did not know exactly what I had to do to get out of the plane. But in the moment when the flames licked my face, I did know at once what to do!'

Second to save his life, just two days later, was the great German ace Ernst Udet, whose credited sixty-two victories were eventually to rank second to the eighty of Richthofen, in whose flying circus he commanded a squadron. In an encounter with a French Breguet observation machine Udet's controls were blasted out of action. He decided to bale out of his Albatros. But when he unfastened his safety belt and stood up on the seat things didn't go well. The 100mph slipstream blew him out of the cockpit. As he hurtled back along the top of the fuselage his parachute harness caught on the forward tip of the rudder. He hung there believing his last moment had come, dragged down to crash with the aeroplane. In those seconds, he wrote, he thought of his girlfriend, Eleanor 'Lo' Zink. 'Lo will cry ... I think, Mother, I will be unrecognisable ... I have no papers on me ... they're shooting like mad down there ... the ground is coming at me fast.'

But with superhuman strength Udet managed to grip the rudder and, at barely 250 feet above the ground, to break off the tip, 'A jerk – I am free. The machine drops off below me. A sharp pull and I float on the

straps like a swimmer. Immediately after, a jolt, and I have landed. The
parachute had opened at the last moment.' He found himself in a bleak
'crater landscape' between the French and German lines. Shrapnel was
bursting all around him. 'I unhook the parachute and start running. The
shell bursts come closer as though they were racing toward me. A large
clod of earth hits me in the back of the head like a fist. I fall down, clamber
back up and continue running.' Udet reached a German gun position.
The artillery officer was in the middle of ordering an ear-bursting salvo
of firing that convulsed the ground.

'"Cigarette?" I say with dry lips. "Bayer," he introduces himself, salutes,
and produces a cigarette case. "Udet," I say, and for a moment the drum-
fire doesn't exist, so strong are the rituals of upbringing that even war
can't obliterate.'[11] Udet survived the war to marry 'Lo', though it was to
be a short-lived marriage, and to join the Nazi party. In the Second World
War he was a senior general responsible for aircraft development and
procurement in the German Air Ministry, a job that was to end in his
suicide.*

By July 1918 German and Austro–Hungarian Air Service parachute
escapes had become routine. The Heinecke chutes were not perfect and
sometimes failed to operate safely. Some were destroyed by fire before
they could open, and occasionally, as they swayed gently down to earth,
pilots faced the further peril of being shot at by Allied fighters. Ira Jones
had no compunction in doing this. 'My habit of attacking Huns dangling
from parachutes led to many arguments in the mess,' he said. 'Some
officers of the Eton and Sandhurst type, thought it "unsportsmanlike".
Never having been to a public school, I was unhampered by such considerations of "form". I just pointed out that there was a bloody war on,
and that I intended to avenge my pals.'[12]

According to German records, there were forty-five bale-outs between
June and late October 1918, including several escapes from mid-air col-
lisions, with a success rate of over 80 per cent.[13] The Flying Corps pilots
would have welcomed these as more than fair odds. In the autumn their
hopes were temporarily raised when the Air Council announced it had
finally been persuaded that the Guardian Angel was reliable enough for

*Udet was blamed by the Luftwaffe's chief, his old WWI pilot colleague Hermann
Goering, for Germany's failure to win the Battle of Britain with adequate aeroplanes. In
November 1941, he shot himself at his Berlin villa. In a note written in red pencil he left
an anguished last message for Goering: 'Iron One, you are responsible for my death.' He
had called his girlfriend and pulled the trigger while on the phone to her.

general introduction. Hundreds of aircraft in France were to be fitted.

It never happened. When, to his delight, in September 1918, Calthrop was given an initial order to supply 500 Guardian Angels to front-line squadrons in France, it was too late. The parachutes had not been attached to a single aeroplane before the war ended. They were only ever used, in a small quantity with black canopies, for dropping agents behind the enemy lines at night. Nor did the French or US air services ever introduce parachutes for pilots.

With the immediate urgency ended, the Air Ministry's parachute investigators resumed their default position: the search for the infallible device. And when this finally came into service in 1925 it was an American chute, worn by the pilot and self-operated with a ripcord. Calthrop remained bitter to the end that thousands of young British lives had been needlessly wasted in the last two years of the war. 'No one in high quarters,' he wrote cynically, 'had any time to devote to investigating the merits of an appliance whose purpose was so ridiculously irrelevant to war as the saving of life in the air.'[14]*

Disillusionment with the callous attitudes war produced extended far beyond the bungling of the parachute issue. By the autumn of 1918, as the conflict headed for its fifth winter, a much wider disenchantment pervaded the offensive spirit of many front-line pilots. As the chairs continued to empty with depressing regularity, some of them were daring to ask what it was all about. Sending his wife news of the deaths of a fresh cluster of colleagues, Arthur Gould Lee wrote: 'Today's list of killed makes one wonder why such good chaps are the ones to die. Bonar Law [the son of the British chancellor of the exchequer and future prime minister Andrew Bonar Law] who'd probably have been a big public man like his father, or Armie and Warbabe, who'd scarcely started life. You ask yourself, what are fellows like these, and hundreds of thousands more, giving their lives for? I hope it's not just to make England safe for bolt-holers, profiteers, strikers, fake conchies, ponces and all the rest of the indispensables.'[15]

*Everard Calthrop was said to have been financially and physically drained by his years unsuccessfully promoting his parachute. After the war he went back to railway construction work, but failing health forced him to give this up. He retired to his estate in Essex to re-establish his stable of Arabian horses. He had had most of his original string humanely destroyed rather than see them commandeered to haul guns through the shellfire of the Western Front, where hundreds of thousands of horses were killed. He was seventy when he died in 1927, the unsung inventor of a device that could have brought thousands of pilots back from the war alive.

The fervour that had driven so many of them, the belief that their lives were being sacrificed in a great and noble cause, was increasingly being eroded by the apparent pointlessness of the whole war and concern at what the grinding air combat was doing to them. Lee's once-cheerful letters had begun to reflect his battered state of mind.

> The truth is that the spirit doesn't move me at the moment to write long descriptive tomes. That spell of low strafing has knocked some of the stuffing out of me. I don't get the same thrill out of flying as I used to do. Things have changed so much. So many chaps have gone, and half the people in the mess are strangers. I've been longer in the squadron than anybody and now I realise I've had enough. I feel a sort of waning of the spirit, and I shan't grumble if I'm now for home.[16]

The relentless death toll was even affecting the chaplains. 'Our padre with the MC has left us. He couldn't bear the business of seeing us off at the hangars knowing that some of us wouldn't come back, and has returned to a regiment in the lines. Good for him.'

Lee's long-incubating combat fatigue had taken a sharp turn for the worse by the time 46 Squadron's Camels embarked on one of the most dangerous of all its battle roles: the low-level strafing of German soldiers in their trenches.

> To make sure of your target you have to expose yourself to the concentrated fire of dozens of machine guns and hundreds of rifles. Compared with this, Archie is practically a joke ... I've got to admit it gives me the shakes. With so many guns firing you feel every time you dive that it's bound to be your last.
>
> Even Thomson is feeling it, and nobody in the squadron has more guts than him. He lives in the next cubicle to me, and last night, about midnight, I was awakened by awful screeching noises. It was Tommy. I took a torch and went in to him. He was struggling and sweating and shouting in the throes of a nightmare. The chaps in the other two cubicles heard and came in, and we awakened him. He was very shamefaced. He'd just been shot down in flames, he said.[17]

The same thing was soon happening to Lee. 'I had proof last night that this darned trench-strafing had begun to get on my nerves. I performed a show like Thomson's – maybe it's catching. Apparently I was yelling in a nightmare and <u>he</u> had to come into my cubicle and waken <u>me</u>. I was shaking and sweating with it. I was diving, diving into a black bottomless pit with hundreds of machine guns blasting up endlessly at me. I didn't like it a bit.'[18]

Fortunately Lee's squadron commander noticed his battle fatigue, grounded him and recommended a posting back to England. The medical officer reported that he was 'run down physically and won't be able to do any more useful flying until I've had a good spell of leave'. He was gone within days. 'They gave me a whale of a farewell last evening,' he wrote. 'Gallons of booze. Too many speeches. All the old songs ... These are tunes I shall never forget, they're part of 46, part of me ... And so it's all over, and I'm for home.'[19]

Elliott Springs, who had rushed across the Atlantic to join the British Flying Corps with no higher purpose than the adventure it promised, had long ago lost his fervour. 'War is a horrible thing, a grotesque comedy,' he declared. Springs had moved from the RAF to the US Air Service to command its 148th Aero Squadron flying Camels and now had sixteen victories to his credit. 'This war won't prove anything. And it is so useless. The worst thing about it is that it takes the best. If it lasts long enough the world will be populated by cowards and weaklings and their children.' The young pilot from South Carolina compared the present conflict with the Civil War. 'Look what it did for the South. It wasn't the defeat that wrecked us. It was the loss of half our manhood and the demoralisation of the other half.'

The devastated France over which he flew was 'too horrible to describe. It looks from the air as if the gods had made a gigantic steamroller, forty miles wide, and run it from the coast to Switzerland, leaving its spike holes behind as it went.' He listed the dozens of his colleagues who had died over this infernal scar and continued:

It's only a question of time until we all get it.

I'm all shot to pieces. I only hope I can stick it. I don't want to quit. My nerves are all gone and I can't stop. I've lived beyond my time already.

It's not the fear of death that's done it. I'm still not afraid to die. It's this eternal flinching from it that's doing it and has made a coward out of me. Few men live to know what real fear is. It's something that grows on you, day by day, that eats into your constitution and undermines your sanity ... Here I am, twenty-four years old [he was actually twenty-two], I look forty and I feel ninety. I've lost all interest in life beyond the next patrol ... I've even lost my taste for licker.

Springs, who took to flying with a bottle of milk of magnesia in one pocket and a flask of gin in the other, described the stress of waiting for an afternoon patrol. 'I keep watching the clock and figuring how long I have to live. Then I go out to test my engine and guns and walk around and have a drink and try to write a little and try not to think. And I move my arms and legs around and think that perhaps tomorrow I won't be able to.' He said he'd lost over a hundred friends 'but to me they aren't dead yet. They are just around the corner, I think, and I'm still expecting to run into them any time. I dream about them at night.'

His great fear was that he might 'turn yellow'. 'I've heard of men landing in Germany when they didn't have to. They'd be better off dead because they've got to live with themselves the rest of their lives. I wouldn't mind being shot down. I've got no taste for glory and I'm no more good – but I've got to keep on until I can quit honourably. All I'm fighting for now is my own self-respect.'[20]

'I frankly liked it less and less,' recalled the Australian pilot Bill Taylor at 66 Squadron. He wrote of his growing disgust at the job he had to do. One incident, in which he shot down a German reconnaissance machine, was so distressing the images haunted him for the rest of his life. 'A black object detached itself from the blazing Rumpler; a grotesque thing with loose and waving ends. The rear gunner had jumped from the death by fire to which my action had condemned him. He appeared to fall quite slowly, passing my machine as though he were almost floating in space; and then he was gone, invisible against the dark earth.' Taylor watched the Rumpler hit the ground with a great explosion.

For the first time, I was horror-stricken by the result of war in the air. I had seen aircraft go down in flames, break up in the air and flutter down in tattered shreds, go down out of control and hit the ground with a shattering crash. But somehow before it had all remained impersonal. Not an aeroplane with a man in it, but a dangerous creature of the air to be destroyed. For some reason this Rumpler was different – or perhaps I had been in France too long. But this now was no triumph. It was a horror from which I wanted to fly away.

Taylor contrasted the simple pleasure he got from flying his Sopwith Pup with the lethal use to which he was required to put it.

Why, with this God-given thing, did I have to kill the German crew of the Rumpler? They were probably people like myself. The horrible waving thing in the air had a home, parents, someone who loved him. Now he was dead, lying crumpled on the earth, killed by me. Returning from this encounter, I had for the moment no more taste for war. I began to think my way over the world, to my home in Australia; to Lion Island with my boat moored off the beach; the tent by the banksia trees, the red gums sprawling over the sun-bleached sandstone rocks, the call of the little penguins coming in from the sea at night.[21]

When Taylor landed back at Estrée Blanche he was taken out to the wrecked Rumpler. 'I was still sick with the whole thing but, somewhat inconsistently, I went with the others in the tender, mainly to avoid the embarrassment of explanations. A few tin-hatted soldiers were standing around. One of them came over to me and said, "Want to see the bloke? He's under that sack." The thing under the sack had been the German pilot. I turned away.'*

Another Australian pilot, Charles Kingsford Smith, had already endured shellfire on the Gallipoli beaches and been blown up as a dispatch rider on the Western Front when he transferred to the Flying Corps and found himself strafing German infantry. He described the shock of his first experience unleashing this slaughter – the initial bloodlust and satisfaction and, afterwards, the disgust. Spotting a long column of hundreds of German troops resting on a roadside, 'in one mass of humanity' on their march up to the front line, he decided that 'my business was to kill'.

My mind was completely occupied with one desire. Over my sights I could see men moving down the road, but there were too many of them to move quickly. I pressed the trigger. Tracer bullets zipped along the road and I saw men falling, and hundreds of them scrambling to get out of the way.

I was filled with an unearthly joy. I kept my finger pressed hard on the trigger. Then I turned and roared back with my machine gun spitting death. I saw dozens of men bowled over and I remember screaming at the top of my voice . . . I roared up to the other end of

---

*Bill Taylor was knighted in 1954 under the full name he disliked – Patrick Gordon Taylor – for a succession of the epic pioneer oceanic flights he continued to make throughout his life. In 1934 he was co-pilot and navigator of the first eastbound trans-Pacific flight from Australia to America. In 1939 he captained the first across the Indian Ocean from Australia to Africa, and in 1951 the first across the South Pacific from Australia to Chile.

the road, turned quickly and back again, until my gun was empty, then streaked for home. All the way back I had nothing but these thoughts of quite unholy joy. I had killed – undoubtedly killed – lots of men.'

But when he climbed out of the cockpit back at his 23 Squadron base Kingsford Smith was overcome by revulsion. 'After the noise of the engine and the gun everything, all of a sudden, was quiet. I could hear birds whistling and men talking and laughing. Contact with these realities suddenly made me realise the horror of the thing I'd done. I leaned against the fuselage and vomited. I was twenty years old. I had just killed many men and I hadn't the faintest idea why. For those few minutes I had gone completely insane. Now I felt miserable and hated my weakness for doing what I did.'[22] In a letter to his parents back in Australia he wrote: 'We are doing frightful quantities of work now and couldn't keep it up indefinitely or our nerves would go to pieces.' He was saved from collapse when, in combat a few weeks later, he had part of his foot shot off, a wound that permanently ended his front-line flying.*

For a few of the pilots combat stress became so disabling they reached a point where, despite the disgrace it would bring, they even lost the ability to push themselves to go on patrol.

Harold Balfour described one particularly tragic case, diplomatically referring to the flight commander merely as 'Captain A'. In Balfour's judgement he was an above-average pilot but his patrols 'were not led with any keenness or desire to cross the lines if it could possibly be avoided', while 'on the ground his conversation was defeatist, unhealthy and not likely to induce any *esprit de corps* in the breasts of the younger pilots'. Ordered to lead a dangerous low-level bombing raid on an enemy aerodrome, Captain A told his squadron commander

that he did not feel he could take part. He was asked if he definitely declined to go. He replied in the affirmative.

---

*Despite the loss of three toes Charles Kingsford Smith went on to become one of the world's greatest pioneer trans-ocean fliers. In 1928 he captained the first aircraft to fly the Pacific from America to Australia and the first to fly across the Tasman Sea from Australia to New Zealand and back; in 1930 the first non-stop westbound flight across the Atlantic from Ireland to North America; in 1934 the first eastbound trans-Pacific flight from Australia to California. He made numerous record-breaking solo flights in both directions between England and Australia. Knighted in 1932, he was killed on a 1935 flight from England to Australia when his aircraft crashed into the sea off the coast of Burma.

The squadron commander told him to return to the office in one hour's time and meanwhile communicated the refusal to Head-quarters. At the end of an hour Captain A reported and was informed that he was to proceed to the Base the following morning. He asked if this meant that he would probably be court-martialled and was informed that this was likely to occur. He left the office and within an hour had gone into the officers' lavatory and shot himself with a bullet through the head.

I record this incident as it has always seemed to me inexplicable as to how Captain A had the courage and nerve deliberately to shoot himself, and yet could not bring himself to lead the raid where he had an excellent chance of surviving, with the probability that, if he did, he would be awarded a Military Cross for his gallantry, and if he did not his fate would be no different from that which he was deliberately choosing.[23]

Squadron commanders were expected to recognise in their pilots the classic indications of imminent collapse. 'Shaking hands unable to pick up cups of tea. Twitching eyelids. Men constantly glancing at the clock or unable to keep still. A double Dubonnet before a patrol. Lapses of memory and blurred vision. Meals returned untouched. Sudden flare-ups, showing the hint of hysteria beneath the calm.'[24]

The leave they longed for didn't always provide the emotional solace they sought. On one of his leaves back in London Arthur Gould Lee was upset to find a widespread lack of true comprehension of life on the front lines. 'They talk glibly about danger and bravery and so on, but these are just words, they don't mean a thing. They ask you how many Fritzes you've shot down, old bean, as though it's a cricket score. They just don't realise that a machine destroyed means a life ended, some unfortunate devil, British or German, smashed to pulp, or burned alive.' He was actually relieved to return to his squadron. 'As soon as I entered the mess and was greeted by the chaps, I had a sensation of coming home. The familiar cheerful faces, the smiling mess servants, my batman ... and later the NCOs and the men in the flight – they all made me feel I belonged here, and not to the selfish mob in London.'

Even the seemingly resilient Ira Jones, who'd watched the emotional collapse of Mick Mannock and was soon to record his thirty-seventh victory, was struggling. He wrote in his diary on 4 August 1918: 'This bloody war has now been on for four years. I wonder if it will ever finish? Personally, I don't care much now. Having lost so many of my pals, life somehow has lost its lustre. I feel almost a coward living; yet it's Kismet, I suppose.'[25]

When Jones wrote these depressing words on 4 August 1918 he had no means of knowing that, within days, the tide of war would be turning again. And in less than three months it would all be over.

Chapter 30

The Eleventh Hour of
the Eleventh Day

In the late summer of 1918 the Allied Army commanders began preparing a battle campaign that would take the war into 1919. What they hadn't expected quite so soon was a bid for peace from their enemies. After four years of growing hardship the morale of the German and Austro–Hungarian civilian populations and their millions of war-weary soldiers had, with dramatic suddenness, collapsed.

The great German spring offensive Operation Michael, launched in March with such initial devastating success, had run out of steam by the end of June. With the arrival in France, at long last, of the American expeditionary force of more than a million men, German hopes of victory on the Western Front had finally died. The Allies, now joined by more than forty US divisions including squadrons of their own air service flying British and French machines, had taken the offensive and launched counter-attacks on all fronts.

The British, together with French divisions, had delivered the first blow on 8 August in a surprise assault in heavy fog to the east of Amiens. The Canadian and Australian units that spearheaded the offensive, supported by tanks and an immense force of 800 bombing and low-flying, ground-strafing RAF aircraft, had sown panic and confusion among the defenders. In a spectacular advance of twelve miles, during which aeroplanes laid a smokescreen in a rolling carpet ahead of the tanks, the Allies had taken such a huge toll of General Ludendorff's troops that they were driven back to the Hindenburg Line. It was the first outright defeat the Germans had suffered in four years of fighting. When the sun set that day they had lost 27,000 men.

There were Allied losses, too. The RAF paid an appalling price for its supporting role in the first day's assault. It lost a hundred aeroplanes and eighty-six airmen, the highest number in a single day of the entire war. But for Germany the Battle of Amiens was a watershed. 'August 8th,' Ludendorff wrote, 'was the black day of the German Army in the history of the war. This was the worst experience I had to go through.' Three days later he offered his resignation to the Kaiser. It was not accepted.

But Wilhelm II had seen the writing on the wall. He now uttered the momentous words: 'We have nearly reached the limit of our powers of resistance. The war must be ended.'

It wasn't to end for another three months. In what became known as the Hundred Days Offensive, the Allies forced the German armies back across the Hindenburg Line, but they remained a brave and dangerous enemy. By early September they had inflicted a further 300,000 losses on the British and French.

It was not only the German armies on the Western Front that were crumbling. Since 1917 the German nation and its staunch allies, Austria–Hungary and Bulgaria, had been steadily descending into internal chaos and the Turkish Ottoman Empire, heavily occupied in Iraq and Palestine by British troops, was suing for peace. The Allied naval blockade had inflicted desperate shortages of resources and food on the German population. Hungry people were rioting on the streets of cities across the country. The same was happening in Austria–Hungary whose army, on its southern front, was being decimated by Italian, British and French forces. Austro–Hungarian soldiers were deserting en masse. On the Western Front wounds were being dressed with paper bandages.

In Germany, where the greatest fear was invasion and occupation of the Fatherland itself, the Prussian military regime that had driven the war was overthrown and the country teetered on the edge of revolution. 'Slowly the revolt against autocratic militarism was rising. The martial bands still played and flags waved as usual, but there was a hollow something in the cheering. The cry was no longer from the heart.'[1]

In the first week of October, as the Allied divisions poured across the Hindenburg Line, seizing hundreds of thousands of prisoners and guns, a new social democratic German government proclaimed the country a republic and sent armistice proposals. Arranging the terms of a suspension of hostilities, however, proved a slow process. For more than four weeks the peace settlement notes passed back and forth while fighting raged on and at least half a million more Allied and German men were killed or wounded. During these weeks, as the world held its breath, the RAF's missions continued, met in the air with undiminished ferocity by the surviving squadrons of the shrinking German air circuses.

The once much-feared and still active Richthofen wing, Jagdgeschwader 1, was now commanded by a twenty-five-year-old pilot, Hermann Goering, credited with twenty-two victories – not all of them, according to aviation historians, adequately substantiated. In 1918 the future chief of the RAF's Fighter Command, Sholto Douglas, found himself in combat with the future Reichsmarschall of Nazi Germany.

'I encountered Goering quite a few times in the air, chasing him around the sky when he was not chasing me,' Douglas wrote. 'But neither of us was ever able to get his gun-sights on the other. Whatever his subsequent crimes, Goering as a young man was undoubtedly a brave and good fighter pilot. I have wondered many times about the extent to which the course of history might have been changed if, in one of our encounters, I had managed to draw a bead on him long enough to finish him off. It would have saved the world, and me, a lot of trouble many years later.'[2]

In the autumn of 1918, as his country headed for defeat, Goering had a far more pressing concern than fighting: the urgent need to prevent the capture of his elite wing of pilots and aeroplanes. The Jagdgeschwader had been re-equipped with one of the finest fighters to emerge from the war, the Fokker DVII. Fitted with a big BMW engine, it could travel at nearly 120 miles an hour, was exceptionally easy and safe to fly and accounted for most of the Richthofen wing's victories in the final months of combat. But if the German Air Service had once again, in a final flourish, introduced a technically superior machine, the squadrons of the new Fokkers were by this point hopelessly outnumbered by the swarms of Allied aeroplanes they faced. They were also now facing, perhaps rather too late in the day, a new breed of British fighter pilot.

Gone at long last were the days when schoolboys arrived in the front-line squadrons with no more than twenty-something hours in their logbooks and not the least understanding of the forces that kept their aeroplane in the sky. One of the Flying Corps' great eccentrics, Robert Smith-Barry – an Irishman of aristocratic descent who had been dismissed from Eton for academic laziness but had gone on to command 60 Squadron – had become so outraged by the lack of basic flying skills with which new pilots arrived in France that he had badgered Trenchard with a radical plan for a more scientific approach to the crude and casual training process. Trenchard had eventually listened.

At Gosport in Hampshire Smith-Barry had been given his own training squadron and a uniquely free hand to develop his techniques. The results, which saw him hailed as 'the patron saint of flying instruction', were startling. Introducing full dual controls and communication between instructor and pupil through voice tubes fitted to their helmets, he revolutionised pilot training the world over. The fundamental principles of his methods are still in use to this day. Throwing the hit-or-miss approach out of the window, he taught his pupils every manoeuvre they might ever need to call upon: how to stall, recover from spins, make steep turns, take off and land in crosswinds. He taught instructors how to fly properly and introduced the 'patter', the vital running commentary that accompanied their demonstrations. The accident rate in France began to drop.

Improved training could not, however, do a great deal to minimise the danger inherent in many missions. Among the most vulnerable flight crew, right to the end, were those of Trenchard's strategic bombing force on their long day and night flights from their base near Nancy to raid German cities. These fleets of biplanes with open cockpits, single-engined de Havilland and four-crew Handley Page twin-engined machines with 30-metre wingspans, were the primitive forerunners of the aeroplanes of Bomber Command that would follow little more than twenty years later. Unlike the devastating operations of their successors, which helped bring Nazi Germany to her knees, the damage inflicted on target cities by Trenchard's tiny force was negligible and had no effect at all on German war industries. It merely sustained terrible losses in men and machines. One in twelve of them never returned.

The raids on the Rhine cities were epics of endurance for the crews lumbering through the night against headwinds that could reduce their homeward progress to 30 miles an hour on their eight- or nine-hour missions. Using primitive navigational instruments, debilitated by cold that produced icicles on their faces, they flew through dense curtains of cloud that blotted out the stars above and the earth four miles below. Seventy-four bombers were lost in the last three months of their operations. 'Nearly half were claimed by the vagaries of wind, fog and storm. Some, circling low with empty fuel tanks and exhausted or badly wounded pilots at the controls, were wrecked within earshot of home airfields shrouded in the mists that so often rose without warning in the hills and bogs of that half-tamed wilderness.'[3]

Perversely, it seemed that the longer the peacemakers' negotiations dragged on, the more savage the air war, in its dying weeks, became. One of its worst days, 30 October 1918, saw another horrendous catalogue of casualties. On this one day the British claimed to have shot down sixty-seven German aircraft at the cost of forty-one of their own. Through the early days of November, as the German armies were routed, they were mercilessly harassed from the sky. There was, one historian wrote, little 'magnanimity in victory'. Certainly 46 Squadron's Camel pilots showed little as they pursued the fleeing columns.

'On a squadron sweep,' one of its American pilots, Lieutenant Richmond Viall, recalled, 'we found a long straight road filled with retreating German supply trains. We saw horse-drawn artillery, motor trucks, infantry and other military equipment. We formed a big circle and as we went down this road we fired our machine guns and dropped our 25lb bombs. When we got through with that road it was one unbelievable scene of chaos, with dead horses, lorries and dead soldiers all over the road. As I went down the last time to use up what was left of my ammunition and bombs, the two planes in front of me collided.'[4]

Even the glorious flying circus that still bore Richthofen's name was being overwhelmed. 'Hour after hour,' wrote Karl Bodenschatz, the group's adjutant, 'the enemy now hurls at the Front the endless abundance of men and machines streaming in from around the world. On the ground and in the air, the sheer weight of this unparalleled numerical superiority gradually crushes any possibility of fighting it in a meaningful way. A swarm of squadrons of every kind: bombers, infantry support planes, fighters. It is becoming more and more difficult to carve a piece from this vast wall of aeroplanes.'[5]

By the last week of October the disintegrating German nation was imploding into anarchy. A naval mutiny, in which crews of the High Seas Fleet at Wilhelmshaven refused to take their ships to sea, spread to revolution and looting in the cities. As soldiers deserted their spirit-broken army units in droves, workers and soldiers' councils, hoisting red flags, seized power in the style of the Russian Soviets. Early in November, the supreme warlord, Kaiser Wilhelm II, forced to abdicate, fled into exile in Holland.

On the morning of 9 November a group of German armistice negotiators crossed the battle lines and arrived in the Forest of Compiègne, fifty miles north-east of Paris. They were escorted into the private railway coach of the Supreme Allied Commander, General Foch, who presented them with the terms the Allies were demanding. They were ruthless. Germany to evacuate immediately Belgium, France, Luxembourg and Alsace-Lorraine and the Allies to occupy the west bank of the Rhine and a neutral zone on the east bank. The German Army to surrender most of its weapons and vehicles, its entire force of aeroplanes and a huge assortment of its railway locomotives and wagons. All German troops in the East to withdraw behind the 1914 frontiers, all captured merchant ships to be returned and all German submarines and hundreds of battleships to be handed over. And, finally, there was a demand for financial reparations for damage inflicted on Belgium and France. Five months later, the Treaty of Versailles would impose even harsher terms.

At 5.10 on the morning of 11 November the chief German delegate, although protesting that these immediate conditions alone would create famine and civil disorder in his country, accepted them and reluctantly signed. Foch sent a message to all Allied commanders: 'Hostilities will cease on the entire front November 11th at 11am French time.' Yet right to the last seconds there was no let-up. Intense fighting in one final, murderous cataclysm went on, pointlessly, until the stroke of eleven. The last British soldier to be killed was shot dead at 10.58am. On that historic morning there were 11,000 more Allied casualties.

On the front lines British officers 'had their watches in their hands and the troops waited with the same grave composure with which they had fought', wrote the novelist John Buchan. 'At two minutes to eleven, opposite the South African brigade, a German machine-gunner, after firing off a belt without pause, was seen to stand up beside his weapon, take off his helmet, bow, and then walk slowly to the rear.' Buchan described how, as the watch hands reached eleven, 'there came a second of expectant silence, and then a curious rippling sound which observers far behind the front likened to the noise of a light wind. It was the sound of men cheering from the Vosges to the sea.'[6] On the eleventh hour of the eleventh day of the eleventh month, the guns on the Western Front had fallen silent at last.

The news didn't immediately reach all the RAF's bases in France. That morning at Reckem, several aircraft of 48 Squadron were within minutes of setting off on a patrol.

> The engines were ticking over and the observers were in their cockpits. Already two or three Rolls engines had roared as they were run up, when the tall figure of our CO was seen hurrying from the squadron office. His long arms were swinging and the ends of his scarf flapping as he came striding across to the hangars. 'Morning, major' several voices greeted him as he approached. 'Morning, lads!' he called out and waved both arms. 'Wash-out, everybody. The war's over. Hostilities cease at eleven ack emma today!' The engines were speedily switched off. For a moment there was silence, then someone raised a cheer and we all joined in. After that we talked in excited groups for a while and then, feeling rather lost, wandered back to our huts.[7]

At Senlis a flight of 94 Squadron SE5s, ordered to escort some bombers to the front line, taxied out at around 9am and were lining up for take-off when an aircraft suddenly arrived over the aerodrome. 'It was flying very low and firing off red lights,' remembered one of the pilots, Arthur

Capel. 'So I thought I'd better wait and see what this was all about. He landed and came up to me and said, "You are not to go off. The war is finishing at eleven o'clock today."' The squadron had arrived in France only ten days earlier and its pilots were bursting to get into action. 'Believe it or not,' Capel said, 'we were in a state of fury that we hadn't done one operation.'[8]

The pilots of 74 Squadron had gone out that morning, hoping for some final kills. But there was not an enemy aircraft to be found. 'We later learned,' Ira Jones recalled, 'that the German Air Force ... was too busy destroying its machines or flying homewards to risk conclusions with us ... For the last time, 74 Squadron turned back towards its own lines. As each aircraft reached the aerodrome its pilot stunted wildly, diving, looping, zooming, rolling, spinning at minimum safety height before landing from his last patrol. And so ended duty well done.'[9]

At Bircham Newton in Norfolk three huge new Handley Page strategic bombers were on the verge of taking off to attack Berlin for the first time. The four-engined, 38-metre-wingspan biplane giants, called V/1500s, which operated with a crew of six in open cockpits, were Britain's response to the German Staakens. They could stay in the air for fourteen hours and carry a ton of bombs into the German heartland. Around forty were built. The first three had been delivered to 166 Squadron and scheduled for an inaugural Berlin raid on the night of 8 November, but engine problems on one machine had forced the cancellation of the mission. The raid had been re-scheduled for the following day, but again abandoned because of technical problems. At last the three super-bombers were ready to go and were about to taxi out when an excited mechanic ran out to stop them.

In London church bells pealed and people swarmed into the streets. Harold Balfour, who had earlier been repatriated from France with shattered nerves and now, as a twenty-one-year-old major commanded a training squadron back in England, joined the celebrations with three other pilots. At Piccadilly Circus they climbed to the top of Eros from which platform Balfour, 'forgetting entirely that I was wearing the uniform and the gold-peaked cap of a major in the Royal Air Force', had begun to 'harangue the crowd'. Persuading them to sing 'It's a long way to Tipperary', he soon had them 'shouting out the chorus and weeping with emotion'. The four pilots were arrested by the military police and threatened with court-martials 'for conduct unbecoming that of officers and gentlemen'. They were thrown into police cells and kept in custody for three weeks before being released in the absence, Balfour wrote, 'of any evidence that our conduct had really been in any way so unbecoming'.[10]

Meanwhile the world was counting the colossal human cost of the war. 'All the horrors of the ages were brought together,' Winston Churchill wrote.

> No truce or parley mitigated the strife of the armies. The wounded died between the lines; the dead mouldered into the soil. Merchant ships and neutral ships and hospital ships were sunk on the seas and all on board left to their fate, or killed as they swam. Every effort was made to starve whole nations into submission without regard to age or sex. Cities and monuments were smashed by artillery. Bombs from the air were cast down indiscriminately. Poison gas in many forms stifled or seared the soldiers. Liquid fire was projected upon their bodies. Men fell from the air in flames, or were smothered often slowly in the dark recesses of the sea . . . After years of struggle not armies but nations broke and ran. When all was over, torture and cannibalism were the only two expedients that the civilised, scientific Christian states had been able to deny themselves: and they were of doubtful utility.[11]

The number of deaths in World War I has never been precisely established. But among historians of the conflict there is a measure of agreement that of the more than 60 million men mobilised in all the warring nations the military death toll reached around 8 million, with over 20 million more wounded. Adding the nearly 7 million civilians killed as well, the grand total of dead and wounded approached 40 million. Britain and the Empire lost nearly a million military dead and three times that number wounded.

Right to the end the dreaded green envelopes kept arriving. And other mail brought equally tragic news. Only a few days before the armistice the wife of a 98 Squadron pilot, Lieutenant Edward Lee, had excitedly opened a letter from him only to be numbed by its message.

> My very dear wife, You will only read this if I am killed or reported missing. If not the former you must hope on and be certain that I shall escape if it is at all possible. If I am killed, I know how you love me and it is not possible to put on paper what you are to me . . .
>
> It will be poor consolation, but perhaps some consolation, to know that I still think there is no death I would prefer to dying for

my country and I know my darlings will be brought up in that belief.
You have to bear the burden, but I am perfectly convinced that our
souls do not die. So try hard and be cheerful and brave so that when
you meet me again in the spirit world, which we all feel must exist,
there may be no regrets.

Remember I leave you something better than money – two precious children whom, together with you, I love more than anything
that this world has to offer . . . Give my darlings kisses from me and
always remember that you have made my life as happy as it has
been and it is now your hard duty to live for our darling children.
Your loving husband, Teddie.[12]

Lee, and several other pilots in his flight, had been killed on 30 October –
the day after he wrote the letter. They had been shot down while returning
from a bombing raid.

Trenchard, still commanding the Independent Bombing Force when
the armistice came, had seen the army's tiny military wing of four squadrons of rudimentary unarmed flying machines that had arrived in France
in 1914 blossom into a huge and sophisticated air force of over 200 squadrons (nearly a hundred of them in France), around 300,000 men, more
than 22,000 aeroplanes and over 14,000 aircrew. He had presided over the
development of primitive 40mph aeroplanes into technically advanced
fighters with 200-horsepower engines that could dive in battle at 200 miles
an hour. The total of 16,600 pilots and observers who had been killed,
wounded, or taken prisoner in the four years and three months of the
war appeared insignificant against the mountain of casualties borne by
the British Army on the ground. But the army's unwanted appendage,
whose airmen had fought an equally grim and terrifying war, had become
one of its most indispensable arms. It had changed the face of warfare for
ever. No future major conflict would be fought without aeroplanes. On
the Western Front, where cavalry reconnaissance had been neutered by
the great trench barrier, the flying squadrons had become 'the cavalry of
the clouds'. Although the first great air war was for ever after to be
represented by the dazzling aerial dogfights of the pilot aces, the true
stars were the reconnaissance crews, the unsung heroes who much less
spectacularly spent their doomed lives dodging ground fire and destructive enemy fighters at vulnerably low levels over the front lines.

But had the arrival of air power and the sustained heroism and suffering
of its pilots and observers affected the course of the war at all? In any
significant way, probably not, most military historians believe. They cite

the possible exception of the crucial early warning reconnaissance aeroplanes gave the ground commanders. In 1914 it alerted the Allies to the swift movements of the German armies as they swept through Belgium to threaten the Channel ports and Paris, thwarting an early defeat that might have ended the war in its first three months. The same year aircraft assisted the cavalry in leading German commanders to spot so accurately the enormous Russian armies marching into Prussia. Their observations helped the German generals encircle and resoundingly defeat the Russians at the great August 1914 Battle of Tannenburg, a success that prolonged the war on the Eastern Front for around three years.

What the aeroplane had become, for both sides, was an indispensable battlefield adjunct to the land armies. The primary weapon of the war had remained the target-pulverising artillery for whom the flying machine had become its far-reaching eyes. But the war had ultimately been won by the sheer superior power of the Allied land armies along with the Royal Navy's blockade that helped to bring the German nation to its knees.

Replaced earlier as the RAF's field commander in France by Major-General John Salmond, Trenchard was intensely relieved in November 1918 to hand to a successor command of the bombing force in which he'd never really believed and of which he was to say, witheringly, 'a more gigantic waste of effort and personnel there has never been in any war'. For the moment the job of the man who, ironically, was later to become a strident advocate of the crucial role of heavy strategic bombing was done. Despite the wide criticism he had drawn for the casualties of his implacable insistence on offensive operations, often in the face of overwhelming odds, he was also seen as someone without whom the RAF might never have been created as a military force in its own right. Although he hated the title, which many historians believe really belongs to Sir David Henderson, Trenchard would come to be described as 'the father of the Royal Air Force'. On 20 November he left France for the last time. As he drove, with Maurice Baring, out through the great iron gates of the château near Nancy that had served as his headquarters, an emotional surprise awaited him, just possibly arranged by his faithful assistant.

The frank astonishment on his face yielded to a rarer and softer look as the car moved down the main street. The narrow pavements were lined with cheering men. All had come of their own accord from miles around to demonstrate their affection for a man who had unwittingly earned it. He had never expected to carry away from Autigny-la-Tour more than the memory of their magnificent loyalty and achievement, and he could only wave back in acute embarrassment, muttering at intervals to Baring: 'I don't believe it. There must be some mistake.'[13]

Chapter 31

Silence of a Desolate Land

The days before the armistice had brought widely different experiences to the flying squadrons of victor and vanquished. Duncan Grinnell-Milne, who had become a flight commander at the elite 56 Squadron, by then based at La Targette, east of Cambrai, had continued to lead patrols in search of enemy aircraft. There were few to be found. 'I tried to force a fight upon a formation of Fokkers,' he wrote, 'but they would have none of it.' On 7 November he handed the dawn patrol over to another pilot and went off on his own to look for targets among the retreating German columns. He flew in his personal SE5, emblazoned with the highly provocative German insult 'Schweinhund' (pig-dog). He had painted the word on the noses of a succession of machines. Finding an enemy observation balloon, 'I dived steeply in *Schweinhund III* and her streamlined rigging screamed Wagnerian music. The result was the same: the enemy hauled down his balloon.'

Two days later Grinnell-Milne went out on another lone patrol. All he could track down on the ground in the war-ravaged landscape was a 'handful of men in faded grey uniforms'. They were struggling to push a heavily laden handcart out of the firing line – 'of the might of a great nation, of its arrogance and military pomp, the sole remnants'. As he approached them, 'I saw one unsling his rifle and throw it up to his shoulder. Standing firm, legs apart, and aiming well ahead of my machine, he looked like a statue of exasperated humanity firing its small thunder at the mute uncomprehending heavens. One of his shots cracked past, close to my head. I did not reply. It was no longer worth while."[1] But the aerial fighting wasn't completely over for 56 Squadron. That same day, it lost its last pilot.

Lieutenant James Crawford was shot down by Leutnant Rudolf Stark, the commander of Jasta 35b, in one of the final air combats of the war. Stark, an ace who claimed this as his sixteenth victory, movingly described in his memoirs how the suddenness of Germany's collapse had shocked his squadron. Swept up in the retreat, they'd had to find, with just hours' notice, new aerodromes, each one further east, every few days. It had begun in late October when they had paused briefly at Givry near Mons in southern Belgium. There long columns of German wagon trains, hauled by exhausted horses, rumbled incessantly past the airfield in thick autumn fog. 'The mud in the streets smothers all sounds; we can hear neither the creaking of the wheels nor the beat of the horse-hoofs,' Stark wrote. 'The mist spews up colourless forms and then swallows them again. They pass by us like an army of ghosts and disappear into the grey. The retreat continues.'

The constant relocation of aircraft, mobile hangars, vehicles, work-shops and accommodation tents was becoming more and more difficult as their lorries started to break down under the strain. With com-munications failing they began to lose contact with their group com-manders and news of the whereabouts of the military front line, which was shifting by the hour, grew 'scantier and vaguer'. Everywhere, said Stark, the German Army was fighting rearguard actions.

> Every evening we learn that more ground has been lost. Then we draw new lines on our map and mark the date. When we take off in the morning and fly over the ground where the front lines ought to be, we see English troops below us and know that our men have been forced to give up yet another piece of ground.
>
> We have grown very lonely; in fact we feel that we are super-fluous. There is nothing more to reconnoitre and no spotting to do for the artillery. Likewise we are unable to help our infantry because we never know their positions. We feel that the end is near, but we dare not speak of it.

Stark's spirits were raised by a letter from his girlfriend, 'written on dainty paper. For a long time I held it poised in my hand, When I opened the envelope, faded petals fell out – dried asters. It is autumn, and some-where at home a beautiful woman has plucked her asters. But there is also a linden bud between the sheets, and the written lines bore a message of hope and yearning for the spring ... But autumn is around us. This will be our last autumn; then comes a winter which will be our end and our grave.'[2]

The day before the armistice, 10 November, as the columns of infantry and artillery continued to pour rearwards through the fog past the aero-drome, the telephones stopped working. Orders ceased to come. Stark now knew 'we must act on our own initiative'. By now they had only two serviceable lorries. He sent his adjutant to group headquarters to discover where they should go. 'The news he brings is horrible – it is the end.

Rumour and truth – complete breakdown. Armistice, retreat to Germany. Mutiny at the base, the fleet under the red flag, soldiers' councils, revolution at home ... We must at least try to save the machines.'

The ground staff loaded the remaining two lorries with everything they could. 'My big trunk finds a space there,' wrote Stark. 'In the course of time I have acquired a lot of property. I have a lot of valuable things in my trunk – all my many photos among them; their loss would be irreplaceable. Shall I ever see my things again? The lorry is ready. Schlüssler puts the gramophone and its records on top of everything. He cannot bear to leave them behind. The lorries rumble off. It is like a funeral procession.'

When Stark went to say goodbye to the pilots of another squadron on the field he was shocked at what he discovered. 'There is a look of sad desperation in their eyes when they tell us that they cannot fly because their men have cut all the bracing wires and controls on their machines. It sounds so impossible ... but it is the truth.' Stark asked his own mechanics why they hadn't done the same. 'That makes them really angry. How dare we think them capable of such a mean trick, they reply.'

The squadron had paraded for the last time.

> I pass along the ranks and gaze into the familiar faces. Suddenly my heart grows very heavy. I speak a few words of farewell – not many, for the pain of it quivers about my lips and chokes my words. Then I shake every man's hand. Huge tears are running down little Meyer's chubby cheeks ... I have to turn away, otherwise there will be tears running down my own cheeks.
>
> The sergeant-major makes a speech and thanks me in the name of the Staffel. But I can hardly hear his words; only with difficulty can I control my emotions. Then three cheers resound across the field.

After the lorries had departed the pilots climbed into their aircraft, loaded with their most precious possessions. 'Their aeroplanes look more like beasts of burden than war machines. One has a trunk tied on to its undercarriage, another has a handbag buckled on to a strut. The cockpits are loaded up with all sorts of luggage.'

As the twelve machines took off for the last time, heading southeast for Bavaria, the ground party set fire to all their tents and to the unserviceable aeroplanes they'd had to abandon. They hoped to refuel at Metz near the German border and then fly to an air base near Munich. But they got trapped between low cloud and a carpet of fog that obscured all sight of the ground and were unable to check their compass course and drift. Just when their fuel was nearly exhausted Stark spotted a hole in the fog. He led the formation down to land on a meadow that was so rough three of the machines were too damaged to go any further. They had drifted, they discovered, more than fifty miles off course to the north – but they were in Germany, close to the city of Trier. They flew the undamaged machines to an air base there. It was not the homeland to which they had expected to return. When they touched down they were puzzled to find the place strangely deserted. 'I go into one of the sheds, accost a group of mechanics that are lounging about idly and ask them to direct me to the officer on duty,' Stark recalled. '"There are no officers here," is the answer. "There's a soldiers' council in charge now."'

No one would give them any petrol and they were warned that if their officers' epaulettes were seen they would probably be attacked by revolutionary mobs in the streets. 'Was that,' Stark asked, 'our thanks for having kept the enemy out of the country for so many years?' Concealing their ranks under their overcoats, they spent the night in a hotel. Next morning they calculated that there was just enough petrol left in all their tanks to take two machines to Bavaria. They redistributed the fuel and damaged the other seven to make them unflyable. 'For a long while we stand beside our machines; it is so inexpressibly hard to part from them.'

Only one of the two remaining aircraft ever made it back to Munich. Stark and the other pilots went home by train. They were bewildered by what had happened to their country. At Munich station

heavily armed sailors and other fellows in uniform stood at the barrier. They wanted to search us for concealed weapons and called on us to remove our fur coats. We did not vouchsafe them a word, but our threatening looks sufficed to make them open up a passage for us at once ... How we despised and loathed those fellows!

We parted outside the station. A last handshake; then each went his own way. We strode through an alien, empty town ... Home has become a strange land to us ... We live in a strange country that we cannot know. Our home – our home is dead. And this home of ours was the Staffel.[3]

Meanwhile Duncan Grinnell-Milne had returned to France from leave in England, where he'd heard the news of the armistice. He had doubted it would hold. 'It seemed incredible that Germany should have collapsed so suddenly and completely. We thought it more than likely that, back on his own soil, rested, reorganised, strengthened, the enemy would make a stand, defy us to come farther. The Armistice would be denounced, there would be a flare-up of fighting from the embers of war.' But there wasn't. He assumed command of 56 Squadron – 'the Squadron', as he proudly called it – which had moved east of Cambrai to Béthencourt. But 56 was no longer a squadron at war. He had been promoted merely to preside over its last days in France.

> The place was silent now, too silent ... the land was desolate, deserted, for the armies had moved on, the French civilians not yet returned. Sometimes at the end of a misty autumn afternoon the silence would become appalling – like the grave, like being buried alive. Amid the wreckage of a war that was over, with the litter of equipment, the shell holes, the scattered crosses all about one, there seemed to be more than just silence in the air. It was as though from each day of the Four Years some ghostly event were rising to call to us, to remind us of the dead past; as though the dead themselves were calling us back ... We made a great deal of noise in the mess to drown such mournful sounds, and spent as much time as possible in the air.[4]

Grinnell-Milne's *Schweinhund III* had survived the war, 'although the wind hummed through her wires more gently now. Without Archie's startling cough or the sharp crackle of machine-gun bullets there was no need for them to sing too loud a song. But I made them scream again when the troops moved forward; dived at abandoned German aerodromes, hedge-hopped over liberated Belgium, overtook joyfully waving infantry advancing with the Army of the Rhine.'

For two and a half years of the fighting Grinnell-Milne, forced down in 1915 with engine failure behind the enemy lines, had been a prisoner in Germany. The long absence from the air war had probably saved his life. But in the summer of 1918 he had escaped, crossed into neutral Holland and eventually in the last months of the conflict, returned to France to fly with 56 Squadron. Now at liberty to roam the German skies as he pleased, he decided one day to tour from the air the places of his incarceration. He flew to the Rhine, roaring at low level along the river to Cologne, zooming over the cathedral and the railway station 'where, a prisoner, I had spent many cold and depressing hours'. He followed the railway to Aachen, circling the town in which he'd been held and from where he had finally escaped. Then he flew on to the Dutch border he had crossed to freedom, banking over the wood in which he had hidden that night.

'A triumphant return! But somehow, even as I looked down at that little corner of the earth which I had been at such pains to reach, an inexplicable fit of melancholy seized me. The Dutch frontier, the war, even flying seemed to have lost their meaning. Things which for years had mattered more than life itself were no longer of great importance – to me, or to anyone else.' On impulse he decided to satisfy some immediate demands of the flesh. 'Banking the *Schweinhund* steeply I turned away and, without looking back, laid a straight course for Brussels, wine and women . . .'[5]

Back at Béthencourt, as demobilisation got under way through the winter of 1918, 56 Squadron rapidly shrivelled.

> With gathering speed it began to dwindle like a community stricken by the plague. Each morning in the office I would find a fresh list of those to whom release had come. The orchestra played 'The Dark Town Strutters' Ball' for the last time and were dispersed. Skilled mechanics vanished one by one, men who had been in the squadron from the start, ever since the day when, proud of its new SEs, it had come to France to put fear into a strong and determined enemy. Pilots flew for the last time and packed up their kits; the mess grew smaller. Young Canadians, South Africans, Americans whom we had just had time to understand and to like disappeared from our lives forever. The silence became so much the heavier that at length we were too few to lift it.

> In February 1919 'the final blow fell. Our beloved SEs which we had come to regard as our personal property to endow with all the affection men give to ships, were taken away from us – flown down to a depot to be, in the official phrase, "reduced to produce", destroyed.' Soon, of the original twenty-three, only three officers remained on the base with a handful of clerks and drivers. Grinnell-Milne, the adjutant and an American pilot, Johnny Speaks, went on sentimental tours of the surrounding country on the squadron's motorbikes – the bikes on which dispatch riders had once roared in with the often dreaded daily orders for the next morning's patrols. They visited the graves of colleagues who had been killed and, in Cambrai, Grinnell-Milne found 'the gateway where I had caught a company of sheltering Germans; bullet holes and scratches from my machine-gun fire showed up plainly – marks that would not soon be erased'.

The adjutant was the next to leave and then one morning in the middle of March 1919, when snow lay thick upon the old battlefields, Grinnell-

Milne said goodbye to Speaks, who was taking the remains of the squadron back to the base depot before going home to the US.

'What are you going to do when you're demobilised?' he asked the American.

'Try to get a flying job somewhere, I suppose. It's about the only thing worth doing right now.'

Johnny looked slowly over the whitened hills towards the little village where his friend Larry B---- [Lieutenant Laurence Bowen] now slept beneath the cross of his own propeller.

'Funny, after a rotten war like this, how hard it is to leave.' He sighed. And then smiled quickly to hide his feelings. 'War's all wrong, I guess, but – ah well, them *was* the happy days, them was! Goodbye, G-M.'

The lorries, taking the last of the men and equipment, rumbled away towards Cambrai. 'I watched them go,' Grinnell-Milne said. 'I, the only one left of all the men in that once powerful squadron . . . Everything that had given zest to life seemed to have gone too.'

He stood there in the snow, the solitary remaining presence of a squadron that had known the voices of Albert Ball, Cecil Lewis, James McCudden and Arthur Rhys Davids, and so many other equally brave young men. 'The deep rumble of the lorries died away, and in the wintry silence which then fell, the only sound I could hear was the faint humming of telegraph wires – a feeble echo of past endeavour.'

Epilogue

The air war that had taken the lives of so many young pilots had disrupted those of thousands of others. They were, said Cecil Lewis, very young men who suddenly found they 'had no place, actual or prospective, in a peaceful world. We walked off the playing fields into the lines. We lived supremely in the moment. Our preoccupation was the next patrol, our horizon the next leave. Sometimes jokingly, as one discusses winning the Derby Sweep, we would plan our lives "after the War". But it had no substantial significance. It was a dream conjecturable as heaven, resembling no life we knew. We were trained with one object – to kill. We had one hope – to live. When it was over we had to start again.'[1] Many found it extraordinarily difficult to do so.

Cecil Lewis, who ended the war with eight victories, was unable to stick with anything for very long. His life became a kaleidoscope of restless activity. He taught Chinese pilots to fly in Beijing; he became, in 1922, a founding executive of the BBC, then a Hollywood screenwriter, a beachcomber in Tahiti, a Second World War RAF instructor, a farmer in South Africa, a television producer and a successful author. He bought a boat and, at the age of seventy-one, sailed it to Corfu, where he lived until his death in 1997, when he was almost ninety-nine. His memoirs, *Sagittarius Rising*, are still regarded as the finest, most lyrically expressed factual record of the life of the first air war's pilots on the Western Front. To the end he retained an extraordinary vigour. In his ninety-fourth year he flew a Tiger Moth, making a perfect landing in a 15-knot, 90-degree crosswind.

Ira 'Taffy' Jones, who finished the war credited with thirty-seven victories and five gallantry medals, was recommissioned at the outbreak of the Second World War. He became a group captain commanding a fighter operational training unit and, in his mid-forties, unofficially flew a Spitfire on several offensive sweeps over France. Returning to Wales and an inglorious job with the Ministry of Pensions, he became a local war celebrity, striking up a friendship with the Welsh poet Dylan Thomas, with whom he would indulge in long afternoon drinking sessions at a pub in Llangrannog on Cardigan Bay. His death at sixty-four in 1960 was a good deal less heroic than the one he'd been spared in the sky over the Western Front. Working on his roof at home, he was killed falling off a ladder.

Duncan Grinnell-Milne, who had turned the lights out at 56 Squadron, stayed on with the RAF, becoming assistant British air attaché in Paris before he retired, with more than 2,000 flying hours, in 1926. He became a successful author and in the Second World War rejoined the RAF to fly Wellingtons on bombing operations against the Italians in Libya. After being pronounced medically unfit he left the air force for a wartime job at the BBC. He died in 1973.

For the rich and flamboyant American pilot, Elliott Springs, whose hedonistic spirit had driven the boozing and womanising activities in London of the 'Three Musketeers', the war ended with sixteen victories, stomach ulcers and such acute post-traumatic stress that he scarcely cared whether he lived or died. Back in America he found it hard to settle to anything. Haunted by the terrors of air combat and the thrill of the kill, he told his fiancée: 'I have been a nervous wreck ever since the war. I still wake up at night with the sound of screaming wires and the smell of brimstone.'[2] When he reluctantly decided to enter the family cotton business, and married his fiancée, the daughter of a rich industrialist, he became so bored he turned to writing to escape the tedium. His reminiscences in *War Birds*, the hugely successful account of his experiences as a fighter pilot, brought him the enormous fortune of $500,000 (worth around US$6 billion today). It also brought down on his head the wrath of his father, who denounced the book for its startling revelations of debauchery and conducted a symbolic burning of copies in the middle of the main street of the family's home town, Lancaster, South Carolina.

Nearly a century later some of the First World War's pilots are still being honoured on the anniversaries of their deaths. At the small town of Annoeullin in northern France where Albert Ball is buried in the World War I German military cemetery, he remains an enduring local hero, remembered to an unusual degree for a foreigner. On Armistice Day every year the townspeople lay wreaths on his grave as a band plays the British national anthem. Even greater honour was paid him when a new high school was opened in Annoeullin in 1999. The 800 students, asked to vote on the school's name, placed his, the only non-French one, top of the list. He was seen as a symbol of courage and self-sacrifice. At the inauguration of Le Collège Albert Ball that year there were speeches by French ministers and pilots of 56 Squadron, now flying supersonic

Tornados. A contingent of Ball's descendants came from Nottingham, including a great-great niece and nephew who presented the school with acorns to grow commemorative Albert Ball oaks. And nearby, at the small stone memorial marking the spot where he crashed in the middle of the sugar-beet field, still owned to this day by the Ball family, a wreath was laid. A permanent exhibition of Ball's life and combat successes today stands in the college hall. Among the photographs is one of Flora Young, the woman he had scarcely known but had hoped to marry. In 1925 she had become the wife of an army officer, Charles Thornhill.

At Canterbury in England, where Mick Mannock spent some of his early years, he is actively remembered. On a wall in the town's great cathedral there is a memorial plaque. On 26 July, the anniversary of his death in 1918, a brief service is often still held there by the RAF Association, joined by uniformed cadets of the Air Training Corps. But the event doesn't make news any more in a town where few have ever heard of him.

The Red Baron lay in a succession of graves. Twice exhumed, his body finished up in 1925 at the Invalidenfriedhof, the traditional burial ground of Prussian military heroes in what became East Berlin. The Berlin Wall was later built so close to his grave that the tombstone became pockmarked by bullets fired at escapees trying to flee to the West. Today the Baron lies in the Richthofen family plot in Wiesbaden, where he joined his mother, Kunigunde, and his sister Ilse. In Schweidnitz, now in Poland and renamed Świdnica, where Lothar and his father Albrecht are buried, the old family mansion still stands. Between the wars, the Baroness, widowed in 1920, fell on such hard times she was forced to convert part of the great house into a museum filled with artefacts associated with her two famous sons. However, when the Soviet armies occupied Schweidnitz in the Second World War and Kunigunde fled west to Wiesbaden, the Russians took possession of the exhibits, which have never been returned. They included a portrait of Albert Ball, whom Lothar von Richthofen mistakenly continued to insist he had shot down. When the town was returned to Poland after World War II there was little local interest in the home of two former enemy pilots. But a Polish journalist decided to honour them by placing a stone memorial in the garden of the once-famous house, now converted into six apartments occupied by elderly people. Among military aviation enthusiasts the mystique that clings to the Red Baron refuses to die. Nearly a century later, visitors still make the pilgrimage to his crash site on the Somme. They come to photograph the memorial plaque that marks the exact spot in a field beside the derelict Sainte-Colette brickworks on the Corbie–Bray road.

Some of the First War pilots went on to military greatness. The dour and shy Major Hugh Dowding, who had cast such a gloom over Duncan Grinnell-Milne's first squadron in France and who later clashed with Trenchard over the need to rest his exhausted pilots, became an air chief marshal and head of RAF Fighter Command. In the late summer of 1940, in the desperate months when Britain stood alone against the daily onslaught of Luftwaffe bombers and the imminent threat of German invasion, his small force of Spitfires and Hurricanes saved the nation from certain defeat. The heroes of the air battle were the pilots of No. 11 Group responsible for the defence of London and the south-east of England. The group's commander was a twenty-victory World War I ace, Air Vice-Marshal Keith Park, the New Zealander who had voiced his strong views that all his 48 Squadron pilots should enjoy commissioned rank. He and Dowding came to be regarded as the joint saviours of Britain.

Dowding's successor at Fighter Command was Sholto Douglas who, in 1914, had arrived at No. 2 Squadron on horseback. Knighted and promoted to air marshal, he was later to be elevated to the peerage as Lord Douglas of Kirtleside and to the air force's highest rank of marshal of the RAF. At the end of the Second World War he had become head of British forces in Germany and military governor of the British zone, a role that brought him a 'distasteful task': one of a panel of four, he was obliged to sit in judgement on the appeal by Hitler's deputy, Hermann Goering, against his death sentence for war crimes. They had not been able 'to get conclusively to grips with each other in fair combat in the air' when they were young men, Douglas wrote. 'But it was a very different matter when, twenty-eight years later, and outraged as I was over what he had become, I found myself compelled by a circumstance over which I had no control to sign his death warrant.' In the event Goering had evaded the gallows by swallowing poison.

Arthur Harris, who had had to call upon the influence of his uncle Charlie to get into the Flying Corps, remained in the RAF to become, as a result of the enormous death and destruction he was ordered to wreak on German cities in World War II, one of its most controversial figures. But as commander-in-chief of Bomber Command he made a substantial contribution to the Allied victory. His crews, who looked down in awe at the carnage they were delivering from out of the darkness, paid an enormous price. The missions they flew night after night were as terrifying and stressful as the combats endured by the pilots of the First World War and their chances of survival as tragically small. Between 1939 and 1945 more than 55,000 of them were killed on operations or in training accidents.

The demands that 'Bomber' Harris made on his Lancaster and Halifax crews were likened to those imposed so relentlessly by Trenchard on his Flying Corps pilots. Both men have been described as unfeeling apostles of the bludgeon. Harris, nicknamed by his crews 'Butch', short for 'Butcher' Harris, for his willingness to spend their lives, was said by some to have been a disciple of Trenchard.

As for Trenchard himself, he was persuaded in 1919 by the air minister, Winston Churchill, to return to the job of the RAF's chief of air staff from which he had resigned in a huff the previous year. Through the 1920s, he presided over the reshaping of a greatly shrunken air force, scaled back dramatically in the belief that Britain wouldn't have to face another major war for at least a decade. The very need for a third independent force was questioned by the War Office and the Admiralty, who fought hard to dismember it and carve it up between them. The fact that it survived at all to fight another war owed much to Trenchard's tenacity in fending off the predators and persuading the government to preserve the RAF intact. Regarded with what today seems like extraordinary reverence, he continued during the 1939–45 war, though now long retired, to try to wield air-strategy influence from behind the scenes. He lobbied Churchill. He played a much-criticised covert part in hastening the sacking of Dowding from Fighter Command. He haunted Harris's bomber squadrons, inviting himself to their bases. In his old air marshal's uniform he would arrive with his trademark foghorn voice, bushy white moustache, confusingly garbled speech and notorious ability to get people's names mixed up. Yet he was received by the young aircrew as an aviation deity.

'One day Trenchard came, a charming, paternal old gentleman, who endeared himself to them at once. Listening to him lecturing them all in a great semi-circle outside a hangar was like hearing Moses himself, after so many years in which they had learned to think of him as the exalted prophet of bombing.'[3] Few of the young bomber boys enraptured by the informal discourses of this seventy-year-old legend, who talked of an air war in which pilots had fought in small open-cockpit machines with frostbitten hands and icicles on their faces, knew of his background except in the broadest terms. They would have been surprised to learn of the toll that the first air war had taken on this elderly figure.

Within days of his return to the Air Ministry in 1919 Trenchard had fallen ill, stricken by the Spanish influenza raging across the world and killing thousands a week. As a man who hated sickness and sick people he went on working, spurning suggestions of medical help, turning his sickroom into an office and continuing to dictate letters from his bed in his lonely West End flat. But when he collapsed with acute pneumonia he was at last concerned enough to call his wartime amanuensis, the recently demobilised Maurice Baring. The doctor Baring immediately summoned saw that Trenchard, gasping on his solitary lung, was so seriously ill there was a strong probability he wouldn't recover.

'Trenchard's method of acknowledging this was not uncharacteristic of a man suddenly brought face to face with utter loneliness. Through his batman, he sent a series of urgent messages to Katharine Boyle, the one woman for whom he secretly cared.'[4]

Katharine Boyle was the widow of an old army friend of Trenchard's, the Honourable Captain James Boyle, son of the Earl of Glasgow. When James was killed in action in France in 1914 Katherine had been left with three young children to support. Though she and Trenchard had met only once or twice he had formed a secret attachment to her. 'But never until now,' said his biographer, 'had he admitted even to himself the depth of his feeling for her.'

Unfortunately, when the call came Katharine, who had become a Red Cross nurse, was in France visiting her late husband's grave. When she arrived back late one night, exhausted from her journey, Trenchard's message begging her to come was waiting for her. Fearing that he might be dying, she immediately got in a taxi and, still in her nurse's uniform, hurried to his flat which, she was amazed to discover, had become a sort of satellite Air Ministry office.

The door was opened by a bald, politely solemn man in a white overall ... He was unwilling at first to admit her, saying that the patient was too ill for visitors. Then his face brightened.

'Are you by any chance the new nurse?' he asked. 'The patient has already got rid of three.' She explained that she had come at the patient's request. She was a friend.

Several RAF officers sat reading or talking on a row of chairs in the hallway, which reminded her of a dentist's waiting room. Outside Trenchard's bedroom her quaint guide whispered that though the patient was still conscious, he could hardly speak. He was in a bad way with his chest, found difficulty in breathing, and helped nobody, least of all himself, by his reluctance to stop talking and working.[5]

Trenchard didn't immediately recognise the attractive woman who stood there at the foot of his bed.

Was she a mirage, he wondered, or just another uninvited nurse? He recognised her only when she removed her hat, and he pulled the sheet over his unshaven face in a clumsy gesture of embarrassment. Remarking that it would be better if he lay quite still, Katharine took his temperature. It was over 104 [40 degrees Centigrade]. He did not protest at her injunction to lie still and seemed too tongue-tied to comment when she added that the officers outside ought to leave. As she gathered up the litter of papers strewn over the counterpane and bedside-table, putting them neatly out of reach, Trenchard remained strangely docile. Katharine Boyle gave a few nursing instructions to the stranger who had shown her in, assuming that he must be some sickroom orderly. Next day she accidentally overheard that his name was Maurice Baring.

For most of March 1919 Trenchard lay inert in bed. The continuous stress and exhaustion he had endured through all the years of the war had finally sapped his stamina. Katharine Boyle came regularly. She later recalled that in all her wartime experience she had never nursed a more unwilling patient. She was also witness to something intensely private: the evidence of the post-traumatic stress from which even the commander-in-chief had not been immune.

She was present on several occasions when he fell into a restless sleep and his pent-up worries came tumbling deliriously off his lips. Always it was a variation on the same theme: grief at the new and hateful duty of abandoning so many of the survivors he had once led, grief at remembering the violent ends of the many more who had not survived. His anguish was all the more harrowing because of his helplessness. It told her more vividly than any words what the war had cost this man.[6]

Trenchard survived the crisis. The first thing he did when he was at last able to sit up was to call for pen and paper. He wrote to the air minister. Because he would be inactive for many more weeks he offered to stand down and allow someone else to take over. Churchill was touched. 'I could not think of losing your greatly valued services until I was satisfied you were physically unfit,' he replied. 'I am looking forward so much to working with you.'

Trenchard read this with pleasure. But almost immediately, as he began a long convalescence at the country home in Northamptonshire of the solitary friend he had retained since his schooldays, he sank into something no one had ever seen before: a glum and listless depression. What nobody knew was that he had asked Katharine Boyle to marry him and she had turned him down. 'The thought of marrying again had not occurred to her; and Trenchard, of all possible suitors, seemed utterly incongruous. He had never declared his true feelings; and the current vogue of leading war widows to the altar, out of pity or chivalrous sentimentality, was wholly repugnant to her. How could she know that Trenchard had set her on a high pedestal in his heart and had secretly worshipped her for years? . . . Katharine, in fact, fitted his preconception of the ideal wife.'

Not even Baring, it was said, could plumb the depths of his former master's depression. Trenchard shared it with no one. Instead he tried to bury it in a frenzy of work back at the Air Ministry as he resumed the task of creating Britain's tiny post-war air force and keeping it safe from the hovering generals and admirals. But Baring had decided on his own cure. He arranged a series of matchmaking lunches and dinner parties at which he would place Trenchard next to some eligible woman of rank or wealth. What Baring didn't know was that, in that summer of 1919, Katharine Boyle, out for a Sunday walk in Hyde Park, had spotted the lonely figure of Trenchard sitting on a bench. Deciding it would be heartless to ignore him she had greeted him, and ended up inviting him home to a family lunch at her flat in Knightsbridge. Having agreed to meet again this seemingly friendless man with no apparent interest in anything beyond his work she began to like him, finding him a surprisingly thoughtful and attentive friend who would bring her roses and play on all fours on the carpet with her children. Her feelings developed into affection, and when Trenchard screwed up the courage to propose again she accepted.

They were married in July 1920. He had wanted a small quiet ceremony, out of the limelight, trying to keep it that way by dispatching the invitations deliberately late. Maurice Baring, his best man, had other ideas. The multitude of guests, bristling with the titled and the military great, that he drummed up was so large there was standing room only at the society wedding church of St Margaret's at Westminster Abbey. Outside stood a guard of honour of RAF officers and a Scottish regimental band piped the newlyweds to the reception. The street was besieged by press photographers and cinema newsreel cameramen. Churchill made a heartwarming speech. And to everybody's delight, Baring performed his celebrated party piece, captivating the guests with his time-honoured routines, performed with full wine glass nonchalantly balanced on his bald, domed head.

As the couple departed on their honeymoon at the start of a marriage that would prove not only happy but would bring Katharine the title of viscountess and two more children, Baring escorted them to the station. When the whistle blew and the train began to pull away Trenchard leaned out of the window. 'All right, Baring,' he rumbled. 'You may go. This is a journey I shan't want you on.'

Acknowledgements

Although one of them lived on until 2009 and the astonishing age of 113, all of those who participated in the first great air war had gone when my research for this book began. But these men, most of them born in the mid 1890s, left behind, or generated, a rich body of personal literature. Not only in their private letters, diaries and memoirs, but in the numerous biographies others have published about their lives, many of which were so brief. In addition to these sources I was to discover the existence of two specially helpful and astoundingly knowledgeable WWI aviation historical organisations. The information they provided about the Allied and German air forces materially contributed to the detail and accuracy of this book. Between Cross & Cockade International, the First World War Aviation Historical Society in England and its sister organisation, Over the Front, the League of WWI Aviation Historians in the US, there seemed to be no question about the operations of the air war, its history, personalities, politics, technology, strategies and tactics, that could not be answered promptly and in great detail.

A number of the encyclopaedically well-informed enthusiasts who responded to my appeals were themselves authors of WWI aviation biographies and reference books. Some of these works were true labours of love in which up to twenty years of research had been invested. One of the weighty tomes (*Above the Trenches* by Christopher Shores, Norman Franks & Russell Guest) that sat on my desk throughout was a complete record of every combat fought by every British ace with five or more victories, showing the date, time, place, squadron, aircraft type and registration number, the enemy machine type, its fate and often the German pilot's name along with those of the British airmen with whom the victory was sometimes shared. The authors of these priceless reference books had even gone to the trouble of matching many of the British squadron combat records with those, accessible after the war, of the German jastas. Some Flying Corps squadrons had attracted full-length works of their own and a whole series of guide books, with devotedly researched maps and aerial photos, existed, I discovered, to help modern visitors to the battlefields of northern France track down the now all-but-disappeared RFC aerodromes of eighty to ninety years earlier.

To some of these historians and writers I owe a very special debt. To Nick Forder, curator (Air & Space) of the Museum of Science & Industry in Manchester, and to WWI aviation historian and author, Alex Revell in Cornwall, both of whom, with wonderful helpfulness and patience, continued for more than two years to respond to my queries with screeds of important information. To Alex Revell, who was also kind enough to check the final manuscript for accuracy, I am further grateful for his permission to quote from the family correspondence reproduced in his book *Brief Glory* about the life of Arthur Rhys Davids.

My enormous thanks go to curator Gordon Leith at the RAF Museum's archives in Hendon who regularly searched, with diligence far beyond the call of duty, for elusive Flying Corps facts. And to retired British Airways 747 and Concorde pilot and WWI aviation author Mike O'Connor for his unrivalled knowledge of the French airfields and the aces who flew from them. Also to American aviation historians Howard Fisher (San Diego, California), James Streckfuss (Cincinnati, Ohio), Steve Ruffin (Annapolis, Maryland), Jack Herris (Indio, California) and Steve Suddaby (Annandale, Virginia) all of whom shared their surprisingly vast knowledge of the operations and pilots of the British air forces in the First World War. Steve Ruffin's deeply researched articles in *Over the Front* magazine about the horrors of WWI combat flying and the tangled authorship history of Elliott Springs' classic air war diaries were rich sources.

I am indebted to three doctors who generously helped my understanding of the debilitating mental illness to which most of the pilots and observers eventually succumbed and of other medical problems experienced by WWI aviators. Group Captain Geoff Reid, as defence consultant adviser in psychiatry at the British Ministry of Defence, went to great efforts to introduce me to the specialist world of aviation psychiatry and the much bigger understanding that exists today of combat stress disorder. Australian consultant physician and Great War historian Dr Geoffrey Miller shared the fruits of his research into such diverse areas as the medical cause of the Red Baron's death and the treatment of venereal disease on the Western Front. New Zealand psychiatrist Dr Sue Mackersey made enlightening studies for me of the fertile fantasy world of Billy Bishop and the singular character of Albert Ball.

Specially grateful thanks go to Oxfordshire genealogist Keith Winters for his remarkable detective work in successfully tracking down scores of descendants of WWI airmen. To Anja Weller for the great interest she took in the stories of the German pilots and her splendidly idiomatic translations of their writings. To Marta Kielkowicz for her research in Poland into the post-war history of the Red Baron's house in Świdnica. To Sylvestre Bresson of Terre de Memoire in Peronne for the efficient Pas de Calais guided tour he gave me of Flying Corps WWI airfield sites where the ghosts of the pilots still seemed to walk. To my daughter Paula, and to Tasmanian pilot and aviation historian John Darcy Williams, for their enthusiasm and kindness in spending days researching first air war records for me in various London archives. To my creative son David for his major contribution to the design of the book's cover. To my French-speaking wife, Caroline, for her long-distance research into the events in Annoeullin that continue to honour the death there of Albert Ball. To English teacher Françoise Vandenberghe at the Collège Albert Ball for explaining why the British pilot continues to remain the town's hero. To Ball's niece, Paddy Armstrong, for her perceptive comments about the character of her famous uncle. And to Ball's great-niece, Vanda Day, for her account of the opening ceremony of the French college, about which military historians Cliff Housely and Mike Pearce also contributed helpful information. My thanks also to the efficient and friendly staff of the Nottinghamshire Archives for the small mountain of letters Ball wrote to his family and to Flora Young.

For their permission to draw on copyright material I have to thank a number of organisations and people: Lord Avebury for the quotations from the letters of his uncle, Captain Eric Lubbock, and to the Hon. Lyulph Lubbock for his hospitality, his kindness in sharing with me the Lubbock family papers and for the tour he gave me of the High Elms Country Park in Kent where the Flying Corps pilot grew up. To Nola Wyllie for the diaries of her uncle-in-law, Lieutenant-Colonel Harold Wyllie. To William Morley for the letters of 2nd Lieutenant Geoffrey Wall, held by the RAF Museum. To Gillian Clayton for the letters of her uncle, Captain Aidan Liddell, and to Peter Daybell from whose biography I drew some of the pilot's letters. To Professor Nicholas Severs for the 1917 correspondence exchanged by the fathers of Lieutenant Alfred Severs and Lieutenant Norman Knight first published in a 2004 article by Professor Severs in *Cross & Cockade International*. To the Imperial War Museum, where I received much helpfulness from the keeper of documents, Rod Suddaby, and archivists Sabrina Rowlatt and Emma Goodrum.

In Canada, which supplied nearly a third of the Royal Flying Corps pilots, I owe thanks in Ottawa to Carol Reid, archives collections manager at the Canadian War Museum, and to Claire Banton at the Library and Archives of Canada. For information about the contemporary view of Billy Bishop I am grateful to Mary Smith, museums manager, Owen Sounds Museums in Ontario, and to retired Lieutenant-Colonel David Bashow, associate professor of history at the Royal Military College of Canada. Diane Bennett, the widow of Canadian author Alan Bennett, sent me valuable extracts from her husband's then unpublished biography of Captain Roy Brown. And Dr Steve Harris, chief historian at the Canadian National Defence Directorate of History and Heritage, produced for me dozens of the letters Billy Bishop wrote to his fiancée.

For assistance in tracing the papers of Flying Corps pilots from other Empire countries I am indebted in South Africa to Audrey Portman of Rhino Research, Johannesburg, Gerda Viljoen at the South African National Museum of Military History and Jean Marsh of the South African Military History Society; in Australia to the Australian Society of WWI Aero Historians, Craig Berelle and Jessie Webb at the Australian War Memorial research centre in Canberra and Margot Vaughan, associate curator of collections at 2nd Lieutenant Geoffrey Wall's old school, Wesley College in Melbourne; in New Zealand to Vincent Orange, Errol Martyn and the Air Force Museum of New Zealand.

My research into the use of parachutes was greatly aided by Jonathan Rooper, a grandson of the British chute inventor Everard Calthrop. In my quest for information about the long-forgotten Padre Bernard Keymer I was rewardingly assisted by two descendants: his grandson, David Greenway, and great-grandson Edward Keymer, both of whom undertook prodigious family research for me. I must also thank Matti Watton, Church of England archivist at Lambeth Palace library, for information about Padre Keymer's clerical career.

Many people contributed to my investigations into the award of the controversial Victoria Cross to Billy Bishop, especially Brian Best, secretary of the Victoria Cross Society and Didy Grahame, secretary of the VC and George Cross Association. Anthony Staunton cleared up for me the longstanding mystery surrounding the presentation of Edward Mannock's posthumous VC. From the Liddle Collection at the Brotherton library at the University of Leeds I drew on an amazing trove of letters, diaries and transcripts of interviews with WWI airmen, for which I must thank the collection's enterprising creator, Peter Liddle, and its manager, Richard Davies. The complex patent infringement lawsuit brought against Anthony Fokker over his propeller/machine-gun-synchronising device was painstakingly unravelled for me by two intellectual property lawyers: my son-in-law Guy Yonay in New York and Christian Harmsen in Düsseldorf.

A surprisingly large number of organisations which have been involved in the event sent me information about the annual memorial services at Canterbury Cathedral to honour Mick Mannock. They included the Cathedral staff, the Western Front Association, 85 Squadron Association, the Air Training Corps and the Royal Air Forces Association, whose local councillor, Robin Green, was kind enough to send me a photograph of the 2009 ceremony.

When I began my search for the letters and diaries of WWI's aviators I was staggered by the sheer quantity that had survived in museums and libraries. So many were of compulsive reading that the book's first draft was seriously over length. To my two dauntingly professional editors, Stacey McNutt and Caroline North, I owe enormous thanks for their great skill and objective grasp of the subject that helped in the painful task of compressing it. I am grateful for their encouragement and enthusiasm, for the production contribution of my third editor, Martha Ashby and for the guidance and generous support for the project of my publisher, Alan Samson and my military history wise agent, Ian Drury.

I wish to express my gratitude to the following people and organisations who also helped me with information:

Christiane Botzet archivist, Bundesarchiv-Militärarchiv, Freiburg, Germany.

British Library Newspaper Archive, Colindale, London.

Camden History Society, London.

Neil Chippendale, Hornsby Shire Council, NSW, Australia.

Mick Davis, managing editor, *Cross & Cockade International*.

Air Vice-Marshal Peter Dye, Director-General RAF Museum and president of Cross & Cockade International.

Peter Elliott, senior keeper, Department of Research and Information Services, RAF Museum, Hendon.

Tony Mellor Ellis, for his generosity in sharing with me his collection of WWI air war photographs.

Suzanne Fischer for enlightenment on the burial history of the Red Baron and the fate of his Schweidnitz home.

Norman Franks, aviation historian and author.

Dr Dieter Gröschel, Charlottesville, Virginia, for German combat fatigue information.

Jeff Jefford, retired RAF wing commander, aviation historian and author, for his kindness in supplying from his collection a copy of the book's ninety-four-year-old cover picture and, amazingly, the name of every one of the fifteen 45 Squadron men in it.

Peter Kilduff, Manfred von Richthofen biographer.

Joshua Levine, for generously sharing combat-fatigued RFC pilots' medical records.

London Metropolitan Archives.

Barry Marsden, for details of the lives of William Bond and Aimée McHardy.

Museum of Army Chaplaincy, Amport, Hampshire.

Patrizia Nava, McDermott Library Special Collections, University of Texas, Dallas.

Nick Peacey, for copious information about the Spencer parachute used by balloon observers.

Parliamentary Archives, Houses of Parliament, London.

David Reed-Felstead for permission to quote from his grandfather Arthur Gould Lee's book *No Parachute*.

Royal College of Psychiatrists, London.

The Aerodrome Forum.

The National Archives, Kew.

Wellcome Library, London.

Colonel Professor Mark Wells, Department of History, USAF Academy, Colorado Springs.

Karen Wendland, Pali Text Society, for tracking down a rare photo of Caroline Rhys Davids.

Jennifer Wilkinson, RAF Centre of Aviation Medicine, Henlow.

WWI Aero magazine.

Select Bibliography

Ash, Eric: *Sir Frederick Sykes and the Air Revolution 1912–1918*, Frank Cass, London, 1999.

Babington, Anthony: *For the Sake of Example: Capital Courts Martial 1914–18, the Truth*, Leo Cooper, London, 1983; *Shell-Shock: A History of the Changing Attitudes to War Neurosis*, Leo Cooper, London, 1997.

Balfour, Harold: *An Airman Marches: Early Flying Adventures, 1914–1923*, Greenhill Books, London, 1985.

Baring, Maurice: *Dear Animated Bust: Letters to Lady Juliet Duff, France 1915–1918*, Michael Russell, Salisbury, 1981; *Flying Corps Headquarters 1914–1918*, G. Bell & Sons, London, 1920.

Barker, Pat: *Regeneration*, Viking, London, 1991.

Barker, Ralph: *The Royal Flying Corps in France: From Bloody April 1917 to Final Victory*, Constable, London, 1995.

Bashow, David: *Knights of the Air: Canadian Fighter Pilots in the First World War*, McArthur, Toronto, 2000.

Bickers, Richard: *Von Richthofen: The Legend Evaluated*, Naval Institute Press, Annapolis, Maryland, 1996.

Bishop, William Arthur (son of Air Marshal William Avery Bishop VC): *The Courage of the Early Morning*, McClelland & Stewart, Toronto, 1965.

Bishop, William Avery: *Winged Warfare*, McClelland, Goodchild & Stewart, Toronto, 1918.

Blunden, Edmund: *Undertones of War*, Cobden Sanderson, London, 1928.

Bodenschatz, Karl: *Hunting with Richthofen: The Bodenschatz Diaries: Sixteen months of battle with JG Freiherr von Richthofen No.1*, Grub Street, London, 1996 (originally published in German as *Jadg in Flanderns Himmel*).

Böhme, Erwin: *Briefe Eines Deutschen Kampffliegers An Ein Junges Mädchen (A German Fighter Pilot's Letters to a Young Girl)*, edited by Professor Johannes Werner, Koehler, Leipzig, 1930.

Bowyer, Chaz: *Albert Ball: The Story of the First World War Ace*, William Kimber, London, 1977; *Handley Page Bombers of the First World War*, Aston Publications, Bourne End, Bucks, 1992; *Royal Flying Corps Communiqués 1917–1918*, Grub Street, London, 1998.

Boyle, Andrew: *Trenchard: Man of Vision*, Collins, London, 1962.

Bruce, John: *The Aeroplanes of the Royal Flying Corps Military Wing*, Putnam, London, 1992.

Calthrop, Everard: *The Horse as Comrade and Friend*, Hutchinson, London, 1921.

Chadderton, Clifford: *Hanging a Legend: The National Film Board's Shameful Attempt to Discredit Billy Bishop VC*, War Amputations of Canada, Ottawa, 1986.

Clark, Alan: *Aces High: The War in the Air over the Western Front 1914–18*, Weidenfeld & Nicolson, London, 1973.

Cole, Christopher (ed.): *McCudden VC*, William Kimber, London, 1967; *Royal Flying Corps Communiqués 1915–1916*, William Kimber, London, 1969.

Cooksley, Peter: *VCs of the First World War: The Air VCs*, Sutton Publishing, Stroud, 1996.

Coombs, Leslie: *Fighting Cockpits 1914–2000*, Airlife, Shrewsbury, 1999.

Cross, Wilbur: *Zeppelins of World War I*, Paragon House, New York, 1991.

Daybell, Peter: *With a Smile and a Wave: The Life of Captain Aidan Liddell VC MC*, Pen & Sword, Barnsley, 2005.

de la Ferté, Philip Joubert: *The Fated Sky*, Hutchinson, London, 1952; *The Forgotten Ones: The Story of the Ground Crews*, Hutchinson, London, 1961.

Douglas, Lord Sholto of Kirtleside: *Years of Combat*, Collins, London, 1963.

Dudgeon, James: *'Mick': The Story of Major Edward Mannock*, Robert Hale, London, 1981.

Ellis, Peter Berresford and Williams, Piers: *By Jove, Biggles!: The Life of Captain W.E. Johns*, W.H. Allen, London, 1981.

Fischer, Suzanne: *The Mother of Eagles: The War Diary of Baroness von Richthofen*, Schiffer Military Publishing, Lancaster, Pennsylvania, 2001 (originally published in Berlin in 1937 as *Mein Kriegstagebuch*).

Fokker, Anthony and Gould, Bruce: *Flying Dutchman: The Life of Anthony Fokker*, Henry Holt, New York, 1931.

Franks, Norman: *Nieuport Aces of World War I*, Osprey, Oxford, 2000; *Sharks Among Minnows*, Grub Street, London, 2001.

Franks, Norman and Bennett, Alan: *The Red Baron's Last Flight*, Grub Street, London, 1997.

Franks, Norman and Giblin, Hal: *Under the Guns of the German Aces*, Grub Street, London, 1997.

Franks, Norman and Saunders, Andy: *Mannock: The Life and Death of Major Edward Mannock*, Grub Street, London, 2008.

Fredette, Raymond: *The Sky on Fire: The First Battle of Britain 1917–1918*, Holt, Rinehart & Winston, New York, 1966.

Fry, William: *Air of Battle*, William Kimber, London, 1974.

Gibbons, Floyd: *The Red Knight of Germany*, Garden City Publishing, New York, 1927.

Gibbs, Philip: *Realities of War*, Heinemann, London, 1920.

Gilbert, Martin: *First World War*, Weidenfeld & Nicolson, London, 1994.

Gollin, Alfred: *No Longer an Island: Britain and the Wright Brothers 1902–1909*, Heinemann, London, 1984.

Graves, Robert: *Goodbye to All That*, Jonathan Cape, London, 1929.

Gray, John: *Billy Bishop Goes to War*, Talonbooks, Vancouver, 1981.

Gray, Peter and Thetford, Owen: *German Aircraft of the First World War*, Putnam, London, 1962.

Greenhous, Brereton: *The Making of Billy Bishop*, Dundurn Press, Toronto, 2002.

Grinnell-Milne, Duncan: *Wind in the Wires*, Hurst & Blackett, London, 1933.

Guttman, John: *SE5a vs Albatros DV: Western Front 1917–18*, Osprey, Oxford, 2009.

Hanson, Neil: *The Unknown Soldier: The Story of the Missing of the Great War*, Doubleday, London, 2005; *First Blitz: The Secret German Plan to Raze London to the Ground in 1918*, Doubleday, London, 2008.

Hart, Peter: *Bloody April: Slaughter in the Skies over Arras 1917*, Weidenfeld & Nicolson, London, 2005; *Aces Falling: War Above the Trenches, 1918*, Weidenfeld & Nicolson, London, 2007.

Hastings, Max: *Bomber Command*, Michael Joseph, London, 1979.

Hearn, Peter: *Sky High Irvin: The Story of a Parachute Pioneer*, Robert Hale, London, 1983.

Holden, Wendy: *Shell Shock: the Psychological Impact of War*, Channel 4 Books, London, 1998.

Howard, Michael: *The First World War: A Very Short Introduction*, Oxford University Press, 2002.

Immelmann, Franz: *Max Immelmann: Eagle of Lille*, John Hamilton, London, 1936.

Insall, Algernon (A.J.): *Observer: Memoirs of the RFC 1915–18*, Kimber, London, 1970.

Jackson, Robert: *Air War Flanders 1918*, Airlife, Shrewsbury, 1998.

Jefford, Jeff: *RAF Squadrons*, Airlife, Shrewsbury, 1988.

Jones, Ira ('Taffy'): *King of Air Fighters: The biography of Major Mick Mannock, VC, DSO, MC*, Nicholson & Watson, London, 1934; *Tiger Squadron*, W.H. Allen, London, 1954.

Kiernan, Reginald: *Captain Albert Ball VC DSO*, John Hamilton, London, 1933.

Kilduff, Peter: *Richthofen: Beyond the Legend of the Red Baron*, Arms & Armour Press, London, 1994.

Layman, Richard (R.D.): *Naval Aviation in the First World War: Its Impact and Influence*, Chatham Publishing, Barnsley, 1996.

Lee, Arthur Gould: *No Parachute: A Fighter Pilot in World War I*, Jarrolds, London, 1968; *Open Cockpit*, Jarrolds, London, 1969.

Leonard, Pat: *The Fighting Padre: Letters from the Trenches 1915–1918*, Pen & Sword Military, Barnsley, Yorkshire, 2010.

Levine, Joshua: *On a Wing and a Prayer*, HarperCollins, London, 2008.

Lewis, Cecil: *Sagittarius Rising*, Peter Davies, London, 1936; *Farewell to Wings*, Temple Press, London, 1964.

Lewis, Gwilym: *Wings over the Somme 1916–1918*, Bridge Books, Wrexham, Clwyd, 1976.

Libby, Frederick: *Horses Don't Fly*, Arcade Publishing, New York, 2000.

Longyard, William: *Who's Who in Aviation History*, Airlife, Shrewsbury, 1994.

Mackersey, Ian: *Smithy: The Life of Sir Charles Kingsford Smith*, Little Brown, London, 1998.

Macmillan, Norman: *Into the Blue*, Duckworth, London, 1929.

Marben, Rolf: *Zeppelin Adventures*, John Hamilton, London, 1931.

Marson, Thomas (T.B.): *Scarlet and Khaki*, Jonathan Cape, London, 1930.

Marwick, Arthur: *The Deluge: British Society and the First World War*, Bodley Head, London, 1965.

Mitchell, T.J.: *History of the Great War: Medical Services*, HMSO, London, 1931.

McCaffery, Dan: *Billy Bishop: Canadian Hero*, Formac Publishing, Halifax, Nova Scotia, 1990.

McCudden, James: *Flying Fury: Five Years in the Royal Flying Corps*, Aeroplane and General, London, 1918.

McHardy, Aimée: *An Airman's Wife*, Herbert Jenkins, London, 1918.

MacLanachan, William (under the pseudonym 'McScotch'): *Fighter Pilot*, George Newnes, London, 1936.

Moran, Lord: *The Anatomy of Courage*, Constable, London, 1945.

Morris, Alan: *The Balloonatics*, Jarrolds, London, 1970.

Morrow, John: *The Great War in the Air: Military Aviation from 1909 to 1921*, Smithsonian Institution Press, Washington DC, 1993.

Moynihan, Michael: *God on Our Side: The British Padres in World War*, Leo Cooper, London, 1983.

Norris, Geoffrey: *The Royal Flying Corps: A History*, Frederick Muller, London, 1965.

O'Connor, Mike: *Airfields & Airmen: Somme*, Pen & Sword, Barnsley, 2002; *Airfields & Airmen: Arras*, Pen & Sword, Barnsley, 2004.

Orange, Vincent: *Sir Keith Park*, Methuen, London, 1984.

Oughton, Frederick (ed): *The Personal Diary of Major Edward 'Mick' Mannock*, Neville Spearman, London 1966.

Oughton, Frederick and Smyth, Vernon: *Mannock VC: Ace with One Eye*, Muller, London, 1956.

Raleigh, Sir Walter and Jones, H.A.: *The War in the Air* (six-volume official British history of the first great air war), Clarendon Press, Oxford, 1922–1937.

Remarque, Erich: *All Quiet on the Western Front*, Little Brown, Boston, 1929.

Revell, Alex: *Brief Glory: The Life of Arthur Rhys Davids*, William Kimber, London, 1984; *James McCudden VC*, Albatros Productions, Berkhamsted, 1987; *Victoria Cross: WWI Airmen and their Aircraft*, Flying Machines Press, Stratford, Connecticut, 1997; *No. 56 Squadron RAF/RFC*, Osprey, Oxford, 2009.

Richardson-Whealy, Elizabeth: *Pilot's Log: The log, diary, letters and verse of Lieutenant Leonard A. Richardson Royal Flying Corps 1917–1918*, Heron Publishing, Victoria, British Columbia, 1998.

Rivers, Dr William (W.H.R.): *Instinct and the Unconscious*, Cambridge University Press, 1920; *Conflict and Dream*, Harcourt Brace, New York, 1923.

Robinson, Douglas H.: *Giants in the Sky: A History of the Rigid Airship*, University of Washington Press, Seattle, 1973; *The Dangerous Sky: A History of Aviation Medicine*, G.T. Foulis, Henley-on-Thames, 1973.

Sassoon, Siegfried: *Memoirs of an Infantry Officer*, Faber, London, 1930.

Saward, Dudley: *'Bomber' Harris: The Authorised Biography*, Cassell, London, 1984.

Scott, Alan (Jack): *Sixty Squadron RAF 1916–1919*, Heinemann, London, 1920.

Shores, Christopher: *British and Empire Aces of World War I*, Osprey, Oxford, 2001.

Shores, Christopher, Franks, Norman and Guest, Russell: *Above the Trenches*, Grub Street, London, 1990.

Slessor, Sir John: *The Central Blue*, Praeger, New York, 1957.

Smith, Adrian: *Mick Mannock Fighter Pilot: Myth, Life and Politics*, Palgrave, Basingstoke, 2001.

Springs, Elliott White: *War Birds: Diary of an Unknown Aviator*, George Doran, New York, 1926.

Stark, Rudolf: *Wings of War*, John Hamilton, London, 1933.

Steel, Nigel and Hart, Peter: *Tumult in the Clouds*, Hodder & Stoughton, London, 1997.

Stewart, Oliver: *Words and Music for a Mechanical Man*, Faber & Faber, London, 1967.

Strange, Lieutenant-Colonel Louis: *Recollections of an Airman*, Aviation Book Club, London, 1940.

Taylor, Sir Gordon: *Sopwith Scout 7309*, Cassell, London, 1968.

Terraine, John: *The First World War 1914–18*, Hutchinson, London, 1965.

Tredrey, Frank (F. D.): *Pioneer Pilot: The Great Smith Barry Who Taught the World How to Fly*, Peter Davies, London, 1976.

Udet, Ernst: *Ace of the Iron Cross* (originally *Mein Fliegerleben*), Berlin, 1935.

van Ishoven, Armand: *The Fall of an Eagle: The Life of Fighter Ace Ernst Udet*, William Kimber, London, 1977.

von Buttlar Brandenfels, Baron Treusch: *Zeppelins Over England*, Harrap, London, 1931.

von Richthofen, Manfred: *The Red Air Fighter* (originally published as *Der rote Kampfflieger*), Ullstein, Berlin, 1917.

Wall, Geoffrey: *Letters of an Airman*, Australian Authors' Agency, Melbourne, 1918.

Warner, Philip: *Passchendaele*, Sidgwick & Jackson, London, 1987.

Wells, Mark: *Courage and Air Warfare*, Frank Cass, London, 1995.

Williams, Alistair: *Against the Odds: The Life of Group Captain Lionel Rees VC*, Bridge Books, Wrexham, 1989.

Winter, Denis: *The First of the Few: Fighter Pilots of the First World War*, Allen Lane, London, 1982.
Wood, Alan: *Aces and Airmen of World War I*, Brassey's, London, 2002.
Yeates, Victor: *Winged Victory*, Jonathan Cape, London, 1934.

Source Notes

Prologue
1. Cecil Lewis: *Sagittarius Rising*, Peter Davies, London, 1936.
2. Ibid.
3. Ibid.

Chapter 1: The Reluctant Inventors
1. Air/1608/204/85/36. National Archives, London.
2. *Daily Mail*, London, 11 July 1908.
3. Alfred Gollin: *No Longer an Island: Britain and the Wright Brothers 1902–1909*, Heinemann, London, 1984.
4. Andrew Boyle: *Trenchard: Man of Vision*, Collins, London, 1962.
5. Sir Walter Raleigh and H.A. Jones: *The War in the Air* (6-volume official British history of the first great air war), Clarendon Press, Oxford, 1922–1937.
6. Martin Gilbert: *First World War*, Weidenfeld & Nicolson, London, 1994.
7. Quoted in Martin Gilbert, op. cit.

Chapter 2: The Aeroplane Goes to War
1. British official history of WWI, quoted by Martin Gilbert in *First World War*, op. cit.
2. James McCudden: *Flying Fury: Five Years in the Royal Flying Corps*, Aeroplane and General, London, 1918.
3. Ibid.
4. Geoffrey Norris: *The Royal Flying Corps: A History*, Frederick Muller, London, 1965.
5. C.E.C. Rabagliati. Imperial War Museum sound archives SR4208, reel 1.
6. Ibid.
7. Cecil King: Imperial War Museum sound archives SR27, reel 3.
8. John Terraine: *The First World War 1914–18*, Hutchinson, London, 1965.
9. Quoted in Martin Gilbert, op. cit.
10. Geoffrey Norris, op. cit.
11. Field Marshal Sir John French's dispatch to Lord Kitchener quoted in Geoffrey Norris, op. cit.
12. John Terraine, op. cit.

Chapter 3: Enter 'Boom'

1. Lord Douglas of Kirtleside: *Years of Combat*, Collins, London, 1963.
2. William Fry: *Air of Battle*, William Kimber, London, 1974.
3. Lord Douglas of Kirtleside, op. cit.
4. Ibid.
5. Vincent Orange: *Oxford Dictionary of National Biography*.
6. Andrew Boyle, op. cit.
7. Cecil King, op. cit.
8. Andrew Boyle, op. cit.
9. Ibid.

Chapter 4: Brave Lives Given for Others

1. Lord Douglas of Kirtleside, op. cit.
2. Peter Cooksley: *VCs of the First World War: The Air VCs*, Sutton Publishing, Stroud, 1996.
3. William Rhodes-Moorhouse: letter to his wife, Linda, 24 April 1915, Air Force Museum of New Zealand.
4. Cecil Lewis, op. cit.
5. Aidan Liddell: letter to an unnamed friend, 29 December 1914, Imperial War Museum PP/MCR/281.
6. Aidan Liddell: letter to his mother, 21 December 1914, quoted in Peter Daybell: *With a Smile and a Wave: The Life of Captain Aidan Liddell, MC VC*, Pen & Sword Aviation, Barnsley, 2005.
7. Aiden Liddell: letter to his mother, 7 January 1915, quoted in Peter Daybell: *ibid.*
8. Oliver Stewart: *The Clouds Remember*, Arms & Armour Press, London, 1972.
9. Lieutenant Dhanis, CO No. 3 Squadron Belgian Air Corps: letter to Major Hoare, 1 August 1915, Liddell Family papers.
10. Major C. Hoare: letter to Aidan Liddell, 2 August 1915, Liddell Family papers.
11. Aidan Liddell's final words quoted in Stonyhurst College magazine.
12. Major Maxwell Rouse: letter to Liddell family, 12 September 1915, Imperial War Museum PP/MCR/281.
13. F.F. Urquhart: letter to John Liddell, 13 December 1915, Imperial War Museum PP/MCR/281.

Chapter 5: The Fokker Scourge

1. Anthony Fokker and Bruce Gould: *Flying Dutchman: The Life of Anthony Fokker*, Henry Holt, New York, 1931.
2. Max Immelmann: letter to his mother, 28 October 1915, quoted by his brother Franz Immelmann in *Immelmann: The Eagle of Lille*, John Hamilton, London, 1935.
3. Duncan Grinnell-Milne: *Wind in the Wires*, Hurst & Blackett, London, 1933.

4. Marshal of the Royal Air Force Sir John Slessor quoted on Trenchard in Raymond Fredette: *The Sky on Fire*, Holt, Rinehart & Winston, New York, 1966.
5. Sir Walter Raleigh and H.A. Jones, op. cit.
6. Quoted in Andrew Boyle, op. cit.
7. Lieutenant-General Sir David Henderson: letter to Brigadier-General Trenchard, December 1915, RAF Museum archives, London, MFC 76/1.
8. Lieutenant-General Sir David Henderson: letter to Brigadier-General Trenchard, 16 March 1916, RAF Museum archives, London, MFC 76/1.
9. Lieutenant-General Sir David Henderson: letter to Brigadier-General Trenchard, March 1916, RAF Museum archives, London, MFC 76/1.
10. Brigadier-General Trenchard: letter to Lieutenant-General Sir David Henderson, 21 April 1916, RAF Museum archives, London, MFC 76/1.
11. Brigadier-General Trenchard: letter to Brigadier-General Brancker, 16 March 1916, RAF Museum archives, London, MFC 76/1.
12. Brigadier-General Trenchard: letter to Brigadier-General Brancker, 4 April 1916, RAF Museum archives, London, MFC 76/1.
13. Major-General Trenchard: letter to Brigadier-General Brancker, 29 June 1916, RAF Museum archives, London, MFC 76/1.

Chapter 6: Public Schoolboys Wanted

1. Colonel Cavendish: letter to Major-General Sir David Henderson, 6 July 1916, RAF Museum archives, AC 71.
2. Major-General Sir David Henderson: letter to Colonel Cavendish, 6 July 1916, RAF Museum archives, AC 71.
3. Cecil Lewis, op. cit.
4. Arthur Harris: Imperial War Museum sound archives SR3765, reel 1.
5. Sir John Slessor: *The Central Blue*, Frederick Praeger, New York, 1957.
6. Geoffrey Wall: letter to his mother in Melbourne, Australia, [17 December 1916?]. All extracts from Wall's correspondence are quoted from *Letters of an Airman*, a volume of his letters published by the Australian Authors' Agency, Melbourne, 1918. Typescripts of many of them are also held in the archives of the RAF Museum, London.
7. Denis Winter: *The First of the Few: Fighter Pilots of the First World War*, Allen Lane, London, 1982.
8. Geoffrey Wall: letter to his mother, 17 December 1916, op. cit.
9. Geoffrey Wall: letter to his mother, 5 February 1917.
10. Ibid.
11. Arthur Rhys Davids: letter to his mother, 10 December 1916. The Rhys Davids family papers are held by the Pali Text Society at the Faculty of Asian and Middle Eastern Studies, Cambridge University, and quoted in Alex Revell: *Brief Glory: The Life of Arthur Rhys Davids*, William Kimber, London, 1984.
12. Geoffrey Wall: letter to his mother, 18 February 1917.

13. Geoffrey Wall: letter to his father, 10 February 1917.

14. Geoffrey Wall: letter to his father, 4 April 1917.

15. Denis Winter, op. cit.

16. Geoffrey Wall: letter to his aunt Christobel, 21 April 1917.

Chapter 7: The Instructors Who Stuttered

1. Albert Ball: letter to his father, Albert Ball, 4 July 1915. Ball's family correspondence is held in the Albert Ball archive, Nottinghamshire County Council archives DD 1180/1. All extracts quoted here are from this source unless otherwise stated.

2. Albert Ball: letter to his father, c. October 1915, quoted in Chaz Bowyer: *Albert Ball: The Story of the First World War Ace*, William Kimber, London, 1977.

3. Albert Ball: letter to his father, 2 December 1915.

4. Albert Ball: letter to his father, c. December 1915, quoted in Chaz Bowyer, op. cit.

5. Albert Ball: letter to his family: 15 January 1916.

6. Albert Ball: letter to his family, 22 January 1916.

7. Albert Ball: letter to his family, 6 February 1916.

8. Ira 'Taffy' Jones: *Tiger Squadron*, W.H. Allen, London, 1954.

9. Sir Gordon Taylor: *Sopwith Scout 7309*, Cassell, London, 1968. All quotations from 'Bill' Taylor are from his book.

10. Central Flying School records, quoted in F.D. Tredrey: *Pioneer Pilot: The Great Smith Barry Who Taught the World How to Fly*, Peter Davies, London, 1976.

11. Harold Balfour: *An Airman Marches: Early Flying Adventures, 1914–1923*, Greenhill Books, London, 1985.

12. Geoffrey Wall: letter to his father, 30 July 1917.

13. Thomas Clark: letter to Mr A.E. Wall, Melbourne, 5 September 1917, published in *Letters of an Airman*, op. cit.

Chapter 8: Unhappiness in Parliament

1. Noel Pemberton-Billing, MP for East Hertfordshire: House of Commons, Hansard, 17 May 1916.

2. Lord Hugh Cecil, MP for Oxford University: House of Commons, Hansard, 17 May 1916.

3. Arthur Gould Lee: letter to his wife, 19 May 1916, reproduced in Gould Lee's war memoir *No Parachute: A Fighter Pilot in World War I*, Jarrolds, London, 1968. All extracts from his letters and diary are quoted from the same source.

4. Arthur Gould Lee: letter to his wife, 21 May 1916.

5. Sir Gordon Taylor, op. cit.

6. Cecil Lewis: *Farewell to Wings*, Temple Press Books, London, 1964.

7. Christopher Addison, Minister of Munitions: *Politics from Within 1911–1918*, Jenkins, London, 1924.

8. Arthur Gould Lee: *No Parachute: A Fighter Pilot in World War I*, op. cit.
9. Trenchard Papers, RAF Museum archive, MFC 76/1/5. Brancker letter to Trenchard, 13 April 1916; Trenchard to Brancker, 14 April 1916.

Chapter 9: Giants Dripping Death
1. Quoted in Ralph Blumenfeld: *All in a Lifetime*, Ernest Benn, London, 1931.
2. Quoted in Rolf Marben: *Zeppelin Adventures*, John Hamilton, London, 1931.
3. Baron Treusch von Buttlar Brandenfels: *Zeppelins Over England*, Harrap, London, 1931.
4. Sources for the story of the fate of Zeppelin L19: Sir Walter Raleigh and H.A. Jones, op. cit.; *The Times*, London, 4 and 6 February 1916; *New York Times*, 3 March 1917; Rolf Marben: 'The L19's Last Message' in *Zeppelin Adventures*.

Chapter 10: Zeppelin Stalkers
1. Arthur Harris, op. cit.
2. Eric Beauman: Imperial War Museum sound archives SR14914.
3. William Leefe Robinson, 39 Squadron RFC: letter to his parents, 22 October 1916, Imperial War Museum archives.
4. Sybil Morrison: Imperial War Museum sound archives SR331, reel 3.
5. William Leefe Robinson, 39 Squadron RFC, letter to his parents, October 1916, Imperial War Museum archives.
6. Pitt Klein: *Achtung! Bomben Fallen!*, Verlag von K.F. Koehler, Leipzig, 1934.

Chapter 11: The 'Fees' Come to France
1. Frederick Libby: *Horses Don't Fly*, Arcade Publishing, New York, 2000.
2. Max Immelmann: letter to his mother, April 1916, quoted by Franz Immelmann, op. cit.
3. Anthony Fokker and Bruce Gould, op. cit.
4. Gwilym Lewis: letter to his parents from St Omer, 31 May 1916, reproduced in his war memoir *Wings over the Somme 1916–1918*, Bridge Books, Wrexham, Clwyd, 1976.

Chapter 12: Terror Above the Somme
1. Cecil Lewis: *Sagittarius Rising*, op. cit. This and all further quotations from Lewis in this chapter are from the same source.
2. *Daily Chronicle*, London, 3 July 1916.

Chapter 13: Morale and the Offensive Spirit
1. General Fritz von Below: memorandum quoted in H.A. Jones: *The War in the Air* vol. 2, 1928.
2. Unnamed German soldier quoted in H.A. Jones, ibid.
3. Maurice Baring: *Flying Corps Headquarters 1914–1918*, G. Bell & Sons, London, 1920.

4. Cecil Lewis: *Sagittarius Rising*, op. cit.

5. H.A. Jones, op. cit.

6. Ibid.

7. Ian Henderson: letter to his mother, Lady Henderson, 14 May 1915, RAF Museum archives AC71/12/422.

8. Ian Henderson: letter to Lady Henderson, 19 April 1915, RAF Museum archives AC71/12/405.

9. Ian Henderson: letter to Lady Henderson, 29 September 1916, RAF Museum archives AC71/12/437.

10. Andrew Boyle, op. cit.

11. H.A. Jones, op. cit.

12. Arthur Gould Lee: 'Trenchard's Strategy of the Offensive', Appendix B to *No Parachute: A Fighter Pilot in World War I*, op. cit.

13. Lieutenant Thomas Hughes: diary, Department of Documents, Imperial War Museum.

14. Andrew Boyle, op. cit.

15. Ibid.

16. Albert Ball: letter to his father, 10 July 1916.

17. Albert Ball: letter to his family, 16 July 1916.

18. Albert Ball: letter to his father, 18 July 1916.

19. Albert Ball: letter to his family, 22 July 1916.

20. Albert Ball: letter to his family, 31 July 1916.

21. Major-General Trenchard: letter to Brigadier-General Brancker, 5 July 1916. The correspondence between Trenchard and Brancker is held in the RAF Museum archives, London, MFC 76/1.

22. Major-General Trenchard: letter to Brigadier-General Brancker, 23 September 1916.

23. Brigadier-General Brancker: letter to Major-General Trenchard, 22 September 1916.

24. Major-General Trenchard: letter to Brigadier-General Brancker, 23 September 1916.

25. Major-General Trenchard: letter to Brigadier-General Brancker, 21 September 1916.

Chapter 14: **Bloody April**

1. Erwin Böhme: letter from Kovel, Russia, to Annamarie Brüning, 16 August 1916. All extracts from Böhme's correspondence are quoted from Professor Johannes Werner (ed.): *Briefe Eines Deutschen Kampffliegers An Ein Junges Mädchen (A German Fighter Pilot's Letters to a Young Girl)*, Koehler, Leipzig, 1930.

2. Manfred von Richthofen: *Der rote Kampfflieger*, Berlin, 1917.

3. Erwin Böhme: letter from France to Annamarie Brüning, 18 October 1916.

4. Manfred von Richthofen, op. cit.

5. Ibid.
6. Ibid.
7. Erwin Böhme: letter from France to Annamarie Brüning, 31 October 1916.
8. Suzanne Fischer: *The Mother of Eagles: The War Diary of Baroness von Richthofen*, Schiffer Military Publishing, Lancaster, Pennsylvania, 2001. Kunigunde von Richthofen's diary was originally published as *Mein Kriegstagebuch*, Berlin, 1937.
9. Andrew Boyle, op. cit.
10. Maurice Baring: *Dear Animated Bust: Letters to Lady Juliet Duff, France 1915–1918*, Michael Russell Publishing, Salisbury, 1981.
11. Andrew Boyle, op. cit.
12. Lord Brabazon: *The Brabazon Story*, Heinemann, London, 1956.
13. Lord Douglas of Kirtleside, op. cit.
14. T.B. Marson: *Scarlet and Khaki*, Jonathan Cape, London, 1930.
15. John Terraine, op. cit.
16. A.J.L. Scott: *Sixty Squadron RAF 1916–1919*, Heinemann, London, 1920.

Chapter 15: Going 'Mad Dog'

1. Maurice Baring: *Dear Animated Bust: Letters to Lady Juliet Duff, France 1915–1918*, op. cit.
2. Manfred von Richthofen, op. cit.
3. Erwin Böhme: letter from France to Annamarie Brüning, 8 April 1917.
4. Quoted by Manfred von Richthofen in *Ein Heldenleben*, Berlin, 1920.
5. Suzanne Fischer, op. cit.
6. Floyd Gibbons: *The Red Knight of Germany*, Garden City Publishing, New York, 1927.
7. Manfred von Richthofen, op. cit.
8. C.S. Knight: letter to Frederick Severs, 2 April 1917, RAF Museum archives, X003–0400/004.
9. Norman Knight: letter from Germany to Frederick Severs, 8 June 1917, RAF Museum archives, X003–0400/005.
10. Albert Ball: letter to his father, 14 August 1915.
11. Albert Ball: letter to his father, 18 November 1915.
12. Albert Ball: letter to his father, 12 March 1916.
13. Extracts from Albert Ball's letters to his parents quoted in Reginald Kiernan: *Captain Albert Ball VC DSO*, John Hamilton, London, 1933.
14. William Fry, op. cit.
15. Cecil Lewis: *Sagittarius Rising*, op. cit.
16. Albert Ball: letter to his parents, 29 September 1916.
17. Albert Ball letter to his mother, Harriet Ball, 5 May 1917.
18. Paddy Armstrong: interview with author, 18 December 2010.
19. Albert Ball: letter to his parents, April 1917, quoted in Chaz Bowyer, op. cit.

20. Albert Ball: extracts from letters to Flora Young, March–April, 1917, Nottinghamshire County Council archives, DD 682/1–21.
21. Cyril Crowe quoted by Ira Jones in: *King of Air Fighters: The biography of Major Mick Mannock, VC, DSO, MC*, Nicholson & Watson, London, 1934.
22. Cyril Ball: interview with Douglas Whetton, *Cross & Cockade Journal* vol. 2, no.1, summer 1961.
23. Harold Balfour, op. cit.
24. Maurice Baring: *Flying Corps Headquarters 1914–1918*, op. cit.

Chapter 16: An Airman's Wife

1. Aimée McHardy: *An Airman's Wife*, Herbert Jenkins, London, 1918. All extracts from the correspondence between Bond and McHardy are quoted from the same source.
2. Sir John Slessor, op. cit.
3. William MacLanachan (writing under the pseudonym 'McScotch'): *Fighter Pilot*, George Newnes, London, 1936.

Chapter 17: The Mothers

1. Arthur Rhys Davids: letter to his mother, Caroline, December 1916.
2. Arthur Rhys Davids: letter to his mother, 18 April 1917.
3. Arthur Rhys Davids: letter to his mother, 29 May 1917.
4. Arthur Rhys Davids: letter to his sister Nesta, 13 May 1917.
5. Arthur Rhys Davids: letter to his sister Nesta, 12 June 1917.
6. Arthur Rhys Davids: letter to his mother, 30 July 1917.
7. Cecil Lewis: *Farewell to Wings*, op. cit.
8. James McCudden, op. cit.
9. Arthur Rhys Davids: letter to his sister Nesta, 28 September 1917.
10. Major Richard Blomfield: letter to Caroline Rhys Davids, 28 October 1917.
11. Caroline Rhys Davids: letter to Major Richard Blomfield, 3 November 1917.
12. Caroline Rhys Davids: letter to her son Arthur, 3 December 1917.
13. Caroline Rhys Davids: letter to CO No. 56 Squadron, 2 March 1918.
14. Major Rainsford Balcombe-Brown: letter to Caroline Rhys Davids, 14 March 1918.
15. Hon. Eric Fox Pitt Lubbock: letter to his mother, Lady Alice Avebury, 23 July 1915. The family's papers are held by the Imperial War Museum, PP/MCR/406 & 97/12/1.
16. Hon. Eric Fox Pitt Lubbock: letter to his mother, 18 September 1915.
17. Hon. Eric Fox Pitt Lubbock: diary entry, 18 September 1915.
18. Lady Alice Avebury: diary entry, 23 September 1915.
19. Robert Loraine, quoted by his widow, Winifred Loraine in her biography of his life, *Head Wind*, Collins, London, 1938.
20. Hon. Eric Fox Pitt Lubbock: letter to his mother, 22 November 1915.
21. Lady Alice Avebury: diary entry, 6 November 1915.

22. Lady Alice Avebury: diary entry, 7 November 1915.

23. Hon. Eric Fox Pitt Lubbock: diary entry, 24 February 1916.

24. Lady Alice Avebury: letter to Hon. Eric Fox Pitt Lubbock, 31 December 1916.

25. Lady Alice Avebury: diary entries, 25 & 26 January 1917.

26. Hon. Eric Fox Pitt Lubbock: letter to his mother, 21 February 1917.

27. Lady Alice Avebury: diary entry, March 1917.

28. Hon. Eric Fox Pitt Lubbock: letter to his mother, 10 November 1915, quoted in a privately published memoir, *Eric Fox Pitt Lubbock* by Alice Avebury, 1918.

Chapter 18: The 'Bloody Wonderful Drunks'

1. Harold Balfour, op. cit.

2. Nigel Steel and Peter Hart: *Tumult in the Clouds*, Hodder & Stoughton, London, 1997.

3. Duncan Grinnell-Milne, op. cit.

4. Cecil Lewis: *Sagittarius Rising*, op. cit.

5. Lord Douglas of Kirtleside, op. cit.

6. Ira Jones, *King of Air Fighters*, op. cit.

7. Arthur Gould Lee: letter to his wife, 25 May 1917.

8. William Arthur Bishop: *The Courage of the Early Morning: A son's biography of a famous father*, David Mackay, New York, 1965.

9. George Coles: letter to Constance Sanderson, 16 August 1918, Imperial War Museum, 03/58/1.

10. Harold Balfour, op. cit.

Chapter 19: They Also Served

1. George Eddington: Imperial War Museum sound archives SR13, reels 5 & 6.

2. Jeff Jefford: 'NCO Pilots in the RFC/RAF 1912–18', *Air Power Review* vol. 7, no. 2, summer 2004.

3. Brigadier-General Brancker: letter to Major-General Trenchard, 20 August 1917.

4. Keith Park quoted by Jeff Jefford, op. cit.

5. *War Birds: Diary of an Unknown Aviator*, George Doran, New York, 1926. A memoir purportedly based on the diary of American pilot John MacGavock Grider, but in fact almost entirely written by his friend, fellow pilot Elliott White Springs.

6. Duncan Grinnell-Milne, op. cit.

7. Corporal William Dalton: letter to Lieutenant Gwilym Lewis, 24 December 1916, quoted in *Wings Over the Somme 1916–1918*, op. cit.

8. Air Mechanic Leslie Tupping: undated letter to a Captain Garland, quoted by Denis Winter, op. cit.

9. Sir Gordon Taylor, op. cit.

10. Bernard Shaw's reaction to 40 Squadron's performance of his play, as described by Frederick Powell, is quoted in Joshua Levine: *On a Wing and a Prayer*, Collins, London, 2008.

11. Geoffrey Wall: letter to his mother, 9 June 1917.

12. Arthur Gould Lee: letter to his wife, 22 May 1917.

13. Quoted in Denis Winter, op. cit.

14. Arthur Gould Lee: letter to his wife, 7 December 1917.

15. Arthur Gould Lee: letter to his wife, 21 September 1917.

16. Quoted in Henri Barbusse: *Le Feu*, Flammarion, Paris, 1917. Published in English as *Under Fire*, Dutton, New York, 1917.

17. Leonard Richardson: letter to his mother, 26 May 1918, quoted in Elizabeth Richardson-Whealy (compiler): *Pilot's Log: The log, diary, letters and verse of Lieutenant Leonard A. Richardson, Royal Flying Corps 1917–1918*, Heron Publishing, Victoria, British Columbia, 1998.

18. Arthur Rhys Davids: letter to his aunt Seda, c. June 1917.

19. William Bond: undated 1917 letter to his wife, quoted in Aimée McHardy, op. cit.

20. Ibid.

21. Ibid.

22. Gwilym Lewis: letter to his parents from St Omer, 23 December 1917, reproduced in his memoirs *Wings Over the Somme 1916–1918*, op. cit.

23. Ellen Keymer: undated letter to her daughter Eleanor Greenway. Copy held by Padre Keymer's grandson, David Greenway.

24. Robert Graves: *Goodbye to All That*, Jonathan Cape, London, 1929.

25. *History of the Great War: Medical Services*, HMSO, London, 1931.

26. Joshua Levine, op. cit.

27. Cecil Lewis: *Sagittarius Rising*, op. cit.

28. Arthur Gould Lee: letter to his wife, 6 October 1917.

Chapter 20: The Majors

1. Denis Winter, op. cit.

2. Duncan Grinnell-Milne, op. cit.

3. Ibid.

4. Lord Douglas of Kirtleside, op. cit.

5. D.W. Warne: introduction to 1990 edition of A.J.L. Scott: *Sixty Squadron RAF*, Greenhill Books, London. First published 1920.

Chapter 21: The Raid That Never Was

1. William Avery Bishop: *Winged Warfare*, McClelland, Goodchild & Stewart, Toronto, 1918.

2. William Avery Bishop: letter to Margaret Burdon, 21 June 1917. Bishop's correspondence is held by the Directorate of History & Heritage, Canadian Department of National Defence, Ottawa: Billy Bishop Collection, 2001/9.

3. William Fry: 'William Avery Bishop VC: Statement by Wing Commander William Mays Fry MC', *Cross & Cockade International* vol. 32, no. 1, 2001.

4. William Fry, *Air of Battle*, op. cit.

5. William Fry: 'William Avery Bishop VC – statement by Wing Commander William Mays Fry, MC', op. cit.

6. Ibid.

7. William Avery Bishop: letter to Margaret Burdon, 14 July 1917.

8. William Avery Bishop: letter to Margaret Burdon, 18 July 1917.

9. William Avery Bishop: letter to Margaret Burdon, 26 July 1917.

10. Evidence to Canadian Senate Standing Committee on Social Affairs, Science and Technology, Ottawa, 1986. Quoted in Clifford Chadderton: *Hanging a Legend: The National Film Board's Shameful Attempt to Discredit Billy Bishop VC*, War Amputations of Canada, 1986.

11. 'Production and Distribution of the National Film Board Production *The Kid Who Couldn't Miss*', the report of the Canadian Standing Senate Committee on Social Affairs, Science and Technology, Ottawa, 1986.

12. Philip Markham: 'The Early Morning of 2 June 1917: Summary of an Unsuccessful Research Project', *Over the Front*, the journal of the League of WWI Aviation Historians vol. 10, no. 3, 1995.

13. 'Nachrichtenblatt der Luftstreitkräfte', German Air Service intelligence report no. 37, 8 November 1917.

14. Philip Markham, op. cit.

15. Ed Ferko: undated 1987 letter to Wing Commander William Fry. Copy held by aviation author, Alex Revell.

16. Brereton Greenhous: *The Making of Billy Bishop*, Dundurn Press, Toronto, 2002.

17. Arthur Gould Lee: letter to his wife, 7 September 1917.

18. Clifford Chadderton, op. cit.

Chapter 22: Gothas

1. Major G. St P. de Dombasle, CO No.1 Squadron RFC: letter to the father of 2nd Lieutenant Hugh 'Toby' Welch, 30 March 1917. The Welch family war correspondence is held by the Liddle Collection, Air 338.

2. Lionel Mars: letter from London to Hugh 'Toby' Welch's father, undated.

3. Hugh 'Toby' Welch: letter from 1 Squadron in France to his mother in England, 16 March 1917.

4. H. Derycke, Curé, Sainghin-en-Melantois, France: letter to the father of 2nd Lieutenant Hugh 'Toby' Welch, 26 July 1919.

5. *New York Times*, 18 June 1917.

6. Raymond Fredette, op. cit.

7. Ibid.

8. Cecil Lewis: *Sagittarius Rising*, op. cit.

9. Harold Wyllie: diary entry, 1 November 1917. Wyllie's diary is held by the Imperial War Museum, 84/5/1.

10. Harold Wyllie diary, 3 November 1917.

11. Harold Wyllie diary, 20 November 1917.

12. Michael Howard: *The First World War: A Very Short Introduction*, Oxford University Press, 2002.

Chapter 23: America Comes to London

1. *War Birds: Diary of an unknown Aviator*, op. cit. All quotations in this chapter are from this anonymously published memoir, now attributed to Elliott White Springs.

Chapter 24: Operation Michael

1. General Johan Smuts: report on Air Organisation and the Direction of Aerial Operations, August 1917, Royal Air Force Museum archives, B404.

2. Lord Beaverbrook: *Men and Power 1917–1918*, Duell, Sloan & Pearce, New York, 1956.

3. Andrew Boyle, op.cit.

4. Eric Ash: *Sir Frederick Sykes and the Air Revolution 1912–1918*, Frank Cass, London, 1999.

5. Field Marshal Sir Douglas Haig: Order of the Day to his army on 11 April 1918, quoted in John Terraine, op. cit.

6. Erwin Böhme: letter from France to Annamarie Brüning, 18 October 1916.

7. Annamarie Brüning: letter from Hamburg to Erwin Böhme, 29 April 1917.

8. Erwin Böhme: letter from Bavaria to Annamarie Brüning, 16 January 1917.

9. Erwin Böhme: letter from Belgium to Gerhard Böhme, 31 October 1917.

10. Erwin Böhme: letter from Belgium to Annamarie Brüning, 31 October 1917.

11. Robert Jackson: *Air War Flanders 1918*, Airlife, Shrewsbury, 1998.

12. Manfred von Richthofen: letter to Gerhard Böhme, 1 December 1917. Quoted in Professor Johannes Werner, op. cit.

Chapter 25: Death of the Red Baron

1. Suzanne Fischer, op. cit.

2. Ibid.

3. Ibid.

4. Ibid.

5. Ibid.

6. Karl Bodenschatz: *Hunting with Richthofen: The Bodenschatz Diaries: Sixteen months of battle with JG Freiherr von Richthofen No.1*, Grub Street, London, 1996. Originally published in German as *Jadg in Flanderns Himmel*.

7. Wilfred May: letter of 9 March 1950, quoted in Peter Kilduff: *Richthofen: Beyond the Legend of the Red Baron*, Arms & Armour Press, London, 1994.

8. Roy Brown: letter to his parents, 21 April 1918. The family's wartime correspondence is in the Canadian War Museum archives, Ottawa, 19790720–001/58A1-7-1.

9. Details from the Richthofen post-mortems are from Dr. Geoffrey Miller: 'The Death of Manfred von Richthofen: Who fired the fatal shot?', *Journal and Proceedings of the Military History Society of Australia* vol. XXXIX, no. 2, June 1998.

10. Roy Brown: letter to his parents, 27 April 1918.

Chapter 26: The Spent Capital of Courage

1. Raymond Collishaw undated letter to Ed Ferko, Ferko Collection, University of Texas, McDermott Library, Dallas.

2. Roy Brown: letter to his father, 27 April 1918.

3. Ibid.

4. Roy Brown: letter to his father, 28 May 1918.

5. Mark Wells: *Courage and Air Warfare*, Frank Cass, London, 1995.

6. Lord Moran: *The Anatomy of Courage*, Constable, London, 1945.

7. Siegfried Sassoon: *Memoirs of an Infantry Officer*, Faber, London, 1930.

8. Stearne Edwards: letter to the father of Roy Brown, 21 July 1918.

9. Roy Brown: letter from the Prince of Wales Hospital for Officers, Staines, to his mother, 23 August 1918.

10. Roy Brown: letter from Horton War Hospital, Epsom, to his mother, 23 November 1918.

11. Ibid.

12. Victor Yeates: *Winged Victory*, Jonathan Cape, London, 1934.

Chapter 27: The Working-Class Heroes

1. Ira Jones, *King of Air Fighters*, op. cit.

2. Adrian Smith: *Mick Mannock Fighter Pilot: Myth, Life and Politics*, Palgrave, Basingstoke, 2001.

3. Christopher Cole: *McCudden VC*, William Kimber, London, 1967.

4. Adrian Smith, op. cit.

5. James Dudgeon: '*Mick': The Story of Major Edward Mannock*, Robert Hale, London, 1981.

6. Lieutenant D. de Burgh: undated letter to Ira Jones quoted in *King of Air Fighters*, op. cit.

7. Edward Mannock: diary entry, 20 April 1917. Extracts from Mannock's diary are quoted from *The Personal Diary of Major Edward 'Mick' Mannock*, introduced by Frederick Oughton, Neville Spearman, London, 1966.

8. Edward Mannock: diary entry, 9 May 1917.

9. Edward Mannock: diary entry, 7 May 1917.

10. Edward Mannock: letter to Jim Eyles, 12 May 1917, quoted by Ira Jones: *King of Air Fighters*, op. cit.

11. Edward Mannock: diary entry, 14 May 1917.
12. Edward Mannock: diary entry, 7 June 1917.
13. Edward Mannock: diary, 14 June 1917.
14. Edward Mannock: diary entry, 20 July 1917.
15. Ira 'Taffy' Jones: *Tiger Squadron*, op. cit.
16. Keith Caldwell quoted in *Mannock VC: Ace with One Eye* by Frederick Oughton and Vernon Smyth, Muller, London, 1956.
17. Ira Jones: *King of Air Fighters*, op. cit.
18. James Dudgeon, op. cit.
19. Wilfred Soltau, quoted in Ira Jones, *King of Air Fighters*, op. cit.
20. Ira Jones, *King of Air Fighters*, op. cit.

Chapter 28: Flamerinoes

1. Ira 'Taffy' Jones: *Tiger Squadron*, op. cit.
2. Ibid.
3. Ibid.
4. Ira Jones: *King of Air Fighters*, op. cit.
5. Ibid.
6. Edward Mannock: letter to Jim Eyles, 29 May 1918, quoted in Ira Jones: *King of Air Fighters*, op. cit.
7. Edward Mannock: letter to his sister Jess, 16 June 1918, quoted in Ira Jones: *King of Air Fighters*, op. cit.
8. Edward Mannock: letter to Mary Lewis, 7 June 1918. Imperial War Museum, Edward Mannock papers 1839.
9. Ira 'Taffy' Jones: *Tiger Squadron*, op. cit.
10. Ibid.
11. Ira Jones: *King of Air Fighters*, op. cit.
12. Ira 'Taffy' Jones: *Tiger Squadron*, op. cit.
13. James Dudgeon, op. cit.
14. *War Birds: Diary of an unknown Aviator*, op. cit.
15. Paul Winslow: diary entry quoted in Alex Revell, *James McCudden VC*, Albatros Productions, Berkhamsted, 1987.
16. James Dudgeon, op. cit.
17. Ira Jones: *King of Air Fighters*, op. cit.
18. Ira 'Taffy' Jones: *Tiger Squadron*, op. cit.
19. Ira Jones: *King of Air Fighters*, op. cit.
20. Donald Inglis quotes from his 85 Squadron combat report in an article he wrote for *Popular Flying* magazine, July 1938.
21. Ira Jones: *King of Air Fighters*, op. cit.
22. Padre Bernard Keymer: letter to Patrick Mannock, 28 July 1918. Quoted in Norman Franks and Andy Saunders: *Mannock: The Life and Death of Major Edward Mannock*, Grub Street, London, 2008.
23. Lieutenant W.E.H. Cushing, 85 Squadron: letter to Patrick Mannock, 28 July

1918, quoted in Norman Franks and Andy Saunders, op. cit.

24. Norman Franks and Andy Saunders, op. cit.
25. Sir Donald Hardman: interview with Peter Liddle, July 1976, Liddle Collection, Air 148.

Chapter 29: Waning of the Spirit

1. Arthur Gould Lee: letter to his wife, 3 January 1918.
2. Ira 'Taffy' Jones: diary entry, 21 April 1918, quoted from *Tiger Squadron*, op. cit.
3. Leonard Richardson diary entry, 16 May 1918, quoted in Elizabeth Richardson-Whealy, op. cit.
4. Everard Calthrop: *The Horse as Comrade and Friend*, Hutchinson, London, 1921.
5. British Air Board statement quoted in numerous WWI air war publications but never dated or identified with any War Office archives reference.
6. Everard Calthrop: letter to Commodore Murray F. Sueter, Air Department director, Admiralty, 8 December 1915, National Archives Air/1/148.
7. Arthur Gould Lee: 'Why No Parachutes?', Appendix C to *No Parachute: A Fighter Pilot in World War I*, op. cit.
8. *War Birds: Diary of an unknown Aviator*, op. cit.
9. Arthur Gould Lee: 'Why No Parachutes?', op. cit.
10. Helmut Steinbrecher, German Air Service: letter to Schroeder & Co., Berlin, 7 July 1918.
11. Ernst Udet: *Ace of the Iron Cross*, originally *Mein Fliegerleben*, Berlin, 1935.
12. Ira 'Taffy' Jones: *Tiger Squadron*, op. cit.
13. Information on WWI German and Austro–Hungarian pilots' use of parachutes from W.K. Puglisi: 'Parachute Notes', *Cross & Cockade* (US) vol. 6., no. 4 and Dan-San Abbott: 'German Parachutes in the Great War', *WWI Aero* magazine no. 207, May 2011.
14. Everard Calthrop quoted in Arthur Gould Lee: 'Why No Parachutes?', op. cit.
15. Arthur Gould Lee: letter to his wife, 5 October 1917.
16. Arthur Gould Lee: letter to his wife, 13 December 1917.
17. Arthur Gould Lee: diary entry, 29 November 1917.
18. Arthur Gould Lee: diary entry, 9 December 1917.
19. Arthur Gould Lee: letter to his wife, 17 January 1918.
20. *War Birds: Diary of an Unknown Aviator*, op. cit.
21. Sir Gordon Taylor, op. cit.
22. Ian Mackersey: *Smithy: The Life of Sir Charles Kingsford Smith*, Little Brown, London, 1998.
23. Harold Balfour, op. cit.
24. Denis Winter, op. cit.
25. Ira 'Taffy' Jones: diary entry 4 August 1918, quoted from *Tiger Squadron*, op. cit.

Chapter 30: The Eleventh Hour of the Eleventh Day

1. Anthony Fokker and Bruce Gould, op. cit.
2. Lord Douglas of Kirtleside, op. cit.
3. Andrew Boyle, op. cit.
4. Interview with Lieutenant Richmond Viall, *Cross & Cockade* vol. II, autumn 1961.
5. Karl Bodenschatz, op. cit.
6. John Buchan: *The King's Grace*, Hodder & Stoughton, London, 1935.
7. Vivian Voss: *Flying Minnows*, Arms & Armour Press, London, 1977.
8. Arthur Capel (later Air Vice-Marshal): interview with Peter Liddle, August 1974, Liddle Collection, tape 285.
9. Ira 'Taffy' Jones, *Tiger Squadron*, op. cit.
10. Harold Balfour, op. cit.
11. Winston Churchill: *The World Crisis*, Thornton Butterworth, London, 1923–31.
12. Edward Lee: letter to his wife, 29 October 1918, RAF Museum archives.
13. Andrew Boyle, op. cit.

Chapter 31: Silence of a Desolate Land

1. Duncan Grinnell-Milne, op. cit.
2. Rudolf Stark: *Wings of War*, John Hamilton, London, 1933.
3. Ibid.
4. Duncan Grinnell-Milne: *Wind in the Wires*, Jarrolds, London, 1971.
5. Ibid.

Epilogue

1. Cecil Lewis: *Sagittarius Rising*, op. cit.
2. Burke David: *War Bird: The life and times of Elliott White Springs*, University of North Carolina Press, 1987.
3. Max Hastings: *Bomber Command*, Michael Joseph, London, 1979.
4. Andrew Boyle, op. cit.
5. Ibid.
6. Ibid.

Index